Accounting in Business

FIFTH EDITION

Accounting in Business

R. J. BULL

BSc (Econ), FCCA

Head of School of Accounting
and Applied Economics
Leeds Polytechnic

FIFTH EDITION

BUTTERWORTHS
London Boston Durban Singapore Sydney Toronto Wellington

First published 1969
  Reprinted 1970, 1971
Second edition 1972
Third edition 1976
  Reprinted 1977
Fourth edition 1980
  Reprinted 1982
Fifth edition 1984

© R. J. Bull, 1984

British Library Cataloguing in Publication Data

Bull, Roger John
Accounting in business.—5th ed.
1. Managerial accounting
I. Title
658.1'511   HF5635

ISBN 0–408–01486–5

Library of Congress Cataloguing in Publication Data

Bull, R. J. (Roger John), 1940–
  Accounting in business.

  Includes bibliographies and index.
  1. Accounting.   I. Title.
HF5635.B9655   1984   658.1'511   84–3248
ISBN 0–408–01486–5

Printed and bound in Great Britain by
The Garden City Press Ltd, Letchworth, Herts.

Preface

The basic objective of this book is to enable the reader to acquire a broad perspective of business accounting based upon a sound conceptual framework. Much of the enthusiasm for writing the original text in 1969 was generated as a result of my year's research for the Department of Education and Science and the Institute of Chartered Accountants in England and Wales which culminated in the report entitled 'Accounting for the Non-Specialist' which became the basis for the accounting guide syllabuses for ONC and HNC issued by the Joint Committee for Business Studies (now the Business Education Council). During that research year I became convinced that the traditional introductory studies to accounting which focused exclusive attention upon the detailed mechanics of bookkeeping failed both to provide an adequate conceptual framework for accounting and to present accounting as an important tool of management.

Considerable emphasis, therefore, has been placed on the integration of the theory with the application, seeking to stimulate independent thought on the part of the reader. This book is not intended to be a reference manual which can provide ready-made solutions to all problems; it does attempt to identify principles which the reader can apply and adapt to meet the needs of fresh and challenging situations. In writing this text, I have striven to present accounting concepts as simply and directly as possible, bearing in mind the needs of different groups of readers.

At the end of each chapter is a list of suggested additional reading on specific topics, designed to extend and deepen the reader's knowledge of the areas introduced by the chapter. No doubt some very excellent references have been omitted either because of the author's ignorance of their existence or because of the sheer wealth of material in a particular area. For this, I apologise, but would hope that these lists will be useful in providing a starting point for further investigation.

Since the publication of the first edition, it is evident that this book has provided, and will continue to provide, a suitable foundation for students pursuing a variety of courses—the Foundation Course, the first part of degree courses, the Business Education Council Higher National Certificate and Diploma Courses, and a range of professional accounting and finance studies. The increasing acceptance of a conceptual and broader approach to accounting is one measure of the profound change which has taken place in accounting education in the last two decades.

The fifth edition builds on the substantial extension and restructuring of the fourth edition, and, apart from minor changes made to update and improve clarity, incorporates several important changes and extensions:

(i) Chapters 10 and 11, which examine aspects of the limited company, have been extensively amended and extended to incorporate the effects of the Companies Act 1981;
(ii) Chapter 13, Value and Income Measurement, now incorporates SSAP 16—Current Cost Accounting, and subsequent criticisms;
(iii) Short-term decision-making (Chapter 18) includes the consideration of limiting factors;
(iv) Business income taxation is no longer a separate chapter, but the effects of taxation on financial accounting and decision-making have been incorporated into the text;
(v) Question material has been reviewed and amended and—by popular request—suggested solutions to numerical questions or parts of questions have been included at the end of the book.

My thanks are due to the Association of Certified Accountants for permission to reproduce some of the questions from their recent foundation examination papers—some of which I myself set during a period as examiner—and also to many of my colleagues at Leeds Polytechnic who have provided through our 'question data bank' some of the other question material.

My thanks must also go to my wife who has so patiently and carefully interpreted my inadequate handwriting, and turned it into legible typescript, quite apart from her willing acceptance of the many hours of work I have spent in preparing the book.

JOHN BULL

Contents

III Financial Planning and Control

Part I

The accounting environment

This introductory chapter reviews the nature and scope of
accounting, setting it in its historical perspective and examining
the environment which helps to shape, constrain and develop
accounting concepts and practices.

1 The scope and environment of business accounting

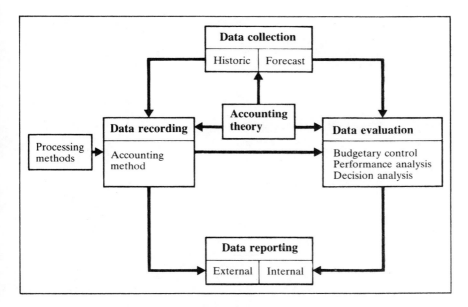

External environment

If a survey were conducted in which people were asked to say what they understood by accounting, the majority would be able to produce some sort of answer. For most people, accounting is 'something to do with figures, working out profits and the like'; perhaps the very vagueness of such answers is indicative of the fact that those concerned with accounting are more adept at explaining what they do, rather than what accounting is, or what are the foundations and uses of their art. In this book we will be concerned with laying the theoretical foundation of accounting and the uses to which accounting can be put in the business world; the methods of accounting, and in particular, that method called bookkeeping, will be treated as a means to an end, rather than an end in itself.

Accounting is in a period of rapid transition, and the changing environment has given rise to changing and ever-widening definitions of accounting. Many of today's definitions would be unacceptable—and almost unrecognizable—to the accountant of a century ago. Even with the past 40 years,

3

definitions of accounting have markedly broadened. According to a 1953 definition:

> 'The central purpose of accounting is to make possible the period matching of costs and revenues.'

By 1966, the American Accounting Association interpreted accounting as:

> '. . . the process of identifying, measuring and communicating economic information to permit informed judgements and decisions by the users of the information.'

For our purpose we will adopt the following definition:

> 'Accounting is concerned with the quantification of economic events in money terms in order to collect, record, evaluate and communicate the results of past events and to aid in decision-making.'

This definition does not confine itself to business accounting; it also embraces national income accounting and local government accounting. While these other areas of accounting are important, we will concern ourselves solely with that part of accounting related to the modern business world.

The scope of business accounting

It is useful to present our definition of accounting in diagrammatic form and then to examine each element a little more closely.

Business accounting

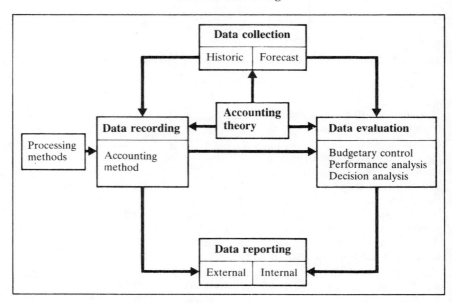

External environment

We use the term 'data' to mean those events affecting the business which are capable of being expressed in monetary terms. Later in this chapter, when we are examining the environment in which accounting operates, we will have to recognize that while the use of 'money terms' is probably essential, it does place important limitations on accounting information.

'Data collection' is the area of activities which provide the raw material of accounting. The data collected is 'historic' in the sense that it refers to events which have already taken place. Until 60 years ago accounting was largely an 'historic' art, concerning itself with what had happened, rather than making any attempt to predict and prepare for the future. The collection of forecast data is the firm's attempt to estimate the likely course of future events.

We must make an important observation here. Historic accounting attempts to describe events in money terms; the money terms are therefore secondary to the event. In other words, although accounting is sometimes said to be central to all business activities—the language of business—it is dependent upon the other functions of business, such as selling and production, to generate the 'event'. In this sense, historic accounting may be regarded as a 'service' function. Where accounting is employed as a controlling or predictive aid, however, it is a prelude to the event, serving the other functions by advising them on the course of action to take.

The historic data, once collected, is recorded in a manner which is in accordance with general accounting theory. The *method* of recording is provided by double entry bookkeeping rules. It is essential that we do not confuse bookkeeping with accounting—unfortunately an all too common misconception. Within our definition of accounting, bookkeeping occupies a small—though important—part. In the diagram, connected with 'data recording' is 'processing methods'. The days of writing the books of account with the aid of a quill pen are long since gone. Manual methods have given way to the mechanical, and, in the larger firms, the electronic computer is the modern equivalent of the ledger clerk.

'Data evaluation' is the most important area of accounting in the modern business. In the diagram we have divided this into three: budgetary control, performance analysis and decision analysis. Budgetary control necessitates the comparison of forecast information with the actual results, with an examination of any variance between the two. Performance analysis investigates the success of the business by testing its profitability, its liquidity— the ability to meet obligations as they fall due, its solvency—the ability to meet interest costs and repayments associated with long-term obligations, and its return on investment. We include in such analysis the use of flow of funds statements—the description of the sources of additional funds available to the business in a given period of time, and the uses to which these funds were put.

Decision analysis is of considerable importance to the business, and will be even more important in the future. It is here that the art of the accountant, the skill of the mathematician and insight of the economist are linked to provide a sound basis for decisions which affect the future of the business. In this book we will examine such issues as pricing, investment in long-lived assets, choosing among alternative course of action, and the relationship between volume of output, costs and profit.

'Data reporting' consists of two parts—internal and external. External reporting refers to the communication of financial information about the business to outside parties—the shareholders, Inland Revenue and various government bodies. Internal reporting highlights the need to communicate the results of financial analysis to management and others in an effective and comprehensible manner.

Accounting does not exist in a vacuum; it reflects the activities of the business which reacts and interacts with the external environment shaped by many different forces—political, social, economic, legal and technological. Traditionally, accounting has particularly related to the economic implications of business activity but now, with a growing awareness of a business's social responsibilities for the environment, for the use of scarce resources, for the provision of employment opportunity, accounting is beginning to reflect a new social awareness—a dimension which promises many exciting developments in the future.

In the centre of the diagram is 'accounting theory'—the foundation stone for the art of accounting. It is important for us that we understand the nature and origins of this theory, and the place which it is to occupy in the practice of accounting.

The nature and place of accounting theory

Accounting has sometimes been defined as 'what accountants do', and this rather inadequate tautology might help us to appreciate why accounting theory was virtually non-existent 50 years ago, and is today the source of much debate and controversy. Theories are conventionally described as either 'positive' or 'normative'. A positive theory is one which attempts to explain or describe what is, and a normative theory is concerned with what ought to be. Theory, in the natural sciences, is expressed in positive terms, because, for example, there is no need to make any value judgements about the boiling point of liquids—it exists as a fact. In the social sciences, however, theories are normative because they take as a starting point a value judgement of what ought to be.

If accounting is 'what accountants do' and we were to take this activity as having some absolute, unchanging basis in fact, then it would be possible to evolve a positive theory of accounting. But accounting, as we have defined it, is concerned with making judgements about the social and economic consequences of business activity, and the central problem of valuation and income measurement depends upon the way in which terms such as 'value' and 'income' are defined. Hence, in accounting, we are seeking to establish a normative theory, a theory by which we can evaluate and guide existing and proposed practices.

We will refer to the particular statements of accounting theory as 'postulates'—sometimes these are also referred to as principles or fundamental accounting concepts. The use of the word 'postulate' is quite deliberate; it means 'a law or rule adopted as a guide to action which rests on general acceptance rather than some basic undeniable truth'. Two words in this definition must be particularly stressed; a postulate is *general* and it offers a *guide*. Accounting postulates do not prescribe *exactly* how economic events affecting the business should be collected, recorded and evaluated; there is an infinite number of possible events, and no rules could hope to prescribe for every eventuality.

In the 'positive' physical sciences it is frequently possible to devise experiments to test any given theory. In the social sciences this is seldom possible, or, at least, it cannot be done in so rigorous a manner, because we cannot control, as in a scientific laboratory experiment, all of the complex variables which influence human and business behaviour. Because we cannot verify accounting postulates in any absolute sense, their acceptance is a process of evolution dependent upon three criteria—utility, feasibility and objectivity. A postulate is *useful* to the extent that it results in meaningful information to those concerned with the business; it is *feasible* to the extent that it can be implemented without unnecessary complication and without excessive cost; and it is *objective* to the extent that the resultant information is not the product of personal bias.

Very often these three criteria are in conflict with one another. For example, the postulates which are the most useful for the purposes of income measurement and decision-making are not those which are the most feasible or objective. The postulates which are currently accepted are those which strike a balance between the three tests. It is useful to bear this in mind, for much of the criticism levelled against accounting postulates attacks their usefulness and ignores completely the two other factors.

Accounting in historical perspective

Acceptance of postulates demands general consent, and the obtaining of general consent is a lengthy, time-consuming process. Contrary to much popular belief, accounting is not the product of the past 100 years but has a long and noble ancestry. It is useful for us, as we begin our exploration of modern business accounting, to spare a moment to place accounting in the context of its historical development.

The earliest attempts to record financial information date back to the Assyria of 3500 BC when it was thought necessary to record the payments made to the armies of the king. The payments, of course, were not in terms of money, but by means of cattle and precious stones. The Egyptian civilization, too, has left us fragments of detailed records relating to the building of the pyramids; the records of one overseer even detail the cost of nails needed to make the slaves' shoes. The records of these early civilizations are erratic in their form, but this is only to be expected in the absence of both an adequate numerical system and money. In any case, trade was not sufficiently developed to necessitate more than a cursory attempt to list some of the transactions which took place.

The Greek and the Roman periods show some advances in the art of record-keeping. The adoption of money as the normal medium of valuation and exchange in the sixth to fifth centuries BC made it possible for transactions to be recorded not as so many slaves, so many bushels of grain or the exchange of so many casks of wine against so many pounds of silver, but in terms of a particular system of currency. Apart from the use of money, however, improvements in methods of accounting were not consistently maintained and were confined to isolated examples. There is no evidence to indicate that there was any use made of what we would call 'double entry' bookkeeping; lists of receipts and payments are often given in narrative form, and even when the figures are clearly segregated from the text there is only occasionally segregation of the receipts from the payments.

It was the Arab traders of the seventh to eleventh centuries AD who provided the stimulus necessary to the eventual use of a double entry system of accounting. The traders who often visited India recognized the merit of a numerical system derived by the Hindus. The system is, of course, our own 'Arabic' notation, or, more properly, 'Hindu-Arabic', which made it possible to add lists of figures in a way which earlier civilizations had found impossible. Once figures began to be disposed in a single column instead of being scattered all over the page, the advantages of having *two* clearly separated columns to facilitate computation would slowly have been realized.

The first double entry bookkeeping records appeared in Italy in the fourteenth century, and the first accounting text appeared in 1494 under the authorship of one Luca Pacioli. His famous 'De Summa' was primarily a treatise on mathematics, but it included one important section on bookkeeping. The ideas expressed in it gradually gained acceptance and slowly became more sophisticated; for example, the practice of ascertaining profit at the end of each year rather than at the end of each trading venture was first proposed in 1605.

The nineteenth century saw a series of economic and social events which gave rise to a tremendous expansion of trade, providing the impetus for the development of a system of bookkeeping into a field of accounting. The extended system of ownership (by means of shares in a limited company) necessitated government legislation to provide for some minimum standards of accounting. Rapid industrialization, with the accompanying heavy investment in plant and machinery and associated complex manufacturing processes, gave rise to the development and expansion of that part of accounting normally referred to as 'cost accounting'.

The formation of the professional accounting bodies in the late nineteenth and early twentieth centuries provided for minimum standards of professional competence; it was not until 1942, however, that a series of statements called 'Recommendations on Accounting Principles' was inaugurated by the Institute of Chartered Accountants in England and Wales. These are intended to be statements of the best practice—and as such they are of great value and importance—but only recently has there been any systematic attempt in this country to develop more definitive statements of practice. The process of establishing accounting standards began in this country in 1969 when the Institute of Chartered Accountants in England

and Wales issued a 'Statement of Intent on Accounting Standards in the 1970s' in which the Institute announced its intention to advance accounting standards by:

(i)   narrowing the areas of difference and variety in accounting practice;
(ii) requiring businesses to disclose the accounting bases on which their published accounts are founded;
(iii) requiring businesses to disclose any departure from established definitive accounting standards; and
(iv) inviting comment from appropriate bodies on any draft proposals for standards.

To give effect to this proposal, the Institute formed in 1970 the Accounting Standards Committee, which by 1976 had been extended to embrace the six major accounting bodies in the UK, being reconstituted as the Consultative Council of Accounting Bodies (CCAB). This new body extended the scope of its activities beyond the development of accounting standards to involve such matters as commenting on company and revenue law changes, and acting as co-ordinators for the UK bodies with respect to international accounting matters. To date, this committee has issued nineteen 'Statements of Standard Accounting Practice' (SSAP) together with a number of 'Exposure Drafts' (ED) which invite comment and criticism before producing a definite statement. It is arguable, however, that these 'standards' are simply rules governing accounting practice rather than any attempt to provide a theoretical framework for accounting. Perhaps their value is more in the debates they engender than in the particular practice which they seek to encourage.

In a wider context, the CCAB is a member of the EEC 'Group d'études des experts comptables' which puts forward the profession's views on proposed EEC legislation which has particular bearing on fiscal matters. The most important example of this is the work on the 'Fourth Directive' much of which has found its way into the 1981 Companies Act. Still broader, is the International Accounting Standards Committee (formed in 1973) which had as its primary objective:

> 'To formulate and publish in the public interest, standards to be observed in the presentation of audited financial statements and to promote their world wide acceptance and observance.'

Although acceptance of IASC standards are not obligatory in the UK, the CCAB now seeks to incorporate relevant standards within the UK standards.

The years since the last war have seen an increasing emphasis on the provision of accounting information for management. Greater analysis and better presentation of historic financial data has been encouraged, and far more attention has been paid to accounting as a predictive device. Record-keeping, the art prescribed by Pacioli, is being placed in its perspective as an essential means to the end of providing management with information to check the results of decisions and predictions.

Increasing, too, is the recognition that business decisions have profound social as well as economic consequences, and businesses are being held to account for the almost endless social implications of their activities. An obvious example is the impact of the business on the environment—pollution, resource depletion, aesthetic qualities—or the extent to which employment opportunities are provided. If this social dimension is important, then it is undeniable that conventional accounting information and reports totally fail to reflect this 'social responsibility' of the business. This area of concern takes us to what some accountants believe to be one of the most exciting frontiers of accounting theory and practice.

References and further reading

AMERICAN ACCOUNTING ASSOCIATION (1966), *A Statement of Basic Accounting Theory*.

ASHTON (1983), UK Financial Accounting Standards. Woodhead-Faulkner.

BROMWICH and HOPWOOD (1983), 'Accounting Standard Setting: An International Perspective', 1983.

BUCKLEY, KIRCHER and MATHEWS (1968), 'Methodology in Accounting Theory', *Accounting Review*, April 1968.

CHAMBERS (1966), *Accounting, Evaluation and Economic Behaviour*. Law Book Co.

ESTER (1973), *Accounting and Society*. Melville Publishing Co.

HARVEY and KEER (1984), *Financial Accounting Theory*. Prentice-Hall.

IJIRI (1967), *The Foundations of Accounting Measurement*. Prentice-Hall.

LITTLETON and YAMEY (1956), *Studies in the History of Accounting*. Sweet and Maxwell.

LITTLETON and ZIMMERMAN (1962), *Accounting Theory: Continuity and Change*. Prentice-Hall.

POPOFF (1972), 'Postulates, Principles and Rules', *Accounting and Business Research*, Summer 1972.

STERLING (1970), 'Theory Construction and Verification', *Accounting Review*, July 1970.

TERLECKYJ (1973), 'Measuring Progress Towards Social Goals', *Management Science*, August 1973.

TINKER, MERINO and NEINMARK (1982), 'The normative origins of positive theories; ideology and accounting thought'. Accounting Organisations and Society, 1982.

WATTS and ZIMMERMAN (1979), 'The Demand and Supply of Accounting Theories: The Market for Excuses'. *Accounting Review*, April 1979.

Questions for discussion

1   Examine a series of job advertisements for accountants, and try to deduce what accounting is from the descriptions.

2   Find a number of different definitions of accounting, and consider the extent to which they coincide or diverge.

3   Normative accounting theories need to be 'generally acceptable' to be

of use. Discuss the extent to which the criteria for acceptability can be in conflict.

4 Outline the major influences on the development of accounting practices from the earliest times to the present day.

5 To what extent should accounting information reflect the impact the business has on the social as well as the economic environment?

6 Accounting is not an end in itself, but aims to help people make decisions. What different groups may need accounting information, and for what purposes?

7 Accounting theory is variously described as setting out 'principles', 'postulates', 'concepts', 'rules' or 'practices'. Is there any difference between these terms, or is this just a matter of semantics?

Part II

Financial accounting theory and practice

Chapters 2–4 explain the basic principles of income measurement and valuation in accounting, and the preparation of income statements and balance sheets. Chapter 5 and, later, Chapter 8 consider the formal bookkeeping used to reflect these concepts. Two major problems in accounting—depreciation and the valuation of stock and other assets—are explored in Chapters 6 and 7, and then the basic concepts and procedures of these early chapters (Chapters 2–8) are extended to partnership accounting (Chapter 9) and company finance, accounting and reporting (Chapters 10 and 11). The section concludes (Chapter 12) with a critical summary of accounting and economic concepts of value and income, leading to a review of the conceptual and operational problems of accounting for inflation.

2 The balance sheet

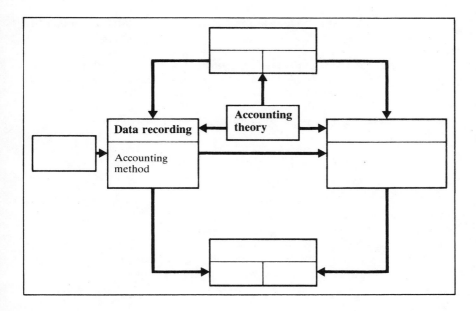

Accounting theory

Data recording

Accounting method

The accounting environment

The environment of the economic, legal, social and political world has provided the general framework for the development of accounting. The boundaries of accounting have been largely prescribed by the varying stages of economic development through which mankind has passed. The economies of the early civilizations depended to a large extent on barter—the exchange of one commodity for another; hence accounting was limited to such things as inventories of the possessions of kings and princes. The feudal system of Europe demanded a check on payments made by way of rent and tithe; accounting was accordingly developed to a stage sufficient to meet this need. The growth of trade in twelfth and thirteenth century Italy saw the birth of double entry accounting; the manorial system of England necessitated the keeping of household accounts; the growth of large industrial complexes in the nineteenth century accelerated the rise of cost accounting. There are many more examples which could be quoted, but perhaps these are sufficient to illustrate how accounting has responded

15

to the needs of the economy, and also helps to explain why the ideas of accounting and economics bear a close relationship to each other.

Accounting, however, is also influenced and constrained by legal considerations in the form of judicial decision and statute law. We may illustrate this point in relation to the limited company, where statute law in the form of the Companies Acts prescribes the keeping of adequate books and accounts, and lays down certain minimum standards in relation to the disclosure of information to shareholders. Judicial decision and statute law has indicated, for example, when the profits of a company shall be available, if so desired, for the payment of dividends.

The influence of taxation legislation has been primarily indirect in nature so far as the larger businesses are concerned. For the small business, however, there is little question that the main use of accounting has been in the preparation of the income tax return—a very restricted use indeed. There are many differences between tax and financial accounting, partly as a result of the use of differing income concepts, and partly because taxation is also used as an instrument of government policy to effect social reform or grant relief to specific industries, or industries in certain geographic areas.

The environmental postulates

The objective of the environmental postulates of accounting is to draw from the broader environment those aspects which are particularly relevant and necessary to the development of accounting. In one sense, these postulates can be no more than general descriptions of parts of our economic environment; however, the very fact that they are *selected* from a range of possibilities means that accounting considers them to be of particular importance. For our purpose we will identify three such postulates:

(1) Economic agents
(2) Business entity
(3) Money measurement.

(1)   Economic agents

An obvious fact about business organizations is that they consist of human beings. Anything that the business achieves is the result of human action, figures in themselves accomplishing nothing. Two firms with identical accounting systems can achieve entirely different results if, in the one, management ignores the information, and, in the other, management utilizes it.

Figure evidence, too, is only partial evidence; no system can describe in terms of numbers all the consequences of human action taken or planned. The postulate of economic agents is an assertion of the human factor which we must be careful not to ignore. It states, in essence, that humans exist, or in more precise terms, that economic agents are 'natural persons engaged in the economic activities of producing, owning, managing, storing, transferring, lending, borrowing and consuming commodities and services'.

(2)   Business entity

The business is an institution which may own and owe economic resources, and which may itself be owned by one or more agents. In accounting, all the records are kept from the viewpoint of the business rather than from that of the owner. In recording data in the accounts the important question is—how does it affect the business? For example, if the owner of a shop were to take cash from the till and put it into his pocket, the accounts would show that the cash had been reduced, even though the owner is himself no worse off.

The business entity postulate states that a distinction can be drawn between business and owner, and therefore that all transactions can be recorded as they affect the business as distinct from the owner. The distinction can be easily maintained in the case of the limited company because the law accords to the business a personality all of its own whereby it can sue and be sued in its own name instead of in the name of all its owners, the shareholders. Distinction is more difficult in the case of a partnership, and even more so in the case of the one-man business—the sole trader. Here, in a very real sense, the man is the business, but, nevertheless, accounting still maintains the separation of business and owner. This means that all the owner's personal affairs—his house mortgage, his expenditure on food, clothing and heating—will not appear in his books of account.

The idea of business entity has a close connection with that of stewardship. The owner is seen as entrusting the business and those who manage its affairs with his funds for which the business must account, that is, act as a steward. The stewardship idea is perhaps rather a narrow view of accounting, for many of the reports prepared are of more use to management than to the owners. Nevertheless, the stewardship idea does help to explain in part the greater emphasis which has been placed on accounting for outside parties.

(3)   Money measurement

In accounting, only those facts which can be expressed in terms of money are recorded, simply because money is accepted both as a store of value and a medium of exchange. The advantage is that a number of widely differing facts can be expressed in terms of a common denominator: what other easily understood means is there of adding together two buildings, ten machines and four vans?

Although money is probably the only practical common denominator, we must observe that there are two major limitations of this unit. In the first place there are a great many facts of vital concern to the business which cannot be expressed in money terms. For example, accounting cannot reveal that the managing director is unwell, or that the chief accountant and the production director are not on speaking terms, or that a strike is about to begin, or that a competitor has recently taken over the best customer.

Secondly, the use of money as a common denominator implies a homo-geneity—that one pound is like any other pound. Most modern economies are in inflationary conditions with prices rising. This means that the £1 of 1984 is not worth the same as the £1 of 1955. In general, accounting assumes the problem away (*see* Chapter 4), and only makes any allowance for changing price levels (*see* Chapter 12) in statements supplementary to the conventional records.

Business entity

The second of the environmental postulates was that of business entity. The concept was seen to be related to the idea of stewardship, namely, that the business is entrusted with funds by the owner for which it must account, that is, act as steward. Given that the distinction between business and owner can be maintained in logic—if not in reality—it follows that what a business owes must necessarily equate with what it owns. In account-ing what a buiness owes is referred to as its liabilities, and what it owns as its assets. The statement of a business's assets and liabilities at a particular moment in time is called the balance sheet.

The balance sheet

Before the assets and liabilities of a business can be recorded in the books of account, one further postulate is necessary. The postulate is that of duality, which states that any economic transaction must necessarily affect two aspects within the accounts. For example, if John Smith were to invest his life savings of £15,000 in a new business venture of, say, a bookshop of which he will be the sole owner and manager, then, from Mr Smith's point of view, he still has his £15,000. However, if we view this situation from the standpoint of the business, which has assumed a fictional life and identity quite separate from that of Mr Smith, the owner, then the result from the accounting point of view will be

John Smith, Bookseller
Balance Sheet as at 1 January 1984

Capital £15,000	Cash at bank £15,000

The business has an *asset* (cash at bank) of £15,000 which is exactly matched by its *liability* to the owner—the capital—of £15,000.

This relationship is also reflected in any balance sheet, a typical example of which is given below:

John Brown and Co.
Balance Sheet as at 31 December 1984

	£	£			£
Fixed Assets			**Capital**		
Buildings	6,000		Ownership interest	19,500	
Plant	5,000				
Vans	2,000				
	——	13,000			
Current Assets			**Current Liabilities**		
Stock	1,000		Creditors	2,500	
Debtors	3,000				
Cash	5,000				
	——	9,000			
		£22,000			**£22,000**

Let us examine the balance sheet in terms of the basic postulates we have identified so far. The 'business entity' involved is that of John Brown and Co. and the balance sheet appertains to that entity rather than to Mr Brown or any other individuals associated with the business. The 'money measurement' postulate is reflected by the fact that each item is expressed in money terms. The duality postulate is evidenced by the fact that the two sides 'balance'. The term 'balance sheet' is sometimes taken to mean that there is something good and significant about the totals contained therein; this is not so—the 'balancing' comes about simply because the duality postulate demands the recording of economic events in such a way that they must necessarily equate.

It will be seen that the assets are divided into two categories—fixed and current assets. The distinction is important because much attention is paid by lenders and others to the total of current assets and its relationship to current liabilities. The essence of the distinction is one of time. Current assets are those assets which within a short period of time—normally one year—will change their form (turnover); thus stock will be transformed by sale either into cash, or if the sale is on credit, into debtors. In their turn, the debtors will settle their account for cash, and the cash will be used to acquire, among other assets, more stock.

The current assets shown in the balance sheet, consist of three items:

(1) 'Stock' means 'the aggregate of those items of tangible property which (1) are held for sale in the ordinary course of business, (2) are in the process of production for such sales, or (3) are to be currently consumed in the production of goods or services to be available for sale'.
(2) 'Debtors' are amounts owed to the business by its customers.
(3) 'Cash' is the fund immediately available for disbursement without any

restriction. Sometimes this item is referred to as the 'unapplied funds' of the business in that it has not yet been used to acquire some other more productive asset.

Fixed assets are long-lived resources, and are normally acquired by the business to be used in the production of goods or services. In this balance sheet the investment in fixed assets consist of buildings, plant and vans.

The liabilities take two forms: the claims of the owners against the business, referred to either as the capital, ownership equity or ownership interest, and the claims of outsiders against the business.

While the individual assets and external liabilities of a business enterprise can be defined and measured independently of other elements in the accounting equation, this is not so with the ownership equity. The figure presented in the balance sheet of John Brown and Co. represents the original capital plus retained profits—which are ascertained as a result of the methods employed in measuring the specific assets and liabilities. To the extent that these items are under- or overvalued, and to the extent that non-monetary assets are omitted, e.g. the goodwill, or the skill of the management team, the total recorded amount of ownership equity will not represent the current value of the rights of the owners.

The liabilities to outside parties are normally claims against all the assets of the business rather than claims against specific assets. Current liabilities are obligations which fall due in the near future, normally within the next year. The Accounting Principles Board defines the term current liabilities as being 'used principally to designate obligations whose liquidation is reasonably expected to require the use of existing resources properly classifiable as current assets, or the creation of other current liabilities'. The particular current liability in our example, creditors, refers to the claims of suppliers and others.

The nature of assets

In describing the assets of John Brown and Co. we focused our attention on the *types* of assets rather than the *nature* of assets themselves. Although in accounting attention has been focused on classification and valuation of assets, there is a need to identify characteristics that are common to all assets. Sprouse and Moonitz defined assets as representing 'expected future economic benefits, rights to which have been acquired by the enterprise as a result of some current or past transaction'.

This definition identifies four essential characteristics:

(1) There must be a specific right which can, if necessary, be enforced legally. A machine on loan to a firm would not be regarded as an asset of the lessee.
(2) The benefits to be derived must be future; if an asset can no longer prefer any future rights and services then it is no longer an asset. Thus an item of equipment which is completely worn out and which has a zero scrap value is not an asset.
(3) The benefits must normally accrue to a specific entity, thus permitting

the exclusion of others. Any business has the right to use the roads, but this right does not result in an asset of the business.

(4) The rights must have been acquired as the result of a 'current or past transaction'. The firm must have incurred either a money sacrifice or a liability; if nothing was incurred in the acquisition of a particular item, then usually this item will not appear in the accounting records as an asset. A business's good reputation with customers will not appear as an asset.

The valuation of assets

Each of the assets of John Brown and Co. had monetary values assigned in them. It is important to recognize that this does not signify their 'worth' in the normally accepted meaning of the term—their market (realizable) value. Rather, the money values assigned to them are derived from the 'cost postulate' of accounting. In its crudest form this postulate states that an asset is worth the price (cost) paid to acquire it; thus assets are recorded in the books of account at their original purchase price, and this cost is the basis for all subsequent accounting for the asset. The emphasis in accounting is placed on input values rather than on output values as in economics.

There may, of course, be a correspondence between accounting values and market values in the case of certain assets. The asset 'cash' is an obvious example. In general, the longer an asset has been owned by the company, the less likely the accounting value is to correspond with the market value.

The cost postulate does not mean that all assets remain on the accounting records at their original cost. The input value for an asset that has a long but limited life is systematically reduced over that life by a process called depreciation which will be discussed in detail in Chapter 6. Depreciation is concerned with gradually reducing the cost of the asset by allocating part of the cost to expense—thus reducing profit—in each accounting period. There is no necessary relationship between depreciation and changes in the market value of the asset.

'Valuation' and 'value' are terms much used in accounting; indeed, it may be said that valuation lies very much at the centre of accounting. There are, however, numerous theories related to valuation and value in economic literature, but the complexity of the problem may be illustrated by considering a simple, everyday problem.

Assume that a student buys a textbook on accounting for £5. One notion of value may be to associate value with purchase price (as does accounting), and value the book at £5. But having purchased the book, and having used and annotated the copy, he may wish to sell it, obtaining a resale price of, say, £2. In the meantime, however, the purchase price of a new book has risen, because of inflation, to £6, and, also because he had purchased a first edition personally signed by the author, there may be some special value attached to the book. What then is the 'value' of the book? This is a question which may have no single correct answer, because it is closely related to the reasons for wanting a value and the particular circumstances at the moment of valuation. In such an unstable and subjective situation, one can perhaps sympathize with the accountant who wishes to cling to an apparently stable and objective measurement of value—that of purchase price or historic cost.

The consequences of determining the value of an asset by reference to its acquisition cost are explained more fully in Chapter 12, but the problems that this concept of value raises are so important that we must note some of these at this stage:

(1) If an asset has no acquisition cost, it is not an asset in the accounting sense, and hence does not appear in the accounts. The accumulated skills and co-operation of a management team, the near-monopolistic control over a large segment of its market, or the good reputation with customers—all are assets in the sense that they will generate future income, but, because of the cost postulate, they will not be recorded as such.

(2) If the value of an asset is determined by reference to its cost, and we depreciate that asset by reference to that cost, there comes a point when the asset will vanish from the records altogether, even though the business may continue to use that resource. Perhaps the most startling example of this was the one-time practice of the banks to reduce all of their buildings and sites to a 'value' of £1—clearly an absurd travesty of economic reality.

(3) The use of acquisition cost in determining profit is not a reliable measure. For example, Alan Smith is in business buying and selling tennis rackets. He buys five rackets for £20 each and sells them at £25 each. He then wishes to buy five more, but discovers that the acquisition price is now £22 per racket. If he had spent all of his 'profit' of £25, leaving him with his original £100, he would not be able to buy five more rackets. Hence, dependence upon historic acquisition cost can lead to unreal measurement of profit.

(4) Connected with this last point is the more general problem of inflation. The changes in the general purchasing power of money, and also in the specific value of individual assets in relation to money, mean that historic cost does not provide any dependable guide to the current value of an asset.

The nature of outside liabilities

As with assets, the discussion of outside liabilities centres on the classification and description rather than the inherent characteristics. Liabilities may be defined as 'the existing obligations of the business to provide money, goods or services to an agent or entity outside of the business at some time in the future'. This definition would include the following characteristics:

(1) The obligation must exist at the present time. An obligation which will not be incurred until some future date (normally referred to as a contingent liability) will not be included in the balance sheet.

(2) Normally there must be a known maturity value and the expectation that payment will certainly be required at some time in the future.

The balance sheet equation

Returning once more to the balance sheet of Mr Brown, we observed that the duality postulate necessarily led to the 'balancing' of assets and liabilities. The balance sheet equation simply states therefore that

Assets = Liabilities

or

$$\Sigma A = \Sigma L$$

Sometimes, the equation is written in a way which distinguishes between the liability to the owner and outside liabilities. Thus:

A = Proprietorship + Outside liabilities

The liabilities of the business provide the sources of funds which are then employed in acquiring various assets. In a sense, the asset cash is an unemployed fund because it has not yet been employed or applied in obtaining more productive assets.

We can represent these concepts diagrammatically:

Application of funds and unapplied funds	Sources of funds
Assets	Liabilities

$$\Sigma A = \Sigma L$$

The balance sheet is, of course, essentially a static representation of the firm's affairs; it presents the position of the business at one moment in time. In economic terms, it is concerned with *stocks* of wealth rather than *flows* (which accounting attempts to measure in the income statement).

It is convenient, however, to consider what effects transactions will have on the balance sheet in order to demonstrate how the basic equation of Assets = Liabilities can always be maintained. Beginning with Mr Brown's balance sheet let us consider what effect the following will have on the balance sheet:

(1) Let us assume that the business buys stock for £500 cash. This means

that cash will be reduced by £500, and that the item stock will be increased by £500.
(2) One of the debtors pays the business £300. Debtors will decrease by £300, and cash will increase by £300.
(3) The business buys on credit stock for £200. Creditors will increase by £200, and stock will increase by the same amount.
(4) Stock which cost £100 is sold for cash at £150. This transaction will affect the stock, the cash and also the ownership interest—because the transaction involves the making of a profit. It will be observed that the profit is a *liability* of the business—perhaps quite contrary to normal usage—because the business owes its owner the amount of the profit. In terms of the balance sheet, cash will increase by £150, stock will decrease by £100 and the ownership interest will be increased by £50.
(5) The business acquires a new machine for cash—£400. Cash will be decreased by £400 and plant will be increased by £400.

These transactions will produce a new balance sheet as follows:

		(1)	(2)	(3)	(4)	(5)	Total
Fixed Assets	£	£	£	£	£	£	£
Buildings	6,000						6,000
Plant	5,000					+400	5,400
Vans	2,000						2,000
Current Assets							
Stock	1,000	+500		+200	−100		1,600
Debtors	3,000		−300				2,700
Cash	5,000	−500	+300		+150	−400	4,550
	£22,000	—	—	+200	+50	—	**22,250**
Ownership interest	19,500				+50		19,550
Current Liabilities							
Creditors	2,500			+200			2,700
	£22,000	—	—	+200	+50	—	**22,250**

References and further reading

ACCOUNTING STANDARDS COMMITTEE (1971), *Disclosure of Accounting Policies*, November 1971.
CHAMBERS (1966), *Accounting, Evaluation and Economic Behaviour*. Law Book Co.
HENDRIKSEN (1982), *Accounting Theory*. Irwin.
MATTESSICH (1982), *Accounting and Analytical Methods*. Irwin.
MOONITZ (1961), *Basic Postulates of Accounting*. AICPA.
PERKS and BUTLER, *Accounting Standards in Practice; The Experience of SSAP 2 in Accounting and Business Research*, Winter 1977.

SPROUSE and MOONITZ (1963), 'Comments on a "tentative set of broad principles for business enterprise"', *Journal of Accounting*, April 1963.

Questions for discussion

1 'With inflation running in double figures, the accounting use of money and purchase price as a concept of value is so obviously misleading that it makes accounting quite useless.' Do you agree?

2 Make a list of your major possessions. What value do you place on them? Explain and justify your basis of valuation. Are you 'better off' now than you were a year ago? Explain and justify your answer.

3 The use of 'historic cost' as a concept of value is sometimes defended on the grounds that it is objective. Can you think of some examples where this is not so, and, if so, is the defence justified?

4 Why does a balance sheet balance?

5 Define carefully the terms 'asset' and 'liability'. How clear-cut is the distinction between 'fixed' and 'current' assets? How would you categorize the following:

(i) An investment in the shares of a subsidiary company.
(ii) An investment in the shares of a company which is the main source of your own company's raw material.
(iii) Expenditure incurred in forming a company, e.g. legal fees.

6 Prepare a series of sequential balance sheets from the following data:

(i) M. Brown commences business with cash of £10,000 which he deposits in a business bank account and uses his car, valued at £2,000, solely for business purposes.
(ii) He purchases for cash some business premises at a cost of £6,000.
(iii) Purchases on credit some stock for £1,500.
(iv) Sells stock which cost £700 on credit for £900.
(v) Pays office wages £100.
(vi) Pays some of his creditors £400.
(vii) Withdraws £200 for his own personal use.

7 Obtain several sets of published company accounts. Examine the balance sheets and discover:

(i) What types of assets are shown?
(ii) What is the basis of valuation of those assets?
(iii) To what extent (if any) are the balance sheets presented in different ways?
(iv) Who are the 'owners' of the company, and what, apparently, does the company owe to them?

8 What do you understand by the 'entity concept'? How do you reconcile the fact that records are kept from the viewpoint of the 'entity' with the fact that the business belongs to its proprietors?

9 If I own my own business, how can my capital invested in it be a liability?

10 To what extent does a balance sheet disclose what a business is worth?

11 What different groups of people may be interested in the balance sheet of a business? To what extent are their needs for information (a) similar and (b) different? Can all of the different needs be met by one balance sheet based upon a single set of principles?

12 (a) Draw up two balance sheets for 1983 and 1984 from the following information, inserting the necessary 'missing' item:

	1983	*1984*
	£	£
Cash at bank	2,500	2,900
Stock of goods	2,900	3,200
Freehold shop	13,500	13,500
Wages owed to staff	175	180
Amounts owed to suppliers (creditors)	1,600	1,800
Amounts owed by customers (debtors)	2,125	2,650
Cash in till	100	50
Delivery van	2,000	2,000

(b) Comparing the two balance sheets, what conclusions, if any, can you derive about the activities of the business during 1984?

(c) Would your conclusions be affected if you knew the proprietor had withdrawn £2,000 from the business for personal use?

(d) Does the value attached to the van in 1984 surprise you? If so, why?

13 From *The Times* 26 August 1976:

'Reginald Bosanquet, the news reader, phoned me yesterday with an intriguing sidelight on the question of suspect works of art. In particular, he was interested in the offer by the Colnaghi Gallery in London to refund the purchase price of an alleged painting by Samuel Palmer if it could be proved not to be his work.

'Bosanquet had a similar difficulty with a drawing of cattle in landscape, bought as a Gainsborough from the Colnaghi Gallery in 1955. It was a wedding present from one of his former wives, so he is not sure how much was paid for it, though he thinks it may have been £40. (That seems improbably low, even for 1955.)

'The painting came equipped with a certificate from Colnaghi that it was a genuine Gainsborough. Some time later, though, he discovered that it was in fact by Gainsborough Dupont, the master's nephew and pupil. Two years ago he approached Colnaghi and was duly offered his money back. But what incensed him was that he was offered only the low sum paid in 1955. He thinks he should have been offered something nearer the real value of a genuine Gainsborough drawing today.

'"After all, if I had put the money into shares or almost anything it would be worth a lot more" he pointed out.

'Colnaghi's do not see it the same way. "We will give him his money back but we have no obligation to offer him a profit", said Alex Wengraf, one of the firm's directors. "We have never denied our responsibilities in this area, but we don't exceed them.

'"In any case, if he were to offer it at Sotheby's or somewhere as a Gainsborough Dupont he would get a lot more than £40. Even without seeing it I think I can say I would be happy to pay more than that."

'Bosanquet, though, points out that the painting still has Colnaghi's certification that it is a genuine Gainsborough. Naturally, the firm are anxious that he should not sell it with that still attached. He thinks that he is entitled to some consideration for removing it.

'It is, as art dealers have been saying ever since the disputed Palmers came to light, a difficult area. If I were Bosanquet I should simply hang on to the drawing and enjoy it.'

Discuss the concepts of value inherent in this article, and advise Mr Bosanquet.

14 T.W. commenced business on 1 January with capital in cash of £7,500. Show the balance sheet at the start and after each of the following days' transactions:

			£
Jan.	1	Bought lease of a shop	5,000
	2	Bought goods for cash	300
		Bought goods from Weston and Sons on credit	1,250
	7	Cash sales (of goods costing £250)	360
		Bought goods on credit from P. Green	320
		Paid wages to assistant	60
	14	Sold goods on credit to M. Potts (cost £160)	300
		Cash sales (cost £100)	150
		Paid wages to assistant	60
	20	Goods returned by M. Potts (cost £30)	70
	21	Paid Weston and Sons on account	1,000
		Paid wages to assistant	70
	26	Received cash from M. Potts	230
	28	Cash sales (cost £300)	560
		Bought office fixtures on credit from Roneo Ltd	500
		Paid wages to assistant	60

Note: There is no need in this question to distinguish between cash in hand and cash in the bank.

3 Income measurement—expense

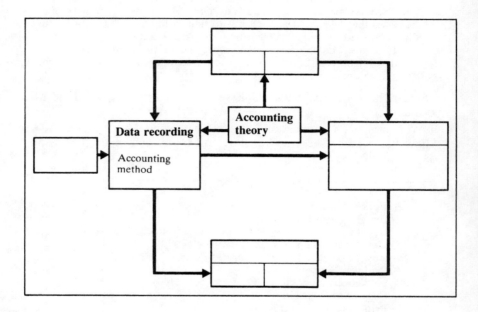

The nature of profit

In the example of the previous chapter we observed that when the item of stock which cost £100 was sold for £150, the resulting difference of £50 was the profit (or income). The measurement of profit is central to the art of accounting, and it demands the identification of the revenues and expenses of a business, and a system by which they can be matched to determine profit. Because of this centrality, we might legitimately expect that accounting has evolved some precise concepts to achieve this end. This is not so, perhaps mainly because income is in itself an elusive concept. Because of the practical importance of the measurement of income in very many everyday affairs, extensive rules have been developed by accountants, by the courts of law, by Inland Revenue and by other regulatory bodies. The various rules emanating from these authorities are often in conflict, since each has used a concept of income suited to his own purpose.

A year's income, fundamentally, is the maximum amount that a person can dispose of over the course of a year and still remain as well off at the end of the year as at the beginning. This definition in itself begs two questions: how do we measure wealth (value) at the beginning and the end of the year, and what is meant by 'as well off'? Essentially the measurement of value and the meaning of 'well offness' involve the making of subjective judgements. The accountant, who tries to remain objective, has sought to eliminate the element of subjective judgement from the determination of income. He has tried to focus attention not on the stocks of wealth, but on the flows of wealth, i.e. the revenues and expenses attributable to business transactions, and, in so doing, has established as nearly as possible hard and fast rules of calculation to eliminate the guesswork and to ensure precision. The precision is spurious in so far as it can only result in an approximation to income in a business world where prices and business prospects are continually fluctuating.

The procedures of accounting measurement of income are everywhere permeated by the assumption that the monetary unit is a constant and reliable measure. The assumption of stable money values—so evidently contrary to our own experiences in an inflationary economy—is probably necessary in the practical situation where innumerable transactions take place, but in making this assumption—in the name of objectivity and feasibility (*see* Chapter 4)—the accountant is evading the problem.

We must not suppose from the foregoing that the accountant's calculations should be discarded on to the rubbish heap. They do provide some measurement of income—and some measurement is better than none at all; secondly, if we can understand the accounting postulates of income measurement and know their weaknesses, it is possible to adapt the accounting information to provide a result more appropriate to our own subjective concept of income. With this in mind, we turn our attention to the first of the income postulates—that of accrual.

The accrual postulate

The accrual postulate states that income (profit) arises from events which affect the owner's equity and *only* from such events. The acquisition of a machine (*see* page 24) merely resulted in a transformation of assets, whereby the machine was substituted for cash. If we look at our example again, and reconsider the sale of stock, which cost £100, for £150, this transaction can be broken into two parts. The first effect is to reduce the asset stock and hence reduce the liability to the owner by £100. Thus the position in column (4a) below is

	(1/2/3)	(4a)	(4b)	Total
Fixed Assets	£			£
Buildings	6,000			6,000
Plant	5,000			5,000
Vans	2,000			2,000

(*continued*)

(*continued*)

	(1/2/3)	(4a)	(4b)	Total
Current Assets	£			£
Stock	1,700	−100		1,600
Debtors	2,700			2,700
Cash	4,800		+150	4,950
	£22,200	−100	+150	**22,250**
Capital				
Ownership interest	19,500	−100	+150	19,550
Current Liabilities				
Creditors	2,700			2,700
	£22,200	−100	+150	**22,250**

The sale of the stock for £150 increases the asset cash and increases the liability to the owner—column (4b). The net effect is to increase the ownership interest by £50, exactly balanced by an increase in assets of £50.

Any increase in owner's equity resulting from such transactions is called a *revenue*; any decrease is called an *expense*. *Income* (or *profit*) is the difference between revenue and expense. Restating the transactions above, the £150 is a revenue, the £100 an expense, and £50 the profit. One of the most important purposes of financial accounting is to relate or match revenue with the associated expense. This 'matching concept' may at first sight seem a matter of simple common sense, but two examples may serve to alert us to the difficulties encountered in achieving a 'match'.

Assume that a business buys for resale 200 cans of soup at a cost of 10p per tin. A little later on, a further 300 tins are purchased at a higher cost of 12p per tin. So far, the business has spent

		£
200 @ 10p	=	20.00
300 @ 12p	=	36.00
		£56.00

The business then sells 400 tins at a price of 15p per tin, a revenue of £60. How much profit has been made? The problem is in deciding what is the relevant expense to match with the revenue. Do we assume that we sold the first 200 tins first, for in that case the profit is £16, viz.:

				£
Revenue	400 @ 15p	=		60.00
Expense	200 @ 10p	=	£20.00	
	200 @ 12p	=	£24.00	44.00
Profit				£16.00

On the other hand, it could be argued that the tins most recently acquired were sold first—simply because they were stacked at the front of the pile. Hence the profit would be £14, viz.:

				£
Revenue	400 @ 15p	=		60.00
Expense	300 @ 12p	=	£36.00	
	100 @ 10p	=	£10.00	46.00
Profit				£14.00

Which, then, is the 'right' profit?

Another illustration of the problems of matching revenue and expense is occasioned by the sort of expense which is not easily and directly attributable to any particular revenue or sale. For example, expenditure on such things as advertising or research and development poses particular problems. If, towards the end of a financial year, a business spends heavily on an advertising campaign which its marketing director thinks will be of benefit for several months, how much of that expenditure should be 'matched' with the revenue earned within the financial year in order to ascertain the 'right' profit?

This last illustration leads us naturally to the problem of the 'accounting period', the artificial division of the total life of the business into short segments of time.

The accounting period

Considered over the whole life of the business, net income is simply the difference between what the owners put into the business at its inception and what they get out of it in the end—an amount that can be easily determined. But businessmen cannot wait until the business has ended to know how much income has been earned; they need this information at much shorter intervals to help them decide if they should continue. In accounting, the intervals, or accounting periods, are normally one year, although for management purposes reports (often called interim statements) are prepared at much shorter intervals. The use of a yearly period is now deeply entrenched in custom and law; the Companies Act and the Income Tax Acts require annual statements of profit, and both national and local government run their affairs on an annual cycle.

Businesses are living organisms, and the act of dividing the flow of events into time intervals is necessarily arbitrary, since business activities do not halt or change in any measurable way as one time period ends and another begins. If there is need for such a division, then it may make greater sense to relate the period to the production cycle of a business or some multiple thereof. For example, the natural flow of events in a capital-intensive industry such as shipbuilding is clearly different from that in the newspaper industry or in a retail undertaking, yet the accounting period for which income is measured is usually of a year's duration.

We can view the accounting period diagrammatically:

The life of the business has been cut into time intervals (T_0, T_1). At T_0 a balance sheet will have been prepared, as also at T_1. The problem of accounting is to identify and measure the stream of revenues and expenses which relate to the interval (T_1-T_0). The measurement of revenue will be discussed in the next chapter, and we turn our attention here to the measurement of expense in a given accounting period.

Definitions

We must first ensure that we understand the meaning which accountants attribute to certain key terms—'cost', 'expense' and 'expenditure'. Accountants often use these terms loosely, partly because there is no universal agreement on their meaning. For our purpose we will make use of the following definitions:

(1) 'Cost' means a money sacrifice or the incurring of a liability in pursuit of the business objectives. For example, the payment in cash for office salaries involves a money sacrifice, and the acquisition of stock on credit necessitates the incurring of a liability.
(2) 'Expenditure' means a money sacrifice, and is thus a more restrictive term than 'cost'.
(3) 'Expense' means an expired cost, that is a cost from which all benefit has been extracted during a given accounting period.

The relationship between cost and expense

We can distinguish three categories of events in considering what 'expense' is properly attributable to a given accounting period:

(1) Costs of this year which are also expenses of this year. This is the simplest—and most common—of all. If an item or service is acquired

during the year (either through money payment or the incurring of a liability) it is a cost; if it is consumed during the year it is also an expense.

(2) Cost of earlier years which will become (a) wholly or (b) partly expenses of this year:

(a) There are two principal types of costs in this category. The first of these is the stock of goods for resale which were acquired last year but not sold till this year. Last year they were a cost, but this year, at the time of sale, they become an expense.

The second type is that of prepaid expenses. These represent services acquired prior to this year but not yet used up when the year begins. They become expenses in the year in which the services are used up. For example, rent paid in last year in respect of this year will be a 'cost' (or 'prepaid expense') of last year, but an expense of this year.

(b) The second category is that of long-lived assets. Most fixed assets (with the exception of land) have a limited useful life. They are acquired with the expectation that they will be used in the business in future periods, and will in part become expenses in each of those periods. The mechanism used to convert these assets to expenses over a number of accounting periods is called depreciation, and is described in Chapter 5.

(3) Costs of this year which become either (a) partly expenses of this year or (b) wholly expenses of later years:

(a) In this category there will appear all those goods and services whose benefit will be consumed only partly in this year. All fixed assets acquired in the current period will normally fall into this category. Items such as rent and rates often refer partly to this period and partly to later periods, i.e. are partly 'prepayments'.

(b) The most important item in this category is that of stock which will be sold in a later accounting period.

The accounting equation

The basic accounting equation, arising out of the entity concept, was stated in Chapter 2 as Assets = Liabilities, or $A = L$. In the example at the beginning of the present chapter we analysed the sale of stock which cost £100 for £150 into its two component parts. First we noted that the reduction in stock of £100 was exactly balanced by the reduction in the owner's equity of £100. Secondly, the sale of the stock for £150 gave rise to a revenue of £150, increasing the owner's equity, exactly balanced by the increase in the asset cash. The net overall effect was to increase the assets by £50 and the liabilities by £50.

In practice, we would not wish to draw up a new balance sheet every time such a transaction took place, so we store and accumulate all such expenses and revenues, only matching the aggregate values when we wish to ascertain the profit for any given accounting period. Returning both to our equation and example, we have

(i) $A = L$

and, after the sale of the stock which cost £100,

(ii) $A - £100 = L - £100$

or

$A - E = L - E$

which, rewritten, becomes

(iii) $(A - E) + E = L$

Turning to the revenue aspect of the transaction, we have

(iv) $A + £150 = L + £150$

or

$A + R = L + R$

which, rewritten, becomes

(v) $(A + R) - R = L$

Putting equations (iii) and (v) together, we have

(vi) $A + (R - E) = L + (R - E)$

so that the change in the assets (i.e. by $R - E$) is exactly matched by the change in the liabilities (i.e. $R - E$), where $R - E$ has been previously defined as profit.

It is convenient, however, if we wish to store all the revenue and expense values to note that the value of the assets *after* incurring a revenue or expense plus the incurred expense exactly equals the sum of the liabilities plus the revenue earned, i.e.

(vii) $A_{R, E} + E = L + R$

We normally abbreviate this (in a rather inexact way) as

(viii) $A + E = L + R$

but it must be remembered that the assets have been adjusted for the revenues and expenses earned and incurred.

It may appear slightly odd that assets and expenses are added together, but a moment's reflection will show that expenses are no more than expired assets (or 'costs' as defined above), i.e. assets from which some or all benefit has been consumed.

The diagram in Chapter 2 can now be extended:

Application of funds and unapplied funds		Sources of funds	
Balance sheet	Assets	Liabilities	
Income statement	Expenses	Revenues	

$$\Sigma A + \Sigma E = \Sigma L + \Sigma R$$

This diagram can now be used to illustrate the relationship between cost and expense outlined in the previous section.

(1) Costs of this year which are expenses of this year

We may take as our example the item of rent. Let us assume that the rent is £120 per annum which is paid during the accounting period. We have a cost which is also an expense, and on the diagram it can appear thus:

Cash	−120	
Rent	+120	

$$\Sigma A + \Sigma E = \Sigma L + \Sigma R$$

The asset cash is reduced by £120, and the expense of rent is increased by £120. If during the year we had only actually paid £80, the cost (and expense) to us in the accounting period would still be £120, i.e. £80 through money payment and £40 through the incurring of a liability. Thus:

Cash	−80	Accrual	+40
Rent	$\begin{cases} +80 \\ +40 \end{cases}$		

$$\Sigma A + \Sigma E = \Sigma L + \Sigma R$$

The cash payment of £80 reduces cash by that amount, and the rent expense is increased similarly. Since the total cost (and also the total expense) applicable to the accounting period is £120, we increase rent by £40, and correspondingly increase the liability of the business in the item 'accrual' by £40. Accruals are normally included with the creditors on the balance sheet and described as 'Creditors and accruals'.

(2)   Costs of earlier years which will become (a) wholly or (b) partly expenses of this year

In category (a) we identified two main subdivisions—stock and prepayments. We will deal firstly with the item of stock.

Let us assume that at the beginning of the accounting period the balance sheet of a firm is as follows:

Balance Sheet as at 1 January 1984

	£		£
Fixed Assets	10,000	**Capital**	14,000
Current Assets		**Current Liabilities**	
Stock	5,000	Creditors	3,000
Debtors	1,000		
Cash	1,000		
	£17,000		**£17,000**

At the end of the last accounting period the firm had incurred a cost for stock of £5,000. This stock remained unsold at 31 December 1983, and hence was an asset at that date. At the start of the new accounting period it is assumed that this initial (opening) stock will be sold prior to any additional stock acquired during the accounting period. (This assumption will be discussed in Chapter 7.) The result is that the cost of the last accounting period wil! become an expense of this one. In terms of our diagram:

Stock −5,000	
Cost[1] of goods sold +5,000	

$$\Sigma A + \Sigma E = \Sigma L + \Sigma R$$

We must note at this point that any stock acquired during the year (normally referred to as purchases) is often treated immediately as an expense, and any adjustment for stock unsold at the end of the year (i.e. the third category of cost items) is made when the income statement is prepared.

The second type of cost in this category is that of prepayments—costs incurred last year on such items as rent or rates which become expenses of this year because they were paid in advance. Let us take as an example the balance sheet of a firm as at 1 January 1984:

Balance sheet as at 1 January 1984

	£		£
Fixed Assets	10,000	**Capital**	13,000
Current Assets		**Current Liabilities**	
Stock	2,000	Creditors	2,000
Debtors	1,000		
Prepayments	100		
Cash	1,900		
	£15,000		**£15,000**

Since the item of prepayments will become an expense of this year, all

---

1   Strictly speaking the 'expense of goods sold', but this expression, which is in common usage, is an example of loose terminology.

benefit from it having been exhausted, the effect will be

Prepayment	100 − 100	
Rent	+100	

$$\Sigma A + \Sigma E = \Sigma L + \Sigma R$$

In category (b) there will appear the long-lived assets acquired in previous accounting periods which are apportioned to expense over succeeding periods by the process of depreciation. In this chapter we will not explore the concept or process, but merely observe, in terms of our quadrant, what the effect will be:

Plant	10,000 − 500	
Depreciation	+500	

$$\Sigma A + \Sigma E = \Sigma L + \Sigma R$$

Assuming that the depreciation appropriate to the period is £500, the book value of the asset plant will be reduced by that amount, and the item depreciation will be charged as an expense.

(3)   Costs of this year which become either (a) partly expenses of this year, or (b) wholly expenses of later years

In the first category will appear long-lived assets acquired during the current accounting period; the depreciation element will be treated in the manner indicated above. Also will appear those services paid for in the current year but which partly relate to the following year. A rent payment of £120 may relate £80 to this year and £40 to the following year. The effect of this can be illustrated thus:

	(i)	*(ii)*	
Prepayment		+40	
Cash	−120		
Rent	+120	−40	

$$\Sigma A + \Sigma E = \Sigma L + \Sigma R$$

Initially the entire payment will be treated as though it were an expense. This is purely a procedural device, because it would be unnecessarily cumbersome to treat the payment as an asset and release a portion of the cost to expense every day. At the end of the accounting period the various service expenses are inspected to establish whether part of the payment should be more properly treated as a prepayment. The adjustment is then made as illustrated in column (ii).

The second category includes the most important item of stock unsold at the end of the year. It will be recalled that when discussing the second type of expense we observed that stock acquired during the year was initially, for procedural convenience, treated as an expense (purchase). At the end of the year an adjustment is made for the stock on hand (closing stock). The full position of stock will be as follows:

	(1)	*(2)*	*(3)*	*(4)*		*(1)*
Stock	2,000	−2,000		+500	Liabilities	7,000
Cash	5,000		−3,000			
Purchases		+2,000	+3,000	−500	Revenues	

$$\Sigma A + \Sigma E = \Sigma L + \Sigma R$$

(1) The opening position shows the assets of cash and stock equating the liabilities.
(2) The opening stock is assumed to be sold first; thus the cost of stock is treated as an expense.
(3) Additional stock is acquired during the period, but is initially treated wholly as an expense.
(4) The stock at close is treated as an asset, i.e. purchases are reduced by the amount of the closing stock.

In the income statement, the position is normally described as

	£	£
Opening stock	2,000	
Purchases	3,000	
	———	5,000
Less: Closing stock		500
Stock sold during the period		**£4,500**

Recording transactions in the quadrant

As each business transaction occurs, it is necessary to record the effect each has on the assets, expenses, revenues and liabilities of the business. It follows from the entity postulate that any single transaction will be recorded twice, in order to keep the equation balanced. For example, if Mr Brown commenced business with cash of £1,000, the transactions are recorded thus:

Asset		**Liability**	
Cash	+1,000	Capital	+1,000

If he then buys goods for resale (stock) for £150, the result is

Asset		**Liability**	
Stock	+150	Capital	+1,000
Cash	+1,000 − 150		

It is convenient to separate the pluses and minuses for each asset, etc., so that we have a layout in the form

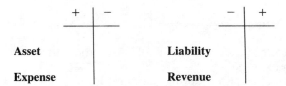

For reasons which will be explained in Chapter 5, the plus and minus has been reversed on the opposite sides of the balance sheet.

Applying this to a fuller illustration, we may record the following transactions relating to J. Brown and Co.:

(i)   J. Brown starts business with cash of £1,000.
(ii)   Buys furniture for shop—cash £300.
(iii) Buys goods for resale—cash £150.
(iv)   Buys more goods for resale on credit from Smith at £180.
(v)   Sells goods for cash—£120.
(vi)   Pays wages of assistant—cash £10.
(vii) Sells goods on credit to Jones—£90.
(viii) Pays Smith cash on account—£120.
(ix)   Pays rent in cash £12.

In terms of our quadrant the result is

		£	£			£	£
(ii)	Furniture	+ 300		(i)	Ownership interest		+1,000
(vii)	Debtors	+ 90		(iv)	Creditors		+ 180
(i)	Cash	+1,000		(viii)		−120	
(ii)			−300				
(iii)			−150				
(v)		+ 120					
(vi)			− 10				
(viii)			−120				
(ix)			− 12				
(iii)	Purchases	+ 150		(v)	Sales		+ 120
(iv)		+ 180		(vii)			+ 90
(vi)	Wages	+ 10					
(ix)	Rent	+ 12					
		+1,862	−592			−120	+1,390

We may extract the final balance for each of the items to draw up what is usually referred to as a 'trial balance'—a check to see that our equation still balances. A fuller consideration of the trial balance will be given in Chapter 5.

J. Brown

	£	£		£	£
Assets			**Liabilities**		
Furniture	300		Capital	1,000	
Debtors	90		Creditors	60	
Cash	528			——	1,060
	——	918			

J. Brown *(continued)*

	£	£		£	£
Expenses			**Revenue**		
Purchases	330		Sales	210	210
Wages	10			——	
Rent	12				
	——	352			
		£1,270			£1,270

i.e.

$$£918 + 352 = 1060 + 210$$

or

$$A + E = L + R$$

The income statement and balance sheet

Once the trial balance has been extracted, it is then necessary to make any required adjustments to the 'expense' items, as illustrated earlier in the chapter.

We may consolidate these ideas by considering a further example which begins at the point of a trial balance, pausing momentarily to acquaint ourselves with some of the, as yet, unfamiliar terminology used:

(1) 'Returns inwards' refers to goods sold which have been returned to John Brown and Co. by customers; this expense is deducted from the sales revenue to enable the effective sales to be clearly stated.
(2) 'Returns outwards' refers to goods (purchases) acquired which have been returned to the suppliers; it is deducted from the purchases.
(3) 'Carriage inwards' are delivery charges incurred in acquiring the purchases; this item is added to the purchases.
(4) 'Carriage outwards' are delivery charges incurred in getting goods to customers.
(5) 'Discount allowed' are the expenses incurred in allowing a percentage reduction to debtors who settle their account within a specified period.
(6) 'Discount received' are the converse of 'discount allowed'.
(7) 'Drawings' relates to the cash taken from the business by the owner. This item is *not* an expense, but is deducted from the owner's equity, i.e. reduces the indebtedness of the business to the owner. Drawings are normally thought of as being an anticipation of profit, and as such they are not an expense of the business.

John Brown and Co.

	£		£	£
Land and buildings	9,000	Ownership equity	14,000	
Plant	7,000	*Less:* Drawings	3,000	
Cars	2,000		———	11,000
Stock	4,000			
Debtors	3,000	Creditors		2,000
Cash	6,000			
	£31,000			**£13,000**

	£		£
Purchases	17,000	Sales	42,000
Returns inwards	500	Returns outwards	400
Carriage inwards	200	Discount received	600
Carriage outwards	300		
Wages	5,500		
Rent	400		
Rates	300		
Insurance	400		
Discount allowed	400		
	£25,000		**£43,000**

$$\Sigma A \quad + \quad \Sigma E \quad = \quad \Sigma L \quad + \quad \Sigma R$$
$$£31,000 \quad + \quad 25,000 \quad = \quad 13,000 \quad + \quad 43,000$$

As indicated in the text above (pages 35–39), the firm will examine its revenues and expenses to ascertain whether any adjustments are necessary before calculating the net profit of the year. Let us assume that on investigation it is discovered that

(1) Stock on hand at close is £3,800 (category 3b).
(2) Rates owing for the year but not yet paid amount to £80 (category 1).
(3) The rent paid (£400) includes rent of £60 which relates to next year (category 3a).
(4) Professional fees owing amount to £100 (category 1).
(5) Depreciation of £700 is to be provided for the plant (category 2b).

The income statement, more usually called a 'profit and loss account', will be as follows:

Income Statement for the period ended 31 December 1984

	£	£	£	£
Revenues				
Sales		42,000		
Less: Returns inwards		500		
		———	41,500	
Discounts received			600	
			———	42,100

Income Statement for the period ended 31 December 1984
(*continued*)

	£	£	£	£
Expenses				
Opening stock		4,000		
Purchases	17,000			
Less: Returns outwards	400			
	16,600			
Carriage inwards	200			
		16,800		
		20,800		
Less: Closing stock		3,800		
			17,000	
Carriage outwards			300	
Wages			5,500	
Rent (400 − 60)			340	
Rates (300 + 80)			380	
Insurance			400	
Discounts allowed			400	
Professional fees (+ 100)			100	
Depreciation (+ 700)			700	
				25,120
Net Profit				**£16,980**

The balance sheet will appear as follows:

John Brown and Co.
Balance Sheet as at 31 December 1984

	£	£	£		£	£	£
Fixed Assets				**Ownership Equity**			
Land and				Balance 1.1.84			
buildings		9,000				14,000	
Plant	7,000			Net profit	16,980		
Less:				*Less:*			
Depreciation	700			Drawings	3,000		
		6,300				13,980	
Cars		2,000					27,980
			17,300				
Current Assets				**Current Liabilities**			
Stock		3,800		Creditors and			
Debtors and				accruals			2,180
prepayments		3,060					
Cash		6,000					
			12,860				
			£30,160				**£30,160**

References and further reading

BACKER (1966), *Modern Accounting Theory*. Prentice-Hall.

BAXTER (1971), *Depreciation*. Sweet and Maxwell.

BAXTER and DAVIDSON (1962), *Studies in Accounting Theory*. Sweet and Maxwell.

HENDRIKSEN (1982), *Accounting Theory*. Irwin.

Questions for discussion

1   Explain why a profit is represented by an equivalent increase in assets.

2   It is possible, after making appropriate adjustments, to measure profit by calculating the change in capital between two dates. Why then is it necessary to prepare an income statement (or profit and loss account)?

3   Make a list of the main sectors of British industry and try to ascertain a typical 'production cycle' in each. How well does the accounting year match up with these cycles? What problems may any 'mismatch' occasion?

4   Examine a number of published company accounts and ascertain the date of the accounting year-ends. Can you find any explanation for the selection of a particular year-end date?

5   Define carefully the terms 'cost', 'expense' and 'expenditure'. Collect other definitions from alternative sources, and consider the extent to which they are in agreement.

6   'An expense is an expired asset'. Make a list of the main categories of assets and consider to what extent the statement is correct.

7   The following expenditure in the year to 31 December 1984 relates to motor vans owned by a small haulage company:

Petrol, oil and repairs	£800
Licences—year to 31 March 1983	80
Tyres	90
Insurance—year to 31 March 1983	100

On 31 December 1984, the stock of tyres amounted to £40, and petrol bills unpaid amounted to £43.

(a) Ascertain the 'expense' for the year ended 31 December 1984.

(b) How might the value of the tyre stock at 31 December have been established? What are the difficulties in establishing a value for year-end stock?

8 Complete the following table, to show how costs incurred during the year ended 31 March 1984 affect the expenses of that, and the subsequent, year:

Details	Payment during 1983/84	Expenses 1983/84	Unexpired expenses 31.3.84	Expenses 1984/85	Unexpired expenses 31.3.85
	£	£	£	£	£
(a) Goods bought and sold during 83/84 (i.e. 1.4.83–31.3.84)	500				
(b) Goods bought during 83/84 sold April 84	220				
(c) Typewriter bought April 83 expected to last five years	180				
(d) Insurance premium paid on 1.1.84 for one year in advance	96				
(e) Freehold land bought in 83/84 expected to rise in value by 10% each year	8,200				
(f) Advertising campaign expenditure 30.9.83 results likely to be effective for two years	2,400				

9 The following data relate to the transactions of H. Smith, a sole trader, for June 1984:

June 1 Started business with £600 in the bank and £50 in hand
    2 Bought £500 goods on credit
    3 Sold goods on credit for £143
    4 Bought goods for cash £23
    5 Bought old delivery van paying by cheque £500
    7 Paid for petrol by cheque £18
    9 Sold goods on credit for £115
   11 Bought goods on credit for £366
   13 Sold goods for cash £200 which was then paid into the bank
   14 Paid sundry expenses in cash £15
   15 H. Smith took £15 cash for his own use

18 Paid some creditors on account by cheque £300
23 Collected cheques from debtors and paid the money into the bank
24 Sold goods for cash £60
27 Sold goods on credit for £400
28 Paid by cheque one month's rent of the office £90
30 H. Smith drew £20 in cash for his own use

Stock at close was valued at £329

Required:

(a) Make a list of the various types of assets, liabilities, revenue and expenses found in this data, e.g. assets include bank, cash, stock, van, etc.
(b) Using the 'quadrant' illustrated in this chapter, record each of the transactions in turn, making sure that after each transaction the equation $(A + E = L + R)$ still balances.
(c) Prepare an income statement for June 1984, taking care to make the necessary adjustment for the closing stock.
(d) Prepare a balance sheet as at 30 June 1984.

10 The following list of balances was extracted from the books of Clifton, a trader, at 31 December 1984:

	£	£
Capital		15,000
Land and buildings	7,000	
Furniture and fittings	1,400	
Stock (1.1.84)	6,100	
Purchases	58,700	
Sales		69,300
Debtors and creditors	5,850	5,545
Rent received		415
Discounts allowed	1,320	
Discounts received		925
Bad debts	325	
Wages and salaries	7,045	
Drawings	1,600	
General expenses	865	
Bank	680	
Rates and insurances	300	
	£91,185	**£91,185**

The following matters are to be taken into account:

(i)   Stock at 31.12.84, £8,500.
(ii)   Wages outstanding at 31.12.84, £415.
(iii) Rates paid in advance at 31.12.84, £50.

(iv) Depreciation on furniture and fittings is to be provided for the year ended 31.12.84 at 10% of the balance at 1 January 1984.

Required:
Prepare an income statement for the year ended 31 December 1984 and a balance sheet as at that date.

4 Income measurement—revenue

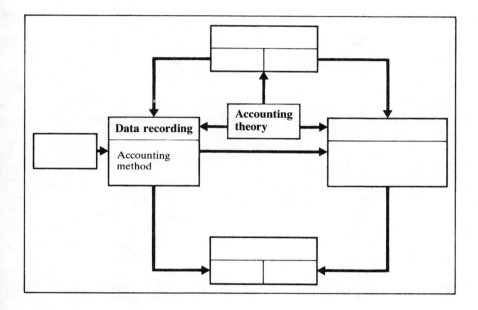

We have now examined the manner in which accounting recognizes expense and associates it with a particular accounting period. In determining the net income of a period expenses were matched with revenues; in so doing, we assumed that the revenues were those properly to be associated with expenses in that same period. We must now examine this assumption, and explore the accounting postulate which enables us to identify and match revenue with expense in a satisfactory and logical manner.

The nature of revenue

Just as we found it necessary to define the key terms of 'cost', 'expense' and 'expenditure', we must attempt to define what the accountant normally means by 'revenue'. Revenue may be defined as the aggregate exchange value of the products or services of the business. The exchange value may be expressed by the inflow of cash (receipts) or by the increase of another asset—normally 'debtors'.

49

The realization postulate

We must now associate the revenue or exchange value with a particular accounting period; the recognition of revenue is established by the realization postulate. According to this postulate, revenue is recognized as soon as (a) it is capable of objective measurement, and (b) the asset value received in exchange is reasonably certain.

This postulate gives rise to four categories, the first of which is the most important. While we will take note of the other three, it is this category which will occupy most of our attention.

(1)   Recognition of revenue at time of sale

This is the general—and most common—category. In the case of tangible property, revenue arises on the date when goods are furnished to the customer in exchange for cash or some other valuable consideration—normally the creation of a legally enforceable debt. Accounting normally does not involve itself in the legal problems of the passing of a title, but recognizes the revenue on the date of invoicing or the date of shipment whichever is the earlier. The invoice provides the objective measurement—the 'test of the market place'—required in (a) above, and the asset value (the debtor) is certain to be turned into cash, subject perhaps to some expense provision for defaulters in relation to the aggregate of debtors.

We may note here an important distinction between economics and accounting. The economist considers profit to accrue at each stage in the manufacturing process; he argues, quite rightly, that additional value over and above input value (cost) is created continually, and does not arise abruptly at some specific moment in time. The accountant only recognizes the *costs* of manufacturing as adding to the value of the property; all the profit arises when revenue is recognized at the date of sale. This difference is explained by the accounting convention of 'objectivity'. The accountant does not deny the validity of the economist's argument, but he points out that there is normally no objective way of measuring profit created at each stage. He requires some tangible evidence, and this is provided by the 'test of the market place'—the acceptance by an outside party of the price placed on the goods.

This search for 'objectivity' can, at times, lead to absurd results. For example, a builder buys two adjacent plots of land in a desirable residential area for £4,000 and, later, obtains planning permission. He sells one site for £5,000 and retains the other for sale at a later date. From an accounting viewpoint the land sold is worth £5,000, yielding a profit of £3,000, but the unsold land, which is equally as valuable, is recorded as being worth only £2,000.

Unrealized gains are not recorded, so that accounting distinguishes between two types of 'profit'—'operating' or 'trading' gains which are realized as a result of selling assets and are recorded, and 'holding gains' which are increases in value obtained by retaining an asset—and are not recorded.

(2) Recognition of revenue during production

Revenue is recognized at each stage of the creative process if there is a simultaneous increase in the claim against the customer or client; the amount of the claim must usually be determined by prior agreement or contract. There are two broad types of revenue within this category:

(a) Rent, interest, commissions and personal services performed on a time basis.

(b) Long-term contracts (e.g. for erection of a building) where a percentage of the ultimate contract price is recognized as revenue during each accounting period.

For example, a building consortium enters into a contract to build a new factory over a three-year period for an agreed contract price of £6 million. At the end of the first year, an independent firm of quantity surveyors certifies that one-quarter of the work is complete, and hence, on the so-called 'percentage of completion' basis, one-quarter of the revenue, i.e. £1.5 million, will be recognized at the end of the first year.

(3) Recognition of revenue at the completion of production

The main criteria for such recognition are (a) the existence of a sure market price, and (b) no substantial costs of marketing. These criteria are often fully met in the case of precious metals, but it is also acceptable for agricultural and other mineral products if selling costs (which should be deducted from the sales price (revenue)) can be adequately determined.

(4) Recognition of revenue subsequent to sale

The fourth category involves the recognition of revenue when cash is received. The 'cash basis' of revenue recognition is acceptable if there is considerable doubt at the time of sale as to the amount of cash that will eventually be received or if additional material expenses which cannot be adequately determined are likely to be incurred in respect of the sale. The most obvious example is that of hire purchase transactions where revenue is recognized only as the instalments are received.

If a furniture store offers a set of chairs under the following conditions:

	£
Cost price	200
Cash selling price	250
Total instalment price (10 × 30)	300

we can assume that the 'normal' profit is £50 and that the hire purchase profit of £100 consists of £50 normal margin and £50 interest. If, at the end of the accounting period, two instalments have been paid, then we recognize as revenue only the £60 received, and match the costs on a *pro rata* basis in order to ascertain the profit for that period. Thus:

	£
Revenue	60
Cost of stock sold	
$200 \times \dfrac{2}{10} \dfrac{\text{(Instalments paid)}}{\text{(Total instalments)}}$	40
Profit	20

'Revenue' and 'receipts'

We must carefully observe that the realization postulate is concerned with the recognition of 'revenue' and not with 'cash receipts'. We can note five possible events:

(1) Receipts of earlier years which will become wholly or partly revenues of this year.
(2) Receipts of this year which are wholly or partly revenues of last year.
(3) Receipts of this year which are wholly revenues of this year.
(4) Receipts of this year which are wholly or partly revenues of next year.
(5) Receipts of next year which are wholly or partly revenues of this.

We can examine these possibilities in terms of our quadrant.

(1) Receipts of earlier years which will become (a) wholly or (b) partly revenues of this year

Such receipts represent an advance payment which creates a liability to render a service or supply goods in some future period. On the balance sheet at the end of last year these items will have been described as 'deferred revenues'. Typical examples are rent and insurance premiums received in advance. In terms of our diagram, the deferred revenue of rent becomes a realized revenue of this period:

	Deferred revenues	100 −100
	Rent received	+100

(2) Receipts of this year which are wholly or partly revenues of last year

This occurs in particular when sales made last year (which are therefore revenues of that year) are turned into cash in this year when the debtors settle the account. Such cash receipts have no effect at all on the revenues of this year, the receipts merely cancelling debtors:

Debtors 1,000	−1,000		
Cash	+1,000		

If rent owed to the firm was not paid last year, then a current year receipt may be partly revenues of this year, and partly revenues of last.

(3) Receipts of this year which are wholly revenues of this year

This is the normal situation, but we must observe that this does not require the *simultaneous* recognition of revenue and receipt of cash. Provided cash is received in the same period a time lag is acceptable. We may illustrate this in the case of sales.

(a) Cash sales result in simultaneous revenue and receipt:

Cash	+50		
		Sales	+50

(b) Credit sales will involve a delay (normally 1–2 months) before cash is received. Thus:

	(i)	(ii)			(i)
Debtors	+80	−80			
Cash		+80			
			Sales		+80

(i) The sale on credit will result in an increase in sales revenue and a corresponding increase in the debtors.
(ii) When the debtor settles his account, debtors will be decreased by £80, and cash increased by the same amount.

(4)   Receipts of this year which are (a) wholly or (b) partly revenues of next year

The situation is similar to that described in (1) above. For example, if rent of £100 is received in respect of next year, then there is no revenue; rather cash increases by £100 and there is a liability—'deferred revenue'—created:

	(i)		(i)	(ii)
Cash	+100	Deferred revenue		+100
		Rent	+100	−100

For reasons of procedural convenience the rent is first treated as a revenue (i), but then, on inspection at the end of the year, is adjusted to be treated as in (ii). Deferred revenues are normally shown as a separate item in the 'current liabilities'.

If of the £100 received, £80 is in respect of this year and £20 in respect of next, the £80 is revenue and the £20 is a deferred revenue. Again, the whole sum will initially be treated as revenue:

	(i)		(i)	(ii)
Cash	+100	Deferred revenue		+20
		Rent	+100	−20

(5)   Receipts of next year which are (a) wholly or (b) partly revenues of this

The most important item in category (a) is the credit sales of this year for which cash will not be received until next year. Assuming a credit sales figure of £1,000 the position will be:

Debtors	+1,000		
		Sales	+1,000

In category (b) will appear such items as rent owing to the business. Thus:

Accrued revenue	+50		
		Rent	+50

The rent owing is referred to as 'accrued revenue' to distinguish it from the 'debtors'—the amounts owed to the business by its customers.

Debtors, bad debts and doubtful debts

We noted in our discussion of revenue recognition at the time of sale that the second condition of realization, a certain asset value, is subject to some modification where it is considered that some customers will fail to settle their account.

Accountants do not like to overstate any asset value, and debtors are no exception. If it is certain that a debtor will not settle his account, the debt is treated as 'bad' and the amount lost treated as an expense. In addition, a business will know by experience that a percentage of debtors will probably default, and accordingly a provision is made for 'doubtful debts'.

We can examine these events in terms of our quadrant. Assume that a business has debtors of £2,100, and that it is learned that £100 will never be collected, i.e. a 'bad debt'. The result is

Debtors	2,100 −100		
Bad debts	+100		

A provision for doubtful debts may also be required. Assuming that this amounts to $2\frac{1}{2}$ per cent of debtors, the results will be

		Provision	+50
Provision for doubtful debts	+50		

The provision is properly shown as a deduction from the asset to which it relates. Thus:

	£	£
Debtors	2,000	
Less: Provision	50	
		1,950

If in the following year the provision is to be increased to £80, the expense of that year will be only £30:

	Provision	
	(last year)	+50
	Increase	+30
Provision +30		

Conversely, a reduction in the provision to £30 will necessitate a reduction of the existing provision by £20 and a corresponding increase in revenue—provision no longer required:

	Provision	50
		−20
	Provision no	
	longer required	+20

Since the £20 represents a rather peculiar type of revenue it is more normal to treat this as a reduction of expense for the period.

Gross and net profit

In the previous chapter we defined the accounting equation as being

$$\Sigma A + \Sigma E = \Sigma L + \Sigma R$$

The net profit (income) of the business for a given accounting period was given as

$$\Sigma R - \Sigma E$$

Accounting makes a further subdivision of the income by identifying and distinguishing between the two categories of revenue and expense:

(1) *Trading revenues* (R_T) are those revenues which arise directly from the major activities and aims of the business; such revenues are normally referred to as 'sales'.

(2) *Trading expenses* (E_T) are those expenses incurred in acquiring and placing goods for resale into a saleable condition. Such expenses, normally referred to as 'cost of sales'[1] will include purchases, manufacturing wages, carriage inwards and any expenses (in a manufacturing concern) attributable to the factory, e.g. power, lighting, heating, depreciation of machines, etc.

(3) *Other revenues* (R_O) are those which arise incidentally to the main aims of the business. They will include rent, bank interest, dividends from investments and discount received.

(4) *Other expenses* (E_O) are those which are incurred in providing the administrative, selling and financial facilities which enable the business to realize its trading aims.

With these definitions in mind we can restate the income equation:

$$(R_T + R_O) - (E_T + E_O) = \text{Net profit}$$

or

$$(R_T - E_T) + (R_O - E_O) = \text{Net profit}$$

or

$$(R_T - E_T) = \text{Gross profit}$$

$$\text{Gross profit} + R_O - E_O = \text{Net profit}$$

The gross profit represents the profit margin achieved by the firm before the ancillary revenues and expenses are taken into consideration. Very often this figure is expressed as a percentage of sales and spoken of as the gross margin or the average percentage gross profit made on each good sold.

The net profit represents the extent to which the funds lent to the business by the owner and outside parties have been gainfully employed. We must make two observations about the net profit which a firm has earned:

(1) The success of a firm cannot be judged on the absolute size of the profit. What matters is the relationship between profit and the ownership equity (referred to as the return on capital employed) and

1   This is an example of the loose use of terms mentioned in Chapter 3; strictly we should speak of 'expense of sales'.

whether this relationship is as good as owner could get elsewhere. For example, a net profit of £1,000 on an ownership equity of £2,000 is a return of 50 per cent, which is evidently better than a similar firm earning a net profit of £2,000 on an ownership equity of £40,000—a return of 5 per cent.

(2) Profit has no direct relationship with cash. A firm can earn a profit and still be without any money. This arises because of the way in which accounting measures revenues and expenses; revenue may be equated with cash or it may not, and expenses may arise through the incurring of liability or the expiring of some past cost rather than through a money sacrifice. In addition, money sacrifices in acquiring long-lived assets reduce the cash but are not treated entirely as expenses.

The trading, profit and loss account

We are now in a position to formalize the presentation of the income statement, which we refer to in more conventional terms as the 'trading, profit and loss account'. The trading account section of this statement is given to the ascertainment of the gross profit, and the profit and loss section to the ascertainment of the net profit. We again begin with a statement of assets, liabilities, expenses and revenues and then consider a number of adjustments:

J. Brown and Co.
Year ended 31 December 1984

	£		£	£
Land and buildings	5,000	Ownership equity	14,360	
Plant and machinery	4,000	*Less:* Drawings	1,400	
Vans	1,000			12,960
Stock	2,300			
Debtors	1,700	Creditors		1,100
Investments	500			
Cash at bank	1,460			
Petty cash	40			
	16,000			**14,060**
Purchases	6,000	Sales		12,000
Returns inwards	200	Discounts received		400
Wages (manufacturing)	2,100	Rent received		140
Salaries	1,300			
Salesmen's commission	700			
Rent	150			
Rates	70			
Discount allowed	30			
Insurance	50			
	£10,600			**£12,540**

$$\Sigma A \quad + \quad \Sigma E \quad = \quad \Sigma L \quad + \quad \Sigma R$$
$$£16,000 \ + \ 10,600 \ = \ 14,060 \ + \ 12,540$$

On investigation it is discovered that

(1) Stock on hand at close is £2,500.
(2) Rates owing £30.
(3) Depreciation of £400 is to be provided for the plant and machinery.
(4) Rent owing to J. Brown and Co. is £60.

The income statement will be as follows:

J. Brown and Co.
Trading, Profit and Loss Account for the period ended 31 December 1984

	£	£	£
Sales		12,000	
Less: Returns		200	
			11,800
Opening stock	2,300		
Purchases	6,000		
		8,300	
Less: Closing stock		2,500	
		5,800	
Manufacturing wages		2,100	
			7,900
Gross Profit			3,900
Discounts received		400	
Rent		200	
			600
			4,500
Less:			
Salaries		1,300	
Commission		700	
Rent		150	
Rates		100	
Discount allowed		30	
Insurance		50	
Depreciation		400	
			2,730
Net Profit			**£1,770**

J. Brown and Co.
Balance Sheet as at 31 December 1984

	£	£	£
Ownership Equity			
Balance 1 January 1984			14,360
Net profit		1,770	
Less: Drawings		1,400	
		——	370
Net Capital Employed			**£14,730**
Represented by:			
Fixed Assets			
Land and buildings		5,000	
Plant and machinery	4,000		
Less: Depreciation	400		
		—— 3,600	
Vans		1,000	
		——	9,600
Current Assets			
Investments	500		
Stock	2,500		
Debtors	1,760		
Cash at bank and in hand	1,500		
		—— 6,260	
Less:			
Current Liabilities			
Creditors and accruals		1,130	
		——	5,130
			£14,730

The balance sheet is here presented in a 'vertical' form, as opposed to the 'two-sided' or 'horizontal' form. There are good reasons for this manner of presentation:

(1) It is often confusing for the non-accountant to find 'capital' added to the creditors. Since the accountant should aim to help rather than confuse, the creditors are shown as a deduction from the assets.
(2) The vertical form highlights the funds which the owner has supplied, referred to as the 'net capital employed'.
(3) The current liabilities are deducted from the current assets; if this result is favourable, i.e. the current assets exceed the current liabilities, it is an indication that the business will be able to meet its obligations to creditors as and when they fall due. The difference between the two is often referred to as the 'net working capital'.

Accounting and economic profit

The accounting profit of £1,770 was ascertained by applying the postulates of accrual and realization. These postulates reflect the accountant's wish to be as objective as possible in the measurement of income. The economist, however, points out that the business of Mr Brown has incurred other costs beyond the incurring of money sacrifices or liabilities; these costs are called opportunity costs. An opportunity cost reflects the cost of the alternative foregone—in this instance, what Mr Brown has given up in order to run his business.

In running his business, Mr Brown has forgone the salary he could earn in alternative employment, the rent which he could obtain if he let his business premises, and also interest on his capital. Such costs cannot be objectively measured, and are often referred to as *imputed* costs. Nevertheless, they are very important, for if their sum exceeds the accounting profit, it follows that, on financial grounds alone, Mr Brown should sell his business. For example, if his alternative salary were £1,200 p.a., the rent he could obtain £400 p.a., and the interest on capital (£14,730 − 5,000), £500 p.a., then the economic profit (loss) would be

	£	£
Accounting profit		1,770
Less:		
Imputed salary	1,200	
Imputed rent	400	
Imputed interest	500	
		2,100
Economic Loss		**£(330)**

Whether Mr Brown will actually sell his business will depend on a number of factors such as the firm's long-term prospects and Mr Brown's preference for being his own master.

The assumptions and conventions of accounting

In this and the preceding chapters we have examined the basic postulates which the accountant adopts to enable him to value worth and to measure income. As was emphasized in the first chapter the postulates are general and do not prescribe in detail the action required in every situation. To enable the postulates to be logically acceptable the accountant has to make (and state) certain assumptions; to enable the postulates to be operated the accountant has to prescribe certain conventions which will limit the possible range of interpretation. We turn, first, to the accounting assumptions of (a) stability, and (b) continuity (going concern).

(a) *Stability*. In accounting, the monetary unit is normally assumed to be stable; in other words, the pound of 1984 is assumed to be the same as the pound in 1944. In a world of inflationary economies this is quite evidently not true, and in recent years considerable effort and research has been devoted to finding an alternative base on which to prepare financial statements. There have been numerous reports, successive accounting standards and draft standards, but as yet there has been no resolution to the problem which has met with unanimous approval and support. Some of these suggestions and attempts will be explored in Chapter 12.

It is necessary for the assumption to be stated, however, to make logically possible the preparation of an income statement and also the balance sheet. For example, unless the assumption is explicitly stated it is logically impossible to add together the monetary values assigned to assets acquired at different dates.

(b) *Continuity (going concern).* Unless there is some good evidence to the contrary, accounting assumes that the business will operate for the foreseeable future. The assumption is of considerable importance for it means that the business is viewed as a mechanism for adding value to the resources it uses. The success of the business can be measured by the differences between output values (sales and other revenues) and input values (expenses). Therefore all resources not yet used can be reported at cost rather than at market value.

The importance of the assumption can be seen if an alternative is advanced, namely, that the business will cease to operate within a year. All assets then would have to be measured in terms of what they were *currently worth* to a buyer. This is evidently not the approach adopted by the cost postulate (*see* Chapter 2), so the continuity assumption is seen as a necessary prop to that postulate. However, it may be argued that the assumption that the business has a future is merely another way of saying that value of a business and its assets are a reflection of future earning capacity. If that is the case, then the value of assets should in some way be ascertained by reference to output rather than input values. This leads us back to our repeated criticism of the accounting concept of value as acquisition cost, and it is perhaps slightly paradoxical that the assumption provided as a support can also be used to deny that concept.

SSAP 2, 'Disclosure of Accounting Policies', regards the 'going concern' concept as fundamental to accounting, and as such a company is obliged to apply this concept to their accounts or expressly justify their departure from it. This 'principle' has now been given further force by its inclusion in Schedule 1 to the Companies Act 1981, which requires the directors of a company not only to justify their departure from it, but also to disclose the effect of that on the accounts. Departure from the concept is apparently viewed as moving from input values to liquidation values where there is evidence that a business may shortly cease to trade, a difficult judgement which is aided by addressing a series of questions formulated by the Auditing Practices Committee of the English Institute. For example, if stocks and sales are declining, purchases are being deferred, bank overdraft growing, profitability declining, and there is undue reliance on too few customers, then there is reason to question the continuity of the business, and perhaps change the basis of valuation.

We can identify four conventions of accounting which act as constraints on the interpretation of the postulates of accounting. As has been pointed out, these conventions are designed to limit the possible range of interpretation of the postulates. Nevertheless their very existence is seen by some to lead to greater attention being paid to the reliability of the information rather than its utility. As the conventions do not lead to conformity of treatment their value must come under close scrutiny. The conventions are: (a) objectivity, (b) conservatism, (c) materiality, and (d) consistency.

(a) *Objectivity*. Business operates in an environment of economic change and uncertainty. In the case of uncertainty, the accountant strives to choose data that is as reliable and objective as possible. The term 'objectivity' relates to data that can be independently verified and is not influenced by the personal feelings or judgements of the accountant or any other person within the firm. We may express it another way and say that the accountant strives for 'fact and not opinion'.

We have met one application of the objectivity convention already in this chapter—the recognition of revenue; but the convention also helps to explain the accountant's use of input (cost) values for most assets. We must observe, however, that the convention is often much overstated, for in many important matters—such as the valuation of stock or the ascertainment of depreciation—the accountant can only be said to be objective in the *application* of a particular method of valuation or depreciation, but the selection of the method will be a result of the accountant's judgement or opinion; in other words, the accountant may *objectively* apply a method he has *subjectively* selected.

(b) *Conservatism*. The convention of conservatism or prudence is often stated as 'anticipate no profit, provide for all possible losses'. This convention has two aspects:

   (1) Revenue should not be anticipated—hence the realization postulate which leads to the recognition of operating but not holding gains, but the anticipation of possible losses.
   (2) Where the market price—either for sale or replacement—of an asset has fallen below its acquisition price, the lower value should be selected.

The convention has its origins in the nineteenth century when the emphasis in financial statements was upon the needs of actual or potential creditors. A balance sheet based upon the most cautious view of value and worth would reassure the provider of finance. The convention, however, can lead to a contravention of the cost postulate because it leads to a departure from acquisition cost whenever other 'values' are lower. Moreover, it is a rather strange logic which demands that gains must not be anticipated but that losses should be.

If the overriding need of the users of financial statements—managements, owners, creditors, investors, employees, etc.—is for *reliable* information, then a convention which emphasizes understatement is not the most helpful of rules.

(c) *Materiality*. The convention or doctrine of materiality permeates a great deal of accounting practice, but it is a convention which is singularly ill-defined and relies very much upon the judgement, experience and common sense of the accountant—a strange contrast to the convention of objectivity which seeks to minimize subjective judgement. The convention of materiality is concerned with the manner in which any item is treated in or disclosed by the accounts. For example, if a firm acquires a new doormat for the managing director's office, then as that doormat is likely to be in use for more than one accounting period, i.e. has a 'future economic benefit', then it should be classified as an asset. Every time someone walks on the mat some benefit is consumed, so an expense is incurred. Clearly, the sheer cost of recording this item as an asset and then expensing it greatly outweighs the usefulness of the information derived. It is 'immaterial', and hence will be immediately expensed.

But where is the line to be drawn between material and immaterial events? A possible distinction is to view any such expenditure in relative terms, i.e. to consider the effect on current profit of treating an item as an immediate expense rather than an asset. If a business is reporting a £1 million profit, then the expensing of a £1 doormat has no material effect on the profit. Thus what is material to a small business can be immaterial to a large one.

However, a relative view of materiality may not be enough, because in a very large business the expenditure of £1 million may itself be immaterial or insignificant relative to profits or turnover; yet, instinctively, the accountant would reject any mistreatment of the item, arguing that in absolute terms £1 million is important and relevant.

The doctrine of materiality also extends to the disclosure of financial information in financial reports. In a limited company, for example, disclosure of certain financial features is required by law, but, in addition, items which are likely to have a significant influence on the interpretation of the accounts in question should also be disclosed.

(d) *Consistency*. Uncertainty regarding economic events and the need to choose among alternative methods of valuation and allocation has obliged accounting to insist that the postulates must be interpreted by the firm in the same manner from year to year. Nevertheless, if a change is made to a method that provides more accurate or more useful information, then the effect of that change of method must be clearly stated. Much of the usefulness of financial information rests on the extent to which the report of one year can be compared with that of earlier years and also with that of other organizations. Whilst consistency of treatment, within an organization, is fairly readily achieved, the very looseness of accounting postulates and conventions makes inter-firm comparison fraught with difficulties.

Appendix—the effect of revenue recognition on reported profit

The different categories of revenue recognition change the point of time at which profit is taken. Although over the entire life of a business the total profit will be the same whatever method is applied, the profit attributed to any one segment of time will vary according to the method applied.

Consider a simple set of data relating to business activity over three time periods:

Period		Activity
I	1	Buy a gold mine with £250,000 cash, and invest working capital of £250,000.
	2	Mine 10,000 oz of gold at £10 per oz (cash).
	3	Sell on credit 5,000 oz at £15 per oz.
II	4	Collect cash from debtors—4,000 oz at £15 per oz.
	5	Sell on credit 3,000 oz at £15 per oz.
	6	Mine 2,000 oz at £10 per oz (cash).
III	7	Collect cash from debtors for 1,000 oz at £15 per oz.
	8	Sell on credit 4,000 oz at £15 per oz.
	9	Collect all outstanding debts.

We analyse the transactions by using comparative balance sheets and applying in turn different categories of revenue recognition.

(a) Revenue recognized at point of sale (£'000)

	I			II			III		
	1	2	3	4	5	6	7	8	9
Capital	500	500	500	500	500	500	500	500	500
Profit I	—	—	25	25	25	25	25	25	25
II	—	—	—	—	15	15	15	15	15
III	—	—	—	—	—	—	—	20	20
	500	500	525	525	540	540	540	560	560
Mine	250	250	250	250	250	250	250	250	250
Stock	—	100	50	50	20	40	40	—	—
Debtors	—	—	75	15	60	60	45	105	—
Cash	250	150	150	210	210	190	205	205	310
	500	500	525	525	540	540	540	560	560

(b) Revenue recognized at completion of production
   (£'000)

	I			II			III		
	1	2	3	4	5	6	7	8	9
Capital	500	500	500	500	500	500	500	500	500
Profit I	—	50	50	50	50	50	50	50	50
II	—	—	—	—	—	10	10	10	10
III	—	—	—	—	—	—	—	—	—
	500	550	550	550	550	560	560	560	560
Mine	250	250	250	250	250	250	250	250	250
Stock	—	150	75	75	30	60	60	—	—
Debtors	—	—	75	15	60	60	45	105	—
Cash	250	150	150	210	210	190	205	205	310
	500	550	550	550	550	560	560	560	560

Stock is valued at *selling price* and profit taken at completion of production.

(c) Revenue recognized on receipt of cash (£'000)

	I			II			III		
	1	2	3	4	5	6	7	8	9
Capital	500	500	500	500	500	500	500	500	500
Profit I	—	—	—	—	—	—	—	—	—
II	—	—	—	20	20	20	20	20	20
III	—	—	—	—	—	—	5	5	40
	500	500	500	520	520	520	525	525	560
Mine	250	250	250	250	250	250	250	250	250
Stock	—	100	50	50	20	40	40	—	—
Debtors	—	—	50	10	40	40	30	70	—
Cash	250	150	150	210	210	190	205	205	310
	500	500	500	520	520	520	525	525	560

Debtors are valued *at cost* and profit taken only when cash is received.

The profits reported at each year-end under the different systems are:

Revenue recognized at	Year-end profit (£'000)			Total profit (£'000)
	I	II	III	
Point of sale	25	15	20	60
Completion of production	50	10	—	60
Receipt of cash	—	20	40	60

The table highlights the need for consistent application of the realization postulate; a change in the method of revenue recognition can alter the profit reported for a given accounting period.

References and further reading

BAXTER and DAVIDSON (1962), *Studies in Accounting Theory*. Sweet and Maxwell.

BUCKLEY, KIRCHER and MATHEWS (1968), 'Methodology in Accounting Theory', *Accounting Review*, April 1968.

HENDRIKSEN (1982), *Accounting Theory*. Irwin.

HENDRIKSEN and BUDGE (1974), *Contemporary Accounting Theory*. Dickenson.

HORNGREN (1965), 'How should we interpret the Realization Concept?', *Accounting Review*, April 1965.

POPOFF (1972), 'Postulates, Principles and Rules', *Accounting and Business Research*, Summer 1972.

TRUE and FAIT (1976), 'Going, Going . . .?' Bulletin of the Auditing Practices Committee 1. Autumn 1976.

WHITTINGTON (1974), 'Asset Valuation, Income Measurement and Accounting Income', *Accounting and Business Research*, Spring 1974.

WILLIAMS and GRIFFEN (1969), 'On the Nature of Empirical Verification in Accounting'. *Abacus*, Winter 1969.

Questions for discussion

1   Collect from as many different sources as possible definitions of the term 'revenue'. Consider the extent to which the definitions are in conflict, and explain what effect, if any, this conflict has on the application of the realization postulate.

2   Explain carefully in your own words the conditions which must be satisfied before revenue is recognized.

3   The data below relate to the business of commodity dealer J. Smith:

(i)   Started business with capital in cash of £1,000.
(ii) Bought stock for resale for cash £500.
(iii) Paid expenses in cash £40.

(iv) Sold on credit stock which cost £100 for £200 (this 'mark up' is standard in this type of business).
(v) Collected cash on account from debtor £50.
(vi) Sold on credit further stock which cost £200 for £400.

Required:

(a) Prepare successive balance sheets to show the effect of recognizing revenue (and profit) at:

   (i)   the 'point of sale',
   (ii) the 'completion of production' (i.e. when stock is acquired),
   (iii) the 'receipt of cash'.

(b) Explain carefully the basis of stock and debtor valuation in each of the above examples.

4   The following details relate to two contracts of a civil engineering contractor (year-end 31 December):

	Contract A	Contract B
Started	1 July 1983	1 January 1983
Costs to 31.12.83	£300,000	£600,000
Estimated further costs to completion	£200,000	£400,000
Estimated date of completion	30 June 1984	31 December 1984
Value of work certified to 31.12.83	£340,000	£480,000
Contract price	£600,000	£1,000,000
Cash received to 31.12.83	£306,000	£432,000

Required:

(a) Identify the general principles of revenue and expense recognition and relate them to this situation.
(b) How much profit/loss should be shown for each contract for the year ended 31 December 1983?
(c) How would the contracts be reflected in the balance sheet at 31 December 1983?

5   Mr Green runs a small 'do-it-yourself' business. During the year to 31 December 1984 his sales were: cash sales £10,000, credit sales £5,000.
At 31 December 1984 his debtors, who totalled £800, included:

(i)   £50 owed by J. Bloggs and Co. who had just been made bankrupt.
(ii) £30 owed by Mr Chips who had recently become unemployed.
(iii) £10 owed by a friend of Mr Green who was well known for being slow in paying his debts.

Required:

(a) Explain how you would treat each of these items, and what provision for doubtful debts might be made for the year ended 31 December 1984.

(b) Show the relevant extract from the balance sheet for the year ended 31 December 1984.

6 The following trial balance was taken from the books of Yama Co. as at 31 December 1984.

	£	£
Stock at 1 January 1984	4,400	
Buildings (cost)	6,000	
Fixtures (cost)	2,000	
Bank	4,100	
Debtors	11,000	
Creditors		16,800
Capital		7,000
Purchases	21,600	
Sales		42,400
Depreciation on fixtures at 1 January 1984		600
Administrative expenses	5,800	
Selling expenses	5,000	
Distribution expenses	3,000	
Financial expenses	900	
Drawings	3,000	
	£66,800	**£66,800**

The following information is also to be taken into account:

(i) Stock at 31 December 1984, £6,000.
(ii) Selling expenses owing £600.
(iii) Administrative expenses include rates of £800 paid for the year ending 31 March 1985.
(iv) A provision for doubtful debts of 2% of debtors is to be provided.
(v) Depreciation is to be provided at 10% on the cost of the fixtures at 1 January 1984.

Required:

(a) Prepare a trading, profit and loss account for the year ended 31 December 1984 and a balance sheet as at that date.
(b) Explain whether you think the Yama Co. has been successful during 1984; what additional information would you need to assist you in making such a judgement?

7 The following trial balance was extracted from the books of Fletcher, a trader, as at 31 December 1984:

	£	£
Capital account		30,500
Purchases	56,500	
Sales		70,900
Repairs to buildings	848	
Motor car	950	

	£	£
Car expenses	318	
Freehold land and buildings	20,000	
Balance at bank	540	
Furniture and fittings (cost)	2,000	
Depreciation of furniture and fittings		540
Wages and salaries	8,606	
Discounts allowed	1,061	
Discounts received		814
Drawings	2,400	
Rates and insurances	248	
Bad debts	359	
Provision for doubtful debts, 1.1.84		140
Trade debtors	5,213	
Trade creditors		4,035
General expenses	1,586	
Stock-in-trade, 1.1.84	6,300	
	£106,929	**£106,929**

The following matters are taken into account:

(i)   Stock-in-trade, 31 December 1984, £8,000.
(ii)   Wages and salaries outstanding at 31 December 1984, £318.
(iii)   Rates and insurance paid in advance at 31 December 1984, £45.
(iv)   The provision for bad debts is to be reduced to £100.
(v)   During 1984, Fletcher withdrew goods, valued at £200, for his own use; no entry has been made in the books for the withdrawal of these goods.
(vi)   The item 'Repairs to buildings, £848' includes £650 in respect of alterations and improvements to the buildings.
(vii)   One-third of the car expenses represents the cost of Fletcher's motoring for private, as distinct from business, purposes.
(viii) Provide depreciation on furniture and fittings at 10 per cent p.a. on the cost at 1 January 1984.

Required:

(a) Prepare a trading and profit and loss account for the year 1984, and a balance sheet as on 31 December 1984. Show clearly the gross and net profit for the year.
(b) How 'successful' has Mr Fletcher been during 1984? What further information might assist in evaluating his 'success'?
(c) Mr Fletcher is considering accepting an offer for his business of £40,000, and taking up a part-time job as manager of a local shop at an annual salary of £2,000. Explain what factors might influence him in this decision.

8 Explain carefully the distinction between gross and net profit. Why is the distinction considered important? Indicate whether each of the following items incurred by a manufacturing business affect the gross or the net profit, and give your reasons:

(i)   Import duty paid on goods for resale.
(ii)   Carriage paid to deliver goods sold.
(iii) Discount received from creditors.
(iv)   Employers' National Insurance contributions paid for production workers.
(v)   Holiday pay for production workers.
(vi)   Advertising a product range.
(vii) Advertising for the post of works manager.

9 To what extent, if any, is the distinction between gross and net profit useful in the following organizations? What alternatives can you suggest?

(i)   A veterinary business.
(ii)   A dentist's surgery.
(iii) An accounting practice.
(iv)   A sports club.
(v)   A building society.
(vi)   An insurance company.

10 If we combine the conservatism convention with the realization postulate, we reach the following conclusion:

A current asset has been bought and is shown in the accounts at £100. If we expect it to be sold next year for £60, we value it at £60, the reduction (loss) being treated as an expense of the current year. If we expect it to be sold next year for £150 we value it at £100, the increase of £50 being shown as a profit of next year.

Can this be regarded as consistent?

11 Examine the annual reports of five different manufacturing companies and try to discover from them the basis on which they each have (a) valued stock and (b) measured depreciation. Discuss the extent to which the treatment is consistent and would assist comparison of the companies' performance.

12 During 1982/3, British Leyland spent £110 million developing the new Maestro. How should this be dealt with in the accounts?

5 Accounting records—an introduction to bookkeeping

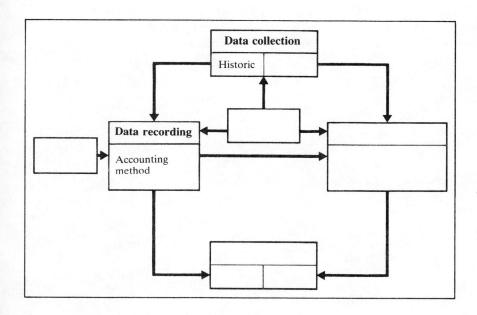

Analysis of transactions using the quadrant

In Chapter 3, we noted that the expanded accounting equation was

$$\text{Assets} + \text{Expenses} = \text{Liabilities} + \text{Revenues}$$

and that any transaction must necessarily be reflected *twice* in order that the equation remains in balance. The crucial decision is the identification of the effect which each transaction has on the assets, expenses, liabilities or revenues of the business; the quadrant used in the earlier chapters has enabled us to record this effect in a systematic manner. In Chapter 3, we used the example of Mr Brown commencing business with a series of transactions, viz.:

(i)   J. Brown starts business with cash of £1,000.
(ii) Buys furniture for shop—cash £300.
(iii) Buys goods for resale—cash £150.

73

(iv) Buys more goods for resale on credit from Smith at £180.
(v)   Sells goods for cash—£120.
(vi) Pays wages of assistant—cash £10.
(vii) Sells goods on credit to Jones—£90.
(viii) Pays Smith cash on account—£120.
(ix) Pays rent in cash £12.

In terms of our quadrant the result is

		£	£			£	£
(ii)	Furniture	+ 300		(i)	Ownership		
(vii)	Debtors	+ 90			interest		+1,000
				(iv)	Creditors		+ 180
(i)	Cash	+1,000		(viii)		−120	
(ii)			−300				
(iii)			−150				
(v)		+ 120					
(vi)			− 10				
(viii)			−120				
(ix)			− 12				
(iii)	Purchases	+ 150		(v)	Sales		+ 120
(iv)		+ 180		(vii)			+ 90
(vi)	Wages	+ 10					
(ix)	Rent	+ 12					
		+1,862	−592			−120	+1,390

Debit and credit

In recording these events, we have clearly segregated increases and decreases in the four sectors of the quadrant; this will enable us more easily to make the transition to the conventional methods of recording employed in bookkeeping. Each sector has been divided into two columns; we will label the left-hand column—quite arbitrarily—the *debit* side, and the right-hand column, the *credit* side. Amounts to be entered into the left-hand side are called *debits*, and amounts to be entered into the right-hand side, *credits*.

It is important that we do not attempt to ascribe any moral or ethical significance to the terms debit and credit. The verb 'to debit' means to make an entry into the left-hand side, the verb 'to credit' to make an entry into the right-hand side; *they have no other meaning whatsoever in accounting*. 'Debit' and 'credit' are usually abbreviated to 'Dr.' and 'Cr.'.

We can now transfer these ideas to the quadrant:

	Dr.	Cr.		Dr.	Cr.
ASSETS	Increase	Decrease	**LIABILITIES**	Decrease	Increase
	+	–		–	+
EXPENSES	Increase	Decrease	**REVENUES**	Decrease	Increase
	+	–		–	+

To increase an asset or an expense requires a debit, to decrease requires a credit. To increase a liability or a revenue requires a credit, to decrease requires a debit. This reflects the duality or 'double entry' postulate of accounting referred to in Chapter 2; here we must restate it in the form applicable to the keeping of financial records, namely that for each transaction the debit amount (or the sum of all debit amounts) must equal the credit amount (or the sum of all credit amounts). This is the operational postulate of accounting.

The account

The collecting and recording of financial data is known as 'bookkeeping'. If we refer back to our example we will observe that we have quite naturally subdivided each of the four sectors of the quadrant. The assets have been subdivided into cash, the debtor (Mr Jones) and furniture; the expenses have been subdivided into purchases, wages and rent. Each subdivision is referred to as an 'account' (often abbreviated to 'A/c') and a business will have as many accounts as it considers necessary to provide management with information about particular aspects of the operations. There is no limit, other than the cost of record-keeping, to the proliferation of accounts that may be found in practice. For example, on balance sheets which we have met there has been a single figure recorded against debtors; in practice it is obviously advantageous to maintain a separate account for each individual debtor.

The ledger is a group of accounts. In a small business all the accounts may be contained within one ledger; in the larger business there may be many ledgers—the debtors ledger, the creditors ledger and so on. Originally when accounts were hand-written these ledgers were quite literally books (hence the expression 'books of account' and 'bookkeeping'); in the modern business the ledger may be a set of loose-leaf cards, a set of punched cards or even a magnetic tape which forms part of a computer system. No matter what its form may be, however, the essential nature of the ledger, the account and the rules of debit and credit (double entry) still remain exactly the same.

For example, the first transaction recorded was

(i) J. Brown starts business with cash of £1,000.

This transaction was recorded by showing an increase (debit) in the asset cash of £1,000, and a corresponding increase (credit) in the owner's capital account of £1,000:

Cash A/c		J. Brown—Capital A/c	
Capital	1,000	Cash	1,000

Each account is cross-referenced to its corresponding debit or credit. Hence, if we look at the cash account and find the debit of £1,000, we are informed that the corresponding and balancing entry is to be found in the capital account. In practice, the date of the transaction must also be recorded—an important piece of information if we are to measure income for any stated period of time:

Cash A/c		J. Brown—Capital A/c	
1 Jan.		1 Jan. Cash	1,000
Capital	1,000		

Originally, it was the practice to preface all debit entries by the word 'To', e.g. To Capital, and all credit entries by the word 'By', e.g. By Cash, but this practice has long been abandoned as superfluous.

As a result of this procedure, the arithmetical precision of the recording process can be checked by simply listing and totalling all of the debits in all accounts and comparing them with the total of all of the credits in all of the accounts. If they are not equal, then there has been an error in the recording process.

Returning to our example of Mr Brown, we can record all of the transactions in appropriate accounts.

Analysis of transactions using accounts

Because of the high volume of transactions which take place in the business and the large number of accounts, it is obviously physically impossible to keep a giant-sized quadrant; rather, each account is maintained separately:

Furniture A/c

Cash	300		

Jones A/c

Sales	90		

J. Brown—Capital A/c

		Cash	1,000

Cash A/c

Ownership interest	1,000	Furniture	300
Sales	120	Purchases	150
		Wages	10
		Smith	120
		Rent	12

Smith A/c

Cash	120	Purchases	180

Purchases A/c

Cash	150		
Smith	180		

Sales A/c

		Cash	120
		Jones	90

Wages A/c

Cash	10		

Rent A/c

Cash	12		

The trial balance

The trial balance is merely a list of the balances extracted from all of the various ledger accounts, and is designed to (a) provide a mathematical check on the accuracy of the recording process and (b) act as a set of 'working papers' to facilitate the preparation of the final accounts—the trading, profit and loss account and the balance sheet. We can list the balances extracted from the accounts above:

J. Brown
Trial Balance as at 31 January 1984

	Dr. £	Cr. £
Furniture	300	
Jones	90	
Cash	528	
Purchases	330	
Wages	10	
Rent	12	
Capital		1,000
Smith		60
Sales		210
	£1,270	**£1,270**

It must be noted that, compared with the corresponding trial balance on page 41 which clearly segregates the asset, liability, revenue and expense accounts, no such distinction is made here, and we have to learn from experience and our knowledge of the transactions which gave rise to the accounts, into which category each falls.

The balancing of a trial balance does not prove that the accounts are correct, because several types of error will not be revealed:

(1) Errors of *omission*, where a transaction has been completely omitted from the records.

(2) Errors of *commission*, where an entry has been made in the right class of account but in the wrong account. For example, if A. Smith, a debtor, owed £30, then a debit for £30 in the account of B. Smith would not be revealed by a trial balance.

(3) Errors of *principle*, where an entry has been made in the wrong class of account. For example, the furniture acquired by Mr Brown for £300 was a long-lived asset, and classified as such in the furniture account. If, however, this entry had been made in the purchases account—an 'expense' account—the trial balance would have agreed but contained a mistake of principle.

(4) Errors of *original entry*, where both debit and credit entries are made for the same but wrong amount.

(5) *Compensating* errors, which cancel each other out and thus will not be revealed. For example, if the cash account had been incorrectly added as £538, and the purchases as £320, the errors of £10 would have been self-cancelling.

(6) Errors of *reversal*, where an account is incorrectly credited rather than debited, and the corresponding account is debited rather than credited. For example, if the entries for the furniture bought for £300 had been to debit cash £300, and credit the furniture account for £300, the trial balance would have balanced but been incorrect.

The trading, profit and loss account

Income is the difference between revenue and expense; within the quadrant it was a simple exercise to add up all the revenues, add up all the expenses, and take one from the other. The quadrant facilitated this procedure because all relevant data was assembled in one place, but with the sub-division and separation of the various elements into particular accounts, there is a need to reassemble the data, and this is achieved by the medium of the trading, profit and loss account. All revenue and expense accounts are transferred at the end of an accounting period to this account. The actual transfer can be neatly contained within the double entry system. For example, to transfer the debit balance of £330 from the purchases account to the trading account requires a credit to the purchases account of £330 (thus eliminating that account) and a debit of £330 to the trading account. Thus:

Trading, profit and loss A/c

Purchases	330		

Dr.   Cr.

Operating this mechanism for all revenue and expense accounts which affect the trading account section of the trading, profit and loss account will give us the following:

Purchases A/c

Cash	150	Trading	330
Smith	180		
	330		330

Sales A/c

Trading	210	Cash	120
		Jones	90
	210		210

Any other revenue and expense accounts which affect the profit and loss section can now be transferred:

Wages A/c

Cash	10	Profit and loss	10

Rent A/c

Cash	12	Profit and loss	12

The position of stock

As we observed in Chapter 3, stock acquired during the year is treated initially as an expense, an adjustment being made at the end of the year for the stock then in hand. Assuming a closing stock of £200, within the debit and credit system of bookkeeping the result is as follows:

J. Brown and Co.
Trading, Profit and Loss Account for
the period ended 31 January 1984

Purchases	330	Sales	210
		Closing stock	200

Stock A/c

Trading account	200		

The stock account, being an asset account, is debited with the value of the closing stock, and the trading account credited. A better presentation is to deduct the closing stock from the purchases which has the same effect. The gross profit can now be ascertained, the amount being transferred into the profit and loss section of the income statement by debiting the trading account and crediting the profit and loss account:

Trading, profit and loss A/c
for the period ended 31 January 1984

	£	£		£
Purchases	330		Sales	210
Less: Closing stock	200			
	——	130		
Gross Profit		80		
		——		——
		210		210
		——		——
Wages	10		Gross profit	80
Rent	12			
	——	22		
Net Profit		58		
		——		——
		80		80
		——		——

The net profit can now be ascertained; as the profit accrues to the owner the £58 is credited to John Brown's capital account:

J. Brown—Capital A/c

		Cash	1,000
		Profit and loss	58

Asset and liability accounts

We have now reduced the revenues and expenses of the business to a single figure of net profit. The accounts remaining must be either assets or liabilities. The amounts standing to the debit or credit of these accounts reflect the position of the business at the end of the current accounting period and also at the beginning of the subsequent period. The amounts (referred to as balances) are therefore 'carried forward'. This means that the various accounts are 'closed' (by debiting or crediting them) to indicate that a balance has been struck, and the individual balances carried forward as debits or credits to the next accounting period. For example, a credit of £300 to the furniture account will 'close' the account, and a corresponding debit of £300 will be 'brought down' as a balance.

The asset and liability accounts will be as follows:

Furniture A/c

Cash	300	Balance c/d	300
	—		—
Balance b/d	300		

J. Brown—Capital A/c

		Cash	1,000
Balance c/d	1,058	Profit	58
			1,058
			1,058
		Balance b/d	1,058

Jones A/c

Sales	90	Balance c/d	90
	—		—
Balance b/d	90		

Cash A/c

Ownership interest	1,000	Furniture	300
		Purchases	150
Sales	120	Wages	10
		Smith	120
		Rent	12
		Balance c/d	528
	1,120		1,120
Balance b/d	528		

Smith A/c

Cash	120	Purchases	180
Balance c/d	60		
	180		180
		Balance b/d	60

Stock A/c

Trading account	200	Balance c/d	200
			—
Balance b/d	200		

The balance sheet

The balances which remain are incorporated into the balance sheet. The balance sheet is *not* part of the double entry system; it is, as the name implies, a list of the balances which remain on the books of account. The balance sheet is drawn up in the manner indicated in Chapters 3 and 4. By convention, if a 'horizontal' statement is prepared the assets are placed on the right, and the liabilities on the left. The reason for this is lost in antiquity, but it seems probable that the use of the 'wrong' sides, e.g. assets on the 'credit' side, was a device to emphasize that the balance sheet does not form part of the double entry system.

The balance sheet will be as follows:

J. Brown and Co.
Balance Sheet as at 31 January 1984

	£	£		£
Ownership Interest			**Fixed Assets**	
Balance at 1.1.84	1,000		Furniture	300
Profit for the period	58			
		1,058	**Current Assets**	
Current Liabilities			Stock	200
Creditors		60	Debtors	90
			Cash	528
		£1,118		**£1,118**

Accruals and prepayments

In Chapter 3 we identified various categories of events in considering what expense is properly attributable to a given accounting period. Among them we discussed the 'accrual' and the 'prepayment'. In terms of the quadrant the accrual was demonstrated as follows:

Cash	−80	Accrual	+40
Rent	+40 +80		

The rent for the period is £120, but only £80 has actually been paid. As the cost (and expense) must be £120, we increase the rent by £40 and correspondingly increase the liability of the business by an accrual of £40.

This event can be neatly contained within double entry bookkeeping. The payment of £80 results in a credit to the cash account and a debit to the rent account:

Cash A/c

		Rent A/c		
Rent	80	Cash	80	

Since the total rent expense must be £120 the rent account will be debited with the additional £40. The corresponding credit of £40 will also be in the rent account, but 'carried forward' as a balance into the next accounting period representing the amount of the liability to the landlord. The full £120 is then debited to the profit and loss account:

Rent A/c

Cash	80	Profit and	
Accrual c/d	40	loss	120
	120		**120**
		Balance b/d	40

The double entry procedure for the accrual is, of course, the reverse of the prepayment procedure. If a business has a rates liability of £100 but during one accounting period actually pays £125, then £25 must be a prepayment. In terms of the quadrant the result is

Prepayment	+25	
Cash	−125	
Rates	+125	
	− 25	

In terms of double entry procedure:

Cash A/c

			Rates	125

Rates A/c

Cash	125	Profit and loss	100
		Prepayment c/d	25
	125		**125**
Balance b/d	25		

Returning to our example of Mr Brown, we may assume that at the end of the accounting period we have discovered that the rent has been prepaid by £2, and that wages owing amount to £4. The two accounts would appear as follows:

Rent A/c

Cash	12	Profit and loss	10
		Prepayment c/d	2
	12		12
Balance b/d	2		

Wages A/c

Cash	10	Profit and loss	14
Accrual c/d	4		
	14		14
		Balance b/d	4

The trading, profit and loss account would now become

Trading, Profit and Loss Account for the period ended 31 January 1984

	£	£		£
Purchases	330		Sales	210
Less: Closing stock	200			
		130		
Gross Profit c/d		80		
		210		210
Wages	14		**Gross Profit** b/d	80
Rent	10			
		24		
Net Profit		56		
		80		80

Since this is a different net profit, the capital account would become

J. Brown—Capital A/c

Balance c/d	1,056	Cash	1,000
		Profit and	
		loss	56
	£1,056		£1,056
		Balance b/d	1,056

Both the rent and wages account now have 'balances' left; the rent account having a debit balance is, of course, an asset, and the wages account, having a credit balance, is a liability. The revised balance sheet becomes

J. Brown and Co.
Balance Sheet as at 31 January 1984

	£	£		£	£
Capital					
Balance at 1.1.80	1,000		**Fixed Assets**		
Profit for the			Furniture		300
period	56				
		1,056			
Current Liabilities			**Current Assets**		
Creditors	60		Stock	200	
Accruals	4		Debtors	90	
	—	64	Pre-		
			payments	2	
			Cash	528	
				—	820
		1,120			**1,120**

Provisions

We have so far met two types of provisions, namely, provision for doubtful debts and provision for depreciation. Whatever the type of provision, however, the accounting procedure is similar, and we will use a depreciation provision as a typical example.

Assume that we have to provide a provision for depreciation of 10 per cent on plant costing £2,000 in 1983. The result is as follows:

Plant	2,000 −200	
Depreciation	+200	

In bookkeeping terms this becomes

Depreciation A/c

Dec. 1983 Provision for depreciation	200	Dec. 1983 Profit and loss	200

Provision for depreciation A/c

	Dec. 1983 Deprecia-tion	200

The depreciation expense is written off to the profit and loss account, leaving the provision as a balance which is shown as a deduction from the asset to which it refers. In the following year the additional provision of £200 will be recorded thus:

Depreciation A/c

Dec. 1984 Provision for depreciation	200	Profit and loss	200

Provision for depreciation A/c

	Jan. 1984 Balance	200
	Dec. 1984 Deprecia-tion	200

If the provision is reduced (perhaps because the rate is considered too high), the bookkeeping entries would be

Depreciation A/c				Provision for depreciation A/c			
Profit and loss		Provision for depreciation	50	Deprecia-tion	50	Balance	400
	50						

This reflects the position depicted by the quadrant:

Plant	+2,000	
Depreciation	−400 +50	
		Provision no longer required +50

The journal and day books

In the early period of accounting practice in the fourteenth and fifteenth centuries it was common practice to keep a daily diary or journal listing the various transactions which had occurred. This diary was a comprehensive record which listed for all transactions in chronological order: (1) the date of the transaction, (2) the name of the seller or purchaser, (3) the asset purchased or sold, (4) the value of the transaction, and (5) a short description of the transaction. When the owner of the business had checked his clerk's work, the appropriate entries were then made in (or 'posted' to) the ledger accounts. The journal took a standardized form, viz.:

Date	Transaction	LF	Dr.	Cr.
1 Jan. 1984	Plant A/c	4	580	
	Brown Co. Ltd A/c	47		580
	Purchase of grinding machine on credit			

By convention the debit is listed first, giving specific instructions as to the charge to be made in the plant account, followed by the credit. To help in locating these accounts a reference is given (LF = ledger folio) which indicates the page on which the appropriate account will be found. It is important to remember that the journal itself is *not* part of the double entry system—it is purely a form of diary which authorizes the charging of a ledger account.

Originally there were two major justifications for the use of a journal. In the first place, the risk of omitting a transaction was reduced, and secondly, the possibility of errors, irregularities or fraud can be reduced by demanding an explanation of all entries. With the growth in business activity, however, the journal in its original form became impracticable, if only through the sheer volume of entries, and it became the practice to subdivide the journal into four sections:

(1) Purchases of goods for resale on credit, which became known as the 'purchases day book'.
(2) Sales of goods on credit, which became known as the 'sales day book'.
(3) Cash receipts and payments, i.e. the cash book.
(4) All other transactions and transfers, which became known as the 'journal'.

These records of 'prime entry' contained between them all of the financial facts relating to the business, and it was a strict rule that no entries could be made in the ledger accounts unless there was some initial record in either the sales day book, purchases day book, cash book or journal. The greatest bulk of source data relates to sales and purchases, and these day books were of the form

Sales day book

Date	Name	LF	£
Jan. 1	A. Burgess	2	100
Jan. 2	J. Burnup	5	40
Jan. 3	G. Hulcoop	14	70
Jan. 5	Transferred to sales account	40	210

In the modern business, these day books have given way to copies of the sales invoice, or simply lists of invoices generated automatically when the sale invoices were prepared.

The scope of the original diary or journal has, therefore, been much reduced, and in most businesses today its use is confined to

(1) Correction of errors.
(2) Adjustments—particularly accruals and prepayments.
(3) Closing entries.

(1)   Correction of errors

Inevitably, errors occur from time to time even in the most efficient business. The error may be one of omission (i.e. a transaction has been completely omitted), or of commission (i.e. one side of the double entry has been entered in an incorrect though similar account), or of principle (i.e. a transaction has been entered in a wrong class of account). To effect the correction, an entry must first be made in the journal which authorizes the change in the ledger accounts.

For example, if J. Smith had been debited with an amount properly attributable to R. Smith, the correcting journal entry will be

		Dr.	Cr.
1 Jan. 1980	R. Smith A/c	47	
	J. Smith A/c		47
	Correction of posting error		

(2)   Adjustments

All accruals, prepayments and provision will normally first be journalized. Referring back to our example on page 84, the prepaid rates of £25 will first appear in the journal as

		Dr.	Cr.
31 Dec. 1983	Rates A/c	25	
	Prepaid rates A/c		25
	Rent prepaid during the period		

(3)   Closing entries

The entries closing the revenue and expense accounts to the income statement are normally journalized, as is also the transfer of the resulting profit or loss to the capital account. The transfer of the revenue and expense accounts in the earlier example (see page 84) would be authorized as follows:

		Dr.	Cr.
31 Dec. 1983	Trading A/c	330	
	Purchases A/c		330
31 Dec. 1983	Sales A/c	210	
	Stock A/c	200	
	Trading A/c		410

		Dr.	Cr.
31 Dec. 1983	Trading A/c—Gross profit	80	
	Profit and loss A/c		80
31 Dec. 1983	Profit and loss A/c	22	
	Wages A/c		10
	Rent A/c		12
31 Dec. 1983	Profit and loss A/c—Net profit	58	
	Capital A/c		58

The accounting process

At the beginning of this chapter we emphasized that bookkeeping does not introduce any new postulate but enables transactions to be recorded in an orderly, systematic and practical manner. The process of recording demands a logical sequence which has four stages:

(1)   Analysis of transactions

The primary and most important step is identifying and assigning each transaction in the appropriate manner. This requires judgement to decide which account or accounts should be debited or credited.

(2)   Recording (posting)

The results of the analysis must be recorded (or 'posted') to the ledger accounts either directly or through the journal medium. This is a purely mechanical step.

(3)   Adjusting entries

At the end of each accounting period, judgement is required to identify and adjust for prepayments, accruals and provisions. These are then recorded.

(4)   Financial statement preparation

The income statement and balance sheet are prepared in a manner judged to be most useful and comprehensible. The figures employed are derived from judgements made in stages (1) and (3).

The sources of financial data

As was indicated in the previous chapter, accounting usually seeks independent corroboration of the existence, validity and value to be associated with any transaction—the 'objectivity' postulate. It is obviously possible to derive a totally fictitious set of transactions, record them in an appropriate manner, and produce a perfectly balanced set of accounts. To minimize this possibility, all accounting records are derived from source documents which provide some independent verification of the validity of the record:

(1) Sources of sales data. The basic source of sales data is the sales invoice which itself may originate from a sales order form. The invoice may reflect sales made for cash, or sales made on credit to a customer.

(2) Sources of purchases data. The basic source of this data is the invoice received from the supplier. Before the invoice is paid it will be checked against a purchase order—to ensure that the goods had actually been ordered, and that the price and quantities were acceptable—and against a 'goods received note' which gives proof that the goods have actually been received.

(3) Sources of other expense data. All of the other expenses associated with a business require authentication. For example, entries for wages of employees will require source evidence that (a) the employee exists, (b) he has been paid at the appropriate rate, and (c) the proper deductions, e.g. tax and national insurance, have been made.

(4) Sources of adjusted data. Entries made in the ledgers for accruals, prepayments and provisions require authorization through means of the journal. In a large organization, the clerk actually responsible for making the ledger entries will have no control over the source of the entry—the journal.

References and further reading

LANGLEY (1978), *Introduction to Accounting for Students of Business Studies*. Butterworths.
LEE (1975), *Modern Financial Accounting*. Nelson.
LEWIS and GILLESPIE (1982), *Foundations in Accounting*. Prentice-Hall.
WOOD (1980), *Business Accounting I*. Longmans.

Questions for discussion

1 What is meant by 'double entry' bookkeeping?

2 What is the purpose of a ledger account? Mr Jones is considering running a small sub post office which also will sell newspapers and confectionery. List the accounts you consider he should keep. What factors have governed your choice?

3 For each of the following transactions indicated which accounts will be debited and credited:

(i) Goods purchased on credit from A. Jones.
(ii) Goods purchased for cash.
(iii) Payment to a creditor, M. Smith, less discount.
(iv) Payment for rent by cheque.

(v) Wages paid from cash.

(vi) Purchase of office equipment on credit from J. Watts Ltd.

4   The following are some of the accounts of P. Goodhope:

J. Jones

Balance	27		
Sales	35		

A. Jones

Balance	92		
Sales	28		

Office equipment

Balance	212		
Cash	97		
Cash	12		

Office expenses

Balance	128		
Cash	8		

Wages

Balance	180	
Cash	40	

At this stage, some additional information was discovered:

(i) The goods debited to J. Jones (£35) had been sold to A. Jones.

(ii) J. Jones had recently been declared bankrupt.

(iii) The £12 debited to office equipment had been for a supply of stationery.

(iv) The £40 debited to the wages account was cash drawn by Mr Goodhope.

Required:

(a) Prepare the journal entries necessary to reflect these facts.

(b) Show the corrected ledger accounts.

5   A trial balance extracted from the books of a trader did not balance, and the following errors were discovered:

(i) Sales account undercast by £20.

(ii) Office wages of £180 shown on the credit side of the trial balance.

(iii) Credit sales of £80 to R. Monk completely omitted from the ledger accounts.

(iv) Credit purchases from G. Holden for £75 included in the purchases account but omitted from the personal account.

(v) Goods bought on credit for £40 from M. Loy credited to L. Moy.

(vi) Office equipment bought for £210 debited to the purchases account.

Required:
Show how the correction of each item would affect the trial balance, and establish what was the original difference on the trial balance.

6 Max, a trader, who had been in business many years, rented additional premises from 1 April 1984. The following are his payments:

Date		£
30.4.84	Rates for half-year to 30.9.84	300
10.7.84	Rent for quarter to 30.6.84 (£500 p.a.)	125
10.10.84	Rent for quarter to 30.9.84	125
31.10.84	Rates for half-year to 31.3.85	300
7.1.85	Rent for quarter to 31.12.84	125
7.4.85	Rent for quarter to 31.3.85	125
30.4.85	Rates for half-year to 30.9.85	350
8.7.85	Rent for quarter to 30.6.85 (increased to £600 p.a.)	150
4.10.85	Rent for quarter to 30.9.85	150
31.10.85	Rates for half-year to 31.3.86	350

Max has an accounting year ending 31 December.

Required:
Write up (a) rent account and (b) rates account for the year to 31 December 1984 and the year to 31 December 1985.

7 The following expenditure in the year to 31 December 1984 relates to motor vans owned by Instant Delivery Ltd:

	£
Petrol, oil and repairs	400
Licences—year to 31.3.85	48
Tyres	90
Insurance—year to 31.3.85	100

On 31 December 1984 stock of tyres amount to £22.

Required:
Write up the motor expenses account for the year to 31 December 1984.

8   The following balances appeared in the ledger of J. Smith at the end of the accounting year 31 March 1984:

	Dr.	Cr.
	£	£
Salesmen's commission	2,600	
Insurances	230	
Provision for doubtful debts (1.4.83)		210
Debtors	8,500	
Plant and machinery	32,800	
Provision for depreciation (1.4.83)		9,000
Stock (1.4.83)	3,650	
Rent	390	

At the year end the following adjustments were necessary:

(i)   Closing stock was valued at £4,310.
(ii)   Depreciation is to be provided at the rate of $12\frac{1}{2}$ per cent.
(iii) A £200 debt regarded as wholly irrecoverable is to be written off.
(iv)   The provision for doubtful debts is to be adjusted to make it equal to 2 per cent of the outstanding debtors.
(v)   The salesmen earn a commission of $2\frac{1}{2}$ per cent on sales, and the commission based on last month's sales £20,000 is still outstanding.
(vi)   Insurance premiums have been prepaid to the extent of £60.
(vii) Rent outstanding at 31 March amounts to £96.

Required:
Open up the necessary ledger accounts and make the adjusting entries to the accounts; show the amounts to be transferred to the trading, profit and loss accounts, and the balances to be carried forward.

9   The following transactions relate to the business of Mr Smith:

Jan.	1	Mr Smith commenced business with cash in hand of £500, cash at the bank of £2,500 and a delivery van valued at £1,200.
	1	Paid in cash three months' rent in advance for office premises £180.
	2	Bought by cheque office furniture for £250.
	2	Bought on credit from J. Squires goods for resale £400.
	3	Sold goods on credit to M. Brown £350.
	4	Paid wages to assistant in cash £40.
	5	Sold goods for cash £100.
	9	Bought goods on credit from A. Guy £280.
	10	Cash sales £130.
	11	Paid wages in cash £40.
	12	Mr Smith drew cash for his personal use £60.
	14	Paid in cash sundry expenses £35.
	18	Paid J. Squires by cheque the amount owing less discount of £16.
	19	Paid wages in cash £40.
	22	M. Brown paid £100 on account by cheque.
	24	Sold goods on credit to R. Jones £110.
	26	Paid wages in cash £40.

Required:

(a) List all of the ledger accounts you consider necessary to record the above transactions.
(b) Record the above transactions in the appropriate ledger accounts.
(c) Extract a trial balance as at 30 January.
(d) What further information would you need in order to work out the profit for January?

10 The following transactions are to be entered up in the books for June:

June	1	Started business with £600 in the bank and £50 cash in hand.
	2	Bought goods on credit from C. Jones £130.
	3	Credit sales: H. Heaton £66, N. Norris £25, P. Potter £43.
	4	Goods bought for cash £23.
	5	Bought motor van paying by cheque £256.
	7	Paid motor expenses by cheque £12.
	9	Credit sales: B. Barnes £24, K. Liston £26, M. Moores £65.
	11	Goods bought on credit: C. Jones £240, N. Moss £62, O. Huggins £46.
	13	Goods returned by us to C. Jones £25.
	15	Paid motor expenses by cash £5, and motor insurance by cheque £84.
	19	Goods returned to us by N. Norris £11.
	20	Cash taken for own use (drawings) £10.
	21	We paid the following by cheque: N. Moss £62, O. Huggins £46.
	23	H. Heaton paid us in cash £66.
	25	P. Potter paid us by cheque £43.
	26	Cash sales £34.
	27	Cash taken for own use £24.
	28	Goods returned by us to C. Jones £42.
	29	Paid for postage stamps by cash £4.
	30	Credit sales: N. Norris £40, M. Edgar £67, K. Liston £45.

Required:

(i) Extract a trial balance as at 30 June;
(ii) Prepare a trading, profit and loss account for the period ended 30 June, and a balance sheet as at that date taking into account the following information:

    (a) Stock at close £300,
    (b) The motor van is to be depreciated by £30,
    (c) Rent owing for June £50,
    (d) Motor insurance prepaid £77.

11 Explain what independent evidence you might seek in order to verify the following entries in the accounting records:

(i)   Sales on credit £20,000.
(ii)   Discounts allowed to customers £250.
(iii)   Land and buildings at cost £5,000.
(iv)   Wages £2,500.
(v)   Salesmen's commission £200.
(vi)   Rent £400.
(vii) Goods returned by customer £190.
(viii) Bank balance £870.

6 Income measurement—the valuation and depreciation of fixed assets

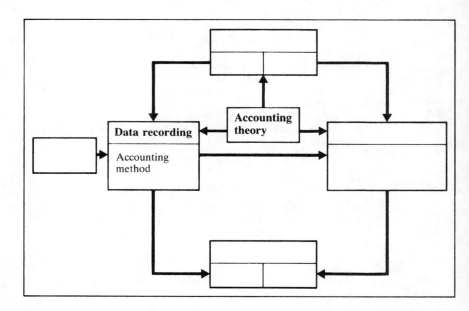

Assets have been defined as representing 'expected future economic benefits rights to which have been acquired by the enterprise as a result of some current or past transaction'. Within this broad definition we observed two categories—fixed assets and current assets. Fixed assets are long-lived resources, and are normally acquired by the enterprise to be used in the production of goods or services. These assets are recorded in the books of account in the manner prescribed by the cost postulate, namely at their original cost of acquisition. This cost, or input value, is systematically reduced over the life of the asset by a process referred to as depreciation, whereby a portion of the cost is allocated as an expense in each accounting period. In this chapter, we will examine the acquisition and valuation of fixed assets and the subsequent depreciation of their costs as expenses of the accounting period benefited.

The nature of depreciation

The term 'depreciation' carries various shades of meaning of which probably the two most important are those which view depreciation as (1) a fall in value and (2) an allocation of cost. The term 'value', as we have already seen, is susceptible to many different interpretations—cost value, exchange value, utility, esteem, etc.—so that linking depreciation to a value concept is fraught with difficulty. Hence, accounting opts for the second view of depreciation, and a useful starting point is the definition employed by the AICPA: 'Depreciation accounting is a system of accounting which aims to distribute the cost or other basic value of tangible capital assets, less salvage (if any), over the estimated useful life of the unit in a systematic and rational manner. It is a process of allocation and not of valuation.' The Accounting Standard SSAP 12 'Accounting for Depreciation' defines depreciation as 'a measure of the wearing out, consumption or other loss of value of a fixed asset whether arising from use, effluxion at time and obsolescence through technology and market changes'. The SSAP 12 has many similarities with the International Accounting Standard (IAS 4), 'Depreciation Accounting', which defines depreciation as 'the allocation of the depreciable amount of an asset over its estimated useful life'.

There are a number of aspects which we must explore arising from these statements:

(1) There is a need to identify the *cost* of the asset.
(2) There is a need to ascertain the *useful life* of the asset.
(3) There is a need to determine the *salvage value* of the asset.
(4) There is a need to select a *method* of depreciation which is *systematic and rational*.

Before considering these in detail there are important points which must be underlined:

(a) Depreciation is a process of *allocation* and not of *valuation*. The process of depreciation is not attempting to measure the value of the asset at any point in time, but trying to measure the value of the service the asset has provided during any given accounting period. The monetary values assigned to long-lived assets represent, therefore, that portion of original cost which has not yet been treated as an expense, i.e. depreciated.
(b) The process of depreciation does not of itself provide funds for the replacement of the asset. A firm may have accumulated large depreciation provisions but have no cash at all. This point will be made clearer when we consider the accounting treatment of depreciation. Not all fixed assets are depreciated, and a distinction is sometimes drawn between depreciable and non-depreciable assets. Where an asset is not susceptible to physical deterioration or obsolence—for example, freehold land—then it is not normally depreciated.

With these points in mind we can turn to the aspects enumerated above, namely: (1) cost of asset, (2) useful life of asset, (3) salvage value of asset, and (4) method of depreciation.

The cost of the asset

In accordance with the cost postulate, fixed assets are recorded at their input cost to the business. The input cost is normally regarded as the summation of all costs incurred in acquiring the asset, installing it and making it ready for use. For example, if a firm acquires a piece of land, the costs associated with it will be the purchase price, plus any legal fees, plus any costs associated with getting the land ready for its intended use. In the case of machinery and equipment, the cost will include the purchase price, any transportation costs and any installation costs.

The measurement of input cost is not always clear cut. In a bulk acquisition of assets, for example, the total cost may be clear, but the allocation to specific assets is a matter of judgement. The solution generally suggested is to allocate the total cost among specific assets in the ratio of the book values carried by the previous owner.

Where an asset is obtained by means of a part exchange, e.g. where a car is obtained in exchange for cash plus an old car, should the 'cost' be measured by the cash plus the book value of the old car, or the cash plus the allowance? The general solution is to use the latter value on the ground that it represents an objective value, whereas the book value (which is that portion of original cost not yet depreciated) represents an estimate dependent upon depreciation.

Where the company constructs a machine or building with its own personnel, the amount to be assigned to original cost (often referred to as the amount to be capitalized) includes all the costs incurred in construction.

Maintenance, improvements and replacements

Maintenance work is done to maintain the asset in good operating condition, or to bring it back to good operating condition if it has temporarily ceased to provide any service. In other words, maintenance (and repair) costs merely maintain the asset in no better condition than when it was purchased. As such, these costs become expenses in the period in which they are incurred.

Improvements are added to the cost of the asset since they result in an increase in the quantity of service provided by the asset. In practice, it is often difficult to draw a distinction between improvements and maintenance; for example, an overhaul of a machine in which some worn out parts are replaced by better ones will partly improve the quality of service and partly maintain the existing quantity. In general, and in the interests of conservatism, some acquisitions which strictly speaking should be treated as improvements (and hence as costs rather than expenses) are treated as expenses of the current period.

Replacements are the most difficult to define and treat properly because they are often similar in effect to maintenance and repairs. The replacement of an entire asset results in the complete expensing of the old asset and the capitalization of the new. The replacement of part of an asset will result in either an expense (as if it were maintenance) or in the capitalization of the replacement cost, the decision depending on how the asset unit is defined. For example, if one firm were to regard a complete lorry as a single unit then the replacement of the engine would be an expense; if another firm regards the body as one unit and the engine as another, replacement of the engine would result in a new asset. The doctrine of materiality may be invoked here: if the firm is large then the cost of a new engine may be immaterial; if the firm is very small, then a new engine is of some consequence.

The useful life of the asset

The estimate of asset life is clearly related to the depreciation process. The cost to be allocated to any particular period is dependent on the ratio of the services received in that period to the total services expected to be received during the anticipated useful life of the asset.

In many instances the estimated useful life of an asset can be little more than an informed guess, with the accountant dependent upon another function—such as production—for the information. In the event of a range of estimates, the accountant must seek to determine the most probable, bearing in mind the doctrine of conservatism which will press for the shortest possible period.

SSAP 12 points out that 'an asset's useful life may be

(a) predetermined, as in leaseholds;
(b) directly governed by extraction or consumption (as in mining);
(c) dependent on the extent of use; and
(d) reduced by obsolescence or physical deterioration'.

Deterioration refers to the physical process of wearing out. In the case of a machine it is connected with the number of machine hours that can be obtained before the machine is completely unusable; in the case of factory buildings a lengthy period will be assumed—normally 40–50 years.

Obsolescence may arise for one of two reasons. In the first place, an asset may lose its usefulness because of the development of improved equipment or processes; it is therefore obsolescence and not deterioration which will determine the life of the asset. In the second place, an asset may become obsolete because the product which it helps to manufacture has become obsolete. For example, the motor industry normally changes its models every four or five years; the machinery which produces those models has not deteriorated in that time, nor has it of itself become obsolete, but the end of the model life brings an end to its usefulness.

The salvage (residual) value of the asset

The net cost of the asset to the firm is its original cost less any amount which will eventually be recovered when the asset is sold at the end of its useful life. It is this net cost that is allocated to expense over the life of the asset. The estimate of salvage value can never be much more than an inspired guess, particularly if the asset has an expected life of more than two or three years. In general, the accountant is not unduly concerned about the lack of precision, primarily because salvage values are normally an extremely small proportion of the original cost and, as such, can be considered immaterial.

The method of depreciation

The basic objective of the various depreciation methods is to provide a 'systematic and rational' basis for allocating the cost of an asset over its estimated service life. Before we can sensibly discuss methods, therefore, we must try to ascertain what is the objective of the allocation of cost. There are several possibilities and we will deal briefly with two of the most important: cost of services and net service contribution.

(1)   The cost of services used

This objective places the emphasis on the measurement of the cost of services provided by an asset during an accounting period. Each asset is regarded as a bundle of potential services which is gradually consumed in the production process. The net monetary value assigned to the asset (i.e. original cost less depreciation) represents the value of unused services.

(2)   The net service contribution

The cost of obtaining each unit of service from an asset includes not only a portion of the original cost but also the associated costs of maintenance and repairs. Since the quality of the output remains constant, it is argued that the input cost must remain in a constant ratio to the output value. Thus, the objective of the 'net service contribution' concept is to hold constant over the life of the asset the total input values of depreciation and associated costs.

Given these objectives, the method of depreciation selected must reflect an attempt to achieve that objective deemed most appropriate to the asset or group of assets in question. In general, the emphasis on measuring the cost of services used is most appropriate when the maintenance and other associated costs are either insignificant or at a constant level over the life of the asset; conversely, where the associated costs are significant and increase as the asset ages, the net service contribution represents the most appropriate objective. SSAP 12 perhaps tends to oversimplify the problem when it asserts that 'the management of a business has a duty to allocate depreciation as fairly as possible to the periods expected to benefit from the use of the asset . . .'.

There are two main patterns of depreciation: (1) the straight line method and (2) decreasing charge methods.

(1) Straight line method

The straight line method assumes that depreciation is a function of time rather than use; the asset is seen as providing an equal amount of service in each year, with maintenance costs either constant or insignificant. The depreciation expense appropriate to each year is given by

$$\frac{\text{Original cost} - \text{Salvage value}}{\text{Useful life}}$$

If, for example, the original cost of an asset was £1,050, the salvage value estimated at £50, and the useful life at five years, the depreciation expense appropriate to each year would be

$$£\frac{1,050 - 50}{5} = £200 \text{ p.a.}$$

Very often, the appropriate depreciation is calculated by means of a percentage rate:

$$\frac{100}{\text{Useful life}}\%$$

In the illustration above the percentage to be applied to the net cost in each year is

$$\frac{100}{5} = 20\%$$

$$20\% \times £(1,050 - 50) = £200 \text{ p.a.}$$

The straight line method is so called because if the depreciation for each year is graphically displayed, the constant charge results in a straight line parallel to the axis:

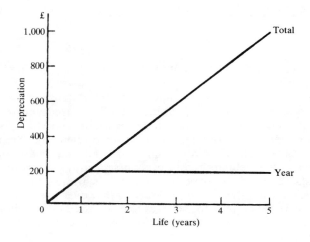

The decline in the book value of the asset will also be a straight line, as the book values at the end of each year will be

Year	Original cost	Depreciation year	total	Book value
1	1,050	200	200	850
2	1,050	200	400	650
3	1,050	200	600	450
4	1,050	200	800	250
5	1,050	200	1,000	50

The book value (sometimes referred to as the written down value or WDV) at the end of year five represents the estimated salvage value. In graphical terms, the result is

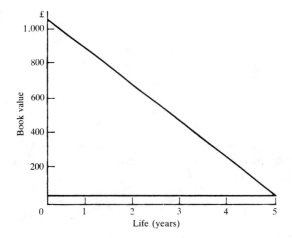

The straight line method is most suited to such assets as patents (legally having a 16-year life) and leases of land and buildings where depreciation is clearly a function of time. It is also applied to freehold buildings where the maintenance costs are normally insignificant compared with the cost of the building. Nevertheless, in so far as the choice of method for allocating the cost should depend upon the pattern of expected benefits obtained in each period the asset is used, the straight line method is seldom appropriate.

This method is also widely applied to other assets, although there is little theoretical justification for so doing. The English Institute's most recently published 'Survey of Published Accounts' reveals that over two-thirds of the 300 companies surveyed employ the straight line method of depreciation for most assets. There are two practical reasons for this; first, it is simple to apply, and secondly, it is argued that so much uncertainty surrounds estimates of life and salvage value that the straight line method is just as likely to result in meaningful information as any other apparently more appropriate method.

(2) `Decreasing charge methods

Decreasing charge methods are closely connected with the objective of measuring for each accounting period the value of the net service contribution. These methods recognize that as an asset (such as a machine) ages, the operating efficiency decreases and the maintenance costs increase. To balance out increasing maintenance costs, the depreciation expense must decrease in each year. We can clarify this in graphical terms:

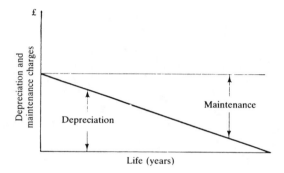

We shall illustrate two such methods, namely, the 'declining balance' method, and the 'sum of the digits'.

(i) *Declining balance.*   The 'declining balance' method applies a depreciation rate to the book value of the asset at the beginning of each period; the result is that, as the book value declines each year, the depreciation expense also decreases. The rate of depreciation to be charged is ascertained by means of the formula

$$r = \left(1 - \sqrt[n]{\frac{S}{C}}\right)\ 100\%$$

where r is the rate of depreciation, S the salvage value, C the original cost, and n the number of years. In the example above

$$r = \left(1 - \sqrt[5]{\frac{50}{1,050}}\right)\ 100$$

$$= (1 - 0.544)\ 100$$

$$= 45.6\%$$

The depreciation expense and the decline in the book value will be as follows:

Year	Original cost	Depreciation		Book value
		year	total	
1	1,050	479	479	571
2	1,050	260	739	311
3	1,050	142	881	169
4	1,050	77	958	92
5	1,050	42	1,000	50

Note that r is applied to the *original* cost less depreciation. In graphical terms, the result is no longer a straight line:

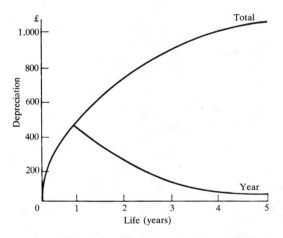

The book value of the asset declines more rapidly in the early years:

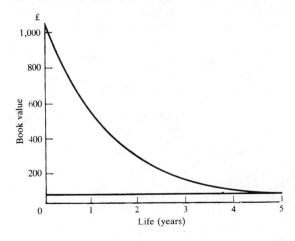

(ii) *Sum of the digits.*   The 'sum of the digits' method is similar in effect to the declining balance method, but is somewhat easier to calculate. Although the method is little used in the UK, it is widely used in North America, and hence it is likely to become more widely used here because of the growth and spread of USA based multi-national companies. The years of the asset's life are the 'digits' which are totalled (summed); the relationship of each year (digit) to the total provides the proportion of the net cost to be treated as depreciation, the digits being arranged in descending order to ensure the higher depreciation in the earlier year. In our example:

Years	Depreciation	Depreciation (year)
5	5/15	5/15 × 1,000 = 333
4	4/15	4/15 × 1,000 = 267
3	3/15	3/15 × 1,000 = 200
2	2/15	2/15 × 1,000 = 133
1	1/15	1/15 × 1,000 = 67
15	15/15	1,000

Thus:

Year	Original cost	Depreciation year	total	Book value
1	1,050	333	333	717
2	1,050	267	600	450
3	1,050	200	800	250
4	1,050	133	933	117
5	1,050	67	1,000	50

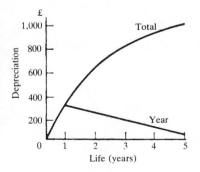
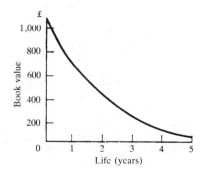

Accounting for depreciation

The method of depreciation chosen makes no difference to the procedure of recording the depreciation. We will use by way of illustration the figures derived from the straight line method. Assuming the original cost of the asset to be £1,050 and the depreciation for the first year to be £200, these values would be recorded as follows:

Asset A/c

19X0			19X0	
1 Jan. Cash			31 Dec.	
		1,050	Balance c/d	1,050
19X1				
1 Jan				
Balance				
b/d		1,050		

Provision for depreciation A/c

19X0			19X0	
31 Dec.			31 Dec.	
Balance			Profit and	
c/d		200	loss	200
			19X1	
			1 Jan.	
			Balance	
			b/d	200

The asset account is debited with the original cost of the asset, and the depreciation provision is accumulated by crediting a 'provision for depreciation' account. The profit and loss account is debited with the annual provision.

In the second year both the asset account and the provision for depreciation account will have opening balances, and the provision account is credited with the depreciation for the second year:

Asset A/c

19X1			19X1	
1 Jan.			31 Dec.	
Balance			Balance	
b/d		1,050	c/d	1,050
19X2				
1 Jan.				
Balance				
b/d		1,050		

Provision for depreciation A/c

19X1			19X1	
31 Dec.			1 Jan.	
Balance			Balance	
c/d		400	b/d	200
			31 Dec.	
			Profit and	
			loss	200
		400		400
			19X2	
			1 Jan.	
			Balance	
			b/d	400

On the balance sheet the asset will appear as

Fixed Assets	£	£
Plant (at cost)	1,050	
Less: Depreciation	400	
		650

Where assets are acquired other than at the beginning of the year the depreciation provision for that year is the appropriate proportion of the charge for the full year.

We can see more clearly now a point made at the beginning of this chapter, namely, that depreciation does not of itself provide funds for the replacement of assets. If this were so, the depreciation provision would reduce the cash—which it clearly does not do. Should the firm wish to provide such funds, it must each year 'earmark' part of its cash equal to the amount of depreciation, or invest that cash outside of the business.

While the depreciation does not directly provide funds, it has an indirect effect on the cash of a limited company. A limited company cannot distribute dividends to its shareholders in excess of its profits; to actually pay the dividends the company must have cash. Depreciation, which is an expense, reduces the profit available, and this restricts the maximum dividend.

We must note in passing that even if depreciation is funded, i.e. cash equal to the depreciation is set aside, this will only provide adequate funds for replacement if an identical asset is acquired and prices have not risen. Both assumptions are clearly unreal in an era of technological change and economic inflation.

Accounting for the disposal of fixed assets

Suppose that at the end of three years the firm sells its plant which it believed had a life of five years. At that time (assuming straight line depreciation) the accumulated depreciation will be £600. If the plant is sold for £250, the result is

	£
Plant at cost	1,050
Less: Depreciation	600
	450
Less: Cash	250
Loss on plant	**200**

The loss on the plant is clearly an expense of the business, but of which period? In one sense it is arguable that the 'loss' reflects the fact that the total amount of depreciation recorded was less than it should have been; in past periods, therefore, the profits have been overstated because the expense of using the asset was understated. The 'loss' should partly reduce the opening balance on the owner's equity (which includes past profits) and partly increase the depreciation expense for the current year. More normally, however, the 'loss' is treated as an expense of the current period on the grounds that if the asset had been used for five years, as originally planned, the residual value—and therefore the depreciation—would have been correct; the loss is something unusual. Indeed, SSAP 12 requires that 'where fixed assets are disposed of for an amount greater or less than the book value, the surplus or deficiency should be reflected in the results of the year'.

The bookkeeping procedure for the sale of an asset is to open a 'sale of asset' account, and to (a) debit it with the original asset cost, (b) credit it with the depreciation accumulated thereon, and (c) credit the account with any cash received for the sale, taking the resulting profit or loss (surplus or deficiency) to the credit or debit of the profit and loss account:

Asset A/c

19X2		19X2	
1 Jan.		31 Dec. Sale	
Balance		of asset	
b/d	1,050		1,050

Provision for depreciation A/c

19X2		19X2	
31 Dec. Sale		1 Jan.	
of asset	600	Balance	
		b/d	400
		31 Dec.	
		Profit and	
		loss	200
	600		600

Sale of asset A/c

19X2			19X2	
31 Dec.			31 Dec.	
Asset	1,050		Provision for deprecia-tion	600
			31 Dec.	
			Cash	250
			31 Dec.	
			Deficiency (Profit and loss A/c)	200
	1,050			1,050

Valuation of fixed assets

As we have observed, fixed assets are normally valued at original cost less depreciation, but whilst this rule applies to industrial buildings, plant and machinery, furniture and fittings, motor vehicles and miscellaneous equipment, there are categories of fixed assets to which the rule is less directly applied:

(1) *Land.* Land is valued at cost, and is not generally regarded as requiring depreciation. Indeed, land may well appreciate in value. Appreciation is only recognized when there is an objective and relatively certain measurement. When this arises in the market, i.e. the asset is sold, then the appreciation is recognized as revenue; when there is no market test but the asset is valued by some outside party the increase in value is treated as an 'unrealized profit' and added, in the case of a sole trader, to the ownership interest. To be an asset of the business, the land must strictly be owned by the business (*see* Chapter 2), but, conventionally, land acquired on a long lease is regarded as 'owned' for this purpose. Where the value of land is adversely affected by changing circumstances, e.g. population shifts which have either a social effect or make labour less available to the business using the land, then it should be depreciated.

(2) *Investments.* Investments are defined as the acquisition of shares or other legal rights in another business, and may, in fact, be held for either a long or a short term. Investments are recorded at their cost of acquisition, and short-term market fluctuations in value—whether up or down—are ignored. However, in the case of a limited company (*see* Chapter 10) a note has to be appended to the balance sheet stating the market value at balance sheet date. If there appears to be a significant and permanent diminution in value, then this loss will be written off to the profit and loss account.

Investment properties are defined as those properties held for the income they yield rather than for use in the business and are subject to the provisions of SSAP 19. Under this accounting standard, investment properties should not be depreciated, but revalued annually on an 'open market' basis. Any surplus on revaluation is treated as 'unrealized profit' and hence as capital rather than income, but any deficit is, by application of the convention of conservatism, treated as an expense and written off through the profit and loss account.

(3) *Intangible assets.* Intangible assets are non-physical long-term assets which represent certain legal rights or competitive advantages. They include such things as patents—a right over an invention; trademarks—a distinguishing product mark; research and development costs—expenditure on the development of future products; and goodwill—the excess of the purchase price paid for a business over the intrinsic value of the assets acquired.

Research and development expenditure is the subject of an accounting standard, SSAP 13, and, for the first time has explicit mention in the new 1981 Companies Act. The particular concern about 'R and D' expenditure is perhaps highlighted by the collapse of the Rolls-Royce company in the late 1960s. Rolls-Royce invested heavily in R and D, and treated most of this expenditure as an asset. This led it to report substantial trading profits out of which it paid dividends to its shareholders. However, the company did not really have the cash for this purpose—it had spent the money on R and D—and thus was soon experiencing the problems of acute cash shortage.

The Companies Act 1981 now requires companies *not* to treat the cost of research as an asset in the balance sheet, and only in special circumstances to treat development costs as an asset. The distinction between 'research' and 'development' is set out in the SSAP 13, and while it is beyond the scope of an introductory text to explore the many and often complex problems associated with the valuation of these items, as a generalization it is usually prudent to expense (depreciate) these items to zero as soon as they are incurred.

References and further reading

BAXTER (1971), *Depreciation*. Sweet and Maxwell.

BAXTER and DAVIDSON (1962), *Studies in Accounting Theory*. Sweet and Maxwell.

COMINSKEY (1971), 'Market Response to Changes in Depreciation Accounting', *Accounting Review*, April 1971.

HENDRIKSEN (1982), *Accounting Theory*. Irwin.

NOKE (1979), 'The Reality of Property Depreciation', *Accounting*, November 1979.

Questions for discussion

1   Depreciation accounting has alternatively been defined as (a) a process of allocation and (b) a process of valuation. Contrast and compare these alternative definitions.

2   'Depreciation provides for the replacement of assets.' Explain why this indicates a misunderstanding of the depreciation process.

3   A small retail business with a turnover of £20,000 p.a. has recently purchased the following items for use in the general office:

Item	Cost £	Expected life (years)
Filing cabinet	140	5
Stationery	180	1½
Pencil sharpener	15	5
Desk	80	8
Chair	30	8
Typewriter	160	5
Dictaphone	70	5
Tapes for dictaphone	12	2

Required:

(a) Explain which (if any) of these items would be treated as fixed assets (capitalized) and which as expenses of the year concerned.
(b) What is the consequence of the decision to capitalize or expense?
(c) Can you offer the business any general rules to guide them in their decision?

4   Jack Jones buys a motor car for use in his business and receives the following invoice:

	£
Basic cost	2,000
VAT	250
Registration plates	10
Road Fund Licence	40
Inertia reel belts	50
Overriders	20
Wing mirrors	24
6 gal. petrol	6
	2,400

Required:

(a) What would you regard as being the cost of this asset for the purposes of depreciation?

(b) Define in general terms what is normally included in the 'cost' of a fixed asset.

5   A new machine has been bought for £5,000. It is expected to last for five years, and have a residual value of £500.

(a) Calculate the charge against profits and balance sheet value for each of the five years, using

(i)   straight line method;
(ii) reducing balance method; and
(iii) sum of the digits method.

(b) Explain carefully the effect of the different methods.

(c) Which method do you consider most appropriate, and why?

6   A.B. Ltd moved to purpose-built office accommodation in 1980. The new building, inclusive of all fixtures and fittings and ready for occupancy, cost £40,000. In 1984 various work was carried out on the building:

(i)   Repainting of exterior   £4,000
(ii) Extension to rear of building   £2,500
(iii) Alteration of interior walls   £600
(iv) Recarpeting of main passages   £1,200

Explain, with reasons, how you would treat these items in the accounts.

7   Smith Ltd has the following fixed assets, according to its balance sheet dated 30 June 1984:

	Cost	Valuation on 30 June 1984	Depreciation	Net
Freehold property	10,000	100,000	—	100,000
Plant and machinery	30,000	—	15,000	15,000
Motor vehicles	25,000	—	15,000	10,000
				£125,000

The company revalues the freehold property every 5 years; provides 10 per cent p.a. reducing balance method for depreciation of plant and machinery; provides 25 per cent p.a. straight line method for depreciation of motor vehicles; calculates depreciation when provided for a whole year irrespective of the date of acquisition. During the year the following items occur:

(i)   An item of plant costing £3,000 purchased on 1 July 1978 was sold on 31 December 1984 for £600.
(ii) An item of plant costing £3,000 purchased on 1 July 1982 was sold on 1 October 1984 for £1,500.
(iii) Plant costing £10,000 was purchased on 1 July 1984.
(iv) On 30 September 1984 a motor car costing £3,000 purchased on 10 August 1978 was part exchanged for a new car. The invoice sent by the garage read as follows:

Cost ex factory	3,800
Delivery charges	40
Road tax	80
Fitted radio	30
Petrol	20
	3,970
Less: Allowance on old car	500
Amount payable	£3,470

(v)   The freehold property was revalued at £150,000 on 30 June 1985.

Required:

(a) A summary of the fixed assets as per balance sheet dated 30 June 1985.
(b) A statement of depreciation charges, profit/losses on disposals and gains on revaluation for the year to 30 June 1985.
(c) The business has a different policy as regards balance sheet value calculations for each of the three types of fixed asset. Discuss briefly why this might be, indicating the advantages and disadvantages of each method as used by Smith Ltd.

8   The following is a summary of a company's motor vehicle register, as at 1 January 1984:

Reg. no	Cost	Date of purchase	Depreciation	Net book value 1.1.84
	£		£	£
Car 1	1,000	1.1.78	1,000	—
Car 2	1,200	1.1.80	1,200	—
Car 3	2,000	1.7.82	1,000	1,000
Van 1	2,000	1.7.78	2,000	—
Van 2	3,000	1.7.83	750	2,250
	9,200		5,950	3,250

Depreciation has always been provided at 25 per cent p.a., straight line basis. A full year's depreciation has been provided in the year of purchase, and no depreciation is provided in the year of disposal. During the year 1984 the following transactions took place:

(i) Car 1 was destroyed in a crash. £100 was received from the insurance company.
(ii) Car 4 and Car 5, which are identical, were bought from a garage which took Car 2 in part exchange, at a valuation of £200. Only one cheque (for £4,800) passed through the company's books relating to this transaction.
(iii) Van 1 was sold for £200 on 31 December 1984.
(iv) Van 3 was bought on 30 September 1984 for £4,000.
(v) Van 2 is an articulated unit, comprising a cab and a separate trailer. The trailer proved too small and on 30 June 1984 the existing trailer (only) was traded in for a larger trailer. The company paid an extra £1,000 cash, and was allowed £500 on the old trailer, this being half of its original cost.

Required:

(a) (1) Prepare a similar summary of the motor vehicle register as at 1 January 1985; (2) state the profit or loss on motor vehicle disposals for the year; (3) state the depreciation charge for the year; (4) what would be the effect on the company's net profit if the company decided to provide a full year's depreciation in the year of disposing of motor vehicles?
(b) As regards the total net book value figure, which appears in the balance sheet: (1) what does it represent?; (2) how useful is it; how could it be made more useful?

9 The A.B.C. Co. Ltd showed the following cost values in its books at the year ended 31 December 1984:

		£
(i)	Freehold land	20,000
(ii)	Freehold buildings	100,000
(iii)	Plant and machinery	75,000
(iv)	Motor cars	15,000
(v)	Office appliances	5,000

The rates of depreciation, as used by the company, are

(ii) 2% fixed instalment.
(iii) 15% reducing balance.
(iv) 25% reducing balance.
(v)   25% reducing balance.

Required:

(a) Show the ledger accounts for each asset as at 31 December 1984 assuming that the whole of the assets were purchased on 1 January 1982 and that depreciation has been taken for each year.

(b) Show the entries required to record the following transactions, all of which took place after three years' depreciation had been charged: (1) an item of plant which cost £500 was scrapped with no residual value; (2) a motor car which cost £800 was sold for £350.

10 During 1984, a manufacturer of garden requisites spent £40,000 on research and development. Investigation of this sum yielded the following information:

(i)   £20,000 had been spent in developing a new plastic moulding process for garden gnomes. It was intended that this new process would come into operation in 1985.

(ii) £12,000 had been spent in trying, without success, to improve the durability of garden hoses, although the research leader was sure that he was 'on the verge of a breakthrough which would revolutionize hose making'.

(iii) £8,000 represented the normal costs of office provision, etc.

Required:
Explain how you would treat each of the above items in the accounts for the year ended 31 December 1984.

7 Income measurement—the valuation of current assets

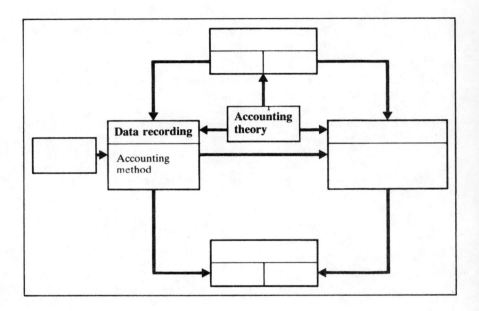

The valuation of stock

The valuation of stock is perhaps one of the most critical areas of income measurement. Consider a typical trading account such as

	£	£
Sales		10,000
Purchases	7,000	
Less: Closing stock	1,000	
		6,000
Gross Profit		**4,000**

The sales revenue will have been measured according to the realization postulate; the purchases treated initially as an expense (*see* Chapter 3) and then adjusted for the value of the stock unsold, thus measuring the cost of goods sold during the period. This expense is then matched with and deducted from the sales revenue to ascertain the gross profit. Accounting can be objective in relation to sales and purchases, but if the closing stock valuation is incorrect then the gross and ultimately the net profit will be over- or understated.

The valuation of stock is no easy task, for, as we shall see, methods of stock valuation which are acceptable for the purposes of income measurement may lead to the distortion of stock valuation in the balance sheet statement of assets; alternatively, acceptable valuation for balance sheet purposes may lead to inadequate income measurement. In addition, the valuation concept employed in accounting, namely that stock shall be valued at 'the lower cost or net realizable value', may of itself lead to inconsistent results.

The nature of stock

In Chapter 2 we observed that the term stock means 'the aggregate of those items of tangible personal property which (1) are held for sale in the ordinary course of business, (2) are in the process of production for such sales, or (3) are to be currently consumed in the production of goods or services to be available for sale'. In less elaborate terms, this means that stock includes (1) finished goods, (2) work in progress, and (3) raw materials. In a retail business stock will normally be entirely composed of finished goods; in a manufacturing company all three categories will exist.

The bases of stock valuation

If we buy an article with the intention of reselling it, then its value can either be expressed in terms of its cost (input value) or in terms of its sales price (output value). Either value may be acceptable in the case of finished goods, but in the instance of work in progress and raw materials (which require considerable economic activity before they can be transferred to customers) the input value may be more appropriate. We must not suppose from this that there is one output value and one input value; there are a number of types appropriate to each category, and we must briefly turn our attention to some of them.

(1) Output values

(a) *Current selling prices*. The use of current selling prices is acceptable as a measure of finished stock valuation when there is in existence a sure market price and no substantial cost of marketing. As we have seen when discussing the realization postulate (*see* Chapter 4), these conditions are met mainly in the case of precious metals.

(b) *Net realizable value*. Net realizable value is the amount at which it is expected that items of stocks and work in progress can be disposed of without creating either profit or loss in the year of sale, i.e. the estimated proceeds of sale less all further costs to completion and less all costs to be incurred in marketing, selling and distributing directly related to the items in question.

(2)   Input values

Input values may be defined as the value of resources required to obtain the inventory and place it in a condition for sale. There are two major types of input values:

(a) *Historic cost*. The input value of stock is seen as the costs incurred in the past to place the stock in its present state. In a business which holds only finished goods as stock, the historic cost is the purchase price; in a manufacturing concern, the historic cost will be the purchase price of the raw materials, the wages of employees directly engaged in the manufacturing process, and a portion of factory expenses (normally referred to as factory overhead) which can be allocated to the product on some logical basis (*see* Chapter 13). Historic cost is the major valuation method employed by accounting. Its main advantage is that it is said to be objective, because cost is based on a past exchange transaction. But costs are not constant over time, and when two or more items of stock are acquired at different times their addition in monetary terms does not result in a meaningful sum. In addition many historic cost computations require the allocation of joint costs (e.g. if a firm buys coal and heats it to produce gas and coke, what is the input value of the two products?), and even the best allocation methods are inadequate.

(b) *Current replacement costs*. Accounting, as we have seen, makes the assumption of continuity. If a business is to continue its operations then there is a perpetual cycle of buying stock, selling it and replacing it. It follows that the cost of using an item of stock is not what was paid for it in the past, but what will have to be paid in the future to replace it. Stock, therefore, should be valued at its current replacement cost; it permits the matching of current input values with current revenues in the income statement, and also the monetary value assigned to stock at the end of the period represents a current cost. Accounting, however, rarely makes use of this input cost, mainly on the grounds that the current replacement prices may have to be estimated, and are therefore not objective. An alternative suggestion is that the most satisfactory valuation basis is the 'deprival' value, which may be interpreted as the lower of replacement cost or expected direct benefits (usually the scrap value). This view has gained implicit recognition in the government report 'Inflation Accounting', which considers that the value of an asset is the amount of loss suffered by the company concerned if the asset is lost or destroyed.

Accounting and stock valuation

The conceptual and practical difficulties of stock valuation are implicitly encapsulated in the preface to SSAP 9, 'Stocks and Work in Progress' which blandly states: 'No area of accounting has produced wider differences in practice than the computation of the amount at which stocks and work in progress are stated in financial accounts'. Prior to SSAP 9, accounting practice required stock to be valued 'at cost or market value, whichever is the lower'. This concept has a long history in accounting, going back to the nineteenth century and before; one of the reasons for its early prominence is the nineteenth century emphasis on the balance sheet as a report to creditors. Without regular and reliable reports on which to base future expectations, creditors emphasized the lowest (and most conservative) value of the assets. When the emphasis was shifted from the balance sheet to the income statement, the concept moved with it, and the result was a conservative statement of income.

The 'lower of cost or market value' dictum was frequently attacked as being ambiguous and inconsistent. 'Cost' could mean historic or replacement cost (both input values) and market could mean selling price, net realizable value (both output values) or replacement cost (an input value). The selection of the lower value simply in the interests of conservatism violates the convention of consistency because it permits a mix of valuation base, i.e. both input and output values. The current accounting standard (SSAP 9, 'Stocks and Work in Progress') merely reinforces the traditional emphasis on conservatism by requiring stock to be 'stated at cost, or, if lower, at net realizable value', and does nothing to remove internal inconsistency. As the Board of Inland Revenue argued in their acceptance of the new standard for tax purpose 'the new standard is . . . merely a refinement and not a change of basis'. The Companies Act 1981, however, has added legal force to SSAP 9, by requiring stock to be valued at 'its purchase price or production cost' or 'the net realizable value' if lower (Schedule 1, Part II), so that ambiguity and inconsistency have been given the sanction of law.

In practice, however, the result is probably not unduly inconsistent because, in an era of rising prices, cost will almost invariably be below net realizable value, however that term is defined. In any business the number of items of stock where net realizable value is below cost will almost certainly be very few, and the convention of materiality may well apply.

Historic cost

In our examination of the problem of stock valuation, we have so far assumed that historic cost, being the most important basis of valuation, is clearly and easily established. This is not so; it is difficult in the instance of a non-manufacturing concern which buys in finished goods for resale; it is even more complicated in the case of a manufacturing concern. This latter problem we will explore in Chapter 13; in this chapter we will focus our attention on the non-manufacturing businesses such as the retail store.

We will concentrate on three methods of valuation, first discussing the concepts involved, and then illustrating these comparatively by means of a simple numerical example. In this analysis we will assume rising prices over time, simply because in today's world this is the normal situation. In a deflationary situation the conclusions drawn would be exactly the reverse.

The three methods are   (1) First in, first out (FIFO).
                                    (2) Last in, first out (LIFO).
                                    (3) Weighted average.

(1) First in, first out

The first in, first out (FIFO) rule is based on the assumption that the stock acquired first will be the first to be sold. For example, if a firm acquires 10 units of stock at £3 each, and 6 identical units at £4 each, and later sells 12 units, the result will be

Purchases	Sales (at cost)	Stock
10 @ £3 = 30	10 @ £3 = 30	
6 @ £4 = 24	2 @ £4 = 8	4 @ £4 = 16
16 = 54	12 = 38	

The 12 units sold will have 'cost' £38 and the stock remaining will be 4 units valued at £16.

The FIFO system represents an approximation to the normal flow of goods, and also ensures that the end stock will be valued at the most recent costs. Depending on the quickness of sale (i.e. rapidity of turnover), and the rate of change in the price level, the closing stock will be shown at a value approaching replacement cost.

While the valuation for balance sheet purposes may be realistic, the FIFO system does not generally meet the objective of matching current costs with current revenues. The greater the time interval between buying and selling stock in a time of changing price levels, the more unrealistic the measure of profit. The danger of this can be easily illustrated.

Assume the following sequence of events:

T_1 Firm begins business with £30 cash.
T_2 Buys 2 units of stock at £5 each.
T_3 Buys 2 more similar units at £10 each.
T_4 Sells 2 units at £8 each.

Under the FIFO system the cost of the units sold will be £10, and the profit £6. If all of the profit is withdrawn, this leaves only sufficient cash to replace one unit at the current price of £10. The prices in the example are, of course, exaggerated; but the danger of matching past costs with current revenues is nevertheless still very real.

The use of the FIFO system is not too unrealistic in a business where there is a rapid turnover of stock; the faster the turnover, the more recent are the 'historic' costs. In a business where the production cycle is lengthy, FIFO can result in unrealistic measurement of profit in a time of changing prices. In this connection, it is perhaps salutary to note that the last three annual 'Survey of Published Accounts' reveal that over half of the surveyed companies use the FIFO method as a basis of stock valuation.

(2) Last in, first out

The last in, first out system of stock valuation assumes that the stock purchased most recently is the first to be sold. Few proponents of the LIFO system consider that this represents the physical flow of goods, but they do claim that LIFO achieves the objective of matching the most currently available costs with current revenues. Using the illustration above:

Purchases	Sales (at cost)	Stock
10 @ £3 = 30	6 @ £3 = 18	4 @ £3 = 12
6 @ £4 = 24	6 @ £4 = 24	
16 = 54	12 = 42	4 = 12

The 12 units sold will have cost £42 (as opposed to £38 under FIFO), and the stock remaining will be valued at £12.

While LIFO may approximate to current costs for the purposes of income measurement, the value of the stock on hand will become more and more unrealistic as time passes. One way round this objection is to indicate by way of a note to the balance sheet what the current input value of the stock actually is, although this compromise is seldom, if ever, adopted.

The LIFO system is often employed by businesses whose pricing system depends on a percentage (mark up) addition to cost. Whether such a system of pricing is either logical or desirable will be discussed in a later chapter, but if such a system is adopted there is evidently much in favour of relating selling price to the most current costs. This should ensure sufficient margin of profit to cover the rising costs of replacement.

(3) Weighted average

One way around the problem of changing prices is to avoid it, and this is the purpose of the weighted average system. Generally, average costs are neutral both in respect of income measurement and balance sheet valuation. All stock acquired during a given period, at whatever price, is reduced to a single representative average cost. Using the figures above:

Purchases	Sales (at cost)	Stock
10 @ £3 = 30		
6 @ £4 = 24		
16 = 54		

Cost per unit = $£\frac{54}{16}$ 12 @ $£\frac{54}{16}$ = £40.5   4 @ $£\frac{54}{16}$ = £13.5

The 12 units sold will have cost £40.5 and the stock remaining will be valued at £13.5.

Historic cost—comparison of methods

We will assume that three similar businesses begin their operations with a capital in cash of £100, and that the same economic events occur during their life span of three years. The basic data is as follows:

Year	Purchases			Sales			Stock at end
	Units	Price (£)	Total (£)	Units	Price (£)	Total (£)	Units
I	10	5	50	8	9	72	7
	5	8	40				
II	6	9	54	9	10	90	4
III	6	12	72	10	14	140	—

Each firm, however, uses a different method of stock valuation, and under these varying systems the results will be

Firm A—FIFO

Year	Revenue £	Cost of sales £	Profit £	Stock at end £
I	72	$(8 \times 5) = 40$	32	$(2 \times 5) + (5 \times 8) = 50$
II	90	$(2 \times 5) +$		
		$(5 \times 8) +$		
		$(2 \times 9) = 68$	22	$(4 \times 9) \qquad = 36$
III	140	$(4 \times 9) +$		
		$(6 \times 12) = 108$	32	

Firm B—LIFO

Year	Revenue £	Cost of sales £	Profit £	Stock at end £
I	72	$(5 \times 8) +$		
		$(3 \times 5) = 55$	17	$(7 \times 5) = 35$
II	90	$(6 \times 9) +$		
		$(3 \times 5) = 69$	21	$(4 \times 5) = 20$
III	140	$(6 \times 12) +$		
		$(4 \times 5) = 92$	48	—

Firm C—Weighted Average

Year	Revenue £	Cost of sales £	Profit £	Stock at end £
I	72	$8 \times \frac{90}{15} = 48$	24	$7 \times \frac{90}{15} = 42$
II	90	$9 \times \frac{96}{13} = 66.5$	23.5	$4 \times \frac{96}{13} = 29.5$
III	140	$10 \times \frac{101.5}{10} = 101$	38.5	—

	I			II			III		
	A FIFO	B LIFO	C W.A.	A FIFO	B LIFO	C W.A.	A FIFO	B LIFO	C W.A.
Capital	100	100	100	132	117	124	154	138	147.5
Profit for year	32	17	24	22	21	23.5	32	48	38.5
Net Capital Employed	**132**	**117**	**124**	**154**	**138**	**147.5**	**186**	**186**	**186.0**
Stock	50	35	42	36	20	29.5	—	—	—
Cash	82	82	82	118	118	118	186	186	186
	132	**117**	**124**	**154**	**138**	**147.5**	**186**	**186**	**186**
Return on Capital Employed	24.2%	14.5%	19.4%	14.3%	15.2%	15.9%	17.2%	25.8%	20.7%

Summarizing the profit position we have

	A FIFO	B LIFO	C W.A.
I	32	17	24
II	22	21	23.5
III	32	48	38.5
	£86	£86	£86

In a time of rising prices, LIFO will tend to delay the recognition of profit as opposed to either FIFO or W.A., and the weighted average will often lead to results in between the other two. We must observe that these are three identical businesses, each carry out identical operations, but the profit for each in each year is a function of the method of stock valuation. Perhaps the point made at the beginning of Chapter 3 takes on new significance—'income (profit) is in itself an elusive concept'.

In Chapter 4 we observed that the success of a firm cannot be judged on the absolute size of the profit, but on the relationship between profit and ownership equity—the return on net capital employed. For each firm we can draw up a balance sheet, and identify the profit and net capital. We will again observe a variation in rates of return which have arisen because of the method of stock valuation employed. We have examined, therefore, some of the problems of stock valuation; we have seen enough to realize how complicated the situation is. There is no one *right* method of valuation; there are a number of possible methods all of which have some advantages and some disadvantages. One last important point must be made; whatever basis of valuation is chosen, it must be applied *consistently* from year to year. Provided this is done, although the profit for any one year may be different from that computed on another basis, the total profit over the whole life of the business will, as we have seen, be the same. If the valuation basis is changed, then profit will be as much a function of the change in method as a change in business fortunes. If a business does elect to change the basis, then in that year profit must be ascertained on both old and new basis in order that a proper comparison can be made.

The valuation of debtors

Debtors are customers to whom short-term credit facilities have been granted, and represent, in effect, short-term loans. The extent to which credit is granted and to whom is an important aspect of working capital management and credit control; this dimension is discussed later in Chapter 18.

The valuation of the amounts due from debtors at the end of an accounting period is not merely a matter of adding up all outstanding invoices, for there is no absolute certainty that all of the customers to whom credit facilities have been granted will, in fact, settle their accounts. If debtors either have or may default, then to include them in the total of debtors would be to overstate the value of the asset, and to fail, in accordance with the convention of conservatism, to 'anticipate any future losses' by writing off the actual or potential defaulters as an expense charged in the profit and loss account.

The debtors known to have defaulted (described as 'bad debts'), and those who may default in the future (known as 'doubtful debts'), are treated separately in the accounts. 'Bad debts', once recognized, are removed from the debtors ledger by crediting the debtors account, and debiting a 'bad debts' account, which at the end of the accounting period is transferred in aggregate to the profit and loss account.

For example, if Mr Smith and Mr Jones, who owe respectively £40 and £70, have been declared bankrupt, the ledger accounts to record this fact will be

Mr Smith A/c

Balance	40	Bad debts	40

Mr Jones A/c

Balance	70	Bad debts	70

Bad debts A/c

Mr Smith	40	Profit and loss	110
Mr Jones	70		
	110		**110**

Profit and loss A/c

Bad debts	110		

All bad debts written off require proper authorization through the journal (see page 89), for it would be only too easy for an unscrupulous clerk to 'write off' the debts of his friends.

The estimation of doubtful debts does not relate to specific debtors; rather it relates to the business's general experience of the proportion of debtors likely to default. This is usually described as X per cent of the total debtors, the particular percentage being established by the custom of the trade and the past history of the business. If the debtors of a business amounted at the end of 1984 to £4,000 and it was anticipated that 2 per cent of the debtors were likely to default, then the accounts would show

Sundry debtors A/cs

1984			1984		
31 Dec.			31 Dec.		
Balance		**4,000**	Balance c/d		**4,000**
1985					
1 Jan.					
Balance b/d	4,000				

Provision for doubtful debts A/c

	1984	
	31 Dec.	
	Provision	
	—profit	
	and loss	80

Profit and loss A/c

1984		
31 Dec.		
Provision		
for		
doubtful		
debts	80	

On the balance sheet, the asset would be shown as

	£	£
Debtors	4,000	
Less: Provision	80	
		3,920

If in 1985 the outstanding debtors rises to £5,000, then the required provision is £100. As £80 has already been provided, the provision for the year is £20. Thus:

Sundry debtors A/cs

1985			1985	
1 Jan.			31 Dec.	
Balance c/d	4,000		Balance c/d	5,000
31 Dec.				
Sales (increase)	1,000			
	5,000			5,000
1986				
1 Jan.				
Balance b/d	5,000			

Provision for doubtful debts A/c

1985			1985	
31 Dec.			1 Jan.	
Balance			Balance	
c/d		100	b/d	80
			31 Dec.	
			Profit and	
			loss	20
		100		100
			1986	
			1 Jan.	
			Balance	
			b/d	100

Profit and loss A/c

1985	
31 Dec.	
Provision	
for	
doubtful	
debts	20

The asset on the balance sheet would be shown as

	£	£
Debtors	5,000	
Less: Provision	100	
		4,900

References and further reading

ACCOUNTING STANDARDS COMMITTEE (1975), 'Stock and Work in Progress', SSAP 9.

BEDFORD and MCKEOWN (1972), 'Comparative Analysis of Net Realisable Value and Replacement Costing', *Accounting Review*, April 1972.

GEMMELL and BROAD (1982), 'SSAP 9 Seven Years on ... and it still means Headaches for the Auditor', *Accountancy*, July 1982.

JOHNSON (1954), 'Inventory Valuation: The Accountant's Achilles Heel', *Accounting Review*, January 1954.

PATTERSON (1979), 'Stock Valuation since SSAP 9', *Accountancy*, April 1979.

UNDERDOWN (1971), 'Logical Principles Needed for Stock Evaluation', *Management Accounting*, July 1971.

Questions for discussion

1   Ivor B. Gunn has just started in the retail business. His transactions in the first period of trading are as follows:

Bought	30 automatic back scratchers at £10 each	6.1.84
Bought	40 automatic back scratchers at £12 each	13.1.84
Sold	50 automatic back scratchers at £20 each	15.1.84
Bought	50 automatic back scratchers at £15 each	18.1.84
Sold	50 automatic back scratchers at £20 each	22.1.84

(a) Calculate the closing stock and gross profit for this period, assuming (1) FIFO, (2) LIFO and (3) weighted average.

(b) The audited accounts of limited companies have to show a true and fair view of the state of affairs, and of the profit for the year.

Which of the three methods do you recommend as best satisfying this legal requirement as regards (1) the stock figure on the balance sheet, and (2) the gross profit—justifying your answer in each case.

2   Accountants generally value stock at 'the lower of cost and net realizable value'.

(a) Define 'cost' as used in this statement.

(b) Define 'net realizable value' as used in this statement.

(c) Do you think your definitions enable precise and correct monetary figures to be calculated?

(d) Do you see any logical inconsistency in valuing stock at 'the lower of cost and net realizable value'?

3   It has been suggested that it would be better if all stocks were valued at current replacement cost:

(a) What alteration would this necessitate in the accountants' usual policy as regards the timing of revenue recognition?

(b) Do you think this method accords with the legal requirements outlined in part (b) of question 1 above?

(c) Do you think this is the best method? Justify your answer in detail.

4   A business includes in its stock three major categories of goods: A, B and C. At 31 December 1984, the following information is available:

Stock item	Historic cost	Replacement cost	Net realizable value
	£	£	£
A	2,000	2,100	1,750
B	3,220	3,050	3,300
C	2,400	2,800	2,500
	7,620	7,950	7,550

What value would you place on the closing stock in order to show a 'true and fair view'?

5   P. Forte commences business on 1 January buying and selling pianos. He sells two standard types, upright and grand, and his transactions for the year are as follows:

| | Upright | | Grand | |
	buy	sell	buy	sell
1 Jan.	2 at £400		2 at £600	
31 March		1 at £600		
30 April	1 at £350		1 at £700	
30 June		1 at £600		1 at £1,000
31 July	2 at £300		1 at £800	
30 Sept.		3 at £500		2 at £1,100
30 Nov.	1 at £250		1 at £900	

You observe that the cost to P. Forte of the pianos is changed on 1 April, 1 July and 1 October, and will not change again until 1 January following.

Required:

(a) Prepare a statement showing gross profit and closing stock valuation, separately for each type of piano, under each of the following assumptions: (i) FIFO, (ii) LIFO, (iii) weighted average.
(b) At a time of rising prices (i.e. using the grand pianos as an example) comment on the usefulness of each of the methods.

6   Rawhide & Co. commenced trading on 1 April 1983. The manager has prepared the following accounts for the first year's operations:

Trading, profit and loss A/c
for the year ended 31 March 1984

	£	£
Sales (80,000 units)		1,200,000
Less: Purchases (100,000 units)		1,000,000
Gross Profit		200,000
Less: Salaries	5,000	
Amount written off motor vehicles	200	
Other expenses	164,800	170,000
Net Profit		**£30,000**

Balance sheet as at 31 March 1984

	£
Motor vehicles	5,800
Investments	10,000
Goodwill	2,000
Good labour relations	5,000
Research and development costs	15,000
Debtors	143,200
Bank	6,000
	187,000
Capital	150,000
Reserves created by inclusion of goodwill and good labour relations	7,000
Net Profit	30,000
	187,000

A friend has commented that these accounts do not observe 'the accounting postulates and conventions', and you are asked to carry out a review. You ascertain the following additional information:

(i)   20,000 units of stock in good condition were on hand at the year-end.

(ii)   Salaries of £2,500 have been misclassified and included in 'other expenses'. The manager was aware of this, but is reluctant to change the accounts since the amount is so small and does not in any case affect the net profit.

(iii) The two motor vehicles purchased on 1 April 1983 for £3,000 each were expected to have a useful life of five years with no residual value. The Managing Director was pleased to see that the quoted trade-in figure was still £2,900 for each car at the year-end.

(iv)   The investments had originally cost £10,000. The market value of half the investments had doubled during the year, but the remaining shares were worthless because of the liquidation of the company involved.

(v)   The manager feels that the company has built up £2,000 of goodwill during the year, in the form of established customers.

(vi)   Rawhide & Co. consider that the research and development expenditure is to be written off in the year it is incurred, and this will be done in future. In view of the results for this first year, however, the manager has decided that this year they should be capitalized.

(vii) Discussions have been going on throughout the year with a competitor to sell the shares in Rawhide's subsidiary, Hatton & Co. Negotiations had almost been completed at the year-end, and the

£20,000 original cost has consequently been included in the bank figure to improve the position.

Required:

(a) Redraft the above accounts in accordance with the recognized accounting postulates and conventions.
(b) Identify the postulates and conventions which had not originally been observed and discuss the basis in each case.

7   You are preparing a company's accounts to 31 December 1984 and are given the following information after you have prepared the draft accounts:

(i) A customer is suing you for damages; your solicitor estimates the potential liability between £50,000 and £80,000.
(ii) A car model has become obsolete and it is estimated that 100 cars (costing £200,000) in stock will be sold for between £100,000 and £130,000.

    (a) How will the foregoing affect the 1984 profit?
    (b) If the claim is settled in 1985 for £65,000 and the cars sold for £115,000, what will be the effect on the 1985 profit?
    (c) What are your conclusions from the foregoing?

8   (i) Flashman, a bully beef trader, started in business on 1 January 1984. During the year to 31 December 1984 he sold on credit some beef to Tom Brown valued at £50, but failed to receive payment as Brown disappeared. On 31 December 1984 Flashman examined the balances of his debtors ledger accounts and summarized them:

	£
Tom Brown (as above)	50
Just William	200
Sundry other customers	5,000
	5,250

Just William is disputing the account and is reluctant to pay as the beef he ate put him in hospital for a fortnight. Although Flashman has had no obvious difficulty with the other customers, he thinks that unless he uses undue violence it is likely that some may fail to pay in these 'hard times'.

(ii) In the year to 31 December 1985, Tom Brown reappeared, paid £10 and then disappeared. Just William paid his account less £170 for doctor's fees (£50 and £120 for removal of his appendix). Other bad debts for the year amounted to £3,000. The turnover (all on credit) for the year was £60,000. The debtors as at 31 December 1985 amounted to £10,000 and, according to Flashman, the 'hard times' environment still exists.

Required:

(a) Discuss the accounting problems of income measurement in (i) 1984 and (ii) 1985. What is the value of the asset 'debtors' in each of the years and what is the expense?
(b) Draft the ledger accounts for the year to 31 December 1984.
(c) Continue the accounts for 1985.

9   The following trial balance was extracted from the books of Fletcher, a trader, as at 31 December 1984:

	£	£
Capital account		30,500
Purchases	36,500	
Sales		50,900
Repairs to buildings	848	
Motor car (WDV)	950	
Car expenses	318	
Freehold land and buildings	20,000	
Balance at bank	540	
Furniture and fittings (cost)	2,000	
Depreciation of furniture and fittings		540
Wages and salaries	8,606	
Discounts allowed	1,061	
Discounts received		814
Drawings	2,400	
Rates and insurances	248	
Bad debts	359	
Provision for doubtful debts, 1.1.84		140
Trade debtors	5,213	
Trade creditors		4,035
General expenses	1,586	
Stock-in-trade, 1.1.84	6,300	
	86,929	**86,929**

The following matters are taken into account:

(i)   Stock-in-trade, 31 December 1984, £8,800.
(ii)   Wages and salaries outstanding at 31 December 1984, £318.
(iii) Rates and insurances paid in advance at 31 December 1984, £45.
(iv)   The provision for bad debts is to be reduced to £100.
(v)   During 1984 Fletcher withdrew goods, valued at £200, for his own use. No entry has been made in the books for the withdrawal of these goods.
(vi)   The item 'Repairs to buildings, £848' includes £650 in respect of alterations and improvements to the buildings.
(vii) One-third of the car expenses represents the cost of Fletcher's motoring for private, as distinct from business, purposes.

(viii) Provide depreciation on furniture and fittings at 10 per cent p.a. on the cost at 1 January 1984, and at 20 per cent on the WDV of the car.

Required:

Prepare a trading, profit and loss account for the year 1984, and a balance sheet as on 31 December 1984.

10 The following is a list of ledger balances in the books of Jim, as at 31 March 1984:

	£
Capital	50,000
Property at cost	50,000
Plant and machinery	
—cost	10,000
—depreciation b/f	6,000
Sales	200,000
Purchases	100,000
Stock	30,000
Trade debtors	40,000
Trade creditors	15,000
Wages	15,000
Heat, light and power	2,000
General expenses	17,000
Discount received	1,000
Discount allowed	900
Carriage inwards	800
Carriage outwards	700
Returns inwards	600
Returns outwards	500
Bad debt provision b/f	400
Sale of plant	900
Cash and bank balance	2,800
Drawings	4,000

Required:

(a) Prepare a trial balance.
(b) Prepare a trading, profit and loss account for the year ended 31 March 1984 and a balance sheet (in vertical form) as on 31 March 1984, incorporating the following details:

   (i)   Closing stock £35,000.
   (ii) An amount of £1,000, included in trade debtors as above, is to be regarded as a bad debt and written off in full. The bad debt provision is adjusted at 31 March each year to be 1 per cent of trade debtors.
   (iii) During the year an item of plant—original cost £1,000, depreciation to date £400—was sold for £900. The bookkeeper did not know how to treat this item, and so had made no adjustments for it. The sales proceeds were credited to a 'sale of plant' account.

(iv)   Included in general expenses are the following: (1) £100 paid to an insurance company for property and equipment insurance, being the premium for the year to 30 June 1984; (2) £25, being the road fund licence on Jim's car for the year to 30 September 1984.

The telephone bill (also included in general expenses) paid in March read as follows: rental charge 1 March to 31 May £12; calls charge 1 December to 28 February £60. No other telephone bill has since been received.

(vi)   Jim has taken for his own use during the year goods costing £100.

(vii) Plant and machinery is to be depreciated at 10 per cent p.a. on the reducing balance. No plant has been bought during the year.

8 Further aspects of financial records

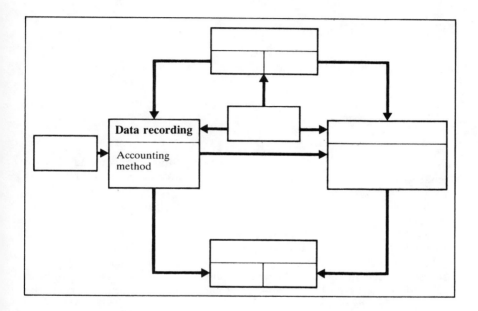

Incomplete records

The system of double entry record-keeping introduced in Chapter 5—a system, incidentally, regarded by the German philosopher Goethe as 'one of the fairest inventions of the human mind'—has an elegance, utility and simplicity which seemingly would make it attractive for any financial record-keeping. However, not all businesses choose to keep their records in this form; some prefer to use a 'single' rather than 'double' entry system. In essence this means that the major record is a cash book, and that information about such items as debtors and creditors can only be obtained by checking through outstanding invoices. Such a system—often referred to as 'incomplete records'—cannot easily provide the information needed for efficient management—analysis of expense, profitability and asset structure for example—and also increases the risk of theft and fraud.

The single entry system, however, does not derive from some distinct set of postulates, but rather is an 'incomplete' or imperfect form of the double entry system. As such, it is possible to convert single entry records into double entry form, and we may easily illustrate this.

If the records of J. Brown and Co. were kept in single entry form, then the basic set of records would be the cash book (*see* pages 74 and 77). His cash account is as follows:

Cash A/c

Ownership interest	1,000	Furniture	300
Sales	120	Purchases	150
		Payments to creditors	120
		Rent	12
		Wages	10
		Balance	528
	1,120		**1,120**

The entry is 'single', i.e. there are no corresponding debits and credits. In practice, the cash book will show an assortment of receipts and payments and it is necessary to analyse the cash book to group like items together; hence, for example, the payment to Smith of £120 has been described as 'payments to creditors'.

Clearly, the cash book does not provide the information necessary to measure profit; we must also have information about the debtor, creditor and stock balances at the date on which we wish to measure profit. These are ascertained in the case of debtors and creditors by checking invoice files and, in the case of stock, by a physical inventory. In our example, the relevant balances were

	£
Debtors	90
Creditors	60
Stock	200

We have observed that profit is measured by matching revenues and expenses, and have stressed that revenues and expenses are not the same as receipts and payments. Hence the sales figure in the cash account reflects only cash received for sales—it does not reflect the revenue position. To discover the revenue position, we must convert the records into double entry form:

Sales A/c

Sales revenue (to trading account)	210	Cash	120
		Debtors balance at end	90
	210		**210**

Debtor balance 90

The cash sales entry is the credit entry corresponding to the debit entry in the cash book; the debtor balance at the end is a debit balance, and is therefore inserted first as a credit balance, and then brought down as a corresponding debit balance. The summation of the cash received and the cash owing (debtors) provides the revenue position—a debit of £210 to the sales account, with a corresponding entry to the trading account.

A similar analysis reveals the purchases position:

Purchases (stock) A/c

Cash	150	Stock unsold at close	200
Creditors (cash)	120	Cost of sales (to Trading A/c)	130
Creditors balance at end	60		
	330		**330**
Stock unsold	200	Creditors balance	60

Inspection of the cash account discloses two other items of expense— rent and wages. In the formal double entry system these would be debited to the expense accounts and then charged to the profit and loss account at the end of the period:

Rent A/c

Cash	12	P. & L.	12

Wages

Cash	10	P. & L.	10

We can now draw up the formal trading, profit and loss account:

J. Brown
Trading, Profit and Loss Account for
the period ended . . . . . .

	£		£
Cost of sales	130	Sales	210
Gross Profit	80		
	210		210
Wages	10	**Gross Profit**	80
Rent	12		
Net Profit	58		
	80		80

The balance sheet of the business reflects all the outstanding balances; to identify those balances we first inspect the cash account to identify all those items which remain, as yet, in single entry form. In this instance the items are

	£
Furniture	300
Cash at close	528
Ownership interest	1,000

In addition, balances remaining on the accounts completed in double entry form are

		£
	Stock at close	200
	Creditors	60
	Debtors	90
and	Net Profit	58

The formal balance sheet will, therefore, be as follows:

J. Brown and Co.
Balance Sheet as at . . . . . .

	£	£		£	£
Ownership Interest			**Fixed Assets**		
Balance at start	1,000		Furniture		300
Profit for the period	58		**Current Assets**		
		1,058	Stock	200	

(*continued*)

J. Brown and Co.
Balance Sheet as at . . . . . . (*continued*)

Current Liabilities			Debtors	90	
Creditors		60	Cash	528	
				—	818
		£1,118			**£1,118**

Let us assume that Mr Brown continues to trade for a further period. Analysis of his cash book at the end of that period reveals the following:

Cash A/c

Opening			Payments to		
balance		528	creditors	250	
Cash sales		130	Cash		
Receipts			purchases	100	
from			Drawings	150	
debtors		150	Rent	20	
			Wages	30	
			Balance at		
			close	258	
		£808		**£808**	

Inspection of the business's records showed that other balances at the close were

	£
Debtors	110
Creditors	50
Rent owing	10
Stock	340

To ascertain the revenue position, we again convert the records to double entry form:

Sales A/c

Opening		Cash	130
debtor		Receipts	
balance	90	from	
		debtors	150

(*continued*)

Sales A/c (*continued*)

Sales revenue (to Trading A/c)	300	Debtor balance at close	110
	390		**390**

It will be observed that the opening debtor balance, as reported in the previous balance sheet, becomes the opening debit entry on the sales account.

Similarly, the cost of sales position is

Purchases (stock) A/c

Opening stock balance	200	Opening creditor balance	60
Cash	100	Cost of sales (to	
Payments to creditors	250	Trading A/c)	200
Closing creditor balance	50	Closing stock balance	340
	600		**600**
Stock unsold at close	340	Creditor balance	50

The remaining items of expense in the cash account are then formally incorporated into the double entry system, and the rent owing inserted as an accrual (see page 84):

Rent A/c

Cash	20	Profit and loss	30
Rent owing	10		
	30		**30**
		Rent owing	10

Wages A/c

Cash	30	Profit and loss	30

Thus, once again we can prepare the formal trading, profit and loss account:

J. Brown and Co.
Trading, Profit and Loss Account for
the period ended . . . . . .

	£		£
Cost of sales	200	Sales	300
Gross Profit	100		
	——		——
	300		**300**
	══		══
Rent	30	**Gross Profit**	100
Wages	30		
Net Profit	40		
	——		——
	100		**100**
	══		══

To draw up the balance sheet we inspect the opening balance sheet to identify all those balances which we have not yet incorporated in the accounts:

Opening balance of ownership interest	£1,158
Furniture	£300

the cash accounts for items remaining in single entry form:

Drawings	£150
Cash at close	£258

and the balances on the accounts completed in double entry:

Debtors at close	£110
Creditors at close	£50
Stock at close	£340
Rent accrued	£10

The balance sheet therefore becomes:

J. Brown and Co.
Balance Sheet as at . . . . . .

	£	£		£	£	
Ownership interest			**Fixed Assets**			
			Furniture		300	
Opening balance	1,058					
Profit for the period	40		**Current Assets**			
	——		Stock	340		
	1,098		Debtors	110		
Less: Drawings	150		Cash	258		
	——	948		——	708	*(continued)*

J. Brown and Co.
Balance Sheet as at . . . . . .(*continued*)

Current Liabilities			
Creditors	50		
Accruals	10		
	——	60	
		£1,008	**£1,008**

Control accounts

In preparing the accounts relating to debtors and creditors, we have quite naturally and properly opened up a separate account for each individual debtor and creditor. Only in this way can a business keep a check on precisely what is owed by or to a particular customer or supplier. However, in the preparation of the final accounts, we aggregated these accounts describing them collectively as 'debtors' and 'creditors'. In order that we can readily ascertain how much is owed by all of the debtors or to all of the creditors at any point in time, it is usual to maintain control or total accounts to which are debited and credited in total all the transactions which have been debited and credited in detail to the individual ledger accounts.

Control accounts have a number of advantages:

(1) It is possible to establish immediately the totals of the balances appearing in the debtors and creditors ledger, thus saving the time and labour of extracting and totalling the individual accounts.
(2) If the balance on the control account is equal to the sum of the balances on the relative individual accounts, this is *prima facie* evidence that the entries in the individual accounts are correct. If a trial balance fails to agree, and the balance on the control account equals the sum of the related individual accounts, then no time need be wasted checking those accounts.
(3) If the control account is maintained by a clerk who has no access to individual accounts, the risk of fraudulent entries in the ledger records can be reduced.

Where control accounts are in use, they form part of the double entry system. The detailed records for each debtor or creditor become supportive or memorandum accounts, providing the fuller details that are required for the day-to-day management of the business. We will illustrate this in the context of debtors, but precisely the same principles apply to the treatment of creditors.

J. Brown makes the following sales on credit during March:

	£
T. Smith	80
R. Jones	110
M. Lord	165
S. Price	95

During the month T. Smith settles his account less 5 per cent cash discount, M. Lord pays £100 on account, and S. Price returns goods valued at £15. The ledger accounts would appear as follows:

Sales day book

		£
March	T. Smith	80
	R. Jones	110
	M. Lord	165
	S. Price	95
	Sales A/c	450

Sales returns day book

		£
March	S. Price	15
	Sales Returns A/c	15

Cash book A/c

	£ Cash	£ Discount
March T. Smith	76	4
M. Lord	100	

Sales A/c

	March Credit sales	450

Sales returns A/c

March Returns	15	

T. Smith A/c

March Sales	80	March Discount	4
		March Cash	76
	80		80

R. Jones A/c

March Sales	110	March Balance c/d	110
April Balance b/d	110		

M. Lord A/c

March Sales	165	March Cash	100
		March Balance c/d	65
	165		165

S. Price A/c

March Sales	95	March Returns	15
		March Balance c/d	80
	95		95

The debtors or sales ledger control account is constructed by the simple process of ascertaining from the books of prime entry—sales day and return books (or, in practice, the copy invoices and credit notes) and the cash book—the total of all of the items entered in the individual debtors accounts:

Debtors control A/c

March Sales	450	March Returns	15
		Cash	176
		Discount	4
		Balance c/d	255
	450		450
April Balance b/d	255		

The balance on the debtors control account must now equal the sum of the individual debtors accounts, viz.:

	£
T. Smith	—
R. Jones	110
M. Lord	65
S. Price	80
Debtors control A/c	255

Verification of the bank account

The debtors and creditors control accounts provide an independent check on the sum of the balances on the individual accounts. As has been pointed out, if the control accounts are maintained by an employee who has no access to entries in the individual accounts, this helps to minimize the risk of fraud. Such internal independence is not so readily possible in the case of the bank account, and in order to verify and confirm the accuracy of that account, it is customary regularly to reconcile the bank account in the ledger with the bank statement produced independently by the bank.

The bank statement and the bank account can differ for a number of reasons:

(1) Cheques paid by the business (and credited to the bank account) may not appear on the bank statement, because the recipient has not yet paid them into the bank and/or the bank's own clearing system has not yet recorded the cheque payment.
(2) Monies paid into the bank by the business may not appear on the bank statement, because the bank has not yet recorded the lodgement.
(3) Items deducted by the bank may not have been recorded by the business. These items include:

   (i) Bank charges and interest, as the amounts will not be known by the business until they appear on the bank statement.
   (ii) Standing orders (i.e. regular payments for such things as rates which the bank has been instructed by the business to make without the need to issue a cheque) which the business has overlooked.

(4) Items increasing the bank balance and added by the bank may not have been recorded by the business. These include:

   (i) Interest paid to the business by the bank, as the amount will not be known until the bank statement is received.
   (ii) Monies received directly by the bank through the direct transfer (Giro) system which does not require the use of cheques.

(5) Errors made by either the business or the bank.

In order to reconcile the balance shown by the bank statement with the balance shown by the bank account, we need to compare the two and identify all of the items which appear on one but not on the other:

Bank A/c

1 Jan.		4 Jan.	
Balance	3,200	Wages	250
2 Jan. Cash		7 Jan.	
sales	900	Smoth	1,420
8 Jan.		9 Jan.	
Blink	150	Mantle	870
10 Jan. Eggs	400	15 Jan. Rent	
19 Jan. Cash		(Emms)	220
sales	1,230	21 Jan.	
28 Jan.		Drubb	940
Down	420	27 Jan.	
		Electricity	310
		30 Jan.	
		Webb	470
		31 Jan.	
		Balance	1,820
	6,300		6,300

Bank Statement

Date	Particulars	Payments	Receipts	Balance
		£	£	£
1 Jan.	Balance			3,200√
2 Jan.	Interest		40*	3,240
4 Jan.	Cash		900√	4,140
6 Jan.	Wages	250√		3,890
8 Jan.	Standing order	50*		3,840
10 Jan.	Blink		150√	3,990
12 Jan.	Mantle	870√		3,120
12 Jan.	Eggs		400√	3,520
13 Jan.	Smoth	1,420√		2,100
21 Jan.	Cash		1,230√	3,330
21 Jan.	Emms	220√		3,110
25 Jan.	Drubb	940√		2,170
29 Jan.	Electricity Board	320		1,850
31 Jan.	Bank charges	20*		1,830

Items ticked appear on both the bank statement and the bank account; hence, the unticked items must explain the difference between the balance on the bank statement of £1,830 and the bank account of £1,820. Before effecting the reconciliation, however, we must, after checking their validity, adjust the bank account for any items which should have been recorded (these are marked with an asterisk on the bank statement):

Amended Bank A/c

31 Jan.			8 Jan.	
Balance	1,820		Standing	
2 Jan.			order	50
Interest	40		31 Jan.	
			Bank	
			charges	20
			31 Jan.	
			Amended	
			balance	1,790
	1,860			1,860

To reconcile the two balances we normally start with the balance as shown on the bank statement:

Bank Reconciliation
as at 31 January

	£	£
Balance as per bank statement		1,830
Less: Cheques drawn and not presented		
Webb	470	470
		1,360
Add: Lodgements made and not yet credited by the bank		
Down	420	420
		1,780
Add: Difference on cheque paid to Electricity Board		
	10	10
		1,790

Matrix accounting

It has been stressed that double entry bookkeeping demands that each transaction is recorded twice—once as a debit and once as a credit. More careful consideration will reveal that the important point about the duality postulate is not the *double recording* but the *double classification*.

Consider the following transactions:

	£
Capital paid in	1,000
Cash sales	400
Credit sales	300
Credit purchase of stock	350
Cash purchase of stock	250
Collection from debtors	150
Cost of goods sold	450
Miscellaneous expenses	50

We assign each of the accounts a code number:

1. Capital
2. Creditors
3. Stock
4. Debtors
5. Cash
6. Sales
7. Cost of sales
8. Expenses

In order to double classify each transaction we set up a 'matrix'. Mathematically, a matrix is a rectangular array of numbers written in the form

$$A = \begin{pmatrix} a_{11} & a_{12} & a_{13} & \dots & a_{1n} \\ a_{21} & a_{22} & a_{23} & \dots & a_{2n} \\ \dots & \dots & \dots & \dots & \dots \\ a_{m1} & a_{m2} & a_{m3} & \dots & a_{mn} \end{pmatrix}$$

Each individual 'cell' is uniquely identified by a subscript; for example, a_{23} identifies the cell which is in the second row and third column. Each row or column of numbers is called a 'vector'.

Since in our example there are eight accounts we will need an 8×8 matrix—i.e. a matrix which has 8 rows and 8 columns. Each row vector identifies the account to be credited, and each column vector the account to be debited. The first transaction (capital paid in £1,000) requires a credit to capital and a debit to cash. This requires a credit to account 1 and a debit to account 5; thus an entry of £1,000 is made in cell a_{15}. The remaining transactions are analysed similarly and the result displayed in the following matrix:

	\multicolumn{8}{c}{Accounts debited}

Accounts credited	1	2	3	4	5	6	7	8
1					1,000			
2			350					
3							450	
4					150			
5			250					50
6				300	400			
7								
8								

These transactions reflect the flow of wealth between two balance sheet dates, and this type of matrix is usually referred to as a 'transition' matrix. It will be observed that such a system obviates the need for a trial balance since every entry is simultaneously both a debit and a credit.

The balance in any individual account can be obtained by summing the debit and the credit vectors and subtracting one from the other. Since, for reasons which will become apparent, we want any excess of credits over debits to have a negative sign, we subtract the debits from the credits, i.e. the row vector from the column vector. For example, the balance in the cash account is found by summing column vector 5 and row vector 5 and subtracting them. We write

$$V_5 = \sum_{a=1} a_{m5} - \sum_{a=1} a_{5m}$$

$$= (a_{15} + a_{25} + a_{35} + a_{45} + a_{55} + a_{65} + a_{75} + a_{85})$$
$$- (a_{51} + a_{52} + a_{53} + a_{54} + a_{55} + a_{56} + a_{57} + a_{58})$$

$$= (1{,}000 + 0 + 0 + 150 + 0 + 400 + 0 + 0)$$
$$- (0 + 0 + 250 + 0 + 0 + 0 + 0 + 50)$$

$$= +1{,}250$$

If we carry out the same operation for each of the accounts we can convert the transition matrix into a transition vector:

$$V_T = \begin{pmatrix} V_1 \\ V_2 \\ V_3 \\ V_4 \\ V_5 \\ V_6 \\ V_7 \\ V_8 \end{pmatrix} = \begin{pmatrix} -1,000 \\ -\ 350 \\ 150 \\ 150 \\ 1,250 \\ -\ 700 \\ 450 \\ 50 \end{pmatrix}$$

The reason for assigning negative values to credit balances is now apparent. If we consider the accounting equation

$$\Sigma A + \Sigma E = \Sigma L + \Sigma R$$

then we can write

$$\Sigma A + \Sigma E + (-\Sigma L) + (-\Sigma R) = 0$$

Our transition vector V_T, which is of course composed of these four elements, satisfies this equation as it sums to zero.

We can further reduce the transition vector V_T by summing those sub-vectors which are either revenue or expense accounts, namely, V_6, V_7 and V_8. We write

$$\begin{aligned} V_P &= \Sigma V_R + \Sigma V_E \\ &= -700 + 450 + 50 \\ &= -200 \end{aligned}$$

The reduced transition vector is, in this instance, the closing balance sheet for the period:

$$V_T = V_{BE} = \begin{pmatrix} V_1 \\ V_2 \\ V_3 \\ V_4 \\ V_5 \\ V_P \end{pmatrix} = \begin{pmatrix} -1,000 \\ -\ 350 \\ 150 \\ 150 \\ 1,250 \\ -\ 200 \end{pmatrix}$$

or, in more conventional form:

Balance Sheet
as at end of period 1

		£
1.	Capital	1,000
P.	Profit	200
2.	Creditors	350
		£1,550

(continued)

Balance Sheet
as at end of period 1
(*continued*)

	£
3. Stock	150
4. Debtors	150
5. Cash	1,250
	£1,550

The end balance is, of course, the opening balance sheet of the next period.
If the transition vector for that period were given by

$$V_T = \begin{pmatrix} V_1 \\ V_2 \\ V_3 \\ V_4 \\ V_5 \\ V_P \end{pmatrix} = \begin{pmatrix} 100 \\ -150 \\ 200 \\ 100 \\ 500 \\ -750 \end{pmatrix}$$

The end balance sheet would be

$$V_{BO} + V_T = V_{BE}$$

$$= \begin{pmatrix} -1,000 \\ -350 \\ 150 \\ 150 \\ 1,250 \\ -200 \end{pmatrix} + \begin{pmatrix} 100 \\ -150 \\ 200 \\ 100 \\ 500 \\ -750 \end{pmatrix} = \begin{pmatrix} -900 \\ -500 \\ 350 \\ 250 \\ 1,750 \\ -950 \end{pmatrix}$$

or

	£
Capital	900
Profit	950
Creditors	500
	£2,350

	£
Stock	350
Debtors	250
Cash	1,750
	£2,350

With the increasing computerization of accounting records, the matrix
methodology is likely to gain increasing acceptance.

References and further reading

LANGLEY (1978), *Introduction to Accounting for Students of Business Studies*. Butterworths.

LEE (1981), *Modern Financial Accounting*. Nelson.

LEWIS and GILLESPIE (1982), *Foundations in Accounting*. Prentice-Hall.

WOOD (1981), *Business Accounting I and II*. Longmans.

Questions for discussion

1   John Doe has recently started a small garage business, and has come to you for advice on what financial records he should keep. 'Surely all I need is a cash book', he says. Explain to him the limitations of single entry records, and advise him what records would assist him to run his business efficiently. Make any assumptions you like, e.g. the business sells secondhand cars, does repairs, employs two mechanics, etc., but clearly state your assumptions.

2   John Doe Ltd maintains a single entry record system, and a partial analysis of the cash book yields the following data:

Cash A/c
for the year ended 31 December 1984

Cash sales	7,200	Cash purchases	5,230
Cash received from debtors	9,790	Cash paid to creditors	6,540

Explain what further information you would need in order to establish the sales and purchases for the year, and how you would obtain that information.

3   Dear Mr Guy,   12 Jan. 1984

I am most relieved that you have agreed to assist me by sorting out the financial affairs of my secondhand business, which as you know commenced on 1 January 1983. Such records as I have kept are, unfortunately, to be found on now rather scruffy scraps of paper stored in a large cardboard box. Doubtless you will want to examine these records for yourself, but I thought it might assist you if I were to summarize my business dealings up to 31 December 1983 as I recall them.

In December 1982 I was lucky enough to win £5,000 on the football pools, and this, together with £1,000 loaned to me by a friend—I agreed, incidentally, to pay him 10 per cent p.a. interest—formed the

initial capital of £6,000. I put £5,500 into the bank immediately—in
a separate business account. I needed a lorry to enable me to collect
and deliver the secondhand goods, and I'm pleased to say I made a
profit of £460 here; a dealer was asking £1,300 for a secondhand lorry,
but I beat him down to £840. I've only paid by cheque £200 of this so
far, but as I will finish paying the full £840 in three more years, it will
be mine before it falls to pieces in another five years from now.

I rent some business premises, and, as they are fairly dilapidated,
I only pay £350 a year. I've paid by cheque this year's rent and also
£50 in respect of next year.

My first bit of business was to buy a job lot of 2,000 pairs of jeans
for £6,000. I've paid a cheque for £4,000 so far, and my supplier is
pressing me for the balance. To date, I've sold 1,500 pairs, and received
£5,800, but I reckon I'm still owed £500, most of which I should be
able to collect. I promptly banked the £5,800 as it was all in cheques.

I bought 800 tee-shirts for £1,200 out of my bank account. I've sold
700 of these for cash—£1,500 in all—but as the remainder have got
damaged I'd be lucky if I get £50 for them.

I managed to get some pocket-calculators cheaply—50 of them only
cost me £400, but I'm rather pleased I haven't paid for them yet, as
I think there is something wrong with them. My supplier has indicated
that he will, in fact, accept £200 for them, and I intend to take up his
offer, as I reckon I can repair them for £1 each and then sell them at
£8 a time—a good profit.

I haven't paid my cash into the bank at all, as the cash I got for the
tee-shirts and my initial float enabled me to pay for my petrol—£400—
and odd expenses—£250. Also, it enabled me to draw £20 per week
for myself. As I've done so well I also took my wife on holiday—it
made a bit of a hole in the bank account but it was worth all £600 of
it.

Perhaps, from what I've told you, you can work out what profit I've
made—only keep it as small as possible as I don't want to pay too
much tax!

Yours sincerely,
BERT HUGGINS

Required:

(a) From the data, prepare a trading, profit and loss account for the
    period ended 31 December 1984, and a balance sheet as at that
    date. Show clearly all your workings and assumptions as notes to
    the accounts.
(b) Write a short report to Mr Huggins highlighting what you consider
    to be the most important features revealed by the accounts you
    have prepared.

4 Mr Wilson, a retailer, has his accounts prepared for the year ending
   30 June. On the morning of 1 July 1984, however, his shop and most

of the business records were destroyed by fire. At the beginning of the year, 1 July 1983, Mr Wilson's assets and liabilities had been as follows:

	£
Fixtures at cost less depreciation	1,000
Stock	950
Debtors	160
Prepayment for rates	30
Bank (asset)	2,565
Cash	90
Creditors—goods	610
—electricity	25
—accountancy fees	65

Mr Wilson's bank was able to provide copies of his bank statements, and an analysis of these revealed the following information for the year to 30 June 1984.

	£
Cash and cheques paid in	16,456
Payments for:	
Goods	16,781
Rates	180
Electricity	110
Income tax (Mr Wilson)	830
Rent	650
Accountancy fees	65
Caribbean Holidays Ltd	490

A letter was sent to all the known customers and suppliers requesting information about monies owed and owing. A summary of their replies indicated that at 30 June 1984, the position was as follows:

	£
Creditors for goods	979
Electricity owing	47
Accountancy fees owing	125
Rent owing	150
Rates prepaid	40
Trade debtors	360

Mr Wilson's insurance company agreed to pay £1,250, which was the cost price of the stock destroyed by the fire (none of which could be salvaged), and £750 for the loss of the fixtures. The money in the till on 30 June amounting to £190 had survived the fire.

Mr Wilson had banked his cash takings after the payment of certain expenses which he estimated at

Sundry expenses	£2 per week	(50-week year)
Purchase of goods	£15 per week	
Shop assistant's wages	£30 per week	

He was uncertain of his personal drawings which he thought were 'usually between £55 and £65 per week'.

Mr Wilson was somewhat inflexible in his business practice, and consistently sold his goods at a 25 per cent mark up on cost of goods sold.

Required:
Prepare a trading and profit and loss account for the year to 30 June 1984 and a balance sheet as at that date. Show all your workings and assumptions.

5   The balances extracted from the records of Perrod and Co. at 31 December 1984 were as follows:

	£
Premises (cost)	7,000
Capital	8,440
Drawings	1,935
Provision for depreciation of office equipment at 1.1.84	480
Debtors control account	1,891
Creditors control account	2,130
Stock at 1.1.84	1,200
Purchases	9,480
Sales	14,003
Returns inwards	310
Office equipment (cost) (balance at 1.1.84)	1,600
Wages	1,540
Commission	160
Discount allowed	210
Discount received	121
Bank (credit balance)	980
Cash in hand	56
Heating and lighting	375
Postage and stationery	224
Bad debts	68

A preliminary trial balance was prepared, but, although no arithmetical errors were made, the trial balance did not balance. In seeking the reasons for the difference, the following facts emerged:

(i)   Debtors control account:

  (a) No entry had been made in the control account in respect of the debts written off as bad.
  (b) A cheque paid by a debtor for £110 had been returned on 31 December 1984 by the bank marked 'return to drawer'. An entry had been made in both the bank account and the debtors account for this, but no entry had been made in the control account.
  (c) Sales on credit of £97 to A. Jones had been correctly entered in his account but nothing had been entered in the control account.
  (d) M. Smith had been allowed a cash discount of £43, but no corresponding entry had appeared in the control account.

(ii)   Creditors control account:
This exceeded the balance of the individual creditors accounts by £12. The difference was caused by

  (a) Goods returned to R. Hardy costing £69 had been entered correctly in the control account, but no entry had been made in Mr Hardy's account.
  (b) An invoice for £56 had been incorrectly entered in the control account as £65.
  (c) Two credit balances of £45 and £27 had been omitted from the list extracted from the creditors ledger.

(iii) Some office equipment which had cost £240 had been debited to the purchase account.
(iv)   The wages (£1,540) included £320 of personal drawings by the owner of the business.
(v)   The provision for depreciation of office equipment had been credited in 1983 with straight line depreciation of 10 per cent, i.e. £160, but the depreciation should have been charged at 12½ per cent p.a.
(vi)   The account for stationery (£224) included £45 of personal note-paper for the owner.
(vii) The returns inwards account had been credited with £90 for some goods returned to a creditor.

Required:

(a) Prepare the debtors and creditors control accounts taking into account, where appropriate, the facts ascertained in (i) and (ii) above.

(b) Prepare journal entries to correct the errors and omissions enumerated in (iii)–(vii) above.

(c) Draw up a corrected trial balance.

(d) Given that Perrod and Co.'s stock at 31 December 1984 was valued at £1,400 and the depreciation on office equipment for the year was £230, prepare a balance sheet as at 31 December 1984, showing clearly the net profit for the year.

6 Explain carefully the purposes of keeping control accounts.

7 The following information relates to a firm for the month of December:

	£
Sales ledger balances 1 Dec.	33,041
Purchase ledger balances 1 Dec.	23,214
Purchase invoices for December	162,175
Sales invoices for December	232,183
Cash and cheques received from customers in December	215,164
Bad debts written off in month	750
Cheque payments in December:	
To suppliers	131,643
To customers (refunds for goods paid for and subsequently returned)	125
Discounts received	1,742
Discounts allowed	2,475
Credit notes issued to customers in month	2,354
Credit notes received from suppliers in month	2,858
Amounts settled by contra.	565

Total of individual balances at 31 December taken from the ledgers:

Sales ledger £44,112
Purchase ledger £48,581

Required:

(a) Prepare sales ledger control account and purchase ledger control account, identifying any differences.

(b) How would you go about finding any differences?

8 On 15 May 1984, Mr Lakes received his monthly bank statement for

the month ended 30 April 1984. The bank statement contained the following details:

Mr Lakes
Statement of Account with Baroyds Ltd
(*balance indicates account is overdrawn)

Date	Particulars	Payments	Receipts	Balance
1 April	Balance			1,053.29
2 April	236127	210.70		842.59
3 April	Bank Giro credit		192.35	1,034.94
6 April	236126	15.21		1,019.73
6 April	Charges	12.80		1,006.93
9 April	236129	43.82		963.11
10 April	427519	19.47		943.64
12 April	236128	111.70		831.94
17 April	Standing orders	32.52		799.42
20 April	Sundry credit		249.50	1,048.92
23 April	236130	77.87		971.05
23 April	236132	59.09		911.96
25 April	Bank Giro credit		21.47	933.43
27 April	Sundry credit		304.20	1,237.63
30 April	236133	71.18		1,166.45

For the corresponding period, Mr Lakes' own records contained the following bank account:

Date	Detail	£	Date	Detail	Cheque No.	£
1 April	Balance	827.38	5 April	Purchases	128	111.70
2 April	Sales	192.35	10 April	Electricity	129	43.82
18 April	Sales	249.50	16 April	Purchases	130	87.77
24 April	Sales	304.20	18 April	Rent	131	30.00
30 April	Sales	192.80	20 April	Purchases	132	59.09
			25 April	Purchases	133	71.18
			30 April	Wages	134	52.27
			30 April	Balance		1,310.40
		1,766.23				1,766.23

Required:

(a) Prepare a statement reconciling the balance at 30 April as given by the bank statement to the balance at 30 April as stated in the bank account.
(b) Explain briefly which items in your bank reconciliation statement would require further investigation.

9 'If I keep my bank account accurately, and the bank does its job properly, there should never be any difference between my records and the bank's.' Do you agree?

10 'Bank reconciliations are rather pointless; if I add and subtract the right things I am mathematically certain to reconcile the bank statement to the bank account.' Is this statement correct, and if so what is the point of a bank reconciliation?

11 Hoddles' cash book on 30 June showed a balance due to his bank of £1,210 on his No. 1 account, and a balance of £706 overdrawn appeared on his bank statement. On investigation you find

(i)   Cheques drawn amounting to £420 had not been presented to the bank for payment.

(ii)   Cheques, £360, entered in the cash book as paid into the bank, had not been credited by the bank.

(iii)   The receipts side of the cash book had been undercast by £100.

(iv)   Bank charges of £76 entered on the bank statement had not been entered in the cash book.

(v)   A cheque for £520 drawn on the No. 1 account had been charged by the bank in error to the No. 2 account.

(vi)   A dividend of £30 paid direct to the bank had not been entered in the cash book.

(vii) A cheque for £70 paid into the bank had been dishonoured and shown as such by the bank but no entry of dishonour had been made in the cash book.

(viii) A cheque drawn for £64 had been entered in the cash book in error as £46.

(ix)   A cheque for £42, drawn by another customer of the same name, had been charged to Hoddles' bank account in error.

Required:

(a) Show the appropriate adjustments to be made in the cash book.

(b) Prepare a bank reconciliation statement for the No. 1 account.

9 The partnership

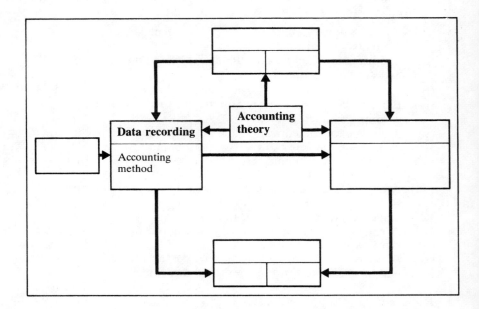

In our considerations so far we have explored the basic postulates of accounting and their interpretation, using by way of illustration the business managed by the individual owner, the sole trader. The accounts of the sole trader were a convenient vehicle for this purpose, primarily because the capital structure is the simplest form possible. Whatever the capital structure, however, be it the capital of one man, or ten partners, or a million shareholders, the interpretation of the basic postulates remains the same. What is required as the number of owners multiply is an adaptation and extension of the form of presentation of accounting information. In this and the following chapter we will examine the changing capital structure as ownership is extended, and the effect which this has on the final accounts.

The nature of partnership

A business partnership exists between persons engaged in any activity in common with a view to profit. As a business grows over time, then for a number of reasons it may be desirable for more than one person to participate in the ownership of the business. The most obvious reason which would compel the sole trader to need a partner is the need for additional capital. The sole trader's major sources of finance are his own savings and his ability to borrow on the security of his business assets or private property or both. While borrowing makes possible a greater scale of operations, it subjects the borrower to such limitations as creditors may impose. To admit a partner or partners will enable the savings of a number of individuals to be combined for a common purpose.

In admitting new capital from a partner, the sole trader is effectively spreading the burden of ownership and sharing the risks. It must be said, however, that in admitting one or more partners to share the risk, the sole trader is also involving himself in two new risk factors. First, he is taking the risk of an error of judgement, or even of bad faith, on the part of a partner, which may mean a loss, or conceivably even deprive him of his own investment in the business. Secondly, the death or withdrawal of a partner can involve him in the obligation of repaying that partner's capital, thus restricting the firm's activities, and even necessitating the selling off of some of the firm's assets.

Generally, however, the expected profit to be derived from the new source of finance far outweighs the additional risks to be borne, and a partnership is formed. The rights and obligations of partners are usually defined by a written partnership agreement called a partnership deed. For the protection of the partners and the stability of the partnership, the agreement usually covers such matters as:

(1) The amount of capital to be contributed by each partner.
(2) The partners' shares in profits and losses.
(3) The rate of interest (if any) to be given on capital.
(4) Salaries to be paid to the partners.
(5) The internal management of the partnership.

Partnerships may also be created by oral agreement, and the existence of a partnership may be inferred from the conduct of the individuals concerned. For this reason and because some written agreements are inadequate, the Partnership Act 1890 provides general rules to be applied in the absence of an express agreement. This provides, among other things, for profits and losses to be shared equally, no interest to be allowed on capital, no salaries to be paid to partners, and for interest at 5 per cent p.a. on any funds provided by the partners in excess of the agreed capital.

Apart from the additional funds available through the introduction of new partners, a partnership is limited to the same sources of finance as the sole trader. With the exception of one type of partnership, known as the limited partnership and registered under the Limited Partnership Act 1907, the liability of the partners for partnership debts is unlimited, so that if they cannot be met out of partnership assets, the separate and private property of each member may become available for the satisfaction of partnership creditors. Even in the case of the limited partnership, there must be at least one general partner whose personal assets are at risk. The limited partner's liability is restricted to the amount that he contributed by way of capital, but to merit this lesser risk, he must take no part in the management of the business.

The proprietary theory

In Chapter 1 we considered the business entity postulate, and saw in the following chapter how this made possible the basic accounting equation of Assets = Liabilities. In this equation, the business is the centre of interest, and profits are assumed to accrue to the business rather than to the owner. The entity theory is most satisfactory in its application to the corporate business where there are several classes of owners and investors, and ownership is separated from management (*see* Chapter 10). The emergence of the giant corporation comes relatively recently in economic history at the close of the nineteenth century. The entity theory evolved with this type of undertaking and in fact owes much of its development to German writers during the first part of the twentieth century. It reflects an economic revolution in which the firm is stripped of the personal involvement of its owners. It is interesting to note that although economic analysis and accounting theory and practice has been conducted in impersonal terms for some years, there has been a recent tendency for both economics and accounting to explore behavioural theories of the firm which reassert the part of the individual or groups of individuals.

It is in this connection that the proprietary theory is of some interest. The partnership demands the personal involvement of the individual owners, and it is therefore difficult in reality to separate the firm from those owners. The proprietary theory places the owners (and not the firm) as the centre of interest. The accounting equation is no longer

Assets = Liabilities

but becomes

Assets − Liabilities = Proprietorship

The assets are owned by the proprietors, and the liabilities are their obligations; the net income of the business accrues directly to the owners— it is theirs by right—and does not require the action of the firm to appropriate it to them. This personal approach to accounting is evident in the majority of bookkeeping texts published in the late nineteenth and early twentieth centuries, where all the accounts are personalized. Cole, for example, writing in 1908 stated 'debit means not merely that something is owned, but that a definite person is responsible for some value'.

It could be said that to distinguish between the proprietary and entity theories is splitting fine hairs. In terms of the practical consequences this is so, yet it nevertheless remains true that the transition from proprietorship to entity reflects a considerable sociological change whereby a large business, by virtue of its size, has tended to obscure the individual owner and employee.

The partnership agreement

We have already observed that any partnership will be operated either within the terms of an express agreement or of the Partnership Act. We must now examine those terms which are of consequence to accounting.

(1)   Capital contributions

There are two broad classes of business obligations and business investments which may be represented diagrammatically:

Time period	Sources of funds	Uses of funds
Long term (fixed)	Owners Deferred creditors (long-term loans)	Land and buildings Plant and machinery, etc.
Short term (current)	Trade creditors Bank loans	Stocks Debtors, cash

The investment of funds in long-term assets requires a reasonable assurance that they will not need to be reconverted into cash in the short run; if this need arose the scale of operations would necessarily have to be reduced. To avoid this difficulty, it follows that the short-term liabilities should not exceed the short-term assets. To put it another way, the long-term sources of funds should be at least sufficient to cover the long-term assets.

The total capital contribution of the partners will be primarily a function of the expected level of investment in long-term assets. In addition any expected excess of current assets over current liabilities will need to be financed by long-term funds. The exact division of the total capital contribution among the partners can be determined only by the partners themselves in the light of funds necessary and available. Normally, the capital contributions of the partners are identified separately from any profit accruing to the partners and not withdrawn.

(2)   Share in profits and losses

The partners are at liberty to prescribe any terms they wish in relation to profit-sharing ratios. In general, it would seem equitable that the share attributable to each partner reflects his contribution by way of capital, skills and work effort to the partnership. Given that the skills and work effort contributed by the partners are similar, it is inequitable for the profits to be shared in the ratio of the capital contributions. Consider the position of two partners who have respectively contributed capital of £10,000 and

£5,000 with a steady increase in profits over time. Thus

	I £	II £	III £	IV £	Total £
Profits	1,200	1,500	1,800	2,400	6,900
Abel (⅔)	800	1,000	1,200	1,600	4,600
Cain (⅓)	400	500	600	800	2,300

Abel received £4,600, or £2,300 more than his partner Cain, for an excess capital of £5,000, an average annual return to the excess of 11.5 per cent. If this return is greater than the return to a similar investment elsewhere, then Abel is receiving a share of profit far more than adequate to encourage him to leave the funds in the partnership.

If we assume that the rate of interest prevailing is 7 per cent, it would follow that Abel would be satisfied if he received £5,000 × 7% = £350 p.a. more than Cain. This can be achieved if both partners are granted interest on their capital, which is deducted prior to sharing the profits equally.

(3) Interest on capital

As we have seen, the granting of interest on capital is an equitable method of achieving a division of profits if the work contributed by each partner is of equal value but the capitals are unequal. Using the illustration above, but sharing the profits equally after charging interest of capital at 7 per cent p.a., the division of profits would become

	I £	£	II £	£	III £	£	IV £	£	Total £
Profits		1,200		1,500		1,800		2,400	6,900
Interest on capital									
Abel	700		700		700		700		
Cain	350		350		350		350		
	—	1,050	—	1,050	—	1,050	—	1,050	4,200
Share of profits									
Abel (½)	75		225		375		675		
Cain (½)	75		225		375		675		
	—	150	—	450	—	750	—	1,350	2,700
		1,200		1,500		1,800		2,400	6,900

Summary:

	Abel £	Cain £	Total £
Interest on capital	2,800	1,400	4,200
Share of profits	1,350	1,350	2,700
	4,150	2,750	6,900

It will be seen that under this scheme Abel receives £1,400 more than Cain, which is the equivalent of £5,000 at 7 per cent p.a. for 4 years—an adequate return (in the partners' estimation) for having invested an extra £5,000 in the firm.

(4)   Salaries

A partner may have some additional responsibility or carry a work load in excess of the other partner. In such circumstances it is usual and more convenient to pay him a salary as recompense rather than adjust the profit-sharing ratio. The salary is deductible before arriving at the balance of profits to be shared in the agreed profit-sharing ratio.

The reason for not adjusting the profit-sharing ratio is evident if we consider the following set of circumstances. Assume that in a given year the profits of a firm are £2,000 and that the two partners, Abel and Cain, have been sharing profits equally. They then agreed that Abel, who has had additional responsibility, should receive £500 more than Cain by way of recompense. This can be achieved in two ways:

	Original position		Revised position			
			Adjusted ratios		Salary	
	Abel	Cain	Abel	Cain	Abel	Cain
Salary	—	—	—	—	500	—
Share of profits	($\frac{1}{2}$)1,000	($\frac{1}{2}$)1,000	($\frac{5}{8}$)1,250	($\frac{3}{8}$) 750	($\frac{1}{2}$) 750	($\frac{1}{2}$) 750

If, in the following year, profits drop to £600, and the revised profit-sharing ratios are employed, Abel will receive £375 and Cain £225, a differential of £150 which is inadequate recompense for the additional responsibility. If the salary of £500 is charged and the remaining profit divided equally, Abel will receive £550 and Cain £50, which is the desired result.

Summary:
In the foregoing we have laid stress on the equitable distribution of profit, but we must remember that the partners are at liberty to impose any terms which they wish upon themselves. In the absence of an agreement, express or implied, the Partnership Act provides for equal distribution of profits, no interest on capital and no salaries to be paid to the partners. Unless the capitals and the responsibilities are equal, the provisions of the Act must result in an entirely inequitable distribution of profits.

The final accounts

The increase in the number of owners and the consequential effect on the distribution of the profit necessitates a modification to the presentation of final accounts. It is important to recognize that the fundamental postulates of accounting and their interpretation discussed in earlier chapters are in no way changed in partnership accounting. The division of the profits between the partners is contained within an extension to the income statement called the appropriation account. All transactions affecting the partners, whether it be salaries, interest on capital or share of profit, are appropriated to them in this account. We may express this another way: the principles of income measurement for the partnership are exactly the same as for the sole trader.

Our quadrant can be extended to accommodate this necessary modification:

Assets	Liabilities
Expenses Appropriations	Revenues

Income will be determined in the normal manner $(R - E)$; the resulting profit will not be added directly to the capital accounts, but will be appropriated in the manner agreed by the partners. The revised income statement will appear in the following manner:

Abel and Cain
Trading, Profit and Loss, and Appropriation
Account for the period ended 31 December 1984

	£	£	£
Sales			85,000
Less: Opening stock	6,900		
Purchases	52,300		
		59,200	
Less Closing stock		7,200	
			52,000
Gross Profit			33,000
Add: Discounts received			500
			33,500
Less:			
Administration		11,400	
Selling expenses		13,700	
Depreciation		4,400	
			29,500
Net Profit			**£4,000**
Abel—Salary			500
Interest on capital (7%)			
Abel		700	
Cain		350	
			1,050
Share of profits			
Abel (½)		1,225	
Cain (½)		1,225	
			2,450
			£4,000

It is important to note that any appropriation prior to the ultimate distribution of profit is made whether there is a profit or not. For example, if there were a net loss of £1,000, then the salary and interest on capital will still be appropriated, increasing the loss to £2,550. This will then be divided among the partners in their agreed profit-sharing ratio.

The capital section of the balance sheet will then appear as follows (the assets and current liabilities will be presented as for the sole trader):

Balance Sheet as at 31 December 1984

	£	£	£
Capital Accounts			
Abel		10,000	
Cain		5,000	
			15,000

(*continued*)

Balance Sheet as at 31 December 1984 (*continued*)

	£	£	£
Current Accounts			
Abel:			
Balance at 1.1.84	900		
Salary	500		
Interest	700		
Share of profits	1,225		
	3,325		
Less: Drawings	2,300		
		1,025	
Cain:			
Balance at 1.1.84	530		
Interest	350		
Share of profits	1,225		
	2,105		
Less: Drawings	1,900		
		205	
			1,230
Net Capital Employed			**£16,230**

Some comments on the above are necessary:

(1) The original capital introduced by the partners is maintained indepen-dent of the accumulated and undrawn past profits.

(2) The current accounts reflect the appropriations of profit to and drawings of the partners. If a partner overdraws his current account this will be shown as a deduction from the current account(s) in credit, i.e. not withdrawn. If this proves insufficient or all current accounts are over-drawn the capital accounts will be reduced, viz.:

	£	£
Capital Accounts		
Cain	10,000	
Abel	5,000	
		15,000
Less:		
Current Accounts		
Cain	(570)	
Abel	(430)	
		1,000
Net Capital Employed		**£14,000**

(3) Notice that the salary attributed to Abel has not actually been paid to him; it has merely been appropriated and (presumably) the actual

payment to him is contained within his drawings. If the salary were actually paid separately, there would be no need of an appropriation, but merely a reduction in cash balance matched by a reduction in the current account.
(4) If one of the partners has made a long-term loan to the business in addition to his capital, then this will form part of the net capital employed, being introduced in the balance sheet as a loan account. The interest thereon will be an expense of the business—and not an appropriation—for the partner making the loan stands as a creditor rather than as a member of the firm. The interest will be added to the current account of the partner.

Capital and current accounts

The double entry procedure can quite readily accommodate the two forms of capital—the long-term investment in the partnership reflected by the capital account, and the shorter term investment, built up out of the accumulated and undrawn profits, reflected by the current account. The capital and current accounts of Abel and Cain would appear as

Capital A/c—Abel

31 Dec. 1984 Balance c/d	10,000	1 Jan. 1984 Balance b/d	10,000
		1 Jan. 1985 Balance b/d	10,000

Capital A/c—Cain

31 Dec. 1984 Balance c/d	5,000	1. Jan. 1984 Balance b/d	5,000
		1 Jan. 1985 Balance b/d	5,000

Current A/c—Abel

31 Dec. 1984 Drawings (Cash A/c)	2,300	1 Jan. 1984 Balance b/d	900

(continued)

Current A/c—Abel (*continued*)

31 Dec. 1984 Balance c/d	1,025	31 Dec. 1984 Appropriation A/c	
		—Salary	500
		—Interest	700
		—Share of profit	1,225
	3,325		**3,325**
		1 Jan. 1985 Balance b/d	1,025

Current A/c—Cain

31 Dec. Drawings (Cash A/c)	1,900	1 Jan. 1984 Balance b/d	530
31 Dec. 1984 Balance c/d	205	31 Dec. 1984 Appropriation A/c	
		—Interest	350
		—Share of profit	1,225
	2,105		**2,105**
		1 Jan. 1985 Balance b/d	205

The admission of new partners—the valuation of goodwill

As the business activities of partnership grow, it may become necessary to seek additional assistance and capital by the admission of a new partner. Such an arrangement requires the consent of the existing partners, and the terms of admission—duties and responsibilities, share of profit, introduction of capital, etc.—are subject in practice to substantial negotiations. A new partner automatically acquires a share in all of the existing assets and the future profits of the partnership, and, therefore, his financial contribution to the partnership must reflect this.

A major difficulty facing the old partners is that the value of the business will, if it is successful, almost certainly exceed the 'book value' of the assets, valued as they are by reference to their historic cost. The location of the partnership, the esteem in which their services or products are held, their entrepreneurial and managerial skills, all will combine to give the business a market value significantly in excess of the balance sheet values of the assets, and this excess is normally known as 'goodwill'.

Conceptually, the value of a business is what someone is prepared to pay now for the expected net future earnings of that business. Economists talk of the 'present value of the future net cash receipts', the general formula being written as

$$V = \frac{P_1}{(1 + r)} + \frac{P_2}{(1 + r)^2} + \frac{P_3}{(1 + r)^3} + \cdots$$

where P is the estimated net cash receipts for future years, and r is the rate of return which reflects current alternatives foregone. This concept of economic theory has found its way into accounting in an imperfect form in what is known as the 'super profit' method of business valuation. Super profit is the excess of future maintainable annual profits over what could normally be earned in a similar but new business. The present value of this stream of super profits is known as goodwill. An established business will have a number of advantages over a new one—it will have such things as established connections in the markets for goods and services it buys and sells; it will have built up working relationships within the business which make for smoother running and more effective working.

We may derive a formula for calculating the value of super profits, goodwill and of the business as a whole utilizing these ideas. We may write

$$V = A + \frac{P - rA}{m}$$

where V is the value of the business, A is the value of the net tangible assets, P is the expected annual future income, r is the normal annual rate of return, and m is the capitalization rate of the super profit.

The tangible assets of a business are those which can be sold separately, thus excluding 'other assets' such as patents and goodwill. The reason for their exclusion is that while a new business could perhaps exactly match the tangible assets of the old, it could not use the patents employed by the established business, nor could it enjoy the other benefits of establishment mentioned above. The tangible assets should be valued at their estimated saleable value; the best estimate of this may in fact be the assets stated in terms of current pounds.

A new business employing such assets can expect to earn a certain rate of return, r; r is usually defined as the long-run rate of return an investor would expect to receive in a business of the type that is being valued. The expression rA, therefore, provides the long-run level of profits which a similar but new business could be expected to earn.

$P - rA$ is a measure of the annual super profits of the established business. It will pay the investor to add to the value which has been set on A an amount equal to the present value of the difference between P and rA;

this difference provides the value of the goodwill. The present value is often expressed crudely as the purchase of 'x years of super profits'. More precisely, we say that $P - rA$ is capitalized at a rate m; $(P - rA)/m$ is the sum which the investor is prepared to invest at rate of interest m to yield $P - rA$ super profits. Since the super profits represent earnings unbacked by tangible assets, they are at a higher risk than normal profits; a higher risk demands a higher rate of return, so m must be greater than r.

It may be helpful at this point to take a numerical example. Assume that the net tangible assets of a business are valued at £20,000, the future profits at £3,000 per annum, the normal rate of return at 10 per cent, and the high risk rate of return at 20 per cent. Then we have

$$V = A + \frac{P - rA}{m}$$

$$= 20,000 + \frac{3,000 - (0.1)(20,000)}{0.2}$$

$$= 20,000 + \frac{1,000}{0.2}$$

$$= £25,000$$

The super profits amounted to £1,000, and by capitalizing these at 20 per cent, the goodwill is valued at £5,000 or 'five years' purchase of super profits'.

In practice, of course, when old and new partners are seeking to establish the value of the goodwill, there will be considerable debate as to the values to be placed on the net current assets, the estimate of future earnings, and how many years' purchase of super profits is a fair representation of the value of the goodwill. There is no one 'right' value—except that to which in the end the parties agree.

The admission of new partners—the treatment of goodwill

Once the value of the goodwill is agreed between existing partners and the incoming partner, there are, broadly speaking, three ways of dealing with this in the accounts of the partnership:

Method 1

The new partner introduces capital into the business, and the old partners are credited with the full value of the goodwill in proportion to their *old* profit-sharing ratios. This means that should the new partnership dissolve and realize the full value of the goodwill, the old partners will receive payment in full for that goodwill.

Assume that A and B are in partnership, sharing profits and loss in the ratio 3:2, and that at 31 December 1979 the balance sheet of the partners shows

Capital A/cs	£		£
A	6,000	Net assets	11,000
B	5,000		
	11,000		11,000

On 1 January 1980, they agree to admit C as a partner who will introduce £2,000 as capital. Goodwill is to be valued at £4,000, and the new profit-sharing ratio is $A:B:C = 4:3:1$.

The new balance sheet will therefore be

Capital A/cs	£		£
A	8,400	'Original' net assets	11,000
B	6,600	Goodwill	4,000
C	2,000	Cash	2,000
	17,000		**17,000**

The goodwill of £4,000 is shared between A and B in the *old* profit-sharing ratios, viz. 3:2, so that A's capital account is credited with £2,400, and B's with £1,600, and the goodwill account is debited with the full value of the goodwill. The capital introduced by C is credited to his capital account and debited to the cash account.

Method 2

The new partner introduces capital and pays for a share of the goodwill, all monies being retained in the business. This has the effect of making additional funds available to the partnership, whilst at the same time allowing the old partners to gain recompense for the goodwill they have established.

Using the data given in Method 1 above, but assuming that C pays for his share of the goodwill, the new balance sheet will be

Capital A/cs	£		£
A	6,400	'Original' net assets	11,000
B	5,100	Cash	2,500
C	2,000		
	13,500		13,500

The goodwill was valued at £4,000, which is now written back to the capital accounts in the *new* profit sharing ratio, viz. 4:3:1. Hence A's account is reduced from £8,400 by 4/8 (£2,000) to £6,400, B's account from £6,600 by 3/8 (£1,500) to £5,100, and C, who has had to contribute £2,000 plus £500 for his 1/8 share of the goodwill, by 1/8 (£500) to £2,000.

Method 3

This is a variant of Method 2, whereby the new partner introduces capital and pays for a share of the goodwill, but the payment for goodwill is not retained in the business but taken by the existing partners in such a way as to reduce their capital accounts to the level prior to the valuation of the goodwill. A and B will respectively receive £400 and £100 which they will withdraw from the business.

The new balance sheet will be

	£		£
Capital A/cs			
A	6,000	'Original' net assets	11,000
B	5,000	Cash	2,000
C	2,000		
	13,000		**13,000**

Partnership dissolution

Partnerships may come to an end for a number of reasons. A partner may die or retire and no successor can be found, leaving the original partner with insufficient funds to continue the business; the partnership may have been formed for a limited duration or purpose, or it may be taken over by another organization, or it may simply have become insolvent. Whatever the reasons, however, a dissolution involves the disposition of all of the assets, payment in settlement of any creditors, with any surplus or loss being shared by the partners in their profit-sharing ratios, the partners being required to make up any capital deficiency from their personal resources. A complication may arise if a partner is unable, because of insolvency, to make good any such loss, for then the remaining partners must make good that loss from their own funds. We will not, however, consider the problem of insolvency at this stage, but focus our attention on the dissolution of a solvent partnership.

The basic accounting procedure for dissolution is relatively straightforward:

(1) Transfer all assets other than cash to a 'realization account' (i.e. credit asset account, debit realization account).
(2) Credit the realization account with the proceeds from the sale of the assets and debit the cash account, or, if a partner has taken an asset, debit the partner's capital account.

(3) Settle any external liabilities (i.e. credit cash, debit external liability) taking any gains (e.g. discounts) to the credit of the realization account.
(4) Settle any loans made by a partner.
(5) Transfer any balances on the partners' current accounts to their capital accounts.
(6) Share any profit or loss on realization—the remaining balance on the realization account—between the partners in their profit-sharing ratios (i.e. debit or credit the realization account, and, correspondingly, debit or credit the partners' capital accounts).
(7) Require any partner whose capital account is in deficit to pay in that deficit to the partnership (i.e. debit cash, credit capital).
(8) Pay to the remaining partners the balance due on their capital accounts (i.e. credit cash, debit capital account).

An example may help to clarify the procedure. The balance sheet of Smith and Jones who shared profits and losses 3:1 at 31 December 1984 was as follows:

	£	£		£	£
Capital					
Smith	10,000		Buildings	8,000	
Jones	7,000		Vehicles	6,500	
	——	17,000		——	14,500
Current A/cs					
Smith	1,500		Stock	6,200	
Jones	100		Debtors	3,100	
	——	1,600	Cash	800	
Loan: Smith		2,000		——	10,100
Creditors		4,000			
		24,600			**24,600**

The partnership was dissolved on 1 January 1985, the assets realizing

Building	£11,000	
Vehicles	£3,500	plus one vehicle taken over by Jones for £1,000
Stock	£5,700	
Debtors	£2,900	

The creditors were paid in full less discounts of £100.

Thus, following the procedure outlined above, we can prepare the accounts relating to the realization of the partnership:

Realization A/c

	£	£		£	£
Sundry assets			Cash		
Buildings	8,000		Buildings	11,000	
Vehicles	6,500		Vehicles	3,500	
Stock	6,200		Stock	5,700	
Debtors	3,100		Debtors	2,900	
		23,800			23,100
Share of profit			Jones (vehicle)		1,000
Smith	300		Capital		
Jones	100		Creditor—discount		100
		400			
		24,200			24,200

Capital A/cs

	Smith £	Jones £		Smith £	Jones £
Realization—vehicle		1,000	Balance b/f	10,000	7,000
			Current A/c	1,500	100
Cash	11,800	6,200	Realization—profit	300	100
	11,800	**7,200**		**11,800**	**7,200**

Current A/cs

	Smith £	Jones £		Smith £	Jones £
Capital A/c	**1,500**	**100**	Balance b/f	**1,500**	**100**

Loan A/c—Smith

Cash	**2,000**	Balance b/f	**2,000**

Cash A/c

Balance b/f	800	Creditors	3,900
Realization	23,100	Loan	
		Smith	2,000
		Capital	
		Smith	11,800
		Jones	6,200
	23,900		**23,900**

(*continued*)

Creditors A/cs

Cash	3,900	Balance b/f	4,000
Discount—			
realization	100		
	4,000		**4,000**

References and further reading

CHAMBERS (1968), *Financial Management.* Law Book Co.
LEE (1981), *Modern Financial Accounting.* Nelson.
WOOD (1982), *Business Accounting I.* Longmans.

Questions for discussion

1   Two antique dealers, currently running separate businesses in the same town, are wondering whether to combine and form a partnership. They seek your help and advice in the matter, and ask you to identify the major factors they should consider.

2   The two antique dealers, having carefully considered your advice, decide to form a partnership, and wish to draw up a written agreement. What are the main points the agreement should cover?

3   In the absence of agreement, the Partnership Act 1890 lays down the way in which profits are to be shared between the partners. In what circumstances would you consider these rules to be inequitable?

4   On 30 September 1984, Alexander and Arnold completed their first year of trading in partnership. They shared profits and losses in the ratio Alexander $\frac{3}{5}$, Arnold $\frac{2}{5}$, and were entitled to 5 per cent p.a. interest on capital. Arnold was also entitled to a salary of £1,490 per annum. They kept a debtors ledger, a creditors ledger for goods purchased, and a single entry record of all other transactions.

A summary of their cash transactions for the year ended 30 September 1984 is given below:

Receipts	£
Cash float for till	20
Cash sales	12,800
Receipts from debtors	44,900
Payments	
Creditors—goods purchased	2,600
Drawings	
Alexander	1,400
Arnold	1,200
Lodgements with bank	52,190

A summary of the partnership bank account for the year ended 30 September 1984 is also available:

Bankings	£
Capital paid in	
Alexander	8,400
Arnold	7,200
Banked from business	52,190
Cheques drawn	
Premises	11,000
Cash float	20
Creditors for goods	50,200
Van	1,600
Sundry expenses	4,720

The partners also supplied the following details:

(i)	Stock in hand at 30 September 1984	6,000
(ii)	Debtors at 30 September 1984	5,400
(iii)	Bad debts written off (already excluded from the debtor-balance)	200
(iv)	Creditors at 30 September 1984	3,000
(v)	Depreciation is to be provided for the van at 10 per cent on cost	
(vi)	Sundry expenses accrued	150

Required:
Prepare the trading, profit and loss and appropriation accounts for the period ended 30 September 1984 and a balance sheet as at that date.

5   Smith and Jones formed a partnership on 1 April 1983, sharing profits and losses in the ratio 2:1. The partnership was formed to manufacture and sell a new type of tin-opener developed and patented by Smith. Smith contributed capital of £8,000 and Jones of £5,000, and it was agreed to pay interest on capital of 6 per cent p.a. As Jones had the business acumen, it was agreed that he was to be responsible for most of the day-to-day work of the partnership, and therefore was to receive a salary of £1,000 p.a.

The initial capital was paid into a bank account. The partnership acquired a 10-year lease of suitable business premises for £6,000. The manufacturing process was relatively simple, and involved stamping out a plastic mould and inserting the patented cutting and opening device which was made under licence by Blades Ltd. The machines for producing the plastic moulds cost £5,000 and were to be paid for on an instalment basis of 10 quarterly payments of £500. This machinery, made by Synthetics Ltd, was estimated to have a working life of 5 years.

Sales made through mail order were on a cash basis and all such cash received was paid immediately into the bank. Some local retailers collected the tin-openers for themselves and were allowed a trade discount of 20 per cent (on the normal price of £1) and a cash discount of 5 per cent if the accounts were settled promptly. These local sales provided a cash float from which some miscellaneous payments were made by cash. These were:

	£
Wages	600
Postage	2,582
Petrol and oil	248
Motor repairs	170

At the end of March 1984 the partnership had £48 cash in hand. A summary of the bank statement for the year to 31 March 1984 showed:

Deposits	£
Capital introduced	13,000
Other bankings	23,590
Payments	
Lease	6,000
Blades Ltd (purchases)	5,400
Purchases of plastic	3,800
Synthetics Ltd	2,000
Gas and electricity	150
Van	800
Insurance	150
Wages	1,500
Packaging material	1,624
Advertising	620
Telephone	760
Drawings	
Smith	2,140
Jones	1,520

A cheque sent out on 31 March 1984 for electricity (£35) had not been cleared by the bank.

Of the tin-openers sold during the year, 5,000 were sold to local retailers and of these 4,800 had been paid for by the end of the year and had been allowed the appropriate trade and cash discounts.

The insurance included £40 for motor insurance which expired on 30 June 1984.

Blades Ltd were owed £250 at 31 March 1984.

At 31 March 1984 the partnership had stock valued at £660.

Required:
(a) Prepare a trading and profit and loss account and appropriation account for the period ended 31 March 1984 and a balance sheet as at that date.

State clearly (by way of notes) any assumptions you make.
(b) Advise the partners on the success (or otherwise) of their first year of business.

6   Webb and Guy are partners sharing profit and losses in the ratio 3:1, and the partnership agreement provided for Guy to receive a salary of £2,000 p.a., and for interest on capital at 5 per cent p.a. The partners' current accounts for the year ended 31 December 1983 were as follows:

	Webb £	Guy £		Webb £	Guy £
Drawings	4,280	3,950	Balance at 1.1.83	900	100
Goods		100	Salary		2,000
			Interest on capital	480	300
			Share of profit	4,500	1,500
Balance at 31.12.83	1,600		Balance at 31.12.83		150
	5,880	**4,050**		**5,880**	**4,050**

The balance sheet as at 31 December 1983 was

	£	£		£	£
Capital A/cs			Premises at cost		10,400
Webb	8,000		Equipment at cost	4,000	
Guy	5,000		*Less:* Depreciation	2,400	1,600
		13,000			12,000

	£	£		£	£
Current A/cs					
Webb	1,600		Stock		2,800
Guy	(150)		Debtors		1,100
		1,450	Cash		200
					4,100
Creditors and accruals		1,650			
		16,100			**16,100**

Investigation of the accounts revealed the following information:

(i)   The goods taken by Guy had been charged at selling price rather than at cost (£65).
(ii) The interest on capital had been provided at 6 per cent p.a.

(iii) The closing stock included some items which had been valued at original cost (£550) but which had deteriorated badly while in store and were considered to have a market value of £200.
(iv) The equipment had been depreciated in 1983 at 10 per cent on original cost, but should have been depreciated at 15 per cent p.a. of the written down value at 1 January 1983.
(v) The partnership agreement had been amended on 1 July 1983 to increase Guy's annual salary to £2,700, but this had not been reflected in the accounts.
(vi) No provision had been made for doubtful debts, but a provision of 3 per cent of debtors is now considered desirable.
(vii) £82 owing for electricity had not been accrued.

Required:

(a) Prepare a statement showing the revised profit for the year ended 31 December 1983.
(b) Prepare the amended current accounts of the partners.
(c) Prepare a revised balance sheet as at 31 December 1983.

7   The summarized balance sheet of A. Jones at 31 December 1983 was as follows:

	£		£
Capital	20,000	Land and buildings	8,000
		Machinery	4,000
Creditors	4,000	Stock	5,000
		Debtors	4,500
		Cash	2,500
	24,000		24,000

During the past five years the net profits had been £2,500, £2,000, £3,500, £4,000 and most recently £5,000. Mr Jones considers that this trend of profits should continue but that the normal rate of return for his type of business is 10 per cent. He is intending to admit T. Smith as an equal partner, and is seeking to establish a value for the goodwill. He and Mr Smith agree that the current value of the land is £12,000, the machinery £3,000 and the stock £4,800.

Required:
Advise Mr Jones on the value of the goodwill, utilizing whatever method you think appropriate, and making any necessary assumptions.

8   Why is it necessary to establish a value for goodwill when admitting a new partner? What are the methods for dealing with goodwill in the financial accounts, and what are their advantages and disadvantages?

9 A and B are equal partners. Their balance sheet at 30 June 1983 is

	£		£
Capital		Premises	24,000
A	20,000	Equipment	8,000
B	20,000	Stock	6,500
Current A/cs		Debtors	3,000
A	1,500	Cash	3,000
B	1,000		
Creditors	2,000		
	44,500		44,500

They agree to admit C as a new partner with effect from 1 July 1983, sharing profits A:B:C,3:3:2. Goodwill is valued at £16,000, and A and B are considering which method of admission would be most appropriate.

(i)   C will introduce £10,000 as capital, but is unable to pay for his share of the goodwill. A goodwill account would, therefore, be created.

(ii) C pays for his share of the goodwill, the balance of his £10,000 being treated as a capital contribution. No account would be raised for goodwill, and the monies would remain within the business.

(iii) The arrangements would be as for (ii) but the payment for goodwill would be withdrawn by the partners.

Required:

Draw up three balance sheets showing the effect of the alternative methods of admission.

10 On 30 June 1983, Campbell was admitted as a partner to the firm of Brown and Allen. He introduced £4,000 by way of capital and, as he could not immediately find additional monies to pay for his share of goodwill, it was agreed to create a goodwill account for £12,000. Prior to his admission, Brown and Allen shared profits and losses in the ratio of 3:1, but the new partnership profit-sharing ratio was agreed at 3:2:1. Interest was allowed on capital at 6 per cent p.a.

At the year ended 31 December 1983, the trial balance, *excluding all entries relating to the admission of Campbell*, was

	£	£
Capital		
Brown		15,000
Allen		12,000
Current A/cs (1 Jan. 1983)		
Brown		1,600
Allen	259	

(*continued*)

(*continued*)

5% Loan—Brown		4,000
Interest on loan	200	
Sales		50,630
Purchases	47,300	
Stock at 1.1.83	9,250	
Discounts allowed and received	650	950
Wages	2,120	
Lighting and heating	860	
Rates	870	
Depreciation		
buildings		3,100
vehicles		4,000
Buildings (cost)	23,000	
Vehicles (cost)	9,000	
Debtors and creditors	5,300	5,300
Provision for doubtful debts		130
Bad debts	150	
Vehicle running expenses	680	
Miscellaneous expenses	471	
Bank		3,400
	£100,110	**£100,110**

The following data is to be taken into account:

(i) Stock at 31 December 1983 was valued at £14,200.

(ii) Wages owing at 31 December 1983 amounted to £80.

(iii) Rates include £80 in respect of 1984.

(iv) Depreciation is to be provided on buildings at 2 per cent on cost, and on vehicles at 10 per cent on the written down value at 1 January 1983. No new vehicles have been acquired during the year.

(v) The provision for doubtful debts is to be increased to 3 per cent of debtors.

(vi) All revenues and expenses can be deemed to accrue evenly through the year.

Required:

(a) Prepare the journal entries (including cash) in relation to Campbell's admission as a partner.

(b) Prepare the trading, profit and loss and appropriation accounts for the period ended 31 December 1983, and a balance sheet as at that date.

10 The public limited company—capital structure and financial reporting

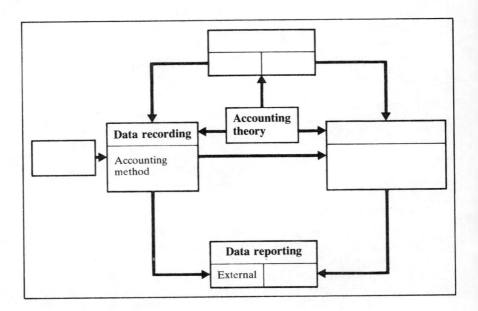

The public limited company, partnership and sole trader—a comparison

A business undertaking may be regarded as an entity separate from the parties who contribute the capital resources or services to it. As we have observed in Chapter 1, the postulate of business entity is artificial in the case of sole traders and partnerships, but in the case of the limited company it is both theoretically convenient and legally correct.

Companies are created and regulated by law, and have a legal personality of their own distinct from the various groups—employees, owners, directors managers—who have an interest in them. This means that a company may enter into contracts, sue and be sued in its own name, and can own property and other assets.

There are now five Acts of Parliament governing limited companies, the Acts of 1948, 1967, 1976, 1980 and 1981. Although consolidated legislation has been promised, none as yet has been forthcoming, and this means that all

Main characteristics of companies, partnerships and sole traders

	Limited companies	Partnerships	Sole traders
Type of ownership interest	Divided into 'shares'. There may be any number of shares from two upwards. Each share carries certain defined legal rights and duties. Shares may be divided into classes with different legal attributes. Any share of a given class is identical with any other as respects legal attributes. A shareholder may hold from one share upwards. Hence very great subdivision of ownership is possible	There normally may be no more than 20 partners. Rights and duties are fixed by agreement. Each partner may have different rights and duties. Subdivision of ownership interest requires agreement of all partners	One owner
Risk to personal estate of owners if business becomes insolvent	Limited to a fixed amount per share, usually paid when the share is first issued	Unlimited. Any partner is responsible for all the debts of the business	Unlimited
Management	In hands of directors elected by shareholders at annual meetings	By agreement between partners	As owner wishes
Information about business available to public	A good deal of information, including annual accounting information, must be registered with the Registrar of Companies and/or sent to shareholders, etc. The public can inspect registered information. The Registrar exercises some supervision over information registered. There must be an annual audit of the amounts, in most cases by qualified accountants	None, except that partners' names must be registered publicly if they are different from the business name	As for partnerships
Withdrawal of funds from the business	Dividends may be paid to shareholders only out of profits. A special legal procedure, involving the consent of the courts, is necessary to repay shareholders' capital	By agreement between partners	At discretion of owner
Financing possibilities	Limited risk, the subdivision of interest, and the law relating to borrowing on the security of 'debentures' makes financing simpler and cheaper than is the case with partnerships and sole traders	Relatively restricted (*see* Companies)	Relatively restricted (*see* Companies)
Constitution	Embodied in formal legal documents copies of which are registered. Alteration requires a special legal procedure, involving the consent of a specified proportion of the shareholders	As agreed between partners. May be informal and need not be in writing	None
Tax on income	Corporation Tax on profits	Income Tax (Sch. D Case I or II)	As for partnerships
Termination	Perpetual succession unless liquidation	By agreement	At will

Acts are in force except where specific clauses or sections have been amended or extended by a later Act—a feature which can result in considerable complexity and confusion. The prime purpose of the Companies Act 1981, however, was to allow the harmonization of company law within the EEC, and in this context, to prescribe the format of published accounts.

The three types of ownership under which a business activity may be exploited are distinguished by the characteristics of their ownership; a summary of these characteristics is given on page 185.

Memorandum and articles

The proprietors of a company are those who own its capital, which is subdivided into units called shares or stock. By acquiring shares, the proprietors become shareholders and members of a company, and receive, as evidence of their legal ownership, 'share certificates'. Companies are usually formed or incorporated by the initiators or promoters lodging certain formal documents with the Registrar of Companies together with the necessary statutory fees.

The formal legal documents consist of Memorandum and Articles of Association.

(1)   The Memorandum

Under the Companies Acts, the Memorandum of Association is of supreme importance in determining the powers of a company. The effect of the Memorandum is to bind present and future members to the observance of its provisions. The Memorandum must state

(a) The name of the company.
(b) The domicile of the company.
(c) The objects of the company.
(d) That the liability of members is limited.
(e) The capital and its division into shares of fixed amounts.

At one time the 'objects' clause was of considerable importance, for this closely defined the activities in which the company could engage, and clearly indicated to prospective shareholders the purposes to which their monies could and would be put. A company which used shareholders' monies for purposes outside of its objectives was deemed to be acting beyond its powers, or '*ultra vires*', and the company's managers or directors who instigated these acts could become personally liable for any resultant losses. However, the effects of this clause is now considerably reduced, for most companies give themselves powers 'to do all such things considered in the best interests of the shareholders'.

The 'capital' clause is the most important clause for our purposes, for it states the numbers, types and value of the shares into which the company will divide its capital and also 'authorizes' the issue of these shares to those wishing to subscribe for them. This clause technically provides the maximum amount which the company may raise by way of share capital, but, in fact, this maximum can fairly readily be increased with the consent of the courts.

The company need not issue all of the authorized capital; that portion of the authorized capital which is sold is referred to as the 'issued capital'. Once shares are issued, the shareholders can freely sell their shares through the Stock Exchange to anyone. The price paid on this transfer is effected between seller and buyer, and the company has no part in nor benefits from such transactions. By law, the company must maintain an up-to-date register of share ownership, the 'Register of Shareholders' being kept at the company's head office.

There are two types of company: those in which the public at large can become members through the ownership of its shares—the 'public' company—and those in which only a restricted or selected number of individuals can own its shares—the 'private' company.

Until the Companies Act 1980, it was impossible to tell from the name of the company whether it was, in fact, a public or a private company. All companies registered under the Companies Acts included the word 'Limited' (usually abbreviated to Ltd) as part of their title. The Companies Act 1980, however, required public limited companies to end their names with 'Public Limited Company' or 'PLC'; any company not so described, i.e. ending its name with the word 'Limited' or 'Ltd', is a private limited company.

In this and subsequent chapters, we will be confining our attention to the public company.

(2)   The Articles of Association

The articles of a company are its internal regulations, and are subordinate to and controlled by the Memorandum. The articles will make provision for the manner in which the company is to be administered, and will have particular reference to matters relating to the raising of capital, directors' remuneration and qualification, dividends and reserves, and accounts and audit. The distinction between ownership and management is one of the features which particularly distinguishes the company from the sole trader or the partnership. The shareholders are the owners of the company and, as such, are the ultimate arbiters of its activities, but the day-to-day management of the company is controlled by the board of directors appointed by the shareholders. In practice, the directors often have considerable shareholdings, but nevertheless they remain accountable to the shareholders at large. The Companies Act 1948 has a model set of articles known as Table A, and most companies either simply adopt Table A, or else adopt part of it and amend some sections.

Shares and share capital

The primary method of raising capital for a company is by the issue of shares. The shareholder, whose rights are evidenced by a share certificate(s), will be entitled to a share in the profits of the company and in the assets of the company if it is wound up.

It is usual for a company's articles to authorize the directors to determine the number of shares to be issued (subject to the total amount authorized by the Memorandum), the issue price of such shares and the income and voting rights of the shareholders. In theory, there can be an infinite variety of classes and subclasses of shares, but in practice there are two main groups—the ordinary share and the preference share.

Ordinary shares

Ordinary shares are the fundamental form of share capital, and many companies have no other class. The ordinary shares represent the claims of these shareholders after all preferential claims have been met. In fact, all claims, whether of preference shareholders, debenture holders, creditors, etc., have precedence over the ordinary shareholder. The ordinary shareholder therefore assumes the greater part of the risks of the enterprise, but in return may also benefit to the greatest extent if the operations are very profitable.

The ordinary shareholder expects to receive an annual income called a dividend, in respect of his investment. As each share carries a nominal or par value, the dividend is declared as a percentage of this value. For example, a dividend of 10 per cent on a share of £1 means that the shareholder will receive an income of 10p (less tax) for every share he holds. The power to declare dividends is vested in the company in the general meeting of its shareholders, but the articles commonly provide that no dividend shall exceed the amount recommended by the directors (e.g. *see* section 114 of Table A of the Companies Act 1948). The directors thus have very wide powers over the disposal of corporate earnings. The market price of the company's shares is closely connected with dividends, however, and any declaration of dividends which adversely affects market price may well lead to a loss in confidence in the company.

When ordinary shares (or any other form of security for that matter) are offered to the public, prospective investors are put in possession of the relevant business facts by means of a document called the prospectus. Company legislation prescribes the minimum amount of information a company may give in a prospectus, which will normally state, among other matters, the issue price, the past record of the company and details of the directors.

Preference shares

The preference share is a device to attract the investor who does not wish to bear the same risks as the ordinary shareholder. The preference shareholder is 'preferred' to the ordinary shareholder both in respect of rights to income and rights to capital in the event of the company going into liquidation.

Preference shares carry the right to a fixed rate of dividend, and are normally 'cumulative'. 'Cumulative' simply means that if a preference dividend is waived in a given year, then it will be carried forward and added to the next or subsequent years' dividends. Like the ordinary shareholder, the preference shareholder only has a legal right to dividends when they are declared—which is the prerogative of the directors. Because the preference shareholder is 'preferred' and carries less risk, his dividend rate is usually less than that of the ordinary shareholder. Some articles give all classes of shareholders equal voting rights, but more usually the voting rights of the preference shareholder are restricted to compensate for the greater security of capital and certainty of income they enjoy by comparison with the ordinary shareholder. For example, the articles may provide voting rights only when the preference dividend is in arrears, or if the directors are proposing a modification of capital structure which will alter the rights of the preference shareholder.

Redeemable shares

A special category of share capital is the redeemable share which provides for the return of capital to the shareholder within a specified period of time. Up till 1981 only preference shares could be redeemable, but section 45 of the Companies Act 1981 now extends that possibility to any class of issued share capital.

There is an important proviso in that a company can issue redeemable shares only if it already has on issue some shares which have not been redeemable. Without this limitation it would be possible for a company to redeem all its shares, and thus end up without any shareholders whatsoever.

Since the repayment of capital necessarily involves the reduction of capital, the law, which seeks to maintain capital intact, requires the company to provide a special reserve equal to the capital redeemed, unless the shares were redeemed out of the proceeds of a new issue (*see* Chapter 11).

Par value and market value

In this country, the law requires each share to carry a nominal or par value. The nominal value need not represent the true worth of the share at the time of issue, and it is highly unlikely to do so after the company has been trading for some time. The main justification for this practice is the argument that dividends can be more easily declared in relation to a fixed, as opposed to the fluctuating, market price. Why it is easier to declare a dividend of X per cent on a nominal value as opposed to a dividend of X pence per share is not at all clear!

The market price of a share will reflect a number of factors both internal and external to the firm. In general, shares are bought for two reasons, namely, income and capital appreciation. Most shareholders want a regular income by way of dividend, and all shareholders will have expectations as to the level of income appropriate to their investment. The rate of return to the investment is measured by the 'yield' of the share. This is based on the dividend expected and the market price of the security. For example, if a dividend of 20 per cent were declared on a share with £1 par value and a market price of £2 the yield would be

$$\frac{\text{Par value} \times \text{Dividend \%}}{\text{Market value}}$$

$$\frac{1 \times 20\%}{2} = 10\%$$

The yield can be expressed gross or net, i.e. before or after tax, since dividends attract income tax at the standard rate. What is an acceptable yield will depend on the other alternatives open to the investor. If the investor considers that the company in which he is to invest is more risky than other options open to him—perhaps because of the nature of the company's activities, or its location in a country with unstable government, etc.—then he will seek a high yield to compensate him for the chance that he may lose his capital. For example, if the desired yield was 25 per cent, it follows from the equation above that as

$$\text{Yield} (\%) = \frac{\text{Par value} \times \text{Dividend} (\%)}{\text{Market value}}$$

then

$$\text{Market value} = \frac{\text{Par value} \times \text{Dividend} (\%)}{\text{Yield} (\%)}$$

Therefore

$$\text{Market value} = \frac{£1 \times 20\%}{25\%}$$

$$= 80\text{p per share}$$

Conversely, if the company was considered to be a good risk in which there was every likelihood that the capital value of the company would appreciate over time, then the investor may settle for a yield of, say, 5 per cent. In this instance

$$\text{Market value} = \frac{£1 \times 20\%}{5\%}$$

$$= £4 \text{ per share}$$

Different investors will have different perceptions of the yield they regard as adequate, so that the actual market price of a share represents the equilibrium point of the expectations and needs of all would-be sellers and buyers of the shares.

A further factor which will affect the shareholder's judgement of risk is the extent to which annual profits 'cover' the dividends proposed. As preference shareholders are 'preferred' or given preference over the ordinary shareholders in the matter of dividend, then reported profits are just seen as 'covering' the preference shareholder:

£1 ordinary shares	£500,000
6% £1 preference shares	£300,000
Net operating profit after tax	£72,000
8% Ordinary dividend	£40,000

The preference dividend is covered

$$\frac{72,000}{300,000 \times 6\%} = 4 \text{ times}$$

and the ordinary dividend

$$\frac{72,000 - 18,000}{500,000 \times 8\%} = 1.13 \text{ times}$$

The preference shareholder's dividend is well secured—it could be paid four times over out of the current profits, but the ordinary shareholder's dividend requires nearly all of the current profit. This means that there is little of the current profits to be reinvested in the company, thus reducing expectations of future growth, which in turn will affect expectations about future profits and dividends.

Share premium

Shares may be issued at par, or at a price above par, by the addition of a premium to the nominal value. Premium issues are normally made when the existing shares of the same denomination are currently bought and sold above their par value. If the market price of the existing shares is above par, this reflects the relationship between desired yield and dividend rate outlined above. The new shareholders cannot expect a higher yield than the old shareholders, and therefore must expect to pay a price above par to place them on an equal footing. Par issues can have the effect of reducing the funds employed per share, and this may make the maintenance of dividend levels very difficult. For example:

	I	IIA	IIB
	£	£	£
Ordinary share capital	200,000	450,000	300,000
Share premium	—	—	150,000
Retained profits	300,000	300,000	300,000
Net Capital Employed	500,000	750,000	750,000
Net profit (available for dividend)	30,000	45,000	45,000
Funds per share	2.5	1.66	2.5
Rate of dividend	15%	10%	15%

In the preceding table the first column represents the initial position of the company. It has built up retained profit in the past of £300,000 and now makes a practice of distributing all current earnings. The funds available per share are £2.5 and the dividend is 15 per cent. The company then increases its net capital by 50 per cent and the rate of profit is expected to increase similarly. In column IIA the additional funds are raised by an issue at par of 250,000 £1 ordinary shares. The result is a decrease in the funds per share employed, and a decrease in the dividend.

If, however, the additional funds are raised by an issue of 100,000 £1 shares at a premium of 150 per cent (i.e. the shares are each issued at £1.50, a premium of 50p per share), the funds per share and the dividend rate are maintained at their previous level. As column IIB shows, the £45,000 profit is distributed to 300,000 shares—the original 200,000 and the new 100,000 shares—so that the rate of dividend is still 15 per cent.

Debentures

A debenture is an acknowledgement of a debt, binding a company to pay a certain amount of money at a future date, with interest being paid at a specified rate. The holder of a debenture, the debenture holder, is *not* a member of the company as is the ordinary or preference shareholder, but stands as a creditor. Debentures are either secured on a specific asset or assets of the company (normally land and buildings) when they are called mortgage debentures, or are secured by a floating charge on all the assets, or are issued without any specific or general security when they are called naked debentures. Debenture holders are preferred creditors and are entitled in the event of liquidation to be repaid their capital interest before shareholders receive payment of their capital. As the security is substantial, the rate of interest is normally lower than the rate of dividend paid to either the preference or ordinary shareholder and is related to the prevailing bank rate. Debenture interest is payable even when there is a loss.

Capitalization

The capital necessary to carry on a business undertaking may be ascertained by estimating the fixed and current assets required plus any non-recurring expenses. Part of this total will be met by short-term finance, e.g. trade creditors and banks, but the balance will have to be found by the issue of long-term securities such as shares or debentures. The capital structure or capitalization of a business is the way in which its long-term funds are distributed between the different classes of owners or creditors.

The capitalization of a business depends on the expected average net income. The potential investor requires the yield to be comparable with yields of other investments subjected to the same risks. Thus, if the expected distributable income of a proposed venture is £30,000 and the yield of similar shares is 10 per cent, then £300,000 of ordinary shares can be issued, i.e. the income is capitalized at 10 per cent. If investors considered that the expectations were less favourable, and therefore the risk was higher, the capitalization rate would be higher. With a rate of 15 per cent

$$\frac{30,000 \times 100}{15} = £200,000$$

of shares could be issued.

If, in this latter situation, funds of £300,000 were required to finance the fixed assets, then some part of the capital would have to be raised other than by ordinary shares. We have already observed that preferences shares and debentures, because they carry less risk, will normally command a lower rate of dividend or interest. The decision as to how the total will be raised will depend on the state of the market in fixed income securities at the time. For example, if the yield on preference shares were 6 per cent, then the following capitalization could be adapted:

Capital		Share of income
166,666	£1 6% preference	10,000
133,334	£1 ordinary at 15%	20,000
£300,000		**£30,000**

The rate at which prospective ordinary share earnings are capitalized will vary, because it is a subjective measure of risks. It will be different for businesses in different fields. If the income is expected to be regular then the rate will be lower than for a more speculative venture where income levels may fluctuate. In addition, the rate will be different for the same firm if general economic conditions change.

Capital gearing

The relationship between ordinary share capital and securities creating fixed interest or dividend charges on income has an important effect on the attitude of prospective ordinary shareholders. The relationship is called 'gearing'; the more ordinary shares a company has issued in relation to other securities the more 'low-geared' it is. For example, a company may wish to raise £1 million and consider three alternatives:

	I	II	III
	£	£	£
5% Debentures	300,000	—	—
6% Preference	300,000	300,000	—
Ordinary shares	400,000	700,000	1,000,000
Gear ratio	1.5:1	1:2.3	∞

In alternative I, the company has £600,000 of fixed interest/fixed dividend bearing capital and £400,000 of equity. This provides a gearing ratio of 6:4

or 1.5:1. In alternative II, the ratio is 3:7 or 1:2.3 and, in III, is 0:£1,000,000 or ∞. The most highly geared alternative is I, and in III there is no gearing at all.

The effect on the market value of ordinary shares of the different gearings will be considerable. We will assume that the yield expected by the ordinary shareholder is 7 per cent, and that in the table below the expected distributable profit is £100,000, £125,000 and £75,000 respectively:

| Scheme | | Profit before interest | | |
		£100,000	£125,000	£75,000
I	300,000 5% debentures	15,000	15,000	15,000
	300,000 6% preference	18,000	18,000	18,000
	400,000 ordinary:			
	available profit	67,000	92,000	42,000
	ordinary rate	16.75%	23%	10.5%
	market price	£2.39	£3.28	£1.50
II	300,000 6% preference	18,000	18,000	18,000
	700,000 ordinary:			
	available profit	82,000	107,000	57,000
	ordinary rate	11.7%	15.3%	8.1%
	market price	£1.67	£2.19	£1.16
III	1,000,000 ordinary:			
	available profit	100,000	125,000	75,000
	ordinary rate	10%	12.5%	7.5%
	market price	£1.43	£1.78	£1.07

Scheme I is the company with a gearing ratio of 1.5:1. £33,000 of its profits are immediately committed: £15,000 to pay interest to the debenture holders and £18,000 to pay dividends to the preference shareholders. This leaves £67,000 available to the ordinary shareholders when total profits are £100,000 before interest and taxation, and £92,000 and £42,000 available if profits are £25,000 higher or lower. Assuming that all of the profit is distributed, then at the three levels of profit, the ordinary dividends are 16.75, 23 and 10.5 per cent, respectively. If the shareholder is expecting a yield of 7 per cent, it follows that the market price of the ordinary share will be £2.39 when the profit is £100,000, £3.28 at £125,000 and £1.50 at £75,000.

A similar analysis has been carried out for alternatives II and III, and the comparative effect on the market price can be summarized as follows:

| | | Profits before interest | | |
| | | £100,000 | £125,000 | £75,000 |
Scheme	Gearing ratio	Market price per ordinary share		
I	1.5:1	£2.39	£3.28	£1.50
II	1:2.3	£1.67	£2.19	£1.16
III	∞	£1.43	£1.78	£1.07

The more highly geared a company, the greater will be the fluctuation in the market price of the ordinary shares in relation to the different levels of distributable profits. When times are good and profits are high the ordinary shareholder will benefit greatly from being in a highly geared company. On the other hand, as profits fall the ordinary shareholder in such a company will do less well, and may feel the need to switch into a low-geared company with a preponderance of equity capital.

Reserves—their purpose

In the case of the sole trader the profit not withdrawn from the business was added to the capital; in the case of the partnership the remaining profit was contained within the current account of the partners. In the limited company, profit not withdrawn by way of dividends is contained within reserves. We might usefully remind ourselves of a point made in Chapter 4—profit, and therefore reserves, has no direct relationship with cash. Generally the increase in funds accompanying the reserve is deployed among all the assets of the company.

The attitude of investors and creditors is probably more influenced by reserves and dividends than by any other feature. We will discuss the question of dividend policy later in the chapter; at this point we will examine the purpose and classification of reserves. Reserves serve a number of complementary purposes, the most important of which are given below.

(1)   Expansion

The expansion of business operations, whether through an increased volume of established activities or through diversification, can be financed through retained funds.

(2)   Contingencies

Reserves will enable the firm to meet any unexpected—and therefore unreserved—contingencies without the erosion of paid-up capital. The firm with the larges reserves will be a position to sustain losses incurred as a result of adverse trading conditions.

(3)   Replacements, improvements, and research

Depreciation provisions reduce the profits available for distribution, and thus help to retain funds for replacement. But depreciation is normally related to historic cost, and replacement prices are continually rising. Savings through reserves can make possible the acquisition of new and improved equipment. Similarly, research can scarcely be carried out unless some profits have been retained.

(4)   Dividend equalization

The retaining of some profits in good years can ensure that, in poor years, dividend levels are maintained by drawing on past profits.

(5)　Long-term debt

Specific reserves (matched by a specific investment of cash) may be necessary to meet the repayment of long-term debt such as debentures.

Types of reserve

Under the Companies Acts there are two types of reserve—the revenue reserve and the capital reserve. The revenue reserve consists of undistributed profit and can be applied in any way in which the directors think fit. They may be used, for example, to maintain the business, pay dividends, absorb losses or issue bonus shares.

The revenue reserve is often subdivided into reserves entitled general reserve, undistributed profit, or profit and loss account balance. It is important to remember that there is, in law, no distinction whatsoever between these sub-categories. The Institute of Chartered Accountants emphasized this in stating that 'the subdivision of such reserves under a variety of headings is unnecessary'.

Capital reserves are *not* available for the payment of dividends. Two categories are distinguishable—reserves related to share capital and reserves arising from unrealized capital gains. There are two types of reserve related to share capital—the share premium and the capital redemption reserve. When shares are issued at a premium, the premium is treated in the same light as paid up capital, and therefore not distributable. The share premium may be used only for

(1) Writing off the formation (preliminary) expenses of the company.
(2) Writing off the expenses of any issue of share or loan capital.
(3) Providing the premium payable on the redemption or purchase of any shares or debentures, provided that those shares were originally issued at a premium (*see* page 225).
(4) Issuing bonus shares.

The redemption of either ordinary or preference shares, as was mentioned earlier in the chapter, requires the establishment of a capital redemption reserve unless redemption was made possible by the proceeds of a fresh issue. This reserve, like the share premium reserve, may be applied in the issue of bonus shares and for no other purpose.

The second category of capital reserve arises from unrealized capital gain. We observed in Chapter 2 that the values assigned to assets arise from the cost postulate, and do not necessarily reflect their market value. If a company wishes to reflect the current values of its assets—particularly its fixed assets—it is perfectly entitled to do so, but any surplus which arises because current values are above the book values does not meet the criteria of realization as laid down in Chapter 4. The surplus, or profit, is unrealized, and therefore cannot be treated as a revenue reserve, since reserves arise from *realized* profits and losses. The surplus is therefore reflected in an asset revaluation reserve—a capital reserve not available for distribution.

The reserves, whatever their type, are the property of the ordinary shareholder unless, very exceptionally, the Articles of Association give the preference shareholder some rights to capital over and above the par value of their shares. A typical balance sheet may reveal

	£
£1 ordinary shares	10,000
6% £1 preference shares	8,000
Reserves	15,000
5% debentures	5,000
	38,000

The par value of each ordinary share is as stated £1, but the book value of each ordinary share is

$$\frac{\text{Issued ordinary shares} + \text{Reserves}}{\text{No. ordinary shares}}$$

$$= \frac{£10,000 + 15,000}{10,000}$$

$$= £2.50 \text{ per share}$$

This means that if the company went into liquidation and all the assets realized their book values, the ordinary shareholders, being the legal owners of the reserves, would receive £2.50 per share.

Dividends

We have already observed that the power to declare dividends is vested in the company in the general meeting of its shareholders, but that the directors normally have the power to determine the maximum amount to be distributed. To pay dividends requires two conditions—the availability of reserves and the availability of cash. Statute law and the judiciary have both been loath to interfere with the discretion of businessmen in determining what may be fairly distributed. Professor Gower in his *Modern Company Law* has suggested that the overriding condition is one of solvency: 'Dividends cannot be paid if this would result in the company's being unable to pay its debts as they fall due.'

Accounting records and the capital structure

(1) Issue of shares

The discussions of the earlier part of this chapter have stressed that the crucial problems connected with the issue of shares relate to the decisions as to the nature of shares—whether preference or ordinary—and the price at which they are to be issued. The detailed procedures for the issue of shares need not concern us for they have become part of a rather specialized aspect of bookkeeping.

When ordinary or preference shares are first issued, it is sometimes the practice to 'call' the monies in a number of stages, viz:

(i)   *On application and allotment.* The public will often apply for more shares than the company has on offer. This means that shares have to be allotted on some *pro rata* basis, and, when allotted, the shareholder will pay the first instalment—say 50p for each £1 share.

(ii) *On first and subsequent calls.* There may be a number of calls requiring the shareholder to pay a further X pence per share of the issue price.

(iii) *On final call.* The shareholder is required to pay the balance of the issue price.

The ultimate result of this procedure is that the company has acquired the long-term funds it needs to sustain and develop its activities. If we assume that a company issues 500,000 £1 ordinary shares at par, the ledger entries will be

Cash A/c

Ordinary share capital	500,000		

Ordinary share capital A/c

		Cash	500,000

If the shares were issued at a premium of 25p per share, the ledgers would show

Cash A/c

Ordinary share capital	500,000		
Share premium	125,000		

Ordinary share capital A/c

	Cash	500,000

Share premium A/c

	Cash	125,000

The share premium account is, as has been previously stated, a *capital* reserve, which means that the monies received cannot be used to pay a dividend to the shareholders, but are retained as part of the long-term funds employed within the company and invested in whatever assets the directors deem appropriate.

When the balance sheet is prepared, the Companies Acts require that certain information must be disclosed, viz:

(i)   The *authorized* share capital, showing the number and value of the shares in each class authorized by the Memorandum.

(ii) The *issued* share capital, showing the number and value of the shares issued to the public in each class, and, if the company is calling the issue price in stages, the proportion of the share price paid up.

(iii) The earliest and latest redemption dates of any redeemable shares.

(iv) The share premium account, if any.

The balance sheet information pertaining to share capital is often presented as follows:

X PLC

	£
Authorized share capital:	
750,000 £1 ordinary shares	
200,000 £1 6% redeemable preference shares (1985)	
Called-up share capital:	
500,000 £1 ordinary shares	500,000
Reserves	
Share premium A/c	125,000
Shareholders' equity	**625,000**

(2) *Issue of debentures*

There is very little difference in the accounting treatment of loan and share capital, but, unlike the issue of shares, it is not uncommon to find that debentures are issued at a discount. The effect of issuing debentures at a discount is that the real rate of interest is higher than the nominal rate.

Debentures are usually issued in units of £100, so that an issue at '95' means that the debenture holder is paying £95 for each £100 unit—a discount of 5 per cent. If the nominal or 'coupon' rate was 10 per cent, then the real rate of interest is

$$10\% \times \frac{100}{95} = 10.53\%$$

When the debentures are redeemed—and unless they are stated to be irredeemable, they are considered redeemable, and must be redeemed according to the terms of the issue—they are normally redeemed at their par value, so that an original debenture holder receives £100 for every £95 he paid for each unit of stock.

As with shares, debentures are recorded at their par value so that any premium or discount is recorded separately. If a company issues £10,000 of 10 per cent debentures at 95, the ledger entries will be

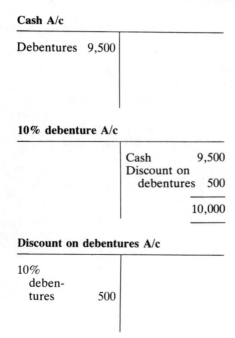

Cash A/c

Debentures 9,500	

10% debenture A/c

	Cash 9,500
	Discount on
	debentures 500
	10,000

Discount on debentures A/c

10%
   deben-
     tures 500	

The discount on debentures can be shown as a rather peculiar asset under the heading 'intangible assets' on the balance sheet (see page 209), but, because of its nature, it is the usual practice to write the discount off as soon as possible by debiting the appropriation account. On the balance sheet, the debentures will be disclosed as 'Creditors amounts falling due after more than one year', or, if redemption is due in the year following the balance sheet date, under 'Creditors: amounts falling due within one year'. Thus:

Creditors: amounts falling due after more than one year

Debenture—loans   £10,000

(3) Payment of dividends

Shareholders are not entitled to a dividend unless it is declared by the directors and approved by the Annual General Meeting of shareholders. Usually, the Articles of Association permit the directors to declare and pay an interim dividend, but the final dividend, and hence the overall distribution for the year, must be ratified by the shareholders. If we assume that in respect of 500,000 £1 ordinary shares, the directors have paid a 6 per cent interim dividend and proposed a 10 per cent final dividend, the ledger accounts will be

Cash A/c

	Interim ordinary dividend	50,000

Interim ordinary dividend A/c

Cash	**30,000**	Appropria-tion A/c	**30,000**

Final ordinary dividend A/c

	Appropria-tion A/c	50,000

Appropriation A/c

| Interim ordinary dividend | 30,000 | |
| Final ordinary dividend | 50,000 | |

As the final ordinary dividend is only a proposal at year end, it is an accrual, and as such will be shown as a current liability on the balance sheet. When it is paid the ledger entries will be to credit cash and debit the final ordinary dividend account.

(4) Payment of debenture interest

As debenture holders are a special type of creditor, interest paid to them is an expense and, as such, is charged to the profit and loss account for the year. The interest is often paid in two equal instalments, and, at the year end, one instalment may not have been paid. Assuming that a company has issued £10,000 10 per cent debentures, and paid half of the interest during the year, the ledger accounts will be

Cash A/c

	Debenture interest 500

Debenture interest A/c

Cash	500	Profit and loss	1,000
Debenture interest accrued c/d	500		
	1,000		1,000
		Debenture interest accrued b/d	500

Profit and loss A/c

Debenture interest 1,000	

The profit and loss account will be charged with the full amount of the interest, the unpaid portion being treated as an accrual and shown on the balance sheet as a current liability.

Valuation of shares

The fundamental principle of traditional accounting in valuing assets is known as the cost postulate. In its crudest form it equates value with the cost or price paid at the date of acquisition. In practice, as we have seen, this version shows several refinements by permitting depreciation, recognizing value decline (lower of cost or market), and exempting certain individual items such as precious metals. In general, however, as we stated in Chapter 2, accounting seeks to identify value with historic input cost, taking profit only when revenue (output value) can be objectively and certainly measured (*see* Chapter 4).

Such a concept of value, it has been claimed, has the virtue of objectivity. This may be true, but by using this concept, accounting violates one of the fundamental constituents of any value theory—the fact that the value of an object or event is bound to time and circumstances. A specific value is a momentary and highly unstable magnitude, and although the cost basis has the virtue of avoiding uncertainty, it also avoids the main problem which the accountant has to solve.

In this section of the chapter, we will specifically consider the valuation of shares. Many lengthy and learned volumes have been written on this subject; all we can do is to provide an introduction which points out some of the pitfalls which can snare the unwary. It is useful constantly to remember that value is always subjective; the value of the business will be different to different people, and different to the same person at different times.

(1) Balance sheet valuation

It is very tempting to value a business on the basis of its assets and liabilities revealed in the balance sheet—so called 'balance sheet' valuation.

Two simple illustrations can show the methodology employed:

Example 1

	£		£
1,000 ordinary shares	1,000	Net assets	1,500
Revenue reserves	500		
	£1,500		**£1,500**

The 'value' of the business is given by the net capital employed, £1,500, and the value of each ordinary share by dividing the net capital by the number of ordinary shares issued:

$$\text{Value of share} = \frac{\text{Net capital}}{\text{No. ordinary shares}}$$

$$= \frac{\text{Net assets}}{\text{No. ordinary shares}}$$

$$= \frac{1,500}{1,000}$$

$$= \underline{£1.50 \text{ per share}}$$

Where there are preference shares and/or debentures, their nominal value should be deducted from the net assets.

Example 2

	£		£
1,000 £1 ordinary shares	1,000	Net assets	4,300
500 £1 6% preference shares	500		
Revenue reserves	800		
Debentures	2,000		
	£4,300		**£4,300**

$$\text{Value of ordinary share} = \frac{\text{Net assets} - (\text{Preference} + \text{Debentures})}{\text{No. ordinary shares}}$$

$$= \frac{4,300 - (500 + 2,000)}{1,000}$$

$$= \frac{1,800}{1,000}$$

$$= \underline{\text{£1.80 per share}}$$

It is doubtful whether this type of valuation can ever have any meaning. The conventional balance sheet assumes stable money values in order to be able to add together the monetary values assigned to assets acquired at different dates. If a balance sheet valuation is to be used, then it is essential to state the input value of the business in terms of their current values.

(2)   Valuation by expectations

The balance sheet method of valuation assumes what is patently not true—that value can be constant over time. More specifically, it fails to take account of expectations. Fundamentally, a business—and, therefore, its shares—is worth what it can earn in the future, and expectations as to its earning capacity will vary from person to person. If expectations are used as a basis of valuation, there can be no unique solution to the question 'what is the business worth?'

Probably the most acceptable conceptual approach is to ascertain the net present value of all anticipated receipts and expenditures, as illustrated:

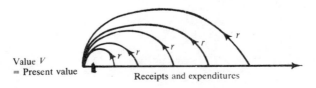

Value V
= Present value   Receipts and expenditures

Each time point of receipts and expenditures is discounted backwards to the time of valuation. The valuation would not be unique because expectations would vary both in respect of receipts and expenditures and also in respect of the rate of interest to be assigned to r.

In practice, expectations of the future are couched in more general terms; a potential shareholder will anticipate future profits and dividends running at an *average* level. The following example illustrates how such expectations may provide a basis of valuations:

	£		£
100,000 ordinary shares	100,000	Net assets	150,000
Reserves	50,000		
	£150,000		**£150,000**

Future profits are estimated at £25,000 per annum, and ordinary dividends at £15,000 (or 15p per share or 15 per cent).

(a) Dividends

We may use dividends as a basis of valuation. The first step is to look at the general market to discover what is the yield of similar shares. Assume that investigation reveals that similar shares should earn 7 per cent. We know that

$$\text{Yield} = \frac{\text{Dividend \%} \times \text{Nominal value}}{\text{Market value}}$$

so, therefore, rewriting the formula, we have

$$\text{Market value} = \frac{\text{Dividend \% } \times \text{Nominal value}}{\text{Yield}}$$

or

$$\text{MV} = \frac{15 \times 1}{7}$$

$$= \text{£2.14 per share}$$

(b) Earnings

There is a relationship between earnings and share value—the price/earnings ratio. This value will differ from the dividend basis of valuation, because it takes into account the fact that the business will employ its non-distributed earnings to enhance future profitability. The valuation procedure is similar to that for dividends. The *P/E* ratio of similar firms is established by investigation of the market. Assuming that the *P/E* ratio is 10:1, i.e. the market is willing to pay £10 for every £1 of earnings per share per annum, the value of the share becomes

$$\text{Future earnings per share per annum} = \frac{25,000}{100,000}$$

$$= \text{£0.25 per share}$$

Therefore

$$\text{Value of shares} = 10 \times 0.25$$

$$= \text{£2.50 per share}$$

The final accounts of public limited companies

Compulsory disclosure through accounts is a method of providing information which was not adopted by the legislature until a comparatively late stage in the development of companies. It was not until 1908 that companies were compelled to publish their balance sheets, and until 1928 there was no requirement to circulate the income statement to members. When a company prepares its final accounts for internal management use, it can do so in whatever form is most appropriate and useful to management. However, as a company is required by law to publish its accounts, there would be little point—and not inconsiderable expense—in adopting internal practices which were at considerable variance with external requirements. The difference between the internal and published forms, therefore, lies primarily in the extent to which detail is disclosed and not in differences of accounting principle or practice.

Until 1981, the successive Companies Acts required the disclosure of more and more information in the published accounts, but did not prescribe the form in which that information should be published. The Companies Act 1981 has dramatically changed that position, for, by bringing the United Kingdom into line with the Fourth Directive of the EEC, the freedom previously allowed to companies to decide upon the form of the accounts has been removed, and now all companies must use the prescribed formats for the balance sheet and profit and loss account. However, there is still an overriding requirement that:

> Every balance sheet of a company so prepared shall give a true and fair view of the state of the affairs of the company as at the end of its financial year, and every profit and loss account of a company so prepared shall give a true and fair view of the profit and loss of the company for the financial year (*Companies Act 1981 Section 1*).

We will deal with the question and some of the detail of disclosure in published accounts later; for the moment we will examine a full (internal) set of company accounts to see how our basic model has to be adapted to the particular needs of the limited company.

Just as the appropriation account of the partnership provides for the distribution of net income among the partners, so the company's appropriation accounts provides, at the instigation of the directors, for the allocation of income to reserves or for the purpose of dividend distribution.

A typical set of final accounts for a limited company is as follows:

Astral PLC

Trading, Profit and Loss, and Appropriation Account for the period ended 31 December 1983

	£	£	£
Sales			800,000
Less: Opening stock	65,000		
Purchases	359,000		
		424,000	
Less: Closing stock		74,000	
Gross Profit			350,000
			450,000
Less:			
Selling expenses		35,000	
Depreciation—vans		20,000	
Salesmen's commission and wages		110,000	
Directors' remuneration (Note 1)		55,000	
Audit fees (Note 2)		11,000	
Depreciation—plant		24,000	
Office salaries		96,000	351,000
			99,000
Add:			
Rent receivable		500	
Dividends received		2,500	3,000
			102,000
Less:			
Debenture interest (Note 3)			6,000
Net Profit before taxation			96,000
Tax on profit (Note 4)			35,000
Net profit after taxation			61,000
Profit undistributed as at 1 Jan 1983 (Note 5)			184,000
			£245,000

('Notes' referred to above are on next page)   (*continued*)

Astral PLC
Trading, P. & L. etc A/c as at 31 December 1983 (*continued*)

Dividends paid (Note 6)		
6% interim ordinary	24,000	
3% interim preference	6,000	30,000
Dividends proposed (Note 7)		
12% final ordinary	48,000	
3% final preference	6,000	54,000
Transfer to general reserve (Note 8)		40,000
Undistributed profits at 31 Dec 1983 (Note 9)		121,000
		£245,000

In the light of this income statement we can observe that:

Note 1   All directors' fees, emoluments and pension contributions will appear as an expense in the profit and loss account.

Note 2   The limited company is required by law to allow an independent authority, the auditors, who are agents of the shareholders, to examine the accounts and books of the company together with all necessary information, in order that the shareholders and other interested parties may be assured that the accounts present a true and fair view. The audit fee is thus an expense in the profit and loss account.

Note 3   As the debenture holder is not a member of the company, the interest attributable to him is a charge (i.e. expense) against and not an appropriation of profit.

Note 4   As a company has a separate legal personality, the company is subject to corporation tax on its taxable profits. At the year end, the tax will not have been paid, i.e. it is a provision, but normally it will be paid within the next accounting year.

Note 5   The undistributed profit accumulated in earlier years is added to the current net profit to establish the profit available for distribution.

Notes 6/7   During the year, the directors may, at their discretion, pay interim dividends, if the trading results are satisfactory. These dividends paid, together with the dividends proposed, will provide the ceiling for dividends and must be ratified by the company in general meeting.

Note 8   The directors are at liberty to transfer profits to special reserves. This reserve is as freely available for dividend as any other revenue reserve.

Note 9   The difference between the profit available for distribution and any dividend or special reserve appropriations is the undistributed profit at the end of the accounting period:

Astral PLC
Balance sheet as at 31 December 1983

	£	£	£
Fixed Assets (Note 1)			
Intangible assets			
Patents and trade marks			19,000
Tangible assets			
Land and buildings		276,000	
Plant and machinery (cost)	628,000		
Less: Depreciation	188,000	440,000	
Vans (cost)	210,000		
Less: Depreciation	119,000	91,000	807,000
			826,000
Current Assets			
Stock of finished goods		74,000	
Debtors		79,000	
Prepayments		9,000	
Investments (Note 2)		54,000	
Cash at bank		90,000	
		306,000	
Creditors—Amounts falling due within one year			
(Note 3)			
Trade creditors	45,000		
Other creditors—dividends	54,000	(Note 4)	
—taxation	35,000	(Note 5)	
Accruals	2,000	136,000	
Net current assets		170,000	170,000
Total assets less current liabilities			**£996,000**
Creditors—amounts falling due after one year			
Debenture loans			100,000
Capital and reserves			
Called-up share capital (Note 6)			
400,000 £1 Ordinary shares		400,000	
200,000 6% £1 Preference shares		200,000	
		600,000	
Share premium account		25,000	
Revaluation reserve		50,000	
Other reserves:			
General reserve		100,000	
Profit and loss account		121,000	896,000
			£996,000

(*'Notes' referred to above are on next page*)

The form used for this balance sheet does, in fact, broadly comply with one of the two alternative formats for published balance sheets provided by Schedule 1 to the 1981 Act. As this format does not differ radically from that to which we have become accustomed, we may as well become acquainted with the slightly different format and terminology at this stage.

Note 1   Fixed assets are divided between 'intangible assets'—assets such as development costs, trade marks and goodwill, 'tangible assets', and, if held in the long term, 'investments', particularly shares in group and related companies.

Note 2   If investments are held long term, then they will be categorized under fixed assets above.

Note 3   Heretofore we have used the term 'Current liabilities' for what the Companies Act 1981 now describes as 'Creditors—amounts falling due within one year'.

Note 4   The dividends proposed will fall for payment within one year.

Note 5   If the taxation is not payable within one year, then it will be included under the later heading 'Creditors—amounts falling due after one year'.

Note 6   There must be shown in the balance sheet or by way of a note the Authorized Share Capital.

Disclosure in company accounts

We have already noted that there is a difference between the internal and external (published) accounts of the limited company, the difference being in the amount of information disclosed, and in the particular format used. The Companies Act 1981 sets out in great detail what must be disclosed in the published accounts, and the form in which those accounts are to be presented. Moreover, successive Acts up to 1981 require the Directors' Report, which must be attached to every published balance sheet, to include statements of fact and opinion on many financial matters. Before looking at some of the statutory requirements, however, it is worth reflecting upon four general questions:

(1) For whom is the information disclosed?
(2) What is the objective of disclosure?
(3) How much should be disclosed?
(4) How should the information be disclosed?

(1)   Disclosure for whom?

It may be argued that all parties who have a direct or indirect interest in the activities of an organization have a right to information about that organization. This view represents a considerable broadening of the corporate responsibilities since the Companies Acts of the nineteenth century when the focus of attention was exclusively the creditor and shareholder.

There are, however, many groups who have an 'interest' in the activities of a company, and these include

(i)   the shareholder;
(ii)   the loan creditor (debenture holder);
(iii)   the employee;
(iv)   the financial analyst;
(v)   the trade creditor;
(vi)   the trade competitor;
(vii)   the government;
(viii) the public at large, e.g. consumers, taxpayers, environmental groups, etc.

A moment's reflection will show that the information needs of these groups are very different, and this leads us to consider the second stage of the problem—the reasons for disclosing information.

(2)   Disclosure for what?

The traditional view of disclosure is that company reports should essentially be an opportunity for the directors to offer an account of their stewardship of the assets entrusted to them. Essentially the directors are seen as protecting and managing the assets and reporting in retrospect to the shareholders on the success or otherwise of their endeavours. That area of company law which is directed towards the disclosure of financial information is almost exclusively based upon the 'stewardship' view, and financial accounting itself is directed towards establishing a 'true and fair' view of the company's financial status based upon historic evidence.

A more sophisticated view of the purposes of disclosure still centres upon the shareholder and potential shareholder as the recipient of the information, but argues that their need for information is to enable them to make rational decisions about their future investment policy—whether to continue to hold their current shares, sell them, or buy additional shares in the company. To make decisions about the future requires predictions about the future, and unless accounts produced to satisfy historic steward-ship needs are regarded as a satisfactory basis for extrapolation, then financial reporting as currently practised does not satisfy this purpose.

The third view of disclosure is that all the interested parties have a need for financial information in order to satisfy their various needs and purposes, and that the public company is accountable as much to society at large as to the relatively small group of its shareholders. This society-wide view of accounting responsibilities is considered in the final chapter of this book, but we must note at this stage that the sheer diversity of the information requirements of the different groups poses substantial problems for the company. It is doubtful whether any one financial statement can reflect the particular needs of all of the groups.

(3)   How much disclosure?

Discussions about the amount of information which should be disclosed by the financial reports of the company tend to centre upon the stewardship view of the purposes of disclosure, but even in this context proves to be a complex and contentious issue. To disclose all information could place the company—and therefore the shareholder—in a detrimental position to compete with unincorporated firms who do not have to disclose anything. Too little disclosure would be detrimental to the shareholder and creditor in relation to the decisions mentioned above. The general criterion would appear to be that information relating to transactions should be disclosed if the knowledge of such information would be significant to an investor.

(4)   Disclosure by what means?

Even if agreement could be obtained upon the audience for the purposes and amount of disclosure, there still remains the need to ascertain the means by which that information should be conveyed. Whatever the vehicle for disclosure, however, the Corporate Report (1975) has set out the characteristics which should pervade any financial reporting. This states that any such reports should be

(i)   relevant, i.e. satisfying the needs of those who use them;
(ii)   understandable, i.e. presented in such a way that the reader will be helped rather than confused;
(iii)   complete, i.e. full enough not to omit any aspect of the company's activities which might cause the recipient to alter his view on the company's past or future performance;
(iv)   reliable, which in general means that the information should have been independently verified;
(v)   objective, or not slanted or biased towards the needs and views of any one of the user groups;
(vi)   timely, in that the information should be published as soon as possible after the end of the period to which it relates;
(vii)   comparable, i.e. expressed in terms which will enable the user to evaluate and compare the performance of the company over time and with other similar companies.

Some of these characteristics may, of course, be in conflict. For example, the need for a report to be understandable may be inconsistent with the need for completeness which requires the incorporation of complex, lengthy information. Or again, if potential investors are seeking guidance as to future income and growth, the relevant information will, of necessity, be a matter of informed opinion rather than independently verifiable fact.

Statutory requirements and published accounts

It is beyond the scope of this text to explore in detail the statutory requirements of the Companies Acts as they relate to the form of published accounts. However, as the Companies Act 1981 has dramatically changed the previous position by laying down not only what *must* be disclosed in the published accounts but *how* it is disclosed, and as published accounts are the major source of information about a company's activities, then some basic knowledge is essential.

The reporting requirements do not apply equally to all companies, for small- and medium-sized companies do not have to file a 'complete' set of final accounts with the registrar of companies. Section 8 of the Companies Act 1981 provides that small companies (i.e total assets less than £700,000, turnover less than £1.4 million and with less than 50 employees) need not file a profit and loss account nor a directors' report, and that medium-sized companies (i.e. total assets less than £2.8 million, turnover less than £5.75 million, and with less than 250 employees) need not provide so detailed a profit and loss account. The observations in the remainder of this chapter, however, deal only with the accounting requirements imposed on large companies.

The 1981 Act provides four alternative formats for profit and loss accounts. We will consider only Format 1, however, because that is closest to the format we have already used for internal purposes. The details of Format 1 will be found in the Appendix on the next page, but it is important to note that the list of items to be disclosed must be displayed in the order laid down. If we apply the format to the example on page 207, we have:

Astral PLC
Profit and Loss Account for the year ended 31 December 1983

	£	£
1 Turnover		800,000
2 Cost of sales		350,000
3 Gross profit		450,000
4 Distribution costs	165,000	
5 Administrative expenses	186,000	351,000
		99,000
6 Other operating income	500	
9 Income from other fixed asset investments	2,500	3,000
		102,000
12 Interest payable		6,000
		96,000
13 Tax on profit on ordinary activities		35,000
14 Profit on ordinary activities after taxation		**£61,000**

The Act prescribes no sub-totals whatsoever, so this is a matter of choice for the company, and also lays down no format for the appropriation account. However, as the Act elsewhere requires the disclosure of movements on reserves and disclosure of dividends paid and proposed, most companies will probably use the format similar to that in the 'internal' accounts (see page 208). This format clearly reduces the detail of the internal accounts, but the

Act goes on to itemize in Schedule 1a requirement to publish 'information supplementing the profit and loss account'. This includes such items as details of interest, auditors' remuneration, depreciation, a breakdown of turnover by classes of activity, and particulars of employee numbers and earnings.

Further disclosure is also required through the medium of the directors' report, and the cumulative effect of successive Companies Acts now adds significantly to the sum of available information. The report must cover, *inter alia*, changes in fixed assets, the market value of land, directors' interest in the shares or debentures of the company, arrangements for securing the health and safety at work of employees, political and charitable contributions made, and the employment of disabled persons.

The Companies Act 1981 permits two alternative formats for the balance sheet, and the layout illustrated on page 209 broadly complies with the requirements of Format 1. However, as with the published profit and loss account, the Act also requires 'information supplementing the balance sheet'. This covers such matters as authorized share capital, details of share and debenture issue, movements on fixed assets and associated depreciation, market values of investments, and details of indebtedness—essentially an analysis of creditors.

There can be no doubt that the Companies Act 1981 has ushered in a new era of disclosure, and that much of the secretiveness embraced and supported in the pre-1948 era has been swept away by a tide of social concern—the company is increasingly seen as being accountable to society at large, and hence is required to display its activities in a more open manner. How much further the process will go depends upon the extent to which the philosophies of 'open government' of environmental and social concern gain ground over the narrower view that the company exists for its shareholders.

Appendix 1

Companies Act 1981—Schedule 1 Part 1
Profit and loss—Format 1

1   Turnover
2   Cost of sales
3   Gross profit or loss
4   Distribution costs
5   Administrative expenses
6   Other operating income
7   Income from shares in group companies
8   Income from shares in related companies
9   Income from other fixed asset investments
10   Other interest receivable and similar income
11   Amounts written off investments
12   Interest payable and similar charges
13   Tax on profit or loss on ordinary activities
14   Profit or loss on ordinary activities after taxation
15   Extraordinary income

16   Extraordinary charges
17   Extraordinary profit or loss
18   Tax on extraordinary profit or loss
19   Other taxes not shown under the above items
20   Profit or loss for the financial year

References and further reading

ACCOUNTING STANDARDS STEERING COMMITTEE (1975), *The Corporate Report.*
BACKER and HASLEM (1973), 'Information Needs of Industrial Investors', *Journal of Accountancy*, November 1973.
BIRD (1973), *Accountability: Standards in Financial Reporting.* Accountancy Age Books.
CARSBERG, HOPE and SCAPENS (1978), 'The Objectives of Published Accounting Reports', *Accounting and Business Research,* Summer 1978.
COMPANIES ACTS 1948, 1967, 1976, 1980, 1981. HMSO.
GOWER (1974), *Modern Company Law.* Stevens.
INSTITUTE OF CHARTERED ACCOUNTANTS IN ENGLAND AND WALES (1982), 'Accounting Requirements of The Companies Acts'. Gee & Co.
PURDY (1973), 'Disclosure of Information', *Accountancy,* December 1973.

Questions for discussion

1   Explain carefully the main differences between a limited company and a partnership. What advantages do you see in turning a partnership into a limited company?
2   Obtain a recent copy of the *Financial Times* in which there is a company prospectus. Ascertain from it:

   (i)   The objective of the company.
   (ii)   The structure of the share capital.
   (iii) The type, number and price of the shares being offered to the public.
   (iv)   The trend of the company profits.

   What factors might influence you in deciding whether to invest in the company?
3   Obtain, from a library, a copy of a company Memorandum and Articles of Association. From the Memorandum, identify the main purposes of the company. From the Articles, ascertain the powers and limitations of the directors.
4   Draw up a table distinguishing between ordinary shares, preference shares and debentures under the following headings:

   (i)   Status of holders.
   (ii)   Rights to dividend/interest.

(iii) Voting rights.
(iv) Security of holders' investment.
(v) Rights to capital in the event of liquidation.

5 Balance Sheet of A Ltd

	£		£
£1 ordinary shares	20,000	Fixed assets	49,000
8% £1 preference shares	12,000		
Share premium	2,000		
Undistributed profit	8,000		
General reserve	10,000	Current assets	14,000
5% Debentures	7,000		
Current liabilities	4,000		
	63,000		63,000

(a) What is the par value of (i) the ordinary share, and (ii) the preference share?
(b) What dividend will the preference shareholder receive? Are the preference shares 'cumulative'?
(c) What is the book value of each ordinary share, assuming that the preference shareholder is entitled to a return of capital only?
(d) Why might the par value, book value and market value of the ordinary shares be different?
(e) If the ordinary shareholders normally received a dividend of 10 per cent and sought a yield of 12 per cent, what would be the market price?
(f) What interest would be paid to the debenture holders? Explain whether this is an expense or an appropriation of profit.

6 A company which currently has a share capital consisting only of 100,000 £1 ordinary shares wishes to raise an additional £50,000 of capital. List the different ways in which the company might raise this sum, and explain what factors would influence the form in which this capital is raised.

7 An abridged balance sheet of B Ltd shows the following:

100,000 £1 ordinary shares	100,000
Reserves	90,000
	£190,000

The company currently distributes all of its profits of £25,000 to its shareholders. It now wishes to raise an additional £80,000 by issuing further ordinary shares, estimating that it will earn a further £20,000 profit from these funds. Explain why the company would issue these new shares at a premium, and calculate the issue price.

8   Using suitable data, explain why the market price of an ordinary share is likely to fluctuate more in a highly geared than in a low-geared company. Why would you prefer to be an ordinary shareholder in a high-geared company when profits are high, even though a low-geared company may be earning the same level of profits?

9   Distinguish carefully between a capital and revenue reserve; explain into which category each of the following falls, and how it may have arisen:
(i)   Share premium.
(ii)   Revaluation reserve.
(iii)   Redemption reserve.
(iv)   General reserve.
(v)   Dividend equalization reserve.
(vi)   Stock replacement reserve.
(vii)   Undistributed profit.

10   A limited company issues the following capital:

50,000 £1 ordinary shares at a premium of 20p per share.
20,000 £1 5% preference shares at a premium of 5p per share.
30,000 10% debentures at a discount of 4 per cent.
(a)   Write up the necessary ledger accounts to record the issues.
(b)   Show how the relevant accounts would be presented on the balance sheet.

11   The company in question 10 above pays and declares the following dividends and interest in 1984:

Interim dividends paid
   5% ordinary
   $2\frac{1}{2}$% preference
Debenture interest paid, 5%

The directors propose to pay the remaining debenture interest, and declare the following final dividends:

$7\frac{1}{2}$% ordinary
$2\frac{1}{2}$% preference

Write up the ledger accounts necessary to record the above.

12   The following list of balances was extracted from the books of Newman PLC on the 31 December 1984:

	£'000	£'000
£1 ordinary shares		250
8% £1 preference shares		50
Share premium		20
General reserve		12
Profit and loss account		58
Stock	66	

	£	£
Sales		964
Purchases	501	
Returns inwards and outwards	28	
Carriage inwards	1	
Carriage outwards	10	
Salesmen's salaries	64	
Administrative wages and salaries	59	
Plant and machinery	125	
Motor vehicles (distribution)	90	
Provision for depreciation—plant		59
—vehicles		30
Goodwill	85	
General distribution expenses	23	
General administrative expenses	23	
Directors' remuneration	30	
Rent receivable		8
Trade debtors	310	
Trade creditors (payable before 31/12/85)		59
10% debentures		20
Cash at bank and in hand	140	
	£1,555	**£1,555**

Notes:
(i)   Stock at 31 December 1984 £90,000.
(ii)   Provide for depreciation of plant and machinery at 20 per cent on cost, and on motor vehciles at 25 per cent of the written down value.
(iii)   Accrue auditors' fees £3,000.
(iv)   Provide for corporation tax of £45,000.
(v)   Debenture interest accrued £2,000.
(vi)   Provide for the preference dividend and an ordinary dividend of 10 per cent.
(vii)   General administrative expenses include rates prepaid £1,000.
(viii) Transfer £40,000 to general reserve.

Required:
(i)   Prepare *for internal use* the trading, profit and loss and appropriation account for the year ended 31 December 1984 and a balance sheet as at that date.
(ii)   In so far as the information provided allows, prepare the final accounts *in published form.*

13   The trial balance of Undercliffe PLC as on 31 December 1984 is as follows:

	£'000	£'000
Ordinary shares (50p)		120
6% £1 preference shares		100
General reserve		90
Revaluation reserve		25
Undistributed profit		40
Stock	220	
Land and buildings (valuation)	200	

	£	£
Sales		900
Returns inwards	22	
Wages and salaries (sales)	60	
Wages and salaries (administrative)	69	
Motor expenses	32	
General distribution expenses	16	
General administrative expenses	18	
Debenture interest	20	
Debentures		160
Royalties		10
Directors' remuneration	38	
Bad debts	6	
Discounts allowed and received	10	
Plant and equipment (cost)	250	
Provision for depreciation (plant)		120
Motor vehicles (used for distribution)	70	
Provision for depreciation (vehicles)		28
Development costs	38	
Goodwill	55	
Trade debtors and creditors	50	65
Bank overdraft		20
Purchases	513	
	£1,687	**£1,687**

Inspection of the company's records yields the following additional information.

Notes:
(i)   Closing stock £288,000.
(ii) Provide for depreciation of plant and equipment at 10 per cent on cost, and on motor vehicles at 20 per cent on cost.
(iii) Provide for corporation tax £60,000.
(iv) Auditors' fees accrued £4,000.
(v)   A provision for doubtful debts is required equal to 4 per cent of debtors.
(vi) The directors propose to pay the preference dividend and an ordinary dividend of 10p per share.
(vii) Transfer £25,000 to general reserve.

Required:
(i)   Prepare, for internal use, a trading, profit and loss and appropriation account for the period ended 31 December 1984 and a balance sheet as at that date.
(ii) If the accounts had been prepaid for publication explain under which heading you would incorporate.ᵒ

   (a) Discounts received.
   (b) Discounts allowed.
   (c) Provision for doubtful debts.
   (d) Bad debts.

14 One of the directors of Loose Leaf Ltd comes to you with the following questions about a set of final accounts which you, the company accountant, have just produced prior to their being audited:

(i)   I'm a bit unhappy about the profits being so high this year, in view of the amount of tax we'll have to pay—can't we transfer some of the profits to reserve and cut down the tax?

(ii)   Reserves are money, aren't they? Then why don't I go and buy some machinery now, and soak up the profits a bit?

(iii) I know you chaps are a bit conservative about things. O.K., well why not charge a bit more depreciation this year since the profits are so good—at least it would be on the safe side?

A year later he is thinking of selling his shares, and he comes to you again with more questions:

(i)   I feel the profits are a bit on the low side. For a start why have you written down one of our investments below cost? After all, you have left freehold land and buildings at cost for years, and their value is rising all the time?

(ii)   If we were to revalue goodwill by £150,000 wouldn't this 'up' the profits. Surely that would be reasonable enough?

(iii) If we were to revalue freehold land and buildings at £950,000 instead of the £250,000 which they cost, at least that would help the profits, wouldn't it?

(iv)   If we sold half the land next year for this sort of amount, would that affect the profit?

(v)   Incidentally the board are a bit unhappy about that auditor chap. He asks too many questions. If he annoys us again this year why don't we get another one? After all, we pay for him.

Required:
Provide explanations in terms the director will understand.

11 The limited company—changes in capital structure and groups of companies

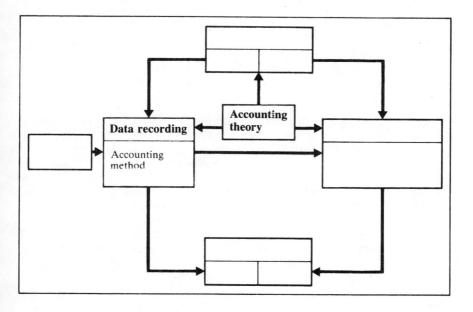

In the previous chapter we considered the legal background of the limited company, the nature of its capital structure, the consequential preparation and presentation of its profit and loss and appropriation account and balance sheet, and some of the issues which surround and underlie the financial reporting of a company's affairs. In this chapter, we shall first further explore the capital structure and the purpose and effect of changes to that structure; secondly, we will consider the accounting problems which occur when companies come together by virtue of one company obtaining a controlling interest in other companies by purchasing their shares to form a group of companies.

Changes in capital structure

In addition to the issue of shares and debentures for cash, there are several ways in which the capital structure of a company may be altered. These are by means of

(1) Bonus or scrip issues.
(2) Rights issues.
(3) Redemption or purchase of shares.
(4) Capital reduction.
(5) Capital reorganization.

(1)   Bonus or scrip issues

In the previous chapter we examined the relationship between the par value and market value of a share, and observed that, in simple terms, the relationship could be described by:

$$\text{Market value per share} = \frac{\text{Par value per share} \times \text{Dividend \%}}{\text{Yield \%}}$$

Over time, it is not uncommon for the market and par values to diverge substantially, because a company does not distribute all of its profits by way of dividend but reinvests them internally. The growing total capital' investment in the company will yield greater and greater profits for the ordinary shareholders. This growth in income, parallelled by a growth in capital, and coupled with a policy of distributing a fixed proportion of the profits, inevitably leads to an increase in the market value of the ordinary shares.

Consider, for example, a company which has a share capital of 100 £1 ordinary shares, an ability to earn a 20 per cent return on the total capital invested, and a policy of distributing one-half of the profits to its shareholders, who are seeking a yield of 10 per cent. The position over three years will be

---

Year 1   Profits: £100 × 20% = £20
Dividends: £20 × ½ = £10

$$\text{Dividend \%} = \frac{10}{100} = 10\%$$

Capital invested
at year end: £100 + (20 − 10) = £110

$$\therefore \text{Market value per share} = \frac{£1 \times 10\%}{10\%} = £1$$

Year 2   Profits: £110 × 20% = £22
Dividends: £22 × ½ = £11

$$\text{Dividend \%}: \frac{11}{100} = 11\%$$

Capital invested
at year end: £110 + (22 − 11) = £121

$$\therefore \text{Market value per share} = \frac{£1 \times 11\%}{10\%} = £1.10$$

Year 3   Profits: £121 × 20% = £24
            Dividends: £24 × ½ = £12

Dividend %: $\dfrac{12}{100}$ = 12%

Capital invested
at year end: £121 + (24 − 12) = £133

∴ Market value per share = $\dfrac{£1 \times 12\%}{10\%}$ = £1.20

With continued prosperity, the percentage dividend grows larger and larger and the market value of the shares diverges further and further from the par value. The growing market value renders them less marketable, because shareholders generally prefer to acquire, say, five shares at £1 each rather than one share at £5. Moreover, shares of lower market value encourage a greater spread of shareholdings which might otherwise become too dominated by a few institutional investors such as pension funds or insurance companies. Since control of a company can be obtained by owning 51 per cent of its equity, the greater the number of shareholders, the more difficult that control is to obtain in a 'takeover' situation.

For these reasons, a company may decide to make a bonus (or scrip) issue of ordinary shares to its existing shareholders, by converting part of its reserves into shares. The mechanics of this are quite simple. Assume that a company has the following capital structure:

	£	£
50,000 £1 ordinary shares		50,000
Reserves		
Share premium	10,000	
General reserve	60,000	
Undistributed profit	45,000	
		115,000
Shareholders' Funds		**165,000**

The company decides to make a bonus issue of two ordinary shares for every one currently held, by capitalizing its reserves. Since the share premium account is a capital reserve (*see* page 196) and cannot be used to effect a dividend distribution, it is usual (and expressly permitted by the Companies Act 1948, Section 56) to exhaust this reserve first before passing to any revenue reserves. The result of the bonus issue is

	£
150,000 £1 ordinary shares	150,000
Reserves	
Undistributed profit	15,000
Shareholders' funds	165,000

It is important to note that the term 'bonus' is rather misleading, for the shareholders, although they have more shares (2 for 1) than before, are no better off because the market value of the shares will fall *pro rata* —the object of the exercise from the company's point of view. The reason for this is that, as the capitalization of reserves does not introduce additional funds into the company, the level of profits and funds available for dividends will remain the same as before. As there are now more shares pursuing the same total dividend, the price of each share will fall.

For example, if before the bonus issue the dividend distribution was 30p (or 30 per cent) per share, and the desired yield was 10 per cent, the market price per share would be

$$\frac{£1 \times 30\%}{10\%} = £3 \text{ per share}$$

and the company would distribute 30p × 50,000 = £15,000 by way of total dividends. After the bonus issue, the £15,000 and no more will be available for dividend, which will fall to 15,000/150,000 or 10 per cent. The market value per share will therefore fall to

$$\frac{£1 \times 10\%}{10\%} = £1 \text{ per share}$$

A shareholder, who previously held 10 shares worth £3 each, £30 in all, will now hold 30 shares worth £1 each, still £30 in all.

(2)   Rights issues

When a company has a long-established reputation and its shares are widely held, it almost always raises new equity capital by inviting existing share-holders to subscribe for additional ordinary shares. This procedure is known as a 'rights' issue, and has the advantages of cheapness (there is no need to issue a prospectus), maintenance of control (the shareholders remain the same), and confirmation of existing members' confidence in the future of the company.

The issue price is usually set below the market price of the existing shares, as an inducement to the existing shareholders to take up their new share in full. This reduced price, however, is rather illusory as, all other things being equal, the market price of all of the shares after the issue will be adjusted to the weighted average of the market price of the old shares and the issue price of the rights issue. This adjustment is, in fact, the result of a complex series of judgements which the market must make, viz.:

(i)   The rapidity to which the new funds can be put to profitable use by the company, and the extent of those profits.
(ii)   The extent to which future dividends per share will be increased, decreased, or held constant.
(iii) The extent to which the changes in the equity of the company increase or decrease the risk being run by the ordinary shareholder, thus affecting the desired yield.

These judgements will cause some adjustments to the 'weighted average' price, which will be reached as follows:

Original shares: 50,000 £1 ordinary
Market value = £1.80 per share
Rights issue (2 for 5): 20,000 £1 ordinary
Issue price = £1.60 per share

$$\text{Weighted average} = \frac{1.80 \times 50,000 + 1.60 \times 20,000}{50,000 + 20,000}$$

$$= £1.7429 \text{ per share}$$

This new price leaves the shareholder, in theory at any rate, indifferent as between taking up the rights offer and selling his rights. Before the rights issue he had five shares worth $5 \times £1.80 = £9$. He then invests a further £3.20 of his own money $(2 \times £1.60)$, making his total investment £12.20. He now, however, holds seven shares each worth £1.7429 per share, or £12.20 in total. If he sells his rights, he will make a profit of $2(1.7429 - 1.60) = £0.2858$, and as his five remaining shares are worth $5 \times 1.7429 = £8.7145$, his profit and his shareholding together total his original worth of £9.

The accounting procedure for recording rights issues is no different from the issue of any shares outlined in the previous chapter. The par value of the issue is taken to the credit of the share capital account, and any premium to the credit of the share premium account.

(3)   Redemption and purchase of shares

The Companies Act 1929 gave companies the power to issue redeemable preference shares, that is shares which were capable of being bought back by the company directly from the shareholders. This provision, re-enacted by the Companies Act 1948, has now been repealed and replaced by the more extensive provisions of Sections 45 and 46 of the Companies Act 1981. Section 45 gives companies the power to issue both ordinary and preference redeemable shares, and Section 46 the power to purchase their own shares, whether redeemable or not, subject in both cases to specified conditions.

It must be noted that whether shares are 'redeemed' or 'purchased' there is still the same outflow of cash from the company, the only difference being the legal one that the buying back by the company of shares stated to be redeemable at their time of issue is 'redemption', and that the buying back of shares not stated to be redeemable at the time of issue is 'purchase'.

Until 1981, the law in the UK was out of step with the rest of Europe and the United States where, for many years, companies had had the power to buy back their own shares. The more restrictive practice of the UK was justified primarily on the ground that creditors might be adversely affected if a company used its available cash to purchase its own shares. Since preference shares were usually the smaller proportion of the issued capital, it was considered that there would be less risk of abuse and potential damage to creditors if the right to issue redeemable shares was limited to preference shares. Although a company can now redeem or purchase its own shares, it can do so only with the proviso that it must still have on issue shares which are not redeemable and must have, after any purchase, at least two members. Without this restriction, it would be possible for a company to redeem and purchase its whole share capital and hence cease to have any shareholders.

Many of the advantages of this provision accrue to the private company where shares are not bought and sold on an open market. It is often difficult, particularly in family businesses, to sell these shares, and hence this provision could encourage a greater range of investors who need no longer fear difficulties in disposing of their shareholding. From the standpoint of the public company, however—which will continue to be our focus of attention—the main advantage will accrue to those with surplus cash who can now return that cash to shareholders by buying back some of its own shares, rather than perhaps seeking to use that cash in uneconomic ways. In addition, public companies can use this power as a strategic device to enable them to change the balance of their capital structure in response to changing market circumstances.

Both past and current Companies Acts, however, have always required a company to 'maintain capital intact' (*see* Section 53, Companies Act 1981). We have already seen the effect of this provision in that dividends cannot be paid out of capital—they can only be paid if sufficient profit and revenue reserves, together with associated cash, are available—but where shares are redeemed (other than out of the proceeds of a new issue) or purchased, the company must transfer to a capital reserve a sum equal to the par value of the shares redeemed.

Since the effects of a redemption or purchase are identical, we may illustrate the effect of this requirement through a redemption of preference shares without a replacement issue by assuming the following data:

AB PLC
Balance Sheet as at 31 December 1984

	£		£
£1 ordinary shares	100,000		
6% preference shares	50,000	Cash	65,000
Share premium	20,000	Other net assets	205,000
General reserve	40,000		
Profit and loss	60,000		
	270,000		270,000

The company then redeems the preference shares at a premium of 5 per cent. This means that the preference shareholders will receive £52,500, of which £50,000 will be transferred from a revenue reserve to the 'capital redemption reserve'—which like any other capital reserve can never be used for the purposes of dividend distribution—and £2,500 will be debited to the share premium account—one of the few uses for which the share premium may be used (*see* 'Bonus or scrip issues', page 222). The ledger accounts will be

Cash A/c

Balance	65,000	Prefer-	
		ence	
		shares	50,000
		Share	
		premium	2,500
		Balance c/d	12,500
	65,000		65,000
Balance b/d	12,500		

Share premium A/c

Cash A/c	2,500	Balance	20,000
Balance c/d	17,500		
	20,000		20,000
		Balance b/d	17,500

6% Preference share A/c

Cash	**50,000**	Balance c/d	**50,000**
Balance b/d	50,000		

Capital redemption reserve A/c

Balance c/d	50,000	General	
		reserve	40,000
		Profit and	
		loss	10,000
	50,000		**50,000**
		Balance b/d	50,000

General reserve A/c

Capital		Balance c/d	40,000
redemp-			
tion			
reserve	40,000		
	40,000		**40,000**
Balance b/d	40,000		

Profit and loss A/c

Capital redemption reserve	10,000	Balance	60,000
Balance c/d	50,000		
	60,000		60,000
		Balance b/d	50,000

After redemption, therefore, the balance sheet will appear as

AB PLC
Balance Sheet as at 1 January 1985

	£		£
£1 ordinary shares	100,000	Cash	12,500
Share premium	17,500	Other net assets	205,000
Capital redemption reserve	50,000		
Profit and loss	50,000		
	217,500		**217,500**

Although in the example above we have written off the premium payable on purchase/redemption to the share premium account, this can only be done if the shares purchased/redeemed were originally issued at a premium. If they were not, then the premium on purchase/redemption must be written off against a revenue reserve (Section 45, Companies Act 1981). This requirement is directed towards capital maintenance, for to use a capital reserve to pay a premium which was not originally part of contributed capital would, in essence, be reducing capital.

(4) Capital reduction

Where a company has for many years been trading at a loss, a debit balance will accumulate on the profit and loss account with the consequential effect that the value of the shareholders' capital has been eroded. If the company were to go into liquidation, then the lower values often obtained by the piecemeal realization of the company's assets may result in greater loss to the shareholders than if they accept some partial reduction in their capital and allow the company to continue to trade on a reduced scale, and, hopefully, more successfully. Such a reduction in share capital must be authorized by the articles and confirmed by the High Court. The court will not permit such a scheme if any creditors object and those objecting cannot receive or be assured that their claim will be met in full.

The elimination of the debit balance on the profit and loss account, by writing down the share capital, is often a very necessary step if fresh investors are to be persuaded to subscribe to any new issue of capital, for there is no prospect of future dividends whilst there is an uncleared debit balance on the profit and loss account. Detailed consideration of capital reduction schemes are beyond the scope of this book, but a simple illustration may help appreciation of the essential elements of such schemes:

XY PLC
Balance Sheet as at 31 December 1984

	£	£		£
100,000 £1 ordinary	100,000		Sundry assets	105,000
20,000 6% £1 preference	20,000			
Share premium	10,000			
	130,000			
Less: Debit balance				
on profit and loss	50,000			
		80,000		
Current liabilities		25,000		
		105,000		105,000

The company proposes to revalue the assets at £75,000, eliminate the share premium account, and to write off the ordinary share capital as required, consolidating the reduced shares into new ones of £1. The effect of these changes is reflected by a capital reduction account, viz:

Capital reduction A/c

	£		£
Profit and loss	50,000	Ordinary share capital	100,000
Sundry assets	30,000	Share premium	10,000
New ordinary share capital	30,000		
	110,000		110,000

This means that for every 10 £1 old shares, the shareholder will now hold 3 £1 new shares—effectively a bonus issue in reverse. The new balance sheet will be

XY PLC
Balance Sheet as at 1 January 1985

	£		£
New £1 ordinary shares	30,000	Sundry assets	75,000
20,000 6% £1 preference	20,000		
Current liabilities	25,000		
	75,000		75,000

(5)   Capital reorganization

A company may sometimes wish to vary the rights of its existing share-holders without recourse to any new issues or repayments of capital. In the 1960s, for example, the tax system was such that it was more beneficial for a company to pay interest to debenture holders where the interest was allowable as an expense against tax, than to pay a dividend to preference shareholders—which was not chargeable against tax. Hence, many com-panies sought to persuade preference shareholders to convert their shares into debentures, often on very advantageous terms. Such reorganization needs the consent of 75 per cent of the affected shareholders and if the minority of 15 per cent or more feel aggrieved they can apply to the High Court to prevent the variation in their rights.

Groups of companies

Business activity is a dynamic process, and many companies expand their activities not only by reinvesting funds within the company—internal growth—but by acquiring the control of and combining with other existing companies—external growth. The reasons for external growth are numer-ous, and any combination is usually the result of a number of equally important considerations. Many companies are seeking economies of scale through the elimination of duplicate marketing or production facilities; combinations are said to be 'vertical' when a company acquires control of its suppliers (backward integration) or its ultimate consumers (forward integration) and 'horizontal' when two similar companies are involved.

Diversification is a motive for some combinations; this is often a device for spreading risk and for acquiring growth potential where the existing market has reached saturation point. The analysis of business combinations is a fascinating study in itself, and the interested reader should refer to the appropriate economic texts. The purpose of this and the following sections, however, is to identify in principle the accounting problems which are the result of business combinations.

A company may gain control of another company either by the acquisition of all the rights of the shareholders of that company or by the purchase of sufficient of those rights to give effective control. In the former case, company X may 'absorb' company Y by paying the shareholders of company Y in cash or by the issue of shares or debentures in company X: company X therefore retains its legal identity, but company Y ceases to exist. Alternatively, companies X and Y may 'amalgamate', in which case a new company Z is formed, and both X and Y cease to exist. The most interesting problem in these circumstances is the valuation to be placed upon the company being absorbed, and, in practice, this is often the subject of protracted negotiations between the management of the two companies. The accounting problems involved once the price is agreed are purely transitory, and, once over, pose no further problems. Hence, our main interest in this chapter is in the second method of control—the acquisition by company X of sufficient of the rights of the shareholders of company

Y to give effective control. In these circumstances, company X is referred to as the 'holding' company, and company Y as the 'subsidiary'.

(1)   Holding companies

Exactly when one company becomes a subsidiary of another is a matter of law. Section 154 of the Companies Act 1948 states:

> 'A company shall . . . . . . be deemed to be a subsidiary of another if, but only if—
> (a) that other either—
> (i) is a member of it and controls the composition of its board of directors; or
> (ii) holds more than half in nominal value of its equity share capital;
> or
> (b) the first mentioned company is a subsidiary of any company which is that other's subsidiary.'

Relationships between companies can be incredibly complex. For example, company A may hold 60 per cent of the equity in each of companies B and C, which in their turn each hold a controlling interest in D and E, and F and G respectively. This 'pyramiding' effect poses considerable theoretical problems of income measurement and valuation, for, by law (Section 151, Companies Act 1948), company A must 'consolidate' the accounts of all subsidiaries and present a consolidated balance sheet and profit and loss account.

There is now (Section 2, Companies Act 1981) an overriding requirement that the group accounts show a true and fair view of the state of affairs and profit and loss of the holding company and subsidiaries dealt with as a whole. It is also worth noting in passing that although the 1981 Act sought to bring the UK into line with European practice, the UK law on the need for consolidated accounts is a good deal tighter than the EEC Commission's Seventh Directive. That directive requires group accounts only where a 'dominant undertaking' exercises in practice a dominant influence on dependant undertakings. The UK law is cast in terms of legal ownership or control, but the EEC directive hinges upon whether that control is actually exercised—a condition often most difficult to determine. UK law is also backed by an accounting standard—SSAP 14 Group Accounts.

This text can do no more than provide an introduction to what is a fascinating but extremely complex subject, and hence the illustrations which follow are grossly simplified, serving only to illustrate in principle the problems which arise.

(2)   The consolidated balance sheet

Let us suppose that A PLC acquires 80 per cent of equity of B PLC at 1 January 1984, and that the balance sheets of the two companies immediately after the merger are

	A £'000	B £'000		A £'000	B £'000
Share capital			Assets	115	86
5% preference	25	20	Investment in B	60	
ordinary	100	50			
Reserves	25	8			
Creditors	25	8			
	£175	**£86**		**£175**	**£86**

The book value of B's equity is

	£	£
Assets		86,000
Less: Creditors	8,000	
Preference shares	20,000	
		28,000
		£58,000

A PLC has acquired 80 per cent of the equity:

80% × 58,000 =	£46,400
but has paid	£60,000
Cost of control (goodwill)	**£13,600**

The excess of the purchase price over the book value, £13,600 is referred to as the 'goodwill'.

Twenty per cent of the equity of B PLC still remains the original shareholders' property. The book value of this must be

Total value of equity in B PLC	£58,000
Less: Value acquired by A PLC	46,400
Value of equity attributable to original shareholders	**£11,600**

This £11,600 is composed of

20% × 50,000 ordinary	10,000
20% × 8,000 reserves	1,600
	£11,600

This remaining equity interest together with the preference shareholders form the 'outside interest' or 'minority shareholding' in the consolidated accounts, some £31,600.

Redrafting B's balance sheet to reflect this information:

	£'000		£'000
Creditors	8	Goodwill of A	13.6
Minority interest	31.6	Other assets	86
Investment by A	60		
	99.6		**99.6**

Substituting for the £60,000 investment which appears in A's balance sheet, the consolidated balance sheet will become

	£'000		£'000
Ordinary shares	100	Goodwill	13.6
Preference shares	25	Assets	201.0
Reserves	25		
Creditors	33		
Minority shareholders	31.6		
	214.6		**214.6**

(3)   The consolidated income statement—dividends and reserves

The minority shareholders are entitled to receive the appropriate proportion of any dividends declared by B PLC, and also participate in any reserves which accumulate after the acquisition date. We may illustrate this, assuming that B PLC declares an ordinary dividend of 10 per cent and a preference dividend of 5 per cent:

	A £	B £
Net trading profit	25,000	9,000
Ordinary dividend declared by B		
(80% × 10% × £50,000)	4,000	—
Profit available for distribution	29,000	9,000

Dividends proposed:

10% ordinary dividend	10,000	5,000
5% preference dividend	1,250	1,000
Retained profits	17,750	3,000
	29,000	**9,000**

The minority interest in the profits of **B PLC** is

Ordinary dividend 20% × 5,000	1,000
Preference dividend	1,000
Retained profits 20% × 3,000	600
	2,600

On consolidation the dividends payable by B PLC and the corresponding dividends receivable by A PLC are eliminated:

Consolidated income statement

	£
Group trading profit	**34,000**
Dividends proposed (A PLC)	
10% ordinary	10,000
5% preference	1,250
Retained profit	
(17,750 + 80% × 3,000)	20,150
Minority interest	2,600
	£34,000

In the consolidated balance sheet the reserves will rise by £20,150 and the minority interest by £2,600.

(4)   The consolidated income statement—inter-company transactions

Inter-company transactions can pose considerable practical and theoretical problems, but the crux of the problem can be illustrated simply.

The basic principle is that there can be no profits on transactions which take place entirely *within* the group. This is totally in accord with the realization postulate since there has been no objective measurement of the worth of the asset so transferred. If, however, after the inter-group transaction the asset is sold outside the group then the profit is realized.

For example, if within the same accounting period, the subsidiary company B transfers to the holding company A goods which cost £100 for £110, and then A sells to an outside party for £120, the realized group profit is £20. If, however, at the balance sheet date A still holds the goods, then the 'profit' of £10 must be eliminated, and the goods shown at original cost £100 on the group balance sheet.

A complication arises, however, when the subsidiary is only partly owned. Assume that A holds 80 per cent of the equity of B, and that B has transferred to A goods costing £100 for £110 which A still holds at balance sheet date. As there is a minority shareholding in B it can be argued that their portion of the 'profit' is properly realized, and that therefore the stock should be shown at £102—the £2 profit being attributable to the minority interest.

The situation is clearly artificial, for the same transaction both does and does not satisfy the realization postulate depending whether one stresses the inter-company nature of the transaction or the position of the minority shareholders. One can further argue that such attribution of profit to the profit is being anticipated in so far as it is assumed that company A will eventually be able to sell the goods to an outside party for at least £102.

References and further reading

ACCOUNTING STANDARDS STEERING COMMITTEE (1975), *The Corporate Report.*

BIRD (1973), *Accountability: Standards in Financial Reporting.* Accountancy Age Books.

CARSBERG, HOPE and SCAPENS (1978), 'The Objectives of Published Accounting Reports', *Accounting and Business Research*, Summer 1978.

COMPANIES ACTS, 1948, 1967, 1976, 1980, 1981 (HMSO).

GOWER (1974), *Modern Company Law.* Stevens.

IAS 3, 'Consolidated Financial Statements', IAS Committee, June 1976.

LEE (1976), *Financial Reporting: Issues and Analyses.* Nelson.

PENROSE (1966), *Theory of the Growth of Firms.*

PURDY (1973), 'Disclosure of Information', *Accountancy*, December 1973.

SSAP 14 Group Accounts, Institute of Chartered Accountants.

Questions for discussion

1   Distinguish carefully between a bonus (or scrip) issue and a rights issue. In what circumstances may a company wish to make either type of issue?

2   The balance sheet of Menis PLC is as follows:

	£		£
Ordinary share capital (£1)	60,000	Sundry assets	195,000
Share premium	20,000		
General reserve	40,000		
Profit and loss	60,000		
Current liabilities	15,000		
	195,000		195,000

The company has normally paid a dividend of 30 per cent, the market price of the shares reflecting the shareholders' acceptance of an 8 per cent yield. The company now proposes to make a scrip issue of two ordinary shares for every three currently held:

(a) What is the purpose of such an issue?
(b) What expenses would be incurred by the company?
(c) What is the effect on future dividends?
(d) What reserves can be used for this purpose?
(e) What is the market value of an ordinary share before and after the issue?
(f) Show the ledger accounts to give effect to the issue.
(g) Draw up a balance sheet after the issue has been made.

3   'Shareholders get something for nothing when a company issues bonus shares.' Do you agree?

4   Explain why the market price of a share may diverge from the par value of that share.

5   The balance sheet of Eaton PLC is as follows:

20,000 £1 ordinary shares	20,000	Sundry assets	35,000
Share premium	2,000	Bank	5,000
Undistributed profit	14,000		
Current liabilities	4,000		
	40,000		40,000

The market price of the ordinary shares is £1.50, and the company proposes to make a rights issue of 1 for 2 at a price of £1.30 per share:

(a) What is the likely market price of the ordinary shares after the rights issue?
(b) Show why an ordinary shareholder is indifferent between taking up the rights offer and selling his rights.
(c) Prepare the ledger accounts to give effect to the rights issue.
(d) Draw up the balance sheet after the issue has been made.

6   Ask your library to supply you with some back copies of the *Financial Times* and find a company which has made a rights issue. Using EXTEL (or some similar source) discover what you can about the company's financial history and capital structure. Discover what the price of the shares was before and after the issue. To what extent does this coincide with the price predicted by the method used in the text? What factors, if any, may have caused the values to diverge?

7   Explain carefully the distinction between 'purchase' and 'redemption' of its own shares by a public company. What limitations and requirements are attached by the Companies Acts to this power?

8 The balance sheet of Tarns PLC is as follows:

	£		£
£1 ordinary shares	50,000	Cash	35,000
6% £1 preference shares	30,000	Other net assets	85,000
Share premium	5,000		
Undistributed profit	35,000		
	120,000		120,000

The company proposes to redeem the preference shares at a premium of 10 per cent by finding the cash from already available internal sources.

Required:

Assuming that the company (i) originally issued the preference shares at a premium of 10p per share, and (ii) originally issued the preference shares at par:

(a) Show the ledger entries necessary to record this redemption.
(b) Prepare the new balance sheet.

9 What are the motives for seeking growth through the acquisition of other businesses?

10 What do you understand by the term 'holding company'?

11 The balance sheet of two companies, A and B, at 31 December 1984, was as follows:

	A £	B £		A £	B £
£1 ordinary shares	200,000	40,000	Assets	195,000	60,000
Reserves	50,000	15,000	Investment		
Current liabilities	20,000	5,000	in B		
			(acquired		
			31.12.84)	75,000	
	270,000	60,000		270,000	60,000

A had acquired 90 per cent of the equity of B on 31 December 1984.

Required:

(a) Calculate the goodwill on acquisition.
(b) What is the value of the minority interest?
(c) Prepare the consolidated balance sheet.

12 The accounts of three companies, A, B and C, at 31 December 1984 were as follows:

	A	B	C
	£	£	£
Net profits after tax	58,500	16,000	(Loss 4,000)
Dividends—proposed	36,000	12,000	
	22,500	4,000	(Loss 4,000)
Balance 1.1.84	29,000	12,000	2,800
	51,500	16,000	(Loss 1,200)

	A	B	C
	£	£	£
Ordinary £1 shares	156,000	80,000	50,000
Retained profits	51,500	16,000	(Loss 1,200)
	207,500	96,000	48,800

	A	B	C
	£	£	£
Fixed assets	80,000	60,000	40,000
Shares in subsidiaries			
B 60,000 £1 ordinary	74,000		
C 30,000 £1 ordinary	40,000		
Stock	38,000	29,000	19,000
Debtors	19,000	18,000	7,000
Cash	14,000	15,000	2,000
	265,000	122,000	68,000
Less:			
Creditors	(21,500)	(14,000)	(19,200)
Proposed dividends	(36,000)	(12,000)	
	207,500	96,000	48,800

A acquired its shareholdings in B and C on 1 January 1984.

Required:

(i) (a) Calculate the minority interest in the *current* profits/losses of B and C;

(b) Calculate the value of the goodwill on the acquisition of B and C;

(c) Calculate the minority interest in B and C at the date of acquisition;

(d) Hence calculate the total minority interest;

(e) Prepare a consolidated profit and loss account showing how the *current* group profit is appropriated;

(f) Prepare a consolidated balance sheet as at 31 December 1984.

(ii) What effect, if any, would the following have on the consolidated accounts:

    (a) If A Ltd had supplied goods to B Ltd for £2,000 (cost £1,500), and those goods had been included in the closing stock of B Ltd?

    (b) If A Ltd had supplied to C Ltd goods for £3,000 (cost £2,400) and half had been sold by C Ltd for £2,000?

    (c) If B Ltd debtors included debit balances for A Ltd £1,000?

    (d) If, when A Ltd had acquired its holding on B Ltd, B Ltd had total revenue reserves of £4,000?

12 Value and income measurement

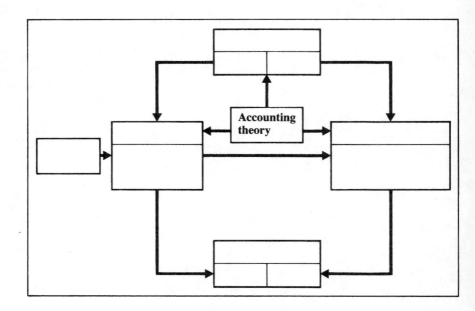

Concepts of value

Value and income measurement lay at the heart of accounting, if we accept the view that accounting information is to enable its users to make rational economic decisions. In Chapter 2 we noted that the concept of value is anything but clear, and the 'value' of an asset is related to the purpose for which the value is to be used. Value relates to the benefit to be derived from having control over an asset or resource—to be able to use, sell or store it as we wish. In essence, there are four different methods which may be applied to asset valuation: (1) historic cost, (2) replacement cost, (3) net realizable value, and (4) net present value.

(1) Historic cost

As we have observed throughout the earlier chapters, value in accounting is closely associated with historic or acquisition cost, or some value derived

240

with reference to that acquisition cost. The equation of value with purchase price has a simplicity and objectivity which has commended it to many generations of accounting practitioners. There are, however, major objections to this basis of valuation, but, as we have discussed many of the problems in earlier chapters (*see* Chapters 2, 6 and 7), we will merely summarize them here:

(a) When applied to assets held for resale (e.g. stock), the use of historic cost can lead to an overstatement of the 'real' profit, and hence to an erosion of capital. For example, an item of stock bought for £1 and sold for £2 does not yield a disposable profit of £1 if, to replace the item, £1.20 has to be spent. Historic cost is only an appropriate concept of value where relative and absolute price levels remain unchanged over time—an unknown occurrence in modern times.

(b) When applied to long-term assets, e.g. plant and machinery, the use of historic cost results in (i) depreciation charges which do not reflect the current costs of consuming the asset and (ii) an asset value which, net of depreciation, bears little if any resemblance to its value now.

(c) Historic cost is not as 'objective' as is sometimes claimed. The valuation of stock, for example, requires a choice of method (LIFO, FIFO, etc) which can lead to different stock values and different profit measurement (*see* Chapter 5). The establishment of the 'cost' of a fixed asset (*see* Chapter 6) may also require judgement, and the estimates and judgement which surround depreciation—asset life, residual value, depreciation method—cannot lead to any ultimately objective measurement of depreciation or of the 'balance sheet' value of the asset.

(d) Many of the crucial decisions made in business are related to its future survival, and these decisions depend upon estimates of future income and value. Historic costs—the records of what was paid yesterday—are not a reliable guide to the future, and hence have little, if any, part to play in assisting the decision-making process (*see* Chapter 16).

Historic cost seems to persist as a basis of value in accounting because:

(i) it is easy to record value based upon independently verifiable transactions;

(ii) it is enshrined in aspects of company and tax law and it would be expensive to maintain separate systems of accounting; and

(iii) it is argued that if accounting starts from a (relatively) objective position, the accounts can be readily adjusted in accordance with any particular view of value one wishes to use.

(2) Replacement cost

Replacement cost is the current cost of replacing an asset with an exactly similar one, which will be put to the same use by the business. This concept of value is an attractive one, for it emphasizes the fact that the value of an asset is what the business would have to pay to replace it; without replacement, the business would cease to exist. This concept of value can also lead to a more satisfactory measurement of profit in times of rising prices. For example, if an item of stock which originally cost £1 is sold for £1.50 but has to replaced at a cost of £1.20, the 'profit' is 30 pence, because if the business spent the 50 pence 'historic profit' it could not afford to replace the item of stock, and hence would no longer be in business.

Replacement cost, however, is only a valid basis of valuation if it is intended to actually replace the asset. For example, if a business owned a highly specialized piece of machinery which it used to manufacture a product which was no longer marketable, then it is highly unlikely it would wish to replace that machine with one similar. Hence, in these circumstances, replacement cost could not be seen as an appropriate basis of valuation. Similarly, if the business carried a stock line which it either did not wish to continue or it could not replace, then the use of replacement cost would again not be appropriate.

In practice, replacement cost can be fairly readily ascertained for goods which are acquired from an outside source, but in a manufacturing concern the replacement cost of partly or even wholly manufactured goods may be more difficult to establish.

(3)   Net realizable value

Net realizable value is the amount for which an asset could be sold less any direct expenses of the disposal. Whereas replacement cost is an input value, net realizable value is an output value, so that this view of value represents a different perspective of business activity, replacement cost emphasizing the need for survival, production and capital maintenance, and net realizable value stressing the selling activity. This view, therefore, equates value with the selling (market) price of the asset.

In the long term, all assets of the business will be sold, so, in theory, there can be net realizable value attached to all. It is, however, difficult to make reasonable estimates of the value of used highly specialized machinery, where markets for such equipment are either very limited or simply do not exist. In addition, if no other business could make use of this machinery, then the net realizable value would be little more than a scrap value, which would be an unacceptable valuation if the firm has no intention of selling and can put the machinery to highly profitable use. Finally, it must be pointed out that realizable value accounting is a short-run concept of income because it implies liquidation values—which is inconsistent with the view of the business as a going concern.

(4)   Net present value

The net present value of an asset is the value of the estimated stream of future net cash flows which will come from holding and using an asset discounted at an appropriate rate of interest. This view of value is most closely associated with economic theories and, for that reason, is extremely attractive. A simple analogy may help to understand this concept. If an individual invests £100 now for two years at 10 per cent p.a. interest, at the end of two years he will have

Year 1 £100 + 10% (100) = £110
Year 2 £110 + 10% (110) = £121

More generally, we write this as

$$V_n = A(1 + i)^n$$

where V_n is the value in n years' time; A the amount invested now; i the interest rate; and n the number of years.

$$V = 100(1 + 0.1)^2$$
$$= 100(1.21)$$
$$= £121$$

If we were to be offered £110 in one year's time, and the current rate of interest was 10 per cent, this would be the same as being offered £100 now, for we could take the £100 and invest it for a year at 10 per cent to give £110 in a year's time.

If we rearrange the formulae we have

$$V_n = A(1 + i)^n$$

or

$$A = \frac{V_n}{(1 + i)^n}$$

Therefore

$$A = \frac{110}{(1 + 0.1)}$$
$$= £100$$

The same would apply if we were offered £121 in two years' time, for

$$A = \frac{121}{(1 + 0.1)^2}$$
$$= £100$$

We say, therefore, that the present value of £121 receivable in two years' time with interest rates at 10 per cent is £100.

The value of a business (as we saw in Chapter 9) is closely related to its future earnings, so that if we were able to ascertain the future stream of net cash flows (receipts less payments) and discount them at an appropriate rate of interest, we can ascertain its net present value. The principal objection to this method of valuation is in the estimation of the future cash flows and in the establishment of an appropriate discount or interest rate. As the future flows become more distant, estimates will become highly subjective, and thus it would be difficult for an external user of financial information to know what reliance to place on such estimates.

A more difficult question is the extent to which this concept of value can be applied to individual assets, particularly fixed assets such as plant and machinery. A machine used in isolation from the business as a whole could not be expected to earn as much income as it would as part of a total, unified production facility. Hence, to attempt to isolate and value particular components of the whole by this method would deny the nature of synergy— the whole is much greater than the sum of the parts.

Value to the business

In considering the various possible concepts of value which can be applied to the valuation of assets, it is noticeable that each one, except perhaps historic cost, is valid in particular circumstances, but each one is inappropriate in other circumstances. The most important attempt to draw these various ideas together into a single, coherent concept of value was made by Bonbright, in *The Valuation of Property*, who defined the value of an asset to a business as: ' . . . identical in amount with the adverse value of the entire loss, direct and indirect, that the owner might expect to suffer if he were to be deprived of that property.'

This idea of 'deprived value' was subsequently developed by Baxter, in *Depreciation*, who pointed out that a business can be 'deprived' by

(1) Selling the asset and not replacing it, in which case the deprival value is the net realizable value, for that is the amount by which the business would be worse off if the asset were 'lost'.
(2) Selling the asset and replacing it, in which case the business suffers the cost of replacement.
(3) Continuing to hold and use the asset, in which case, if the asset were lost, the business would lose the net present value of the future income streams associated with that asset.

Careful consideration of these three possibilities will show that the value of an asset to the business is the 'lower of replacement cost or expected future benefits' from either selling or using the asset. For example, if a machine's replacement cost (RC) is £700, its net realizable value (NRV) is £900, and its net present value from use (NPV) is £800, then the 'deprival value' is £700, for that is all that the business would lose. The relationship may be tabulated thus:

Value concepts	Deprival value
(i) NRV > NPV > RC	RC
(ii) NRV > RC > NPV	RC
(iii) NPV > RC > NRV	RC
(iv) NPV > NRV > RC	RC
(v) RC > NPV > NRV	NPV
(vi) RC > NRV > NPV	NRV

Replacement cost thus becomes the dominant method of valuation for, in practice, the last two possibilities will seldom occur.

In (i) and (ii) in the above table, NRV is greater than NPV, so that the business would be better off selling than using the asset. The sale would necessitate replacement, hence the maximum loss which the business would suffer is the cost of its replacement. In (iii) and (iv), NPV is greater than NRV, so that the business would be better off using than selling. In order to maintain that NPV the business would have to replace the asset, so again the deprival value is the replacement cost. In (v), the RC is greater than the NPV, so the business would not wish to replace the asset, and as NPV is also greater than NRV it is worth using the asset rather than selling it. Hence, the greatest loss to the business is the NPV. In the final case, NRV is greater than the NPV so that the greater loss to the business would be the NRV. If, however, the RC is greater than the NRV the business would not wish to replace, so that the deprival value is the NRV.

The nature of income—an economic view

The concepts of income and value are closely related, for valuation is concerned with the measurement of the stocks of wealth (assets, capital) and income measurement with the flow of benefit from the use of that wealth. The problems of defining income have exercised accountants, economists and lawyer's for many years. The introduction of income tax during the Napoleonic Wars required the government to define the income on which it wished to raise revenue, but, as with all successive tax legislation, there was no attempt to find a general definition, but merely the identification of certain types of income on which tax could be levied, and this division of income into types or schedules remains with us today.

We have to turn to economic literature in order to find a more general definition of income. Hicks, in 1946, defined income as 'the amount which a man can consume during a period and still remain as well off at the end of the period as he was at the beginning'. Unlike accounting, economic income seeks to eliminate the effect of the changing value of money, and, moreover, places emphasis upon measuring changes in the value of assets and capital at the beginning and end of a period, rather than focusing attention upon the revenue and expense transactions which have taken place during the period. Thus the basic definition of income is consumption in the period plus changes in the value of the capital.

The major difficulty in this approach lies in the measure of 'well offness'— the value of the capital stock—at the beginning and end of the period. This value can change because of additional investment during the period, because interest rates change, or because expectations about the future are changed. As economists prefer to regard value as equalling the net present value of future receipts, then, in theory, we can establish the value of a business at the beginning and end of a period by calculating its net present value at those times. In order to measure the income for the period, we merely subtract the opening value from the closing value, making any necessary adjustment for capital introduced or withdrawn.

Even without the introduction of new capital, however, and without any changes in interest rates, changing expectations can lead to two different measurements of income for the same period. Consider the following example:

A firm expects to earn the following net receipts from its investments:

$$
\begin{array}{ll}
& £ \\
\text{Year 1} & 1,000 \\
\text{Year 2} & 1,000 \\
\text{Year 3} & 1,000 \\
\end{array}
$$

The firm considers that these future net receipts represent a return of 10 per cent on the investment; hence, at the beginning of year 1, the net present value of those receipts is £2,486:

	Net receipts at end of year £	Present value factor	NPV at beginning of year 1 £
Year 1 1,000		$\dfrac{1}{1 + 0.1}$	909
Year 2 1,000		$\dfrac{1}{(1 + 0.1)^2}$	826
Year 3 1,000		$\dfrac{1}{(1 + 0.1)^3}$	751
			2,486

At the end of year 1, the expected future value of the receipts will be

	Net receipts at end of year £	Present value factor	NPV at end of year 1 £
Year 1 Cash received	1,000	1	1,000
Year 2 Future Receipts	1,000	$\dfrac{1}{(1 + 0.1)}$	909
Year 3 Future receipts	1,000	$\dfrac{1}{(1 + 0.1)^2}$	826
			2,735

We can therefore ascertain the income for the year by comparing the present value at the end of year 1 with the present value at the beginning of year 1:

	£
Present value at end of year 1	2,735
Present value at start of year 1	2,486
Income (ex ante)	**249**

The income of £249 represents a 10 per cent return on the original opening value of £2,486, and hence we could consume this sum and still be as 'well off' (i.e. £2,486) as we were at the beginning of the period. However, we are calculating the present value of *both* the beginning and end of year 1 in the light of our expectations at the beginning of year 1, and hence this measurement of income from the viewpoint of the beginning of the period is referred to as 'ex ante' income.

If, at the end of year 1, we revise our expectations about the future net cash receipts, then we will, after the first year (or 'ex post'), obtain a different net present value:

	Expected net receipts at end of year revised at end of year 1	Present value factor	NPV at end of year 1
	£		£
Year 1 Cash received	1,000	1	1,000
Year 2 Future receipts	900	$\frac{1}{1.1}$	818
Year 3 Future receipts	900	$\frac{1}{(1.1)^2}$	744
			2,562

Comparing this revised value at the end of year 1 with the value at the beginning of year 1, we have

	£
Revised present value at end of year 1	2,562
Present value at start of year 1	2,486
Income (ex post)	**76**

We can reconcile this with the ex ante income as follows:

	£	£
Ex ante income		249
Original present value at end of year 1	2,735	
Revised present value at end of year 1	2,562	
Ex post adjustment	**173**	173
Ex post income		**76**

Given the uncertainties which surround the measurement of this concept of income—one writer called it 'subjective income'—it is apparent that it cannot be applied on an operational basis. However, the value of such an approach to the accountant is that it serves further to highlight the difficulties intrinsic in income measurement and valuation, and makes him approach the solutions proposed by successive professional committees with caution. We would do well to remind ourselves of an observation made in Chapter 1, namely that accounting principles are accepted on three criteria—feasibility, utility and objectivity. A concept of income which does not lend itself to reasonably objective measurement and which is not operationally feasible is unlikely to commend itself to the accounting world.

Income measurement in accounting

Since the earlier chapters of this book have been very much concerned with identifying and criticizing the conventional approach of accounting to income measurement and valuation, it is not necessary here to review this extensively. Accounting concepts of income and value have been mainly dominated by two postulates—the cost postulate and the realization postulate. The basis of valuation in financial accounting is historic cost or a derivative thereof, which distorts seriously the measurement of income when the value of money is changing. Asset values, depreciation and stock values are all historic and bear little resemblance to their current cost. Profit—in the sense of what could be safely disposed of—is inevitably overstated.

The realization postulate, which requires both objective evidence and reasonable certainty of asset value, means that gains in asset values go unrecorded until they are actually sold. Significant appreciation in land and stock values are often ignored with the result that the balance sheet can be taken as a useful admission of the ownership of assets rather than as a statement of their worth.

Most accountants now agree that there is an urgent need to improve the quality, reliability and utility of financial reporting, but most accountants disagree sharply on how this improvement should be achieved. In the remainder of this chapter we will be examining some of these suggested improvements, many of which have been an urgent response to the growing problem of inflation in the western economies.

Income measurement and inflation

Inflation has become a permanent feature of the Western economies, and although in the UK it has currently declined from its peak of over 20% in 1980 to around 5% in 1983, no government can be other than cautious when forecasting future levels of inflation. Perhaps acknowledgement that inflation will be always with us is to be found in the Companies Act 1981 which recognizes that some companies may take the view that 'historical cost' accounts are misleading and hence may wish to follow what the Act calls 'alternative accounting rules' and value assets at their current cost. Over the last decade, the accounting profession has been preoccupied with the problems of 'inflation accounting', launching a series of initiatives which began in 1973 and culminated in 1980 in the issue of SSAP 16—'Current Cost Accounting'. It is perhaps premature to regard SSAP 16 as the culmination of the debate, for there are strong criticisms of what is both included and excluded by this Standard—criticisms which will almost certainly lead to a modified standard.

The first attempt to devise a way of dealing with inflation in accounts came in 1973, when the profession proposed a system of adjusting costs and revenues by means of a single index measuring price rises generally. This 'current purchasing power', approach or CPP (*see* page 254) had a theoretical justification in that the adjustments measured the amount necessary to preserve the real purchasing power of the shareholders' capital, i.e. to measure the profit which could be consumed (distributed) and leave the shareholder as 'well off' as he was before. The objection to this approach, strongly voiced by industrialists, was that while a single price index, such as the retail price index, might be appropriate to housewives buying similar 'baskets' of commodities, it was inappropriate to industry because:

(1) Inflation affected costs and revenues differently.
(2) Lenders and borrowers are affected in totally different ways by inflation.
(3) Firms vary from the capital intensive to the labour intensive, and inflation has a radically different effect on the different sectors of the economy.

These valid criticisms prompted the establishment of a government committee (the Sandilands Committee) whose report recommended a system of current cost accounting (CCA) (*see* page 258) which basically asserted that 'value' to the business was normally to be equated with replacement cost. Such a proposal met with the support, in principle, of industrialists, and a professional committee (the Morpeth Commitee) was charged with putting Sandilands into practice. Two aspects of this system, however, led to its eventual rejection by the profession. The system totally ignored the effect of inflation on borrowing and lending—a crucial problem, for example, in banking and insurance—and also became so obsessed with the minutia of the adjustments that many felt costs of the system—even if it were feasible for the small company—would substantially outweigh its usefulness. In addition, the Morpeth Committee proposed that the system should completely replace published accounts prepared on a historic cost basis—a proposal which was greeted with complete dismissal in the face of both conceptual and operational difficulties.

Following the downfall of this proposal, a new initiative was proposed in 1977, called the 'Hyde' guidelines. This proposal adopted, in a simplified form, the earlier CCA suggestions—adjustments to cost of sales for inflation in stock prices and to depreciation to allow for rising replacement costs—but in addition proposed a 'gearing' or 'monetary' adjustment to allow companies to take credit for the amount of the other two adjustments which ought to be borne by the providers of loan capital.

Many of the Hyde proposals were incorporated into the accounting standard, SSAP 16, but a further refinement was added by requiring companies to make an adjustment for monetary working capital reflecting the fact that if, for example, there is a net increase in debtors less creditors, then the company is losing by being owed money in a period of inflation. The gearing adjustment reflects the view that if part of the assets is financed by borrowing (e.g. debentures) which is fixed in monetary terms, then there will be a gain to shareholders in a time of rising prices simply because the value of the loan is diminished in real terms.

SSAP 16 will not be the end of the story—of that there can be no doubt; the theoretical and practical complexities will provide a fertile ground for continued debate. No introductory text can do justice to a topic which requires at least one, if not several books, and in order to provide a basic understanding of the problems involved we will illustrate in outline the effect which the various proposals have on reported profit.

The nature of price changes

Prices reflect the exchange value of goods and services in the company, and can be classified as either input prices or output prices. Input prices are the prices of the goods and services acquired for further production or resale; output prices are the prices of goods and services acquired for final consumption. A price change occurs when the price of a good or service is different from what it previously was in the *same* market. If a firm buys a commodity at one (input) price and sells at a higher (output) price, there is no price change. Price changes occur if input prices increase or decrease, or if output prices increase or decrease.

Price changes can be of two kinds: specific or general. Specific price changes relate to the change in the exchange value of a specific commodity (in the absence of general price movements). If the price of a specific asset changes while held by a firm the result is a 'holding' gain or loss. For example, if a commodity has been bought for £10 and later sold for £15 at a time when its current input price (replacement cost) is £12, the operating gross profit is £3, and the 'holding' profit £2.

A general price level change occurs as a result of a change in the value of the monetary unit. A price index is used to express the general level of prices compared with some base period. For example, if the general price index in 1984 is 120 (with 1974 = 100), this means that prices are 20 per cent higher than in 1974. The reciprocal of the price index expresses the change in the value of the pound or the change in purchasing power; in the example above, purchasing power has decreased by (120 − 100)/120, or 16.6 per cent. Purchasing power refers to the ability to buy goods and services with a given quantity of money compared to what that same quantity of money could buy at an earlier date.

Partial solutions to changing price levels

Adjustments for specific price changes can only partially reflect economic reality because the general price changes are ignored. Many proponents of such adustments argue, however, that their methods should be accepted on a number of grounds:

(1) The use of LIFO and replacement cost depreciation will adjust for almost all the error in historical accounting; in fact, the 'partial' adjustment is 95 per cent complete.
(2) Appropriate general price indexes are not available.
(3) General price level adjustments are unduly complicated and confusing.

All the arguments have some force on practical grounds, and we will consider the place of LIFO and replacement cost depreciation as a partial solution to the price level problem.

Last in, first out

In Chapter 7, the effect of LIFO on income measurement was illustrated with reference to a business with a life cycle of three years. It is claimed that LIFO matches current costs with current revenue, and thus measures income more realistically. As a method for adjusting for price level changes, however, LIFO is far from perfect, and may, at best, be considered a stop-gap measure until a better method can be devised. Specifically, the objections to LIFO are:

(1) LIFO results in a distortion of balance sheet values (*see* Chapter 7).
(2) The adjustment is limited to inventories, and ignores all other expenses.
(3) LIFO only approximates to replacement costs if turnover is rapid or price movements are slow.
(4) When sales exceed current purchases, the gap between selling prices and historical costs can be very large.
(5) The administrative work involved in operating LIFO is significantly greater than other systems of stock valuation.

Replacement cost depreciation

The objective of replacement cost depreciation is to charge to expense an amount equal to the depreciation of a similar asset acquired under current conditions. Since the fixed assets of a firm may have been purchased at various times extending many years into the past, price fluctuations cause the expense and asset balance to deviate considerably from current cost. The current cost of the asset is usually determined by applying a specific price index.

For example, if a machine is bought in 1979 for £10,000, with an expected life of 10 years and a scrap value of nil, the straight line depreciation will be £1,000 p.a. The conventional accounts in 1984 will appear thus:

Income Statement (1984)			Balance Sheet (1984)	
		£		£
Net profit before depreciation		2,200	Machinery (cost)	10,000
Depreciation		1,000	Depreciation	5,000
Net Profit		**£1,200**	WDV	**£5,000**

If, however, the price index was 100 when the machine was bought, and 150 on average during 1984, then the current cost of the asset is 10,000 × (150/100) = £15,000; the current cost of depreciation is, therefore, 15,000/10 = £1,500 per annum. The redrafted income statement will now reveal a net profit of £700.

The adjustment of the balance sheet can now proceed in one of two ways. Assume that the balance sheet before adjustment was as follows:

	£	£		£	£
Share capital		5,000	Machine (cost)	10,000	
			Depreciation	5,000	
Revenue reserves					5,000
Profit at 1.1.84	8,000		Net current assets		9,200
Profit for year	1,200				
		9,200			
		£14,200			**£14,200**

(1) The first possibility is not to restate the assets, crediting the excess of price adjusted depreciation over historic depreciation to a capital reserve. This inevitably results in the balance sheet disclosing the machine in terms of 1979 pounds. The redrafted balance sheet becomes

	£	£		£	£
Share capital		5,000	Machine (cost)	10,000	
Capital replacement			Depreciation	5,000	
reserve		500		———	5,000
Revenue reserves					
Profit at 1.1.84	8,000		Net current assets		9,200
Profit for year	700				
	———	8,700			
		£14,200			**£14,200**

(2) Alternatively, both the asset and accumulated depreciation are revalued in 1984 pounds. The surplus on revaluation of the machine £5,000 is unrealized profit, and is displayed as a capital reserve. The adjustment to depreciation is a little more complicated. The current value of accumulated depreciation should now be $15,000 \times 5/10 = £7,500$ (or $£5,000 \times 150/100$); the sum actually accumulated is $£(4 \times 1,000) + 1,500 = £5,500$. The additional £2,000 is not a current expense, and is appropriated from past profits.

	£	£		£	£
Share capital		5,000	Machine (valuation)	15,000	
			Depreciation	7,500	
Revaluation reserve		5,000		———	7,500
Revenue reserves					
Profit at 1.1.84	8,000		Net current assets		9,200
Profit for year	700				
	———				
	8,700				
Less: Appropriation	2,000				
	———	6,700			
		£16,700			**£16,700**

There is no doubt that replacement cost depreciation produces a more meaningful measure of income, and, if the second method is employed, a more meaningful balance sheet. The return on capital measured in current terms is 700/16,700 = 4.2 per cent, as against 1,200/14,200 = 8.5 per cent in money terms. Nevertheless, replacement cost depreciation, even when coupled with the use of LIFO stocks, is incomplete as a means of adjusting for price level changes, for it makes no allowance for the gains and losses on monetary items. We turn to this point now, as we look at adjustments for general price changes.

Adjustments for general price changes

Inflation is known to be beneficial to those who owe money and detrimental to those who are owed money. If a firm borrows £100 and repays it when the price level has increased by 50 per cent, the £100 repaid has only $(150 - 50)/150 = 66.6$ per cent of the purchasing power it had when it was borrowed. Adjustments for general price changes permit the matching of costs and revenues in compatible pounds, the presentation of the balance sheet in 'common' or 'stabilized' pounds, and the evaluation of the gains and losses to the firm of owing and holding monetary assets. The 'current purchasing power' (or CPP) method is concerned with removing the distorting effects of changes in the general purchasing power of money on accounts prepared in accordance with established practice. The illustration appended here simplifies the practical problems involved but seeks to demonstrate that accounts adjusted to show CPP may provide a more meaningful measure of income and operating efficiency by excluding the effects of changing money values.

We assume the following data are given:

(1) Closing stock was acquired during last quarter of 1984 and opening stock during last quarter of 1983.
(2) The land and buildings were acquired, and the capital issued during 1976. The buildings are depreciated straight line over 40 years.
(3) The relevant retail price indices are

(i)	1976 average	60
(ii)	1983 last quarter average	108
(iii)	1983 December 31	110
(iv)	1984 last quarter average	116
(v)	1984 average	114
(vi)	1984 December 31	118

We begin with the unadjusted accounts for 1984 and then restate them in the form of current purchasing power units at 31 December 1984:

Income Statement for the period ended 31 December 1984

	Unadjusted		Factor	Adjusted to current purchasing power basis at 31.12.84	
	£'000	£'000		£'000	£'000
Sales		500	118/114[1]		517.6
Opening stock	80		118/108	87.4	
Purchases	420		118/114[1]	434.7	
	500			522.1	
Less: Closing stock	70	430	118/116	71.2	450.9
Gross Profit		70			66.7
Depreciation (buildings)	5		118/60	9.8	
Administration	25	30	118/114[1]	25.9	35.7
Net Profit		**40**			**31.0**

Balance sheet as at 31 December 1984

	Unadjusted		Factor	Adjusted to CPP basis at 31.12.84	
	£'000	£'000		£'000	£'000
Share capital		200	118/60		393.3
Undistributed profit		200	Residual		292.9
		400			**686.2**
Land		140	118/60		275.3
Buildings	200		118/60	393.3	
Depreciation	45	155	118/60	88.6	304.7
Stock	70		118/116	71.2	
Debtors	40			40	
Cash	30			30	
	140			141.2	
Less: Creditors	35	105		35	106.2
		400			**686.2**

1 Sales, purchases and administration expenses are assumed to occur evenly over the year—and hence at average prices.

The monetary items (creditors, debtors and cash) are not restated because they are already expressed in current pounds.

To evaluate the gains and losses derived from holding monetary assets, the 1983 balance sheet must be related to the 1984 balance sheet. All items must be adjusted, including the monetary items, because the monetary accounts represented the value at 31 December 1983.

Balance Sheet as at 31 December 1984

	Unadjusted		Factor	Adjusted to CPP basis at 31.12.84	
	£'000	£'000		£'0000	£'000
Share capital		200	118/60		393.3
Undistributed profit		160	Residual		262.5
		360			**655.8**
Land		140	118/60		275.3
Buildings	200		118/60	393.3	
Depreciation	40	160	118/60	78.7	314.6
Stock	80		118/108	87.4	
Debtors	20		118/110	21.4	
Cash	10		118/110	10.7	
	110			119.5	
Less: Creditors	50	60	118/110	53.6	65.9
		360			**655.8**

The inclusive net income for the period—inclusive because it includes both the operating profit and gains and losses from money assets—is given by

	Unadjusted	Adjusted
	£'000	£'000
Undistributed profit 31.12.84	200	292.9
Undistributed profit 31.12.83	160	262.5
Net Profit (income)	40	30.4
Net operating income	40	31
∴ Loss from holding money	—	0.6
	40	30.4

The loss from holding money may be formally derived as follows:

Loss from holding money

	£'000
Net monetary assets 31 December 1983 stated in 31 December 1984 pounds	
$(30 - 50)\dfrac{118}{110}$	(21.4)
Increase in net monetary assets	
$[35 - (-20)] \times \dfrac{118}{114}$	57.0
(assumed to occur at average prices)	35.6
Net monetary assets 31 December 1984	35.0
∴ Loss from holding money	**£0.6**

Useful financial ratios can be derived from the adjusted accounts. The unadjusted return on capital is $40/400 = 10\%$, but when the accounts are restated in common pounds the real return is revealed to be $31/686 = 4.52\%$. The unadjusted figures distort both the income and the net capital employed, and the firm can now appreciate in real terms how well it is doing. Moreover a meaningful comparison is now made possible with the firm who have acquired their assets more recently provided they too present their accounts on a CPP basis.

The practical effects of CPP accounting can be seen by examining the published accounts of the 150 or so companies which published supplementary statements, a selection from which is provided below:

Pre-tax profits

	Historical cost basis (£ million)	CPP basis (£ million)
British Petroleum	510	520
Courtaulds	125	98
Grand Metropolitan	33	101
Imperial Chemical Industries	461	338
Rank Organization	62	92
Marks and Spencer	82	103
Allied Breweries	59	83

Casual inspection reveals that differences between the two systems may be large in magnitude which may be either positive or negative. Companies such as ICI, which have invested heavily in plant and equipment, suffer a substantial increase in their depreciation charge under CPP accounting, while companies such as Grand Metropolitan, which have borrowed heavily, show a large net gain on monetary items.

As a measure of how viable a company is, CPP must therefore be treated with some caution. Heavy borrowing—which in inflationary conditions will result in a net monetary gain—requires a heavy outpouring of cash to meet interest charges, with all the attendant liquidity problems. There can be no better illustration of this than to point to the flood of collapses of property companies where overenthusiastic borrowing is at the root of the problem.

Current cost accounting—the Sandilands proposals and ED 18

The important report of the government-sponsored Inflation Accounting Committee (the Sandilands Committee) *Inflation Accounting* criticized CPP accounting for this and other reasons. The report suggests (para. 149) that there are five principal criteria for a unit of measurement underlying an accounting system:

(1) The unit should be equally useful to all users of accounts.
(2) The unit should not change from year to year.
(3) The unit should be the same for all enterprises presenting financial statements.
(4) The unit should preferably be a physical object which could be exchanged by the users of accounts.
(5) The unit should represent a constant 'value' through time.

CPP, in the view of the report, fails to satisfy those criteria and does not remedy the deficiencies of historic cost accounting (paras. 408–415). To remedy these deficiencies it is proposed (para. 519) that all companies should as soon as practicable adopt an accounting system to be known as 'Current Cost Accounting', the main features of which are

(a) money is the unit of measurement;
(b) assets and liabilities are shown in the balance sheet at a valuation;
(c) 'operating profit' is struck after charging the 'value to the business' of assets consumed during the period, thus excluding holding gains from profit and showing them separately.

A crucial feature of CCA is the basis of valuation of assets which is defined as the 'value to the business'. The 'value to the business' of an asset is the amount of the loss suffered by the company concerned if the asset is lost or destroyed. This definition provides only three alternative general bases:

(1) The current purchase price (replacement cost) of the asset (RC).
(2) The net realizable value (or current disposal value of the asset) (NRV).
(3) The present value of the expected future earnings from the asset or 'economic value' (PV).

It follows that the value of an asset to a company is its written down replacement cost except where replacement cost is higher than both the present value and net realizable value, in which case the value of the asset to the company is the present value or net realizable value whichever is the higher. In practice this is likely to mean that in the majority of cases replacement cost will be the correct 'value to the business' (*see* page 244).

The quantification of the 'value to the business' presents many practical difficulties; land and buildings will have to be valued by independent valuers, other fixed assets by application of specific and appropriate price indices, and stock at 'current purchase price (replacement cost) or net realizable value whichever is the lower'. The Sandilands report offers a methodology for arriving at 'the value to the business' which it considers will provide a 'reasonable approximation', but readily and frequently concedes that 'further consideration needs to be given to the practical problems involved'. Much consideration was indeed given to the problems, and in November 1976 the Accounting Standards Committee issued ED 18—*Current Cost Accounting*—together with a detailed guidance manual.

Applying a CCA basis to the illustrative data provided on pages 255 and 256 the result would be as follows:

Income Statement for the period ended 31 December 1984

		£'000	£'000
	Sales		500.0
	Opening stock	80.0	
	Purchases	420.0	
		500.0	
	Less: Closing stock	70.0	
		430.0	
Note 2	Cost of sales adjustment	5.3	435.3
	Current Cost Gross Profit		64.7
Note 3	Depreciation	9.8	
	Administration	25.0	34.8
Note 4	**Current Cost Net Profit**		**29.9**

Balance Sheet as at 31 December 1984

		£'000			£'000	
	Share capital	200.0	**Fixed assets**			
Note 4	Undistributed profit	189.9	Land	275.3	Note 3	
Note 5	Fixed asset revaluation		Buildings	304.8	Note 3	
	reserve	289.9				
Note 2	Stock adjustment reserve	5.3		580.1		
	Shareholders' Interest	685.1	**Current Assets**			
	Current Liabilities		Stock	70.0	Note 2	
	Creditors	35.0	Debtors	40.0		
			Cash	30.0		
		720.1		**720.1**		

Notes

(1) For the sake of simplicity it has been assumed that the specific indices for land, buildings and stock are the same as the general index. The specific indices will provide a measure of the replacement cost appropriate to each class of asset.

(2) The 'cost of sales adjustment' represents a holding gain from stock, and is calculated thus:

		£'000
Decrease in stock holdings at historic cost (70–80)	=	10.0
Decrease in stock holdings at average current cost $\left(70 \times \dfrac{114}{118} - 80 \times \dfrac{114}{110} \right)$	=	15.3
∴ Holding gain arising from increase in stock prices		**£5.3**

The holding gain of £5.3 is credited to the stock adjustment reserve.

An alternative method is to adjust both the opening and closing stock values in the accounts, viz:

	£'000
Opening stock $\left(80 \times \dfrac{114}{110} \right)$	82.9
Purchases	420.0
	502.9
Less:	
Closing stock $\left(70 \times \dfrac{114}{118} \right)$	67.6
Current cost of sales	**£435.3**

This method, however, would require an adjustment in the balance sheet value of stock, which the report recommends should be avoided in the initial implementation of CCA.

(3) The value of the land and buildings is given by

	£'000	£'000
Land $\left(140 \times \dfrac{118}{60} \right)$		275.3
Buildings $\left(200 \times \dfrac{118}{60} \right)$	393.3	
Less: $\left(45 \times \dfrac{118}{60} \right)$	88.5	
		304.8

The current cost depreciation charge for the year is

$$393.3 \times 2\tfrac{1}{2}\% = £9.8$$

(4) So far as the profit and loss account is concerned, the adjustment of stock and depreciation figures to reflect the 'value of the business' of assets consumed during the year is all that is required by CCA. All other items reflect the costs incurred during the year and are therefore the 'value to the business' of those items. The undistributed profit is therefore composed of

	£'000
Balance at 1.1.83	160.0
Current cost net profit	29.9
	£189.9

(5) The fixed asset revaluation reserve reflects the increase in the value of the assets to the business:

	£'000
Opening balance (1983 at 1984 values)	249.9
Increase in gross current value of assets during 1984:	
Land (275.3 − 256.6)	18.7
Buildings (393.3 − 366.6)	26.7
	295.3
Less: Increase in depreciation charge for prior years (88.5 − 73.3) − 9.8	5.4
	£289.9

∴ Increase in year = £289.9 − £249.9 = £40.0

(6) The total gains to the company during the year are

	£'000
Current cost net profit	29.9
Stock adjustment reserve	5.3
Fixed asset revaluation reserve	40.0
	75.2

CCA therefore produces a different result from that of CPP, primarily because of the different treatment of monetary items. CPP, by converting all items in the accounts by means of a general price index, reflects directly the gains from monetary liabilities during a period of inflation. CCA, on the other hand, reflects those gains by measuring the increased value of the assets which the borrowing has helped to finance.

An estimate of the likely effect of CCA on major companies was made by Philips and Drew, showing that the two systems can provide startlingly different 'profits':

	Pre-tax profits on historical cost basis (£ million)	CPP basis (£ million)	CCA basis (£ million)
British Petroleum	510	520	100
Courtaulds	125	98	72
Grand Metropolitan	33.4	101	5
Imperial Chemical Industries	461	338	136
Rank Organization	62.3	92	43
Marks and Spencer	82	103	73
Allied Breweries	59	83	38

SSAP 16, 'Current Cost Accounting'

SSAP 16 has its genesis in the work done by the Sandilands Committee, and emerges from lengthy deliberations upon Exposure Draft 24 published in 1979, itself the creation of the recommendations of the Hyde Committee in 1977. Partly to deflect the criticism of cost and work load imposed by the standard, the standard applies only to listed companies and to other companies which satisfy at least two of the following criteria:

(i)   a turnover of not less than £5 million per year;
(ii) total assets at the commencement of the relevant accounting period of not less than £2½ million; and
(iii) an average number of UK employees of not less than 250 employees.

The current cost operating profit is arrived at by adjusting the historic cost profit by:

(i)   an extra depreciation provision to allow for the current cost of assets consumed—(as for Sandilands above);
(ii) a 'cost of sales' adjustment to reflect the current value of stock consumed (again as for Sandilands above);
(iii) an adjustment for monetary working capital; and
(iv) a gearing adjustment.

Thus the major difference between SSAP 16 and Sandilands lies in the adjustments for what is called 'monetary working capital' and the 'gearing' adjustment. Most businesses have other working capital besides stock tied up in their day-to-day activities. In particular, when sales are made on credit, the business has funds tied up in debtors, and, conversely, when it buys goods or services on credit it is, in essence, borrowing funds. This 'monetary working capital'—debtors minus creditors—will require adjustment to take account of changing price levels, for any increase in monetary working capital (MWC) implies a loss in purchasing power.

The calculation for the monetary working capital adjustment (MWCA) is analogous to that for stock (cost of sales) on page 260. We may illustrate the effect using the data provided earlier in the chapter.

	1984	1983	Increase (Decrease)
	£'000	£'000	£'000
Debtors	40	20	20
Creditors	35	50	(15)
Monetary working capital	5	(30)	35

	£'000
Increase in MWC at historic cost $5 - (-30)$	35.0
Increase in MWC at average current cost	
$\left(5 \times \dfrac{114}{118}\right) - \left(-30 \times \dfrac{114}{110}\right)$	= 35.9
Loss from increase in MWC	**0.9**

Monetary working capital is, in fact, defined by the standard as (a) the aggregate of trade debtors, prepayments and bills receivable, plus (b) stocks not subject to a cost of sales adjustment, less (c) trade creditors, accruals and bills payable. Bank balances are included only in so far as they reflect the consequential fluctuations in items (a), (b) and (c) above together with cash floats needed to support day-to-day operations.

The second adjustment relates to the gearing of the company, and is perhaps the most controversial section of the standard. The net tangible assets of a business will normally be partly financed by borrowings which, being fixed in monetary terms, will provide a gain to the shareholders in a time of rising prices. This view is a significant departure from Sandilands (*see* page 261), where it was argued that gains from such borrowing are reflected through the gain in the value of the assets which they have helped finance and that no further adjustment is necessary.

To make the gearing adjustment, the total of the current cost adjustments is reduced in the proportion which net operating assets financed by net borrowing bear to the total net operating assets. The net operating assets comprise the fixed assets, stock and monetary working capital; net borrowing is the excess of all liabilities (including debentures and tax) but excluding creditors over all current assets excluding stock and debtors. In the illustration we have used throughout this chapter we note that the current cost adjustments are:

	£'000
Cost of sales adjustment	5.3
MWCA	0.9
	6.2
Depreciation adjustment (9.8 − 5.0)	4.8
Total current cost adjustment	11.0

The net operating assets are

	£'000
Fixed assets	295
Stock	70
Debtors	40
	405
Less: Creditors	35
	370

In the data provided there was no 'net borrowing'—there were no debentures—but if we assume that the position was

Debentures	100	
Less: Cash	30	
		70

the 'gearing' adjustment would be

$$11.0 \times \frac{70}{370} = \underline{\underline{\textbf{£2.1}}}$$

and the total current cost adjustment would be reduced by this sum.

The revised income statement would appear as

	£'000	£'000
Net profit as per historical cost accounts (page 254)		40.0
Less: Current cost adjustment		
Cost of sales	5.3	
Monetary working capital	0.9	
	6.2	
Depreciation	4.8	
		11.0
Current Cost Operating Profit		29.0
Add: Gearing adjustment		2.1
Current Cost Profit		**31.1**

All of the adjustments—revaluation surpluses on fixed assets and stock, the monetary working capital and gearing—are to be carried to a reserve called the 'current cost reserve', and the assets are all to be reflected on the balance sheet at their current value to the business. This means that the difference between the historic cost of assets and their current cost value will be credited to the current cost reserve.

SSAP 16, practice and criticism

SSAP 16 came into operation on 1 January 1980 but already there is a groundswell of opinion seeking significant modifications to the standard. Indeed, some opponents argue that as there is no agreement on which particular method of inflation accounting is theoretically or operationally acceptable, we should simply use a cash-flow system of accounting—an entirely factual basis—and leave it to judgement as to what effect inflation has had on the cash flow.

At the operational level, research has shown that costs of sales adjustments are fairly well established and accepted among managers, and that current replacement cost is almost universally used in pricing decision. There is less enthusiasm about the depreciation adjustment, perhaps because its impact is often very substantial, and seems rather remote from the operational level. The adjustments for monetary working capital and gearing have not been well received. In practice, problems have arisen regarding the definition of monetary working capital—how much cash should be included?—the impact of substantial year-to-year fluctuations in debtors and creditors and the choice of an appropriate index. As regards the latter, a survey reported that in published CCA accounts two-thirds of the companies gave no explanation of what index they had used.

Apart from the conceptual difficulties which underlie SSAP 16, there are several detailed matters within it which either need clarification or give rise to practical difficulties. For example, the incorporation of overseas subsidiaries in group accounts can create virtually meaningless accounts if the subsidiary is using a different method of inflation accounting. Or again, if a subsidiary with minority shareholders has virtually no capital gearing, but the holding company is highly geared, the gearing adjustment required on consolidation by SSAP 16 is unduly harsh on the minority interest. SSAP 16 is also in some conflict with SSAP 9, 'Stocks and Work in Progress', which requires the incorporation of fixed as well as variable overhead in stock values. SSAP 16 requires a cost of sales adjustment to this value, but that is correct only if the business has no spare capacity; if it has, then the deprival value of the stock is only the variable costs.

These doubts and reservations led the accounting standards committee to set up a monitoring team to look at the progress of SSAP 16 during the first three years of its life. That team consulted very widely, and in May 1983 it published an interim report on its findings, the most important of which are:

(i) The monetary working capital and gearing adjustments to profit and loss accounts command least support;

(ii)   a current cost balance sheet is widely regarded as misleading;
(iii) few companies which make inflation adjustments for management pur-
       poses follow the SSAP 16 method;
(iv)   historical cost accounts are unsatisfactory but there is uncertainty over
       the purpose of adjusting historical cost accounting for the effects of
       changing prices;
(v)   there is no consensus by those unhappy with SSAP 16 and historic cost
       over what should follow.

As a consequence of its findings, the monitoring team made recommendations of its own, the most controversial of which were that the standard
should permit different methods of calculating the effects of changing prices,
and that an adjusted balance sheet should not be required.

Responding to these findings, the ASC launched yet another set of ideas,
and sought comments on them by Autumn 1983. The current standard
remains in force until 31 December 1984, but it would take a brave man to
predict what will follow.

References and further reading

ACCOUNTING STANDARDS STEERING COMMITTEE (1980), SSAP 16, 'Current
   Cost Accounting'.
BAXTER (1967), 'General or Special Index', *Journal UEC*, **3**.
BAXTER (1971), *Depreciation*. Sweet and Maxwell.
BAXTER and DAVIDSON (1962), *Studies in Accounting Theory*. Sweet and
   Maxwell.
EDWARDS and BELL (1961), *The Theory and Measurement of Business
   Income*. University of California Press.
GOODWIN (1973), 'Fixed Assets in a Period of Inflation', *Accountancy*,
   February 1973.
GYNTHER (1966), *Accounting for Price Level Changes: Theory and
   Procedure*. Pergamon.
HANSEN (1962), *The Accounting Concept of Profit*. North-Holland.
HENDRIKSEN (1982), *Accounting Theory*. Irwin.
HMSO (1975) *Report of the Inflation Accounting Committee*.
HICKS (1946), *Value and Capital*. Oxford University Press.
KENNEDY (1978), 'Inflation Accounting; Retrospect and Prospect',
   Economics Policy Review, March 1978.
NOBES and COOKE (1981), 'Some Complexities in the Use of SSAP 16',
   Accountancy, June 1981 and July 1981.
PRIDDICE (1973), 'Current Value Accounting and Price Level
   Restatements: Where do we stand?', *The Chartered Accountant in
   Australia*, September 1973.
TAYLOR (1975), 'The Nature and Determinants of Income: Some Further
   Comments', *Journal of Business Finance and Accounting*, Summer
   1975.

Questions for discussion

1   Attempt a reasoned defence of historical cost accounting against the criticisms commonly levelled at it.

2   'The valuation of assets can never be more than a subjective process, so that the measurement of profit can be no more than approximate.' Discuss this statement, explaining in particular the link between asset valuation and profit measurement.

3   It is possible to measure profit by calculating the change in capital between two dates. Why, therefore, do accountants consider a profit and loss account is necessary?

4   Critically discuss the major income concepts with which you are familiar.

5   Explain what you understand by 'deprival value'. Why is this concept of value considered to be the most appropriate basis for measuring profit?

6   Consider the following data relating to different points in time:

T0 Buy raw materials for £200.

T1 Add labour for £40; items could now be sold for £300.

T2 Put items in special package for £20; items could now be sold for £400.

T3 Smith (because of inflation) offers £450, if in good condition. Cost to us of making identical item of stock in its special package is now £300 (because of inflation).

T4 Agree to sell to Smith for £450.

T5 Deliver goods to Smith.

T6 Smith signs as having received in good condition.

T7 Smith pays £450.

Required:
Calculate at each point in time as many different measurements of profit as you can, explaining the basis of each calculation. Which 'profit' do you consider to be a 'true and fair view' of the position of the business?

7   There are three possible 'correct' values of an asset—net realizable value, net present value and replacement cost. Explain carefully in your own words the circumstances which may make any one of them the correct 'value to the business'.

8   On 1 January 1983 a company was formed with an issued capital of £100 fully paid up in cash. On 1 January 1983 it purchased for resale a 'widget' for £100, the estimated mark-up being 50 per cent. 'Widgets' are notoriously difficult to turn over and the widget was sold in December 1983 for £180 (there had been a price increase in October 1983 of 20 per cent); another widget was purchased in December 1983 for £120.

(a) On the assumption that all profits are distributed as dividends, show the income statement for 1983 and balance sheet at 31 December 1983 on an historic cost basis (assume all transactions are cash).

(b) Do you think that the income statement is a fair reflection of the operating profit? Does the gross profit percentage reflect the 'terms of trading'?

(c) What will be necessary for the company to carry on the same level of activity?

(d) Is there any alternative system you might consider? If so identify, and draft out the income statement and balance sheet.

(e) Identify the advantages and disadvantages of (d) over historic cost.

(f) Which method (in your opinion) is relevant to the information for a 'decision-making' approach?

(g) Should the holding gain be distributable?

9   (a) If I have capital £1,000 in the bank at the beginning and end of a year, surely I'm worse off if there's been a 20 per cent inflation. How will current replacement cost accounting reflect this?

(b) I understand from my economics that there can be a negative interest cost if I can borrow from the bank at 15 per cent p.a. and there is an inflation rate of 16 per cent p.a. How will this economic reality be reflected in an 'accounting for inflation' system?

(c) If one is trying to assess the performance of managers, what is the problem of separating holding gains from operating gains? Is there a clear distinction in all cases?

(d) Surely it contravenes the conservatism concept to show an asset like stock at current replacement cost when it is higher than historic cost.

(e) Surely I only have a 'real' holding gain on an asset when its specific price rises more than the general price index. If specific price and general price increases are similar, I'm just about breaking even.

10   The balance sheets of Saga Ltd at 31 December 1983 and 31 December 1984 were as follows:

	31 December 83 £'000	31 December 84 £'000
Land and buildings (cost £160)	152	148
Equipment (cost £100)	50	40
Stock	30	40
Debtors	13	28
Bank	(10)	14
	235	270

	31 December 83 £'000	31 December 84 £'000
Ordinary shares	150	150
Reserves	60	70
Debentures 10%	—	20
Creditors	10	15
Dividend proposed	15	15
	235	270

The profit and loss account for the year ended 31 December 1984 was

	£'000	£'000
Sales		100
Opening stock	30	
Purchases	61	
	91	
Less: Closing stock	40	51
Gross Profit		49
Expenses (including debenture interest)	10	
Depreciation—Buildings	4	
Equipment	10	24
Net Profit		25
Dividends proposed		15
Balance carried forward		10

The relevant price indices are

(i)	1982 (average)—Date of building acquisition	105
(ii)	1979 (average)—Date of equipment acquisition and issue of ordinary shares	80
(iii)	1984 (last quarter average)	114
(iv)	1984 (1 January)—debentures issued	116
(v)	1984 (last quarter average)	122
(vi)	1984 (average)	118
(vii)	1984 (31 December)	125

Required:
Prepare the CPP accounts for the year ended 31 December 1984. Comment on your results.

11 Explain why CPP accounting is not considered to be the most appropriate way of accounting for inflation.

12 Saga Ltd (see question 10 above) wishes to adjust its historic accounts to reflect current costs in line with SSAP 16. Assuming that (coincidentally) the 'value to the business' of the assets is given by the price indices above, prepare the accounts on a current cost basis, showing clearly the current cost adjustments for

(i) cost of sales;
(ii) depreciation;
(iii) monetary working capital; and
(iv) gearing.

13 What do you understand by the terms 'ex ante' and 'ex post' income? Using suitable data show how you would calculate and reconcile these two measurements. Why does accounting reject this economic concept of income?

14 Discuss the theoretical and operational criticisms which are levelled at SSAP 16.

15 Acquire (or read in the library) four or five sets of accounts recently published by public limited companies, preferably choosing companies in different sectors of the economy. Compare the historic cost accounts with the CCA accounts, and comment upon your findings.

Part III

Financial planning and control

This section commences with a review of the cost accounting framework (Chapter 13), followed by a brief consideration of the nature of management and the management process providing a framework for an examination of budgetary control and standard costing (Chapters 14 and 15). Long- and short-term decision-making form the focus of Chapters 16 and 17 respectively, with a consideration of the management and control of working capital in Chapter 18. The section concludes (Chapter 19) with an appraisal of the financial performance of businesses by means of ratio and fund flow analysis.

13 Elements of cost accounting

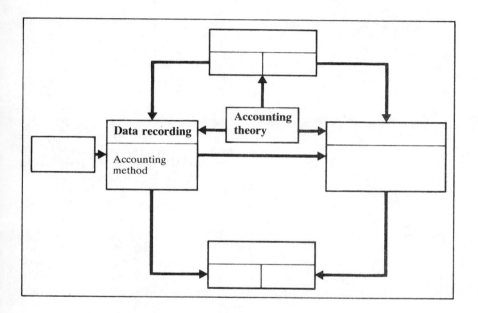

The meaning of cost

The word 'cost' has many meanings in many different settings. In Chapter 2 we defined cost as a 'money sacrifice or the incurring of a liability in pursuit of the business objectives'. For the purposes of income measurement, cost had to be further subdivided in any given time period into expired and unexpired cost. The expired cost was defined as an expense; the unexpired cost as an asset. This notion of cost is an historic one, and perhaps the most fundamental concept of cost in that 'it represents the transformation ratio in production, i.e. that ratio in which the input assets are transformed into the output assets'. Historic cost is the monetary evaluation of this production transformation. As we have seen, in order to make a profit, the firm must ensure that revenues exceed expenses; in other words, the selling price of the output assets must exceed the total transformation cost. In manufacturing industry this transformation cost consists of the raw material costs, wages incurred in the production process

273

and all other expenses necessary to convert the basic material into a marketable commodity, together with administrative and selling expenses.

Such a concept of cost is the basis for balance sheets and income statements which serve the legal, economical and tax needs of an enterprise. It reflects a necessary condition of external reporting, namely, that the recipients of the information—the shareholders, creditors and other interested parties—can be assured that the reports they read are prepared according to some generally accepted set of postulates. If this were not so, it would be impossible for these people to make any sense of the information.

In Chapter 1, we observed that one of the criteria which governed the acceptance of postulates was their utility. Certainly the postulates described are useful to external parties, but they are not necessarily those which are most useful for internal purposes. One of the objectives of the firm is long-run survival; the firm is concerned with its past and current performance, but it is even more concerned with what will happen tomorrow. The costs which are vital to the firm's survival are not past costs—over which management has no control—but the costs associated with the future. The past and future of an enterprise are not entirely unrelated. Most assessments of future cost are derived from adjusting and supplementing the basic historical record of costs. There are two broad categories of future cost which are of importance; costs for planning and control and costs for decision-making. Planned costs are those costs which are reasonably expected to be incurred in some future period or periods. Because these costs represent expectations and not accomplishments, their incurrence is a forecast and their measurement an estimate. Estimates of these costs can be formally incorporated into a comprehensive and co-ordinated plan called a budget. A detailed examination of budgeting will be deferred until Chapter 14. For a plan to be effective, management must know whether it is being followed; hence, for control purposes, there is a need to compare the budgeted expectations against the actual performance.

Costs for decision-making are those which help management to choose between alternative courses of action. To aid in the selection of relevant costs we will draw upon economic analysis for ideas about what costs are appropriate for different decisions. Estimates of these decision-making costs are used only by management, and do not conform to accounting rules, which are designed primarily to assure formal comparability among periods and firms, and to facilitate verification by independent auditors. The use of cost information for this purpose is discussed in Chapter 17.

The present chapter is concerned with the accumulation of historic costs in relation to manufacturing companies. Since historic costs are often adapted and modified for planning and decision-making purposes, it is important to understand the way in which these costs are collected.

The elements of cost

The diagram indicates the elements of cost that are usually associated with manufacturing industries. These are described below.

Direct materials are those which actually become part of the finished product.

Direct labour is the labour applied to the direct materials to transform them into the finished product. These costs can be specifically identified with the products or vary so closely with volume of output that a direct connection is presumed.

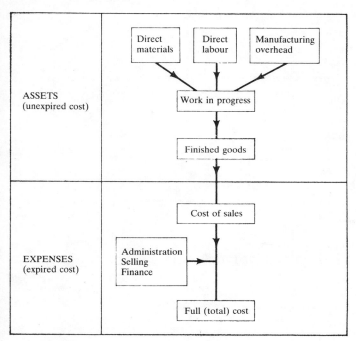

Manufacturing overhead includes all costs (other than direct material and labour) which are associated with the manufacturing process. It will include such items as indirect labour, e.g. supervision and foremen, heat, light, power, maintenance and depreciation. Since there is not any direct association with products, it is usual to apportion or absorb this cost to the product in some logical manner.

The total of these three costs elements in any given period is the factory cost of production. It is the cost which is used for the valuation of work in progress and finished goods. When the finished goods are sold, the cost of these goods becomes an expense, and is charged to the trading, profit and loss account for the period.

The *administrative, selling and finance* expenses are common to all enterprises, whether manufacturing or retail. They are accumulated in expense accounts and charged in the profit and loss section of the income statement. Such expenses are often referred to as 'period costs', indicating that they are considered to be more of a function of time than of volume of production.

Financial records and cost flow

Accounting for manufacturing costs—traditionally referred to as cost accounting—can be maintained as an entity distinct from the double entry system of the financial accounts. However, an integrated accounting system has much to commend it, if only because it ensures that the cost accounts are more than mere memorandum. The accounting flow of costs is illustrated in our costs elements diagram below:

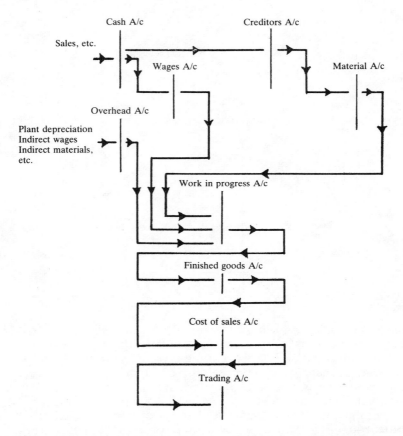

Information relating to materials purchased is recorded in the stock account. As this material is used, the value is transferred to a work in progress account. This account is also charged (debited) with direct labour and manufacturing overhead. As soon as the work is completed the value of the finished goods is transferred to the finished goods account. In the conventional ledger account form the result is as illustrated.

The methods by which the firm determines the monetary values to be assigned to each transfer process will be discussed later in this chapter. For our purposes it is not so important to memorize the details of this procedure, as to understand its nature and significance. The structure reveals a fundamental difference between income measurement in manufacturing enterprises and income measurement in a retail business. In the retail business the costs of wages and depreciation affect net income in the period they are incurred, i.e. they become expenses. This is not necessarily so in the manufacturing concern. The wages and manufacturing overhead associated with the production process initially affect the value of work in progress and finished goods. They affect net income (i.e. they become an expense) in the period when the goods are sold. The larger the stocks in relation to sales (i.e. the slower the turnover rate) the greater the time interval before the costs become expenses.

Income statements for manufacturing businesses

It is evident from the foregoing that, in a manufacturing concern, the development of the cost of goods sold figure is considerably more complex than in a retail organization. While it is possible for the purpose of the income statement to transfer the cost of sales figure to the trading account, omitting all of the detailed build up, it is more customary for internal purposes to produce a detailed statement of the costs of goods manufactured and sold in a statement called the manufacturing account. This is a formal presentation of the data processed through the cost accounting cycle during the accounting period. A typical manufacturing account will appear as follows:

Asta Co. Ltd
Manufacturing Account for the year ended 31 December 1984

	£	£	£
Opening stock of materials	267,000		
Purchases	1,248,000		
		1,515,000	
Less: Closing stock		215,000	
			1,300,000
Direct wages			530,000
Prime Cost of Manufacture			1,830,000
Factory overhead			
Indirect wages		47,000	
Plant depreciation		89,000	
Maintenance		13,000	
Power, light, heat		9,000	
Factory rates		4,500	
Indirect materials		12,500	
			175,000
Work in progress 1.1.84		427,000	
Less: Work in progress 31.12.84		398,000	
			29,000
Factory Cost of Production			2,034,000

Asta Co. Ltd
Manufacturing Account for the year ended 31 December 1984
(*continued*)

	£	£
Finished goods 1.1.84	427,000	
Less: Finished goods 31.12.84	413,000	
		14,000
Cost of Goods Sold		**£2,048,000**

Responsibility accounting

One of management's main objectives with respect to costs is their effective control. To achieve this, it is essential to trace costs to responsible employees, thus assigning the responsibility for their control. Costs are commonly identified with the smallest units of managerial responsibility, called the 'cost centre'. All manufacturing costs are accumulated and recorded on the basis of the cost centre to which they are logically traceable. Some costs, however, such as factory rates, cannot be logically traced to any unit save the factory as a whole; these costs are commonly collected in larger cost centres, and are then allocated on some arbitrary basis to the smaller cost centres. The cost centre, therefore, is an accounting device which may or may not have a physical existence.

The method of assigning costs to the appropriate cost centre varies considerably in practice. It is possible to have a separate account for the cost elements—materials, labour and overhead—within each individual cost centre. Alternatively, a single account may be kept for each cost element, subsidiary records being maintained to identify responsibility for costs by cost centre. Whatever the method, however, the central objective must be kept firmly in mind, namely, the identification of costs with responsible managers and supervisors.

Accounting for materials

Accounting for materials begins when a purchase requisition is issued making a formal request for a required amount. This requisition is often issued when existing material stocks reach a predetermined minimum level. If the requisition is approved, a purchase order will be issued to a selected supplier, itemizing material specifications, price and delivery dates. The supplier complies with this order by delivering the goods and invoicing the purchaser by means of a purchase invoice. After the goods have been checked against the invoice, and the invoice checked against the purchase order, the invoice becomes the basis for the recording procedure, i.e. a debit to inventory and a credit to the creditors (*see* flow chart on page 276).

When materials are needed for production, material requisitions are issued by the production departments; these departments are identified by a cost centre number. The material has now become part of the process of manufacture, and the value is transferred to a work in process account.

If the material issued is indirect material, e.g. maintenance material, etc., which is not incorporated in the finished products its value is transferred to the manufacturing overhead account. All such costs are accumulated in this account prior to allocation to a particular job or process (*see* page 283).

Accounting for labour

There are two aspects of labour accounting; one is concerned with the actual payment to the employee and referred to as payroll accounting; the other is concerned with the problem of identifying the labour costs either directly with production or as an indirect or overhead cost. All labour costs are accumulated by cost centre, by means of records maintained in the individual departments.

The distinction between direct and indirect labour is not so clearly defined as one might imagine. Certainly the wages of foremen, cleaners, watchmen and maintenance workers and others are indirect, for they can in no way be traced logically and practically to the product. But how should the wages of the production workers be treated when they are not engaged on productive work—during holidays, idle time due to machinery break-downs? Equally how should overtime, premiums and bonuses, or higher rates for nightshifts, be considered? The common answer is to consider all these costs as overhead, since these costs are applicable to production as a whole rather than to the production of an individual unit.

Up to the present time, production labour has been regarded as a direct cost, incurred uniquely because of the units of the product manufactured. To the extent that wages have been paid for work done (i.e. piece rate) or by the hour (with the general dictum 'no work, no pay'), wages have varied directly with the volume of production. However, there is a growing trend in wage agreements to pay workers for a given number of hours per week, irrespective of the amount of production. Under such circumstances it is no longer strictly possible to trace labour costs directly to a unit of production; wages have in essence become a fixed cost in the short run. It is obviously still possible to charge these wages to production at some normal rate, i.e. a constant rate per unit of production, and treat any difference as overhead, but this is only an accounting device and makes the cost artificial.

We will return to this point when we discuss the problems associated with fixed and variable costs, and the different means of treating them offered by marginal and absorption costing. Nevertheless, many of the difficulties associated with fixed cost labour are as yet beyond the compass of accounting practice.

Accounting for overhead

As we have seen, all costs connected with the manufacturing process, other than direct labour and direct material, are classified as indirect costs. In our flow chart, we indicated that the overhead associated with a given period was collected in an overhead account and transferred to the work in progress account. There are two interrelated problems: (1) the composition of overhead and (2) the method of charging it to production.

Overhead costs can be classified as variable or fixed. Variable overhead is the name given to those indirect costs which will vary with the volume of production. These costs (along with direct material and labour) are sometimes referred to as product costs. Fixed overhead embraces those costs which are not so much a function of production as a function of time, and are incurred in order to maintain production facilities. These costs remain more or less constant irrespective of moderate changes in the level of activity attained. In a practical situation, it is often very difficult to determine which costs are fixed and which costs are variable. There are a number of costs which contain an element of both, e.g. electricity for power for which there is a basic charge coupled with a charge per unit of consumption. As we shall learn, the distinction is so useful, that it must be made even if it involves a number of approximations.

In economic analysis it is usual to distinguish between the long and short run, i.e. five years and over, and one to two years. In the long run, all costs are variable; for example the 'fixed' rent for a factory can be avoided by the simple expedient of closing down the factory. In the very short run, the variable element may almost completely disappear, e.g. an employee must receive a minimum period of notice. Accounting analysis is normally implicitly conducted in terms of the short run, 'short' in this case signifying the accounting period of one year.

There are two main approaches to accounting for overhead, namely absorption (or full, or total) costing, and marginal (or direct, or variable) costing. Absorption costing, the traditional method of accounting for manufacturing costs, includes all manufacturing costs, regardless of their behaviour with respect to changes in volume, as costs of the product; fixed and variable manufacturing costs are handled in an identical manner. Marginal costing includes only those manufacturing costs which vary with volume in the product cost; fixed costs are treated as 'period' costs. Since in practice all direct material and labour costs are treated as variable under both methods, the only—but crucially important—difference between the two methods is the accounting treatment afforded to fixed overhead. The difference may be illustrated diagrammatically, and is shown on page 282.

Absorption costing

Because overhead is indirect and, in total, does not vary directly with production, it is not possible to charge overhead costs to production in the same way as material and labour. There are a variety of methods for allocating overhead to production, but basically they all require the collection of these costs in production and service cost centres, the apportionment of service costs to production cost centres on some rational basis and, finally, their allocation to the unit of production.

For the sake of simplicity, we will assume that there is only one cost centre—the entire factory—which manufactures one homogeneous product. This assumption will in no way alter the basic concepts involved—it merely reduces the number of accounts to be handled. At a later stage, when considering job and process costing, we will drop this assumption.

Actual overhead is very rarely charged to production; instead a budgeted or normal overhead rate is used. The reason for this is twofold. First, under an actual overhead absorption system, when a job is finished and sent to the customer early in a month, it will be impossible to invoice the customer until early in the following month—clearly an unsatisfactory arrangement for both parties concerned. Secondly, and perhaps more important, any fluctuation in volume of output during the year will result in different monthly overhead rates and, therefore, different total costs per unit. This arises simply because overhead has a fixed and variable component. Assume that for a particular product the overhead consists of £2,000 per month fixed costs, and £2 per unit variable costs. The total overhead absorbed per unit will fluctuate as follows:

Month	Production (units)	Fixed overhead	Fixed overhead per unit	Variable overhead per unit	Total overhead per unit
		£	£	£	£
January	500	2,000	4	2	6
February	800	2,000	2.5	2	4.5
March	1,000	2,000	2	2	4
April	1,500	2,000	1.33	2	4
May	1,000	2,000	2	2	3.33
June	750	2,000	2.66	2	4.66

Overhead absorbed per unit varies inversely with the volume of production, and differences in unit cost will appear even though the product remains unchanged.

A normal overhead rate for the entire factory can be determined quite readily from observations of overhead costs incurred in the past accounting period, with adjustments for changing prices and circumstances. This figure is then divided by the expected (budgeted) volume of output to produce an overhead absorption rate per unit, which is applied to the actual production of the period to obtain an overhead cost which is transferred to work in progress. Under this system if either the actual volume of production differs from expectations, and/or actual overhead costs differ from those anticipated, there will be a difference between the overhead absorbed and the actual overhead. These differences are termed under-applied overhead when actual costs exceed the costs applied, and over-applied overhead when the costs applied are greater than the actual costs incurred. The overhead over or under applied is normally adjusted through the trading account.

282

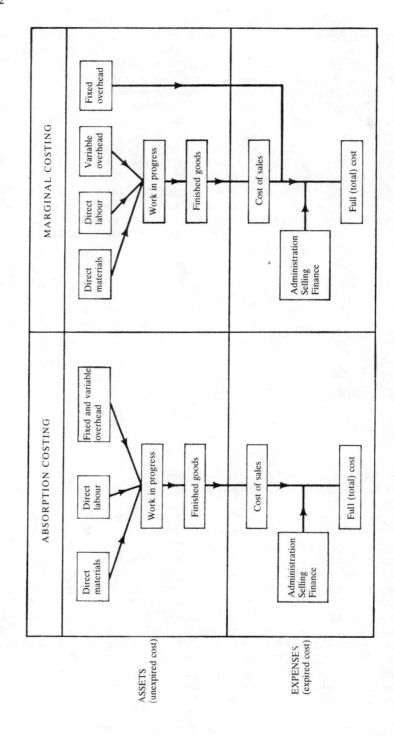

Example 1

At this point, it may be helpful to study a single example with specific production and cost data:

(1) The Askew Manufacturing Co.'s experience indicates that variable overhead should be £0.5 per unit, and that fixed overhead will be £560,000, at 280,000 units—a fixed overhead absorption rate of £2 per unit.
(2) Raw (direct) materials costing £600,000 were acquired on credit.
(3) Materials costing £500,000 were issued at work in progress.
(4) Direct wages amounted to £300,000.
(5) Fixed overhead amounted to £530,000, and variable overhead to £190,000.
(6) Units actually produced amounted to 300,000.
(7) The total cost of completed production was £1,200,000 (the determination of this cost will be discussed later).

Fixed overhead A/c

Creditors		WIP	600,000
Cash	530,000		
Trading A/c	70,000		
	600,000		**600,000**

Materials A/c

Creditors		WIP	500,000
	600,000		
		Balance	100,000
	600,000		**600,000**
Balance	100,000		

Variable overhead A/c

Creditors			
Cash	190,000	WIP	150,000
		Trading A/c	40,000
	190,000		**190,000**

Wages A/c

Cash			
	300,000	WIP	**300,000**

Work in progress A/c

	£'000		£'000
Material	500	Finished goods	1,200
Wages	300		
Fixed overhead	600	Balance	350
Variable overhead	150		
	1,550		**£1,550**
Balance	**£350**		

Finished goods A/c

	£'000	
WIP	1,200	

The fixed overhead transferred to work in progress amounts to 300,000 × £2 = £600,000, resulting in an over-absorption of £70,000. In the instance of the variable overhead the transfer is 300,000 × £0.5 = £150,000, an under-absorption of £40,000.

Marginal costing

Under a marginal costing system, all fixed overhead costs are treated as 'period' costs, and no attempt is made to allocate these to production. At this point we will merely observe the effect of this on the accounts, leaving till later stages a discussion of the relative merits of the two approaches.

Since fixed overhead is not absorbed, the actual cost is transferred to the trading account:

Trading A/c Dr.	£530,000	
Fixed overhead		£530,000

Notice that this results in a substantially lower valuation of both work in progress and of finished goods. The difference in finished goods cost must be the number of units completed multiplied by the normal fixed overhead rate, for the only difference between absorption and marginal costing is the treatment afforded to fixed overhead.

Cost accounting systems—job costing

So far in this chapter we have attempted to obtain an overall perspective of the cost flow cycle. To achieve this, we simplified the analysis by assuming that there was only one cost centre for the entire factory, and only one homogeneous product. While the basic concepts remain, there are two major classifications of costing systems which are employed in practice, job costing and process costing. Within these classifications both absorption and marginal costing can be employed with equal facility.

Essentially, a job cost system collects costs for each physically identifiable job or batch of work as it moves through the factory, regardless of the accounting period in which the work is done. The 'job' may consist of a single unit, or of units of identical or similar products. Such a system is normally used either to undertake specific orders, e.g. in construction, printing and shipbuilding, or where production is a series of different jobs, e.g. furniture-making.

Direct material and labour costs are traced to individual jobs by keeping a job order number, and overhead is applied at a normal rate when the job is finished. All costs are accumulated for each 'job cost sheet', and all costs charged to production during any given period will be equal to the total of all charges to job cost sheets in that same period. Similarly, the costs transferred to finished goods will represent all costs recorded on the completed job sheets. Thus the unit cost on any one job may involve cost data spanning two or more accounting periods.

Materials will be charged to the job on some predetermined basis—LIFO, FIFO or any other acceptable method. Our discussions in Chapter 7 were related to stock of retail undertakings and can be applied to the transfer of materials to work in progress. Direct labour charges will be ascertained by recording the actual hours spent and multiplying by the hourly rate. The use of normal overhead rates is regarded as essential to the smooth functioning of the system.

It is now convenient to drop our simplifying assumption of one cost centre and one product. Obviously in practice there are several production departments (cost centres) and the product is not often homogeneous. Where different products are manufactured in the same factory, it is hardly logical to absorb overhead on some flat rate. One product may, for example, require more man hours and more machine hours than another. When the unit of production is not a suitable 'common denominator' for the application of overhead, the volume of production may be stated in some unit common to all products—usually direct labour hours or machine hours.

We may illustrate the process of setting the overhead rates. The first stage is to accumulate all of the indirect costs by department or cost centre. Some of these costs may be directly traceable to these individual departments (e.g. supervision wages, maintenance wages, indirect materials), and this can be allocated directly, but others (e.g. rent, lighting, heating) will have to be apportioned to the departments on an appropriate basis. What is 'appropriate' depends upon establishing a causal relationship between the cost and a

Overhead analysis

	Production departments		Service departments		Total costs	Basis of allocation/ apportionment
	A	B	C	D		
	£	£	£	£	£	
Supervisory wages	2,000	1,500	1,000	1,200	5,700	Actual
Maintenance wages	1,200	1,300	500	—	3,000	Actual
Indirect materials	800	1,400	300	200	2,700	Actual
Power	700	900	200	—	1,800	HP of machinery
Rent and rates	500	800	200	300	1,800	Floor area
Light and heat	1,000	1,600	400	600	3,600	Floor area
Machinery insurance	800	500	300	—	1,600	Book value of machinery
	7,000	8,000	2,900	2,300	20,200	

department, and this can often be fairly arbitrary. For example, if a factory incurs a heating bill, then it is fairly evident that all departments within the factory should bear a share of that cost. But on what basis? Space occupied, floor area occupied, number of heating points—all could be deemed 'appropriate'. In the end, a judgement has to be made—with the obvious result that a different basis of apportionment will lead to different levels of cost for the same department.

We may illustrate this process by means of an overhead analysis sheet, noting that there are two types of cost centre or department—the production departments which are directly engaged in the manufacturing process, and the service departments which support the activities of the production departments.

The next stage in the process is to apportion the total costs of the service centres to the production departments. To do this, we must be aware of the functions of the service departments in order to find an appropriate basis for apportionment. For example, if Service Department C is a maintenance department, then it could be logical to apportion its costs to the other departments on the basis of the maintenance wages directly allocated to those departments, as this presumably is a measure of time spent by the Maintenance Department in the service of the production departments. Once again, however, there is no 'right' basis—only that which seems to be the most appropriate.

The analysis begun above may continue a further stage by apportioning the service costs to the production departments. Service Department D is assumed to be a stores department and its costs are apportioned on the basis of the value of materials issued to the other departments.

Overhead apportionment

	Production departments		Service departments		Total costs	Basis of apportionment
	A	B	C	D		
	£	£	£	£	£	
Costs per schedule	7,000	8,000	2,900	2,300	20,200	
Department D	736	1,288	276	(2,300)	—	Materials issued
Department C	1,524	1,652	(3,176)	—	—	Maintenance wages
	9,260	10,940	—	—	20,200	

It will be noted that the costs of Service Department D are apportioned in part to Service Department C, simply because a service is provided by D to C. In this example, this causes no difficulty with the final apportionment, because C does not provide a service to D. If it did do so, then we are faced with the problem of reciprocal service costs, where there is an iterative process of apportionment. This can be dealt with by trial and error, or, more sensibly by a mathematical process; perhaps, however, if we bear in mind all of the judgements we have had to make in apportioning many of the costs in the first place, it is not difficult on practical grounds simply to ignore the apportionment of service costs among service departments.

The final stage in the whole process is to calculate for each production department an appropriate overhead absorption rate by which overhead is 'attached' to production. There are several bases for absorbing overhead, and the most important of these may be briefly summarized as follows:

(i) *Material cost percentage rate* given by:

$$\frac{\text{Overhead to be absorbed}}{\text{Total direct material cost}}\%$$

This is appropriate only when material costs form a major part of the total cost and where overheads tend to relate to material costs.

(ii) *Wages percentage rate* given by:

$$\frac{\text{Overhead to be absorbed}}{\text{Total direct wages}}\%$$

This is suitable only when wages form a significant part of the total cost, and the wages give a fair indication of the time taken to do a particular job.

(iii) *Prime cost percentage rate* given by:

$$\frac{\text{Overhead to be absorbed}}{\text{Direct materials + direct wages}}\%$$

This is probably the least equitable of methods, for it requires satisfaction of the conditions which are identified in (i) and (ii) above—a condition rarely occurring in practice.

(iv) *Labour hour rate* given by:

$$\frac{\text{Overhead to be absorbed}}{\text{Number of labour hours}}\%$$

This is appropriate where most work is completed manually or with the aid of machines having a low operating cost in relation to the cost of labour.

(v) *Machine hour rate* given by:

$$\frac{\text{Overhead to be absorbed}}{\text{Number of machine hours}}\%$$

This is appropriate where machine time is the dominant feature of production.

Returning to our illustration, if we assume that we have established a strong correlation between the incurring of overhead and machine hours, then we may calculate the machine hour overhead absorption rate for each of the production departments.

Overhead absorption rates

	Production departments	
	A	B
Total costs	£9,260	£10,940
Machine hours	15,000	10,000
Machine hour rate	£0.62	£1.09

With the overhead absorption rates determined, the cost of any one job may now be ascertained, viz:

Job Cost Sheet No. XZ50

			£	£
Direct materials				50.00
Direct labour:	L. hours	Rate		
Department A	10 @	£2.0	20.00	
Department B	5 @	£1.5	7.50	27.50
Factory overhead:	M. hours	Rate		
Department A	12 @	£0.62	7.44	
Department B	8 @	£1.09	8.72	16.16
Total job cost				£93.66

Thus the cost of this job is £93.66, but we need to remind ourselves that the very precision of this figure can mask and make us forget the many judgements which were made in arriving at it, particularly the selection of 'appropriate' bases for apportionment and absorption. Different bases, all of which may be defensible, will lead to a different total cost—a fact which should make us treat any 'right' figure with considerable caution.

Cost accounting systems—process costing

Process costing regards production as a continuous flow, and this type of system is employed in industries where production processes are of a repetitive and continuous nature. All costs for an accounting period are initially collected without any attempt to attach them to specific units of production. The total cost incurred during the period is divided by the units of production worked on during the period; this provides the cost per unit and is used as a basis of valuing goods transferred to the finished goods stocks, and later on to the cost of goods sold.

Since in a process cost system there are a number of production processes, costs are collected for each process in a cost centre, the overhead rate being calculated in some suitable manner—as, for example, on page 285.

The ascertainment of unit cost requires a calculation of units worked on in a given period. Units worked on include

(1) Units that were both started and completed during the period; plus
(2) Units that were started but not completed during the period; plus
(3) Units that were started in a prior period and completed in this period.

Since 100 per cent of the costs of (1) were incurred in the current period, but only a portion of the costs of (2) and (3), the real production cannot be determined simply by adding up the units worked on. The three types of units must be converted to a common basis called *equivalent production*.

Equivalent units measure the work accomplished in a given period. For example, if 10,000 units were started and completed in a period, 4,000 units were started but were only one-quarter complete, and 3,000 units were completed but were one-third complete at the beginning of the period, the equivalent production is

Units begun and completed	10,000
Units started but incomplete $4,000 \times \frac{1}{4}$	1,000
Units completed but partly started in prior period $3,000 \times \frac{2}{3}$	2,000
Equivalent Production	**13,000**

If the total costs collected in the cost centre were £26,000 then the unit cost is 26,000/13,000 = £2 per unit.

The problem may be further complicated by the fact that not all the cost factors of production are the same fraction complete at any stage. For example, a stock of work in progress may be complete in respect of materials, but a fraction complete in respect of labour and overhead. Thus we may be faced with two or more sets of equivalent units:

	Materials	Labour and overhead
Units begun and completed	10,000	10,000
Units started but incomplete		
Materials $(4,000 \times 1)$	4,000	
Labour and overhead $(4,000 \times \frac{1}{4})$		1,000
Units completed but partly started in prior period		
Materials $(3,000 \times \frac{1}{2})$	1,500	
Labour and overhead $(3,000 \times \frac{2}{3})$		2,000
Equivalent Units	15,500	13,000

Whatever the method used to ascertain the equivalent production (and it must always be related to a particular cost factor to be meaningful) the valuation will depend on the particular cost flow assumption used. If, for example, the unit costs of the previous period had been £1 per unit, then the value of the opening stock (using our first illustration) would have been

$$3,000 \times \tfrac{1}{3} \times £1 = £1,000$$

The cost to complete would have been

$$3,000 \times \tfrac{2}{3} \times £2 = £4,000$$

giving a total cost for 3,000 units of £5,000 and a unit cost of

$$5,000/3,000 = £1.66$$

Example 2

As a simple example, we may specify the following data:

Dept. A—process 1

(1) 30,000 lb of material costing £9,000 were put into the process.
(2) Direct wages amounted to £3,750.
(3) Overhead costs were £1,250.
(4) 22,500 lb were completed and transferred to dept. B.
(5) Of the remaining work in process, all the necessary material has been used, but it is only one-third complete as regards labour and overhead costs.

The equivalent units are

Material	*Units*
Begun, completed and transferred	22,500
Begun, completed but in process	7,500
Equivalent Units	**30,000 lb**

Labour and overhead	
Begun, completed and transferred	22,500
Begun and $\tfrac{1}{3}$ complete 7,500 × $\tfrac{1}{3}$	2,500
Equivalent Units	**25,000 lb**

Unit costs

Material $\dfrac{9,000}{30,000} = £0.30$

Labour $\dfrac{3,750}{25,000} = £0.15$

Overhead $\dfrac{1,250}{25,000} = \begin{array}{c} £0.05 \\ \hline \mathbf{£0.50} \end{array}$

The value of the work in progress is therefore

	Equivalent units	Cost per unit £	Total cost £
Material	7,500	0.30	2,250
Labour	2,500	0.15	375
Overhead	2,500	0.05	125
		0.50	2,750

The process account for dept. A would be as follows:

Dept. A—Process 1 A/c

	Units (lb)	£		Units (lb)	£
Material	30,000	9,000	Transfer to		
Labour		3,750	dept. B	22,500	11,250
Overhead		1,250	Work in progress c/f	7,500	2,750
	30,000	14,000		30,000	14,000

Dept. B—process 2

In dept. B, the second part of the process attracts additional labour and overhead costs. Thus:

(1) Direct wages amount to £5,250.
(2) Overhead costs were £2,800.
(3) 22,500 lb were completely processed.

In the second process, therefore, the equivalent units for material, labour and overhead have a factor of 1, so that the process account would be

Dept. B—Process 2 A/c

	Units (lb)	£		Units (lb)	£
Transfer from dept. A	22,500	11,250	Finished goods A/c	22,500	19,300
Labour		5,250	Work in progress	—	—
Wages		2,800			
	22,500	19,300		22,500	19,300

Two further problems often arise in process costing. The first of these relates to losses during the production process, and the second to the production of joint or by-products of the process.

(1)   Normal and abnormal losses

Lost or spoilt units occur in some manufacturing processes either through natural wastage such as shrinkage or evaporation, or through mistakes which give rise to defective work. Losses which arise through natural wastage are referred to as 'normal' losses, and, although they do not affect the total costs of manufacturing during a given period, they do increase the unit costs.

This increase in unit costs is simply due to the fact that the cost of the work done on the lost units be absorbed by the remaining good units, thus increasing the unit cost of those good units. For example, if the total costs of a process are £20,000 and the material input of 5,000 lb gives rise to an output of 4,800 lb through material shrinkage, the unit cost rises from

$$\frac{20,000}{5,000} = \text{£4 per unit}$$

to

$$\frac{20,000}{4,800} = \text{£4.17 per unit}$$

If we return to our example above, and assume that the normal yield of process 1 is 90 per cent (i.e. the 'normal' loss is 10 per cent of the input), then we may re-calculate the equivalent units and costs. The equivalent units are

Material	*Units*
Begun, completed and transferred	22,500
Begun, completed but in process	4,500
Equivalent Units (normal yield)	27,000
'Normal' loss	3,000
Total input	**30,000 lb**

Labour and overhead	
Begun, completed and transferred	22,500
Begun and $\frac{1}{3}$ complete 4,500 × $\frac{1}{3}$	1,500
Equivalent Units	**24,000 lb**

Unit costs

Material $\dfrac{9,000}{27,000}$ = £0.333

Labour $\dfrac{3,750}{24,000}$ = £0.156

Overhead $\dfrac{1,250}{24,000}$ = £0.052

£0.541

The value of the work in progress is

	Equivalent units	Cost per unit £	Total cost £
Material	4,500	0.333	1,500
Labour	1,500	0.156	234
Overhead	1,500	0.052	78
		0.541	1,812

and the process 1 A/c would be

Dept. A—Process 1 A/c

	Units (lb)	£		Units (lb)	£
Material	30,000	9,000	Transfer to dept. B	22,500	12,188
Labour		3,750			
Overhead		1,250	'Normal' loss	3,000	—
			Work in progress c/f	4,500	1,812
	30,000	14,000		30,000	14,000

Where losses arise during the production process as a consequence of some expected factor, or through error, this gives rise to 'abnormal' losses. In some processes, an 'abnormal' gain may arise because a particular process in any given period turns out to be more efficient than expected. Unlike the 'normal' losses or gains, however, the 'abnormal' loss or gain is not absorbed as part of the total cost of the process, but costed at the 'normal' cost per unit of output.

Modifying again our previous illustration, we may assume that although the normal yield is 90 per cent, the actual output is 22,200 lb, with 4,500 lb remaining in the process. The equivalent units are therefore

Material	Units
Begun, completed and transferred	22,200
Begun, completed but in process	4,500
'Abnormal' loss	300
Equivalent Units (normal yield)	27,000
'Normal' loss	3,000
Total input	**30,000**

Labour and overhead

Begun, completed and transferred   22,200

Begun and $\frac{1}{3}$ complete 4,500 × $\frac{1}{3}$ 1,500

Equivalent Units   **23,700 lb**

The 'normal' costs of the process are as previously calculated, and hence the closing work in progress is valued at £1,812. The transfer to process 2 is valued at

$$\frac{£22,200}{22,500} \times 12,188$$

or £12,026, and the abnormal loss at £162 (i.e. £300 × 0.541). The modified process 1 account would show

Dept. A—Process 1 A/c

	Units (lb)	£		Units (lb)	£
Material	30,000	9,000	Transfer to dept. B	22,200	12,026
Labour		3,750	Normal loss	3,000	—
Overhead		1,250	Abnormal loss	300	162
			Work in progress c/f	4,500	1,812
	30,000	14,000		30,000	14,000

(2)   Joint and by-products

Joint products are two or more products manufactured simultaneously by a common or series of processing operations. The quantity and sales value are such that their production costs cannot be effectively separated. For example, in the oil industry many products—petrol, benzene, naphtha, etc.—are obtained from the basic crude oil. By-products are produced under the same conditions, but are essentially a secondary result of the process, both in terms of quantity and value of output. For example, the main purpose of the gas industry is the production of gas, but that production often gives rise to by-products such as coke, tar and ammonia.

Where joint products are concerned there are three main methods of establishing the 'cost' of the product—on a simple output quantity basis, on a weighted average of sales values, or by some formulae. For example, in the oil industry the proportion of each of the outputs from the refining of crude oil is known, so that material costs can be apportioned on this basis. Where, however, some products are much more valuable than others, then the output is weighted by market price. In copper mining, for example, there are often valuable metals such as silver and gold which are mined at the same time. In chemical processes the split of costs can be done on a 'formulae' split. It is apparent, however, that whatever difficulties there are in establishing the 'cost' of a single product, these problems become magnified in a situation where already 'arbitrary' costs are reallocated to joint products.

Still more complicated is the position of by-products, where the wide variation in the nature and importance of the by-product gives rise to equally divergent accounting treatment. If the value of the by-product is small, the revenue from it is treated as miscellaneous income, and no 'costs' are attached to it. If a by-product requires further processing after separation from the main product, then it is often regarded as only having costs after the point of separation. Sometimes, the by-product is treated virtually as a joint product, and one of the costing methods described above is employed to establish its cost.

The problems of joint and by-product costs are beyond the scope of this text, but this brief comment is designed to highlight yet again the difficulties of establishing the 'true cost' of a product.

Absorption and marginal costing compared

Absorption costing is the generally accepted manner of accounting for manufacturing costs and, specifically, for fixed overhead costs. There are a number of claims advanced for absorption costing, namely:

(1) To control expenditure
(2) To set a selling price.
(3) To value inventory correctly, and so to measure income correctly.

(1)   Control of expenditure

Earlier on in this chapter we discussed briefly responsibility accounting, where costs are identified with the responsible managers and supervisors. Generally, expenditure can best be effectively controlled at the point where it is actually incurred, e.g. the salary of the works manager is best controlled at the point of appointment and not where part of his salary is charged by apportionment to a process or product. Indeed the whole point about fixed overhead is that, as it does not vary with volume of production, any allocation to production is arbitrary.

(2)   Setting a selling price

It is often argued that full cost must be known before the selling price can be fixed. This concept is most attractive at first sight, yet for many industries price is fixed by considerations external to the firm. Secondly, since fixed overhead allocations are subject to a variety of 'acceptable' methods, price becomes a function of method and not of cost.

(3)   Valuing inventory and measuring income

The advocates of absorption costing would argue that it is correct to include fixed overheads in the valuation of stock. Before developing this point, let us consider an illustration which compares absorption and marginal costing in this respect. We will follow the fortunes of a firm for three years. We will assume:

(1) Sales remain annually constant at 35,000 units at £10 per unit.
(2) Variable overhead is £1 per unit, and fixed overhead is £20,000 p.a. For the sake of simplicity we will assume that normal overhead absorption rates and actual overhead costs are the same.
(3) Production in year I is 40,000 units, year II 60,000 and year III 30,000.
(4) Direct labour and material costs amount to £6 per unit.
(5) From (2) and (3) it follows that the fixed overhead absorption rates are in £0.5, £0.33 and £0.66 per unit in the successive years.

Comparative inventory and income measurement

Year I	Units '000	£	Absorption £'000	£'000	£'000	Marginal £'000	£'000	£'000
Sales	35	10			350			350
Cost of goods produced:								
direct labour and materials	40	6.0	240			240		
variable overhead	40	1.0	40			40		
fixed overhead	40	0.5	20			—		
				300			280	
Closing stock:								
direct materials and labour	5	6.0	30			30		
variable overhead	5	1.0	5			5		
fixed overhead	5	0.5	2.5	37.5	262.5	—	35	245
								105
Fixed overhead								20
Gross Profit					87.5			85
Year II								
Sales	35	10			350			350
Opening stock	5			37.5			35	
Cost of goods produced								
direct materials and labour	60	6.0	360			360		
variable overhead	60	1.0	60			60		
fixed overhead	60	0.33	20	440			420	
				477.5			455	
Closing stock								
direct materials and labour	30	6.0	180			180		
variable overhead	30	1.0	30			30		
fixed overhead	30	0.33	10	220	257.5		210	245
								105
Fixed overhead								20
Gross Profit					92.5			85

Comparative inventory and income measurement (continued)

Year III	Units '000	£ '000	Absorption £ '000	Absorption £ '000	Absorption £ '000	Marginal £ '000	Marginal £ '000	Marginal £ '000
Sales	35	10			350			350
Opening stock	30			220			210	
Cost of goods produced								
direct labour and materials	30	6.0	180			180		
variable overhead	30	1.0	30			30		
fixed overhead	30	0.66	20	230		—	210	
				450			420	
Closing stock								
direct materials and labour	25	6.0	150			150		
variable overhead	25	1.0	25			25		
fixed overhead	25	0.66	16.6	191.6	258.4	—	175	245
								105
Fixed overhead								20
Gross Profit					**91.6**			**85**

The basic point of the illustration is that during the three years there were no changes in sales price, sales volume, direct cost per unit and variable overhead per unit, or in total fixed costs. The only change was in the volume of production. Under absorption costing, income fluctuates; under marginal costing, it is constant.

Which is more desirable? The answer to that depends on whether fixed manufacturing costs are incurred to provide productive capacity, or attach to the units of production. To put it another way, are such costs functions of time or of production? As to which of these positions is correct has been and is still argued frequently and strongly. In this country, opinion is divided. Up until 1 January 1976 the ruling recommendation of the Institute of Chartered Accountants (N22) stated: 'The method selected by the management must have regard to the nature and circumstances of the business so as to ensure that the trend of the trading profits will be shown fairly.'

This rather ambivalent attitude has now been clarified by SSAP 9, 'Stocks and Work in Progress'. In the introduction to this standard we find: 'In order to match costs and revenue, "costs" of stocks and work in progress should comprise that expenditure which has been incurred in the normal course of business in bringing the product or service to its present location and condition. Such costs will include all related production overheads, even though these may accrue on a time basis.'

This decisive statement in favour of absorption costing is further emphasized in the statement's 'Definition of Terms', where it is indicated that

'. . . each overhead should be classified according to function . . . so as to ensure the inclusion in the cost of conversion of those overheads (including depreciation) which relate to production, notwithstanding that these may accrue wholly or partly on a time basis.'

The Accounting Standard has therefore come down decisively in favour of absorption costing for the purposes of income measurement and valuation although, as with most standards, there is no attempt to argue the case but merely an *ex cathedra* pronouncement. It will be interesting to see how well the standard stands the test of time.

References and further reading

ACCOUNTING STANDARDS COMMITTEE (1975), SSAP 9, 'Stocks and Work in Progress'.

DIXON (1969), *The Case for Marginal Costing*. I.C.A.

FEKRAT (1972), 'The Conceptual Foundation of Absorption Costing', *Accounting Review*, April 1972.

HORNGREN (1983), *Cost Accounting: A Managerial Emphasis*. Prentice-Hall.

SWALLEY (1974), 'The Benefits of Direct Costing', *Management Accounting*, September 1974.

Questions for discussion

1   Identify the distinguishing characteristics of direct costs. Apply your definitions to distinguish the following items of expenditure by a manufacturing business as either direct or indirect costs:

    (i)   Raw materials used in the product.
    (ii)   Consumable tools used in the production departments.
    (iii)   Employer's National Insurance contributions for production workers.
    (iv)   Overtime earnings for production workers.
    (v)   Foremen's wages.
    (vi)   Wages of labourers engaged on moving and handling raw materials used in the product.
    (vii) Disposal of waste material.
    (viii) Works directors' salaries.
    (ix)   Depreciation of machinery.
    (x)   Cost accounting department's wages.

2   What factors determine whether wages are treated as direct or indirect cost? Illustrate your answer with a suitable range of examples.

3   Bill Jones runs a small manufacturing company. At 31 December 1984.

a trial balance extracted from his records was as follows:

	£	£
Capital		23,400
Reserves		2,000
Creditors		1,000
Sales		37,330
Land and buildings (cost)	12,000	
Machinery (cost)	9,000	
Office equipment (cost)	1,000	
Vans (cost)	3,000	
Cash	700	
Debtors	6,000	
Factory wages	4,980	
Warehouse wages	2,030	
Provision for doubtful debts		420
Depreciation—buildings		4,000
—machinery		3,440
—office equipment		700
—vans		1,200
Purchases—raw materials	7,800	
—finished goods	1,400	
Factory expenses	3,440	
Sales returns	400	
Warehouse expenses	3,000	
Administration expenses	1,550	
Selling expenses	4,000	
Stocks at 1.1.84—raw material	1,400	
—WIP	2,250	
—finished goods	9,760	
Miscellaneous revenue		220
	73,710	**73,710**

The following adjustments are to be taken into account:

(i)	Stocks at 31 December 1984:	
	Raw materials	£1,000
	WIP	£1,500
	Finished goods	£10,500
(ii)	Expenses accrued at 31 December 1984:	
	Factory	£600
	Warehouse	£270
(iii)	Items paid in advance—selling expenses	100
(iv)	Depreciation is to be provided:	
	Buildings	2% on cost
	Machinery	10% on cost
	Office equipment	10% on cost
	Vans	20% on cost

Required:
Prepare the manufacturing, trading and profit and loss account for the year ended 31 December 1984, and a balance sheet as at that date.

4   Outline the procedures which you consider should be followed for the ordering of materials and their subsequent receipt.

5   A firm of building contractors is engaged on repair work on many sites covering a wide geographical area, and the number of employees, although large in total, is small on any one site. Discuss the problems of compilation and payment of wages that might arise in these circumstances and suggest possible solutions.

6   A light engineering company calculates its production overhead absorption rate at the end of each month by dividing the total actual overheads incurred by the total numbers of units produced in that month, applying this rate retrospectively to the month's production. The company produces a variety of products and uses a variety of production methods and equipment for the different products which are subject to seasonal fluctuations in demand and therefore in production activity.

Required:
Discuss the effect of the above system of overhead absorption on the product costs and pricing policy.

7   Distinguish carefully between marginal and absorption costing. What are the advantages and disadvantages of both systems.

8   The following data relates to the XY Co. Ltd which produced a single product for the two years 1983 and 1984:

	1983		*1984*	
	Units No.	*Unit price* £	*Units* No.	*Unit price* £
Sales	5,000	20	8,000	30
Production	6,000	—	10,000	—
Production costs:				
materials		4		5
labour		3		6
variable overhead		2		4
fixed overhead		4		8
Selling costs		3		5

Required:
Tabulate the gross profit for each period under (a) a marginal costing system and (b) an absorption costing system, and comment upon the results.

9   A company has three different groups of machines for which it wishes to establish machine rates. A budget for the year ending 31 December 1985 shows the following overhead:

	£
Consumable supplies:	
machine group 1	200
machine group 2	400
machine group 3	500
Maintenance:	
machine group 1	500
machine group 2	1,000
machine group 3	800
Power	3,000
Rent and rates	600
Heat and light	1,800
Insurance of buildings	300
Insurance of machinery	1,000
Depreciation of machinery	8,000
Supervision	1,800
	19,900

Additional information available:

Group	Effective h.p.	Area occupied (m²)	Book value of machinery (£)	Machine hours
1	15	400	3,000	12,000
2	20	300	9,000	20,000
3	25	500	8,000	8,000
	60	12,000	20,000	40,000

Required:
Calculate a machine hour rate for each of the three groups of machines, showing clearly the basis of apportionment used.

10 A customer requests the production of a product from the company in question 9 above. The company estimates its direct labour and material costs will be £30 and £90, respectively. The job will pass through each of the three machine groups, spending 4 hours in group 1, 7 hours in group 2, and 5 hours in group 3.

Required:
Prepare a job cost sheet for the above job, showing clearly the prime and factory cost of manufacture.

11 Undercliffe Manufacturing Ltd has prepared a budget for its production overhead costs. It has four production departments: A, B, assembly and

packing; and three service departments: maintenance, stores and general. The overhead costs are estimated as follows:

	£	£
Indirect wages and supervision		
A Machine Dept.	7,600	
B Machine Dept.	8,700	
Assembly	8,250	
Packing	4,600	
Maintenance	4,500	
Stores	2,300	
General	4,850	40,800
Maintenance Wages		
A Machine Dept.	2,000	
B Machine Dept.	4,000	
Assembly	1,000	
Packing	1,000	
Maintenance	1,000	
Stores	500	
General	900	10,400
Indirect Materials		
A Machine Dept.	5,400	
B Machine Dept.	7,200	
Assembly	3,600	
Packing	5,400	
Maintenance	1,800	
Stores	1,350	
General	800	25,550
Power		12,000
Rent and rates		16,000
Lighting and heating		4,000
Insurance		2,000
Depreciation of machinery		40,000
		£150,750

The following information is also available:

Department	Effective h.p.	Book value of machinery £'000	Direct labour Hours '000	Direct labour Cost £'000	Area (m²)	Machine Hours '000
Production						
A	80	60	200	56	5,000	100
B	80	80	150	42	3,750	120
Assembly	—	10	150	28	7,500	—
Packing	20	10	100	14	3,750	—
			600	140		220

(*continued*)

Department	Effective h.p.	Book value of machinery £'000	Direct labour Hours '000	Direct labour Cost £'000	Area (m²)	Machine Hours '000
Service						
Maintenance	20	30			1,500	
Stores	—	5			2,500	
General	—	5			1,000	
	200	200			25,000	

Required:

(i) Prepare an overhead analysis sheet for the departments of the factory showing and justifying the basis of apportionment;

(ii) Calculate appropriate overhead hourly absorption rates for each production department, ignoring the apportionment of service department costs among service departments.

12 A concentrated liquid fertilizer is manufactured by passing chemicals through two consecutive processes. Stores record cards for the chemical ingredients used exclusively by the first process show the following data for May 1984:

Opening stock	4,000 litres	£10,800
Closing stock	8,000 litres	£24,200
Receipts into store	20,000 litres	£61,000

Other process data for May are tabulated below:

	Process 1	Process 2
Direct labour	£4,880	£6,000
Direct expenses	£4,270	—
Overhead absorption rates	250% of direct labour	100% of direct labour
Output	8,000 litres	7,500 litres
Opening stock of work in process	Nil	Nil
Closing stock of work in process	5,600 litres	Nil
Normal yield	85% of input	90% of input
Scrap value of loss	Nil	Nil

In process 1 the closing stock of work in process has just passed through inspection, which is at the stage where materials and conversion costs are 100 per cent and 75 per cent complete, respectively. In process 2 inspection is the final operation.

Required:

(a) Prepare the relevant accounts to show the results of the processes for May 1984, and present a detailed working paper showing your calculations and any assumptions in arriving at the data shown in those accounts.

(b) If supplies of the required chemicals are severely restricted and all production can be sold immediately, briefly explain how you would calculate the total loss to the company if, at the beginning of June, 100 litres of the correct mix of chemicals were spilt on issue to process 1.

14 Budgets and budgetary control

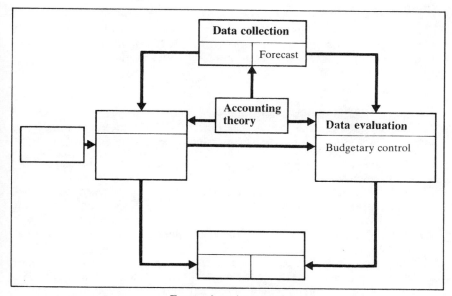

External environment

Planning and control

All organizations, whether economic, social or political, make plans for the future, for an organization without a plan is no longer an organization but an unco-ordinated assortment of individuals. Plans, however, can vary greatly in their degree of sophistication, and the extent to which different organizations plan the future may reflect a philosophical view about the extent to which a firm can be master of its own destiny by virtue of detailed planning as opposed to being at the whim of fickle economic and social forces and thus relying on an ability to 'sense' what is required.

Most organizations normally operate somewhere in the spectrum between these philosophies, and so the term 'plan' embraces the two views. It is possible to plan for factors entirely within the firm's control, e.g. advertising plans, production methods. Such a plan is a declaration of achievable intent. On the other hand, it is possible to achieve certain plans if and only if certain non-controllable conditions materialize; e.g. sales

305

volume can be planned but will only be achieved if the assumptions relating to such things as consumers' income and spending habits, government economic measures, etc., are valid—such plans involve a declaration of expected intent. Planning in practice, therefore, links what can be made to happen with what can be expected to happen. The function of business management is to control what is controllable, and to ensure that it reacts speedily and effectively to changes in the non-controllable conditions.

The management process

The term 'management' is susceptible of many definitions, but it is generally agreed that the management process involves five main activities—planning, controlling, organizing, communicating and motivating.

(1) Planning

Planning is the most important long-term activity in an organization and it is helpful to view this activity as part of the hierarchy of interactive systems. The hierarchy of systems which make up the total systems include:

(i) Strategic systems—decisions what to do, when to do it, and with what resources; overall business objectives stated.

(ii) Planning, control and evaluation systems—the preparation of detailed organization and operational plans, based on the strategic plan, and the control and evaluation systems to check on the attainment of these plans. This includes such systems as budgetary control, credit control, production and stock control, etc.

(iii) Collecting, recording and co-ordinating systems—the sorting and analysis of operational activities for control and evaluation purposes. This embraces personnel records, financial and cost accounting systems, production reporting systems, etc.

(iv) Operating systems—the day-to-day operating activities: production of goods, paying of wages, etc.

These systems do not consist merely of the flow of various pieces of paper through routines; within the total system concept human beings are systems components themselves. It is the human being which makes the business system probabilistic rather that deterministic, dynamic rather than static.

Quite critical to the business system is information; without information none of the subsystems can be fused together to form the whole. The one-man business gains all his information from personal observation and contact; information is taken for granted. But in an organization which is complex, both in terms of technology and size, information is a precious commodity—perhaps the most valuable resource the business has. We must observe here a distinction between data and information. Data is the whole range of facts and statistics available to the business; information is that part of data which is valuable in a particular situation. Very often a manager in a firm receives masses of data whose information content, as far as he is concerned, is nil.

Strategic planning is concerned with the setting of organizational objectives, usually formulated as general statements of policy relating to profitability, financial sources, market penetration, employment, product development and production methods. Such a high level of planning must take into account expected changes in the economic, social and political environment in which the firm operates. As the objectives are general statements (e.g. a profit objective might be to achieve a profit level sufficient to satisfy existing and future shareholders) they need to be turned into quantified and specific goals (e.g. to attain a profit level of 15 per cent before tax on the shareholders' equity) to be achieved within the stated periods of time. In order to achieve these goals, it is necessary for management to set up the necessary control systems.

(2)   Controlling

Control is closely linked to the planning function in that its purpose is to ensure that the strategic plans and goals are achieved. The detailed plans necessary for control are specified in annual budgets, and detailed information which relates to this budget is collected and co-ordinated through the financial and cost accounting record-keeping system (*see* Chapters 5 and 13). The actual results as recorded in these systems are compared with the budget, and under- or over-achievements carefully evaluated. At the base of all of these systems lie the operating systems concerned with the day-to-day operating activities—production of goods, payment of wages, collection of cash, etc. Unless these systems are clearly specified, understood and adhered to, the information recording and control systems will not function meaningfully. No system can be better than the quality of information input into it, so that poor operating systems and procedures can neutralize and deny the most careful strategic plans.

(3)   Organizing

The establishment of control, recording and operating systems as a means of achieving the strategic plan implies that the organization has established the necessary administrative structure. Management's organizing function is to establish an administrative structure which clearly defines responsibilities, duties and lines of authority, and which co-ordinates the many tasks undertaken by the different parts of the administrative structure.

An outline or organizational chart of a typical manufacturing business might be as illustrated on page 308.

Each of the main functional activities—purchasing, production, research, finance, personnel, sales—may well be headed by the appropriate director who has direct responsibility for all of those departments which report directly to him. For example, the managers of the financial, cost and budgetary departments will report to the financial director, and the foreman

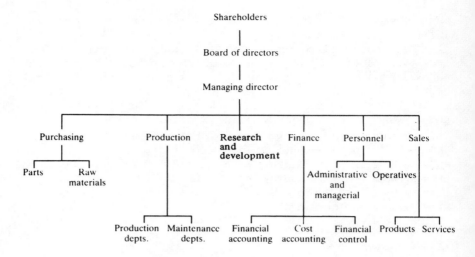

of 'Product Y department' to the production manager who reports to the production director. Apart from these 'vertical' relationships, however, which clearly define levels of authority, there are many 'lateral' relationships—the working relations between executives or supervisors at the same level of responsibility. The smooth working of management calls for collaboration between them on points of mutual interest without reference back to their respective hierarchical seniors.

A major purpose of any organization structure is to facilitate the communication of information, for information, converted into decision and action, is the life blood of the strategic plan.

(4) Communicating

Communication is the exchange of data by two or more persons, and involves a sender, a message, a medium of communication and a receiver. Most businesses transmit vast quantities of data, but all too often the information content—that part of the data which enables the manager to perform his task efficiently and effectively—is very low. The sender may be a person, a computer or machine, the medium of communication may be written, electronic, oral or visual, and the receiver also may be human, electronic or mechanical. Many management reports are written, because such reports may be more readily incorporated into formal procedures, and they provide a point of reference should there be any dispute between the sender and receiver on what was actually communicated. Many communication systems try to reduce the volume of transmission by communicating only 'exceptional' information—data which is actually of use to the receiver. Vast quantities of data tend to cause 'interference' or 'noise' in the system, because the receiver is not readily able to distinguish the vital information from the irrelevant data.

(5)   Motivating

Organizations are created by people for people, so that strategic plans, control systems, organizational structures and communications networks which ignore the human element are likely to be much less successful than those which are concerned to align personal and business goals. The study of motivation is beyond the scope of this book, but the many studies of the patterns of human behaviour in the work situation tend to agree that the business should strive to create a situation in which the business and individual goals coincide to as great a degree as possible.

The nature of budgets

The strategic plans of a business define its long-run goals and objectives, but, in order to realize these plans, it is necessary to convert them into explicit, short-term targets through a process called 'budgeting'.

Although all managers of business enterprises plan, there are considerable differences in the extent to which they do so. Some managers carry plans in their head, some make rough estimates on their cigarette packets, and others express their plans in an orderly and systematic manner. We are concerned with this latter group, for a budget is a comprehensive and co-ordinated plan, expressed in monetary terms, directing and controlling the resources and trading activities of an enterprise for some specified period in the future.

There are some important aspects contained within this definition which we must stress:

(1) *Comprehensive and co-ordinated.* A budget is comprehensive if it embraces all aspects of the organization. Such a budget is the master budget which is the sum of all component or subsidiary budgets prepared by sections of the organization. Sectional plans must be co-ordinated to ensure that their objectives are compatible, for it is obviously pointless to plan to produce a million units of a product if only half a million can be sold.
(2) *Plan.* As we have seen, the term 'plan' embraces two extremes. It is possible to plan for factors entirely within the firm's control, e.g. advertising plans, production methods; such a plan is a declaration of achievable intent. On the other hand it is possible to achieve certain plans if and only if expected conditions materialize, e.g. sales volume can be planned, but will only be achieved if the assumptions relating to such things as consumers' income and spending habits are valid; such plans involve a declaration of expected intent. The business budget is a combination of the two extremes, linking what can be made to happen with what can be expected to happen.
(3) *Resources and trading activities.* The planning of resources involves the planning of investment in all types of assets and the securing of the capital to be invested in these assets. The planning of trading activities requires the forecasting of expected revenues and expenses.

Budgets—objectives and benefits

Essentially the budget has two main objectives—planning and control:

Planning

Good budgeting demands a comprehensive, integrated and co-ordinated plan, not a set of vague, uncommunicated hopes. The plan is not a straitjacket, but can provide the guidelines for improved performance.

Control

In preparing the budget, responsibilities are assigned in relation to the component parts. The budget thus gives the responsible managers a guide to their conduct and a basis for evaluating the actual results. Such a comparison should be made against a budget adjusted for any change in external circumstances; a rigid budget which is blindly adhered to is often worse than no budget at all. Many budgets are flexible in that, by differentiating between fixed and variable costs/revenues, schedules are prepared showing expected revenues and expenses at given levels of activity.

The use of budgets can be seen to be advantageous for a number of reasons:

(1) The preparation of budgets forces management to engage in planning, in looking forwards rather than backwards;
(2) The responsibilities of each manager have to be clearly identified;
(3) Budgets provide a detailed means of controlling all income and expenditure of a business;
(4) The need for capital can be kept at a minimum level consistent with the planned activity, and future needs can be anticipated;
(5) The management team becomes more 'cost conscious', and this can help to eliminate waste and inefficiency;
(6) The managers throughout the different functions are forced to work together and co-ordinate their activities.

Budgets and behaviour

Budgets are neither good nor bad *per se*; they are what the people affected by them view them to be. As we observed in Chapter 1, an obvious fact about business organizations is that they consist of human beings. Certain psychologists believe that all observed behaviour is in response to stimuli; thus the behaviour of the manager or worker is the result of a variety of stimuli affecting him. The budget is a stimulus, and, as such, will evoke some response. The response may be favourable if the recipient has been persuaded that participating is beneficial to him; the chances of budgeting working effectively without mistrust and doubt being dispelled are negligible.

Many budget systems include implicitly or explicitly rewards and punishments for good or bad performances in relation to the budget. Rewards can take the form of bonuses and/or promotion, punishment the reverse.

It is obviously important that the standards demanded by the budget can be achieved without undue physical or mental stress. To set standards too high will discourage rather than encourage, frighten rather than motivate.

The production aspect of budgets relies to a considerable extent on the attitude and motivation of the shop-floor workers. All groups of individuals have their norms—the generally accepted behavioural principles for the group—and worker groups are no exception. Researchers studying their behaviour found that workers may refuse to produce their best performance for fear that budget standards will be revised unfavourably. Equally, on the management side, Dalton described a number of instances where departmental managers acted outside of the budget (persuading other managers to absorb some of their costs) thus freeing funds for goals which the individual managers considered more appropriate.

The manner in which a budget is viewed by employees depends to a large extent on the style of management. Organization theorists identify two extreme styles of management. The one stresses the need for people to be persuaded and controlled so that their behaviour fits the needs of the organization; the other emphasizes the view that people are already self-motivated and that management's task is to so arrange the methods of operation and organization that people can best meet their own needs by working towards the organization's objectives. All employees, as people, have certain needs which have to be satisfied if they and the organization are to have congruent goals. In a work situation, an employee seeks a complex, interrelated set of goals—financial rewards, physical and intellectual stimulation and satisfaction, status and recognition of worth by fellow employees, and the kudos which attaches to being identified with a successful organization.

Any budgetary system, therefore, to be successful must reflect an awareness of these personal needs, but research shows how, all too often, the budget is viewed with much suspicion at many levels of management and supervision. If managers are made answerable for costs over which they have no real control—for example, breakdown of machinery may be due to the processing of defective materials over which the maintenance supervisor has no control—they become hostile and indifferent to the budget. Performance may be reviewed purely in the context of one year, yet the more complex and innovative departments may only see the benefit of good management over a much longer time span. The emphasis on performance in the short run may lead to lowering of standards in order to meet a budgetary target—maintenance can be delayed, lowering costs substantially in one period, but perhaps leading to the need to replace rather than repair in a future period.

All performance evaluation, therefore, should be qualitative as well as quantitative, and there is a need to see management performance in a broad perspective which covers the whole range of duties and responsibilities in both the short and long term. Managers must be full participants in both the planning and the control process, and should be motivated, not pressurized, into achieving their budgetary goals.

The framework and construction of budgets

As we have noted, the attainment of budgetary targets is in part conditional upon factors external to the firm. As we mentioned in Chapter 1, the accounting environment is the social, economic, legal and political world. Social factors will affect the manner in which people act and think, and have an impact on the pattern of demand for consumer products; economic factors will influence seasonal and cyclical trends of demand and supply; legal requirements may alter; and a change in government may result in a fundamentally different attitude to business activities.

To some extent, these conditions are predictable, and thus may provide the framework within which the firm may prepare its own budget. Nevertheless, there remain many unpredictable environmental factors which make even the most carefully planned budgets subject to substantial deviations from reality.

With the framework established, the detailed construction of the budget can proceed. We have already referred to the need for co-ordination, but this does not arise automatically; usually the firm will discover that there is some factor which effectively restricts the total magnitude of operations in any given period. This is referred to as the 'limiting' or 'principal' budget factor. For example, if sales demand is 20 per cent in excess of productive capacity, then there is little point in budgeting to sell non-existent goods. Clearly, whatever the limiting factor is, it is at this point that the planning process should begin.

We will consider budgets under two broad heads; profit budgets which are concerned with the operating activities of the firm, and capital budgets which are concerned with the provision of resources to maintain the firm's operational capacity.

Profit budgets—the sales budget

Price–sales relationships have long occupied a central position in micro-economic theory, yet empirical investigations of the effect of price on sales remain a relatively untouched field of demand analysis. Sales or demand analysis and the associated problem of demand forecasting have a central place in any business planning process. Demand analysis attempts to identify the variables influencing sales, and to indicate how these may be manipulated in planning for profit. We will approach the sales budget by considering (1) the nature of demand analysis, (2) the use of the insights gained by such analysis in demand forecasting, and (3) incorporate illustrative results in a sales budget.

(1)   Demand analysis

In elementary economic analysis, demand is represented as a function of price. Demand curves may be drawn showing either the total industry demand, or the individual consumer's demand, or the demand for a product of an individual firm. We will focus our attention on the last of these.

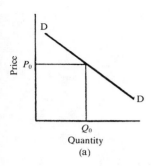

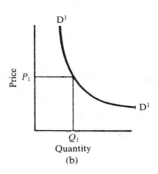

(a)   (b)

In the diagrams, DD and DD^1 are the demand curves for a product Y. At price P_0, quantity Q_0 is demanded; in diagram (b), at price P_1, quantity Q_1 is demanded. The demand curve has been drawn in two ways simply because its shape may vary from product to product. Demand curve D is the common form (in mathematical terms $q = a + bp$); demand curve D^1 has been found more appropriate in certain empirical studies ($q = Ap^a$). Both demand curves, however, have a negative slope, indicating that as price falls more goods are sold. Except for a few special goods and services, this type of demand curve is more readily in accordance with observed experience.

In order to obtain such a demand curve, however, it is necessary to assume that demand is the major, if not unique, function of price. Many other factors will influence demand, however, notably

(1) Changes in consumers' tastes and preferences.
(2) Changes in the prices of related goods.
(3) Changes in consumer income.
(4) Changes in the amount of advertising.
(5) Effect of expected price changes.

A change in any one of these factors will result in a shift upwards or downwards of the whole demand curve.

It is clearly important for the firm to ascertain whether price or one of the variables mentioned above is the major factor determining demand for their product. An important weapon in management's armoury is the concept of price elasticity of demand. For many purposes, management is less interested in how much is bought at the current price, than in how much will be bought if the price is changed. The sensitivity of quantity to changes in price is called price elasticity of demand. The formula for price elasticity is

$$\frac{\% \text{ Change in quantity of product demanded}}{\% \text{ Change in price of product}}$$

or

$$e = \frac{\frac{\Delta q}{q} \times 100}{\frac{\Delta p}{p} \times 100}$$

For example, if a change in price from 5p to 6p results in a change in quantity bought from 20,000 to 18,000 units then the price elasticity of demand is given by

$$\% \text{ Change in } Q = \frac{2,000}{20,000} \times 100 = 10\%$$

$$\% \text{ Change in } P = \frac{1}{5} \times 100 = 20\%$$

Therefore

$$e = \frac{10}{20} = 0.5$$

This means that as prices rise, total revenue will rise; as they fall, total revenue will fall. In our example, total revenue before the price change was $20,000 \times 5p = £1,000$; after the change it was $18,000 \times 6p = £1,080$. The relationship which exists between price elasticity (E) of demand and total revenue (R) can be summarized thus:

	$E>1$	$E=1$	$E<1$
Price rise	R falls	R	R rises
Price fall	R rises	constant	R falls

The methods by which management may obtain data to measure price elasticity will be discussed in relation to demand forecasting, and at this point we must emphasize the policy implications. Management would be foolish to plan for changes in price where price elasticity is one or close to one. More attention might be paid to permitting greater advertising expenditure in the future. Unless price elasticity is relatively high, sales are not sensitive to changes in prices; the 'other factors' are more important in determining demand.

It is possible to apply the concept of elasticity to the other variables, and to derive such measures as income elasticity, advertising elasticity and cross-elasticity of demand. (Cross-elasticity refers to the change in quantity of A demanded when B is changed in price; if A and B are substitutes, e.g. different makes of shoes, cross-elasticity is positive; if they are complements, e.g. bread and butter, cross-elasticity is negative.)

(2)   Demand forecasting

There is a distinction between a forecast and a budget. A forecast is an estimate of the future which may be attained under given conditions; a budget is an objective to be attained and is based on the forecast or a modification of that forecast. It is beyond the scope of this book—and, for that matter, the author—to explore in detail the field of market research, but it is important for the accountant to appreciate how the sales forecast, which is incorporated into the budget, is obtained.

Before considering techniques of demand forecasting, let it be said that there is no method which can guarantee success; forecasting is a combination and interaction of judgement, information, and analysis. Some variables affecting demand have already been mentioned on page 338; to these we must add the need to decide whether the forecast should be general or specific, concerned with the whole or broken down into product lines for all markets. New products create problems different from established products, and special factors concerning the product and the market must be taken into account.

Once these variables have been noted, two approaches are possible to demand forecasting, although the approaches are by no means exclusive. The first is to obtain information by ascertaining buyers' intentions; the second is to project past trends. The former is primarily used for short-term forecasting (i.e. up to one year); the latter is more suitable for the long term.

Field surveys or interviews are the most direct method of estimating sales in the short run. Since it is impossible to question all potential customers, some sampling technique has to be employed. When sales are to industrial producers, the survey is primarily an exercise in persuading those customers to reveal their production plans. To learn the intentions of household consumers is more difficult if only because customers are inconsistent in buying intentions, and are unable accurately to predict what choice they will make when faced with alternatives. Many firms recognizing such difficulties rely on the collective opinions of their sales force. Past experience can often provide some guide to the future, and projections of the past require the application of some mathematical methods. Regression and correlation analysis uses statistical techniques to examine the extent and nature of the relationship between one or more variables. Basically this requires two steps:

(1) Determining a curve (or straight line) which will express the average relationship between variables. This provides a regression equation.
(2) Determining how well the regression equation fits the variables by calculating the degree of association by the correlation coefficient.

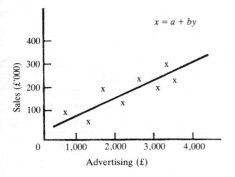

For example, a firm might ascertain from past experience that different levels of advertising expenditure will result in varying levels of sales. The relationship can be plotted on a graph, as shown, called a scatter diagram.

Clearly, from the graph there is an indication that higher levels of advertising are associated with higher levels of sales. The relationship can be more precisely described by means of an equation, such as the linear expression $x = a + by$, where x is the computed value of sales for any given expenditure y.

It is important to appreciate that the equation does not *prove* a relationship between sales and advertising—it presumes it; there are certainly many other factors affecting sales. To introduce other variables requires techniques of multiple regression and correlation where, for example, a relationship may be described as

Sales = (f) National disposable income; Price, Advertising

or

$$X = a + b_1 Y_1 + b_2 Y_2 + b_3 Y_3$$

The more variables introduced, the more perfect is the fit with past data; but as has been observed, the more variables in the equation, the surer the function is to go wrong at some time in the future.

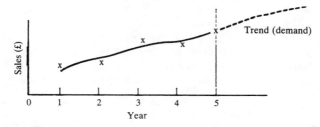

As an alternative to such techniques, time series analysis is often employed. The principle is to establish a growth pattern in the past, and then to extend (extrapolate) the trend into the future, as illustrated.

The trend may be established by means of moving averages, or a regression technique of sales on time (years). The trend line can be then extended to provide an estimate of future sales.

(3)   The sales budget

The forecast is incorporated into the formal budget in total, and with a detailed breakdown by product, area, timing, volume and value. The analysis by product, volume and timing is clearly necessary to prepare the production budget in detail. Area analysis is important as a means of fixing a separate target for each group of the sales force. The timing and value of sales will have an effect on the firm's cash flow which must be incorporated into the cash budget (*see* page 324).

An illustration of a sales budget is given; the first schedule is a summary of monthly total sales forecast by area; the second a monthly breakdown of products A and B.

Astral Manufacturing Co. Ltd—Sales
Budget (Fiscal)
first quarter 1984

| Month | Area | | | | Total |
	West £'000	North £'000	East £'000	South £'000	£'000
January	16	21	37	32	106
February	27	29	52	45	153
March	34	33	68	59	194
	77	83	157	136	453

Sales Budget (Product Volume)
first quarter 1984
(unit in thousands)

| Month | West | | North | | Area East | | South | | Total | |
	A	B	A	B	A	B	A	B	A	B
January	2.4	3.6	2.2	4.8	8.0	4.1	5.7	5.0	18.3	17.5
February	5.1	1.4	5.1	4.8	9.1	6.9	8.2	6.5	27.5	19.6
March	4.3	4.0	6.0	5.0	13.7	8.2	10.3	9.4	34.3	26.6
	11.8	9.0	13.3	14.6	30.8	19.2	24.2	20.9	80.1	63.7

Profit budgets—the production budget

We observed in Chapter 13 that production or manufacturing costs are composed of three elements—material, labour and overhead. The variable costs of these elements are a function of the volume of production multiplied by the price of the various inputs, the volume being determined by the anticipated volume of sales, decisions to increase or decrease stock, and the productive capacity of the enterprise. Taking prices as a constant, it is unlikely that the production levels will be exactly the same from one year to the next. If levels change, it is of critical importance for the firm to identify the relationship which exists between costs and levels of activity.

(1) Cost behaviour

In the previous chapter, we drew a distinction between fixed and variable costs, defining fixed costs as those which are function of time rather than volume of production, and variable costs as those which vary with production. In practice cost types range the whole spectrum from fixed through semi-variable to fully variable, as the diagrams illustrate.

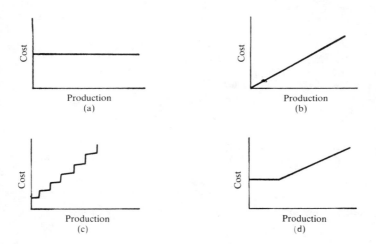

Diagram (a) illustrates a fixed cost such as the rent of a factory which is constant irrespective of the level of activity; diagram (b) shows a cost such as direct materials which vary with production; diagram (c) is a step cost such as the cost of supervision where one supervisor is required for a fixed number of men who each produce a constant output; diagram (d) illustrates a semi-variable cost such as electricity where there is a fixed charge up to a given number of units, and a variable charge after that point.

Although there is a variety of cost behaviour, accounting theory tends to adopt the simple economic distinction between fixed and variable costs, asserting that this approximation will not have much, if any, effect on subsequent analysis. Beyond this point, however, economics and accounting diverge, and very different conclusions are drawn with respect to cost behaviour in the short run.

In economic analysis, the short run is defined as a period in which at least one input factor is in fixed supply. Under such conditions, as additional units of the variable factors are added, the additional output (or marginal product) at first increases, then is constant and eventually decreases. This concept is traditionally illustrated with reference to land, where it would appear intuitively true that the sowing of seed more and more thickly will result in an increased harvest at first, but eventually reach the point where the marginal product will decrease.

If this is so and the concept can be applied to the industrial situation, then the firm's cost schedule could appear as

Input units (variable) (i)	Total output (ii)	Variable cost per unit (iii)	Total variable cost (iv)	Total fixed cost (v)	Total cost (vi)
		£	£	£	£
1	1	10	10	40	50
2	3	10	20	40	60
3	7	10	30	40	70
4	11	10	40	40	80
5	14	10	50	40	90
6	16	10	60	40	100
7	17	10	70	40	110
8	16	10	80	40	120

From this data, important secondary information can be derived:

Marginal product from (ii)	Average variable cost (iv)÷(ii)	Average fixed cost (v)÷(ii)	Average total cost (vi)÷(ii)	Marginal cost per unit (iii)÷marginal product
	£	£	£	£
1	10	40	50	10
2	6.6	13.3	20	5
4	4.3	5.8	10	2.5
4	3.6	3.6	7.3	2.5
3	3.6	2.8	6.4	3.3
2	3.7	2.5	6.3	5
1	4.1	2.3	6.5	10
−1	5	2.5	7.5	—

The tables show the marginal product at first increasing then decreasing; the consequence of this is the U-shaped cost curves of short-run economic analysis. The data may be graphed as illustrated on page 320 (upper).

In most situations, accounting rejects the concept of the eventually diminishing marginal product, and makes the simple linear assumption that each additional unit of input will result in a constant marginal product. The student should reconstruct the tables above under this assumption to ascertain numerically the effect on the average and marginal costs. The results should be constant average variable and marginal costs, which may be graphed as shown on page 320 (lower).

The important question from the point of view of production budgeting is which assumption of cost behaviour is the more realistic? If the economist

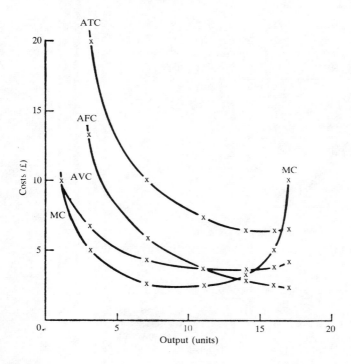

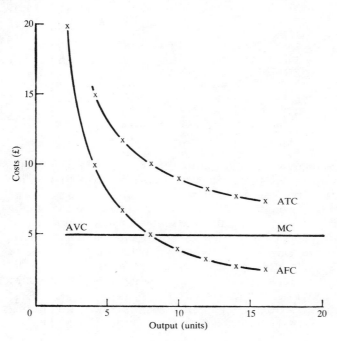

is correct, then the firm will reach a level of output at which average total costs will begin to rise (where MC = ATC). If the sales budget plans to exceed this critical volume, then unless sales prices are increased, the firm may operate at a loss.

However, many empirical studies seem to support the view of the accountant. For example, Johnston concludes that 'two major impressions stand out clearly. The first is that the various short run studies more often than not indicate constant marginal cost and declining average (total) cost as the pattern that best seems to describe the data that have been analysed. The second is the preponderance of the L-shaped pattern of long run average (total) costs that emerges so frequently from the various long run analysis'.

(2)   The production budget

The volume of production required in any period may be ascertained by applying the basic formula

$$\text{Production} = (\text{Planned closing stock} + \text{Unit sales}) - \text{Opening stock}$$

with the provision that planned production cannot exceed the productive capacity. Once the volume of production is ascertained, it is necessary to build up a picture (by cost centre) of expected costs of material, labour and overhead.

As part of the overall production budget, there should be a schedule for the purchases of each category of material used by the firm. The variables influencing the investment in materials are outlined in Chapter 18 and the illustration indicates how the firm will build these factors into the purchase schedule. The cost schedule can be easily ascertained by multiplying the production issues by the anticipated prices.

Astral Manufacturing Co. Ltd
Materials Purchase Budget
first quarter 1984

	Orders	Receipts	Issues to production	Closing stock
Balance 31.12.83	—	—	—	10,000
January	10,000	8,000	7,500	10,500
February	8,000	10,000	9,800	10,700
March	9,000	8,000	7,900	10,800
	27,000	26,000	25,200	—

A comparable exercise is needed to evaluate labour costs. The planned production volumes are expressed in labour hours, and these are then multiplied by the appropriate wage rates to arrive at total direct labour costs. The manufacturing overhead will have to be built up by individual cost centres, both because of differences among costs centres as to the types of overhead costs incurred, and because of the behaviour of those costs with respect to fluctuation in production volume. Overhead rates will be calculated for each cost centre, and while this may be done on an absorption or a marginal cost basis, it is desirable always to distinguish between fixed and variable costs to permit the budget to be adjusted to conform to changing levels of production volume (*see* page 323).

From this data a composite production budget will be prepared, as shown.

Astral Manufacturing Co. Ltd
Production Cost Budget
first quarter 1984

	Material	*Labour*	*Variable overhead*	*Fixed overhead*	*Total*
	£	£	£	£	£
January	15,000	6,500	3,750	1,000	26,250
February	19,600	8,600	4,900	1,000	34,100
March	15,800	6,800	3,950	1,000	27,550
	50,400	21,900	12,600	3,000	87,900

Profit budgets—administration, finance and selling budgets

Budgets for these costs are prepared in essentially the same way as are budgets for manufacturing overhead. As far as possible, costs should be classified as fixed or variable, although, as it is usually difficult to find an adequate measure of volume, most costs of this nature are treated as fixed or period costs.

Budgeted income statement

All the component profit or operating budgets are normally summarized in the form of a budgeted income statement. This is prepared in the same form as the actual income statement, except that the figures represent intents rather than achievements. Since for planning purposes the detailed budgets are often prepared on a monthly basis, the budgeted income statement is detailed by months also.

Flexible budgets

So far, in this chapter, the analysis has been conducted in terms of unique expectations, that is to say a single or fixed volume is anticipated for sales and production. When actual results are compared with a fixed budget they may deviate for two reasons. First, while the actual and budgeted volumes may coincide, there may be a difference between actual costs and budgeted costs; secondly, the actual volume may deviate from the budgeted volume, giving rise to a difference in costs due to volume variations.

From the point of view of management control, the spending variance is more likely to be under the control of the individual department, while the variations in volume usually results from top management's response to changing sales expectations. To aid in cost control, therefore, it is useful to indicate to the various levels of management what costs they should incur at varying levels of activity. Budgets which do provide a basis for determining such costs are termed flexible budgets.

The essence of a flexible budget is the presentation of estimated cost data at various levels of volume, and this requirement makes a knowledge of cost behaviour even more essential. In order to identify such behaviour by department, it is necessary to define volume in a way most meaningful to that department. Volume may be described in terms of units of production, machine hours, direct labour hours or costs, or some other unit of input. The measure selected should be that which offers the greatest degree of correlation with the variable costs.

In the example shown, direct material and labour costs are expressed as a function of units of production, and the variable overhead as a function of direct labour hours. There is no reason why all the components of variable overhead should vary with labour hours; such costs as machine maintenance may be more closely connected with machine hours. It is doubtful, however, whether the additional precision derived from different measures of volume are worth the additional clerical costs involved, and so a single measure of volume has been used.

Astral Manufacturing Co. Ltd
Department Y Budget for January 1984

Cost \ Volume	Per unit £	Per direct labour hour £	Units 5,000 £	Direct labour hours 15,000 £	Units 10,000 £	Direct labour hours 30,000 £	Units 15,000 £	Direct labour hours 45,000 £
Direct material	2.0		10,000		20,000		30,000	
Direct labour	1.5		7,500		15,000		22,500	
Variable overhead		0.2		3,000		6,000		9,000
			3,000	3,000	6,000	6,000	9,000	9,000
Total variable costs			20,500		41,000		61,500	
Fixed overhead			4,000		4,000		4,000	
Total costs			24,500		45,000		65,500	

The example presumes that absorption costing is employed, and the fixed overhead absorption rate will be expressed for the varying levels of activity, e.g. 4,000/15,000 = £0.266 per direct labour hour, or 4,000/30,000 = £0.133 per direct labour hour.

Resource budgets

Resource budgets are directed towards planning the investment in all types of assets needed to maintain the firm's operational capacity. Some asset investment is a necessary corollary to the level of operational activity; for example, the investment in debtors will be a function of credit sales, and the investment in stock a function of the rate of production and sales (*see* Chapter 18). Investment in long-term resources—the fixed assets—will require a more deliberate management decision. However this decision is made—and this will be discussed in Chapter 16—the decision to invest will normally mean an outflow of cash. This outflow, together with the cash receipts and payments associated with trading, will be incorporated into the cash budget.

Earlier in this chapter we indicated that in any firm there will be one or more limiting factors to the scope of the firm's activities. Availability of cash is the limiting factor of many organizations, and cash shortage is a rock upon which many founder. The cash budget will begin with the opening balance of cash on hand, and present a monthly statement of inflows and outflows. The timing of receipts and expenditures is quite critical, and care must be taken to distinguish the revenue from the receipt, and the expense from the expenditure. To do this, the firm will take its budgeted income statement, making adjustments for any time lags, and eliminating any non-cash items such as depreciation; in addition, any planned capital expenditure or any non-operational disbursements such as dividends will require attention.

An example may clarify this point. We will assume that the Starwell Co. Ltd began business on 1 January 1984 with a capital of £30,000 cash. Its budget revealed the following:

	Sales £	Purchases £	Selling and admin. expenses £	Wages £	Rent £
January	6,000	15,000	600	1,000	300
February	8,000	12,000	600	1,000	300
March	11,000	10,000	600	1,000	300
April	12,000	10,000	700	1,500	300
May	12,000	10,000	700	1,500	300
June	12,000	10,000	800	1,500	300

Capital expenditure: January (£3,400) and April (£600)

Debtors will be granted one month's credit, and creditors will grant two months' credit. The rent will be paid quarterly in advance.

The cash budget derived from this data will be as shown below:

Cash Budget
January–June 1984

	January	February	March	April	May	June
	£	£	£	£	£	£
Balance b/f	30,000	24,100	28,500	19,900	15,200	15,000
Receipts:						
Sales	—	6,000	8,000	11,000	12,000	12,000
	30,000	**30,100**	**36,500**	**30,900**	**27,200**	**27,000**
Payments:						
Purchases	—	—	15,000	12,000	10,000	10,000
Selling and admin.	600	600	600	700	700	800
Wages	1,000	1,000	1,000	1,500	1,500	1,500
Rent	900	—	—	900	—	—
Equipment	3,400	—	—	600	—	—
	5,900	**1,600**	**16,600**	**15,700**	**12,200**	**12,300**
Balance c/f	24,100	28,500	19,900	15,200	15,000	14,700

Budget review

We have defined a budget as a comprehensive and co-ordinated plan, expressed in monetary terms, directing and controlling the resources and trading activities of an enterprise for some specified period in the future. We have considered the directing, but management must also know whether the directions have been carried out. The control aspect of budgeting requires periodical budget review reports, comparing actual and budgeted performance. Any variation between actual and budgeted data should be fully explored in an attempt to identify the causes. In the example below, a flexible budgetary system identifies planned costs at a production volume of 10,000 units. The actual costs arising, therefore, are in respect of this volume of output.

Astral Manufacturing Co.
Department Y Budget Report for January 1984
Volume = 10,000 units

	Budget £	Actual £	Variance £
Material	20,000	19,300	700
Labour	15,000	15,100	(100)
Overhead—variable	6,000	5,900	100
—fixed	4,000	4,200	(200)
Total	45,000	44,500	500

The possible causes of the differences between planned and actual costs will be discussed in the following chapter.

Budgetary models

Comprehensive budgeting involves the consideration and integration of all of the activities of the firm. Because every aspect of the firm is interrelated it is impossible to change any one factor (variable) without a consequential change in one or more of the other factors. For example, a donation to a charity will both increase expenses and reduce cash; increased advertising expenditure will increase expense, decrease cash and normally increase sales, which will require either additional production (with the consequential increase in costs) and/or reduction in stocks.

The causal relationships of an enterprise are extremely complex, and therefore the working out of the consequences of a shift in the variable is often costly and time consuming. This is one reason why budgets are normally annual exercises; in large firms they may cost tens of thousands of pounds to prepare, and occupy two or three months of managerial and clerical activity. In recent years, increasing attention has been paid to the possibility of describing the firm in mathematical terms by means of a budgetary model; the model may be derived in aggregate from observation of the accounting process, or it may deal in minute detail with all aspects of management control. Within these two extremes there are many compromise solutions, but the merit of a model—a set of mathematical equations—is that, once established, it is possible with the aid of a computer to experiment with changes in the variables and indicate the likely outcome cheaply and speedily, and many commercial computer packages are available for use, which can be adapted reasonably readily to the particular circumstances of any business.

We will illustrate an aggregative model, using as a starting point a conventional set of accounts for a retail firm:

XY Co.
Accounts

Sales

Trading	1,200	Debtors	1,200

Expenses

Cash		50	Profit and loss	50

Stock

Balance	100	Cost of sales	1,000
Creditors	1,100	Balance	200
	1,200		1,200

Cost of sales

Stock	1,000	Trading	1,000

Debtors

Balance	90	Cash	1,190
Sales	1,200	Balance	100
	1,290		**1,290**

Creditors

Cash	1,088	Balance	80
Balance	92	Stock	1,100
	1,180		**1,180**

Cash

Balance	448	Expenses	50
Debtors	1,190	Creditors	1,088
		Fixed assets	100
		Balance	400
	1,638		**1,638**

Fixed assets

Balance	500	Balance	600
Cash	100		
	600		**600**

Trading, profit and loss

Cost of sales	1,000	Sales	1,200
Expenses	50		
Net profit	150		
	1,200		**1,200**

Capital

Balance	1,208	Balance	1,058
		Profit	150
	1,208		**1,208**

The next stage is to find a coding system to characterize the relationships which the accounts reveal. We will give each account a unique code letter, and describe each transaction by means of those codes. The first code will refer to the account to be credited, the second to the account to be debited. Thus, for example, the entry relating to sales on credit (credit sales and debit debtors) will appear as SD in each account. Two further conventions are necessary at this stage; each opening balance will be prefixed by the letter O, and each closing or ending balance by the letter E (e.g. opening debtors will become OD, and closing debtors, ED). Our accounts rewritten in this form will be as follows:

Sales (S)

TS	SD

Expenses (Ex)

CEx	ExPl

Stock (St)

OSt	StCs
CrSt	ESt

Cost of sales (Cs)

StCs	CsT

Debtors (D)

OD	DC
SD	ED

Creditors (Cr)

CCr	OCr
ECr	CrSt

Cash (C)

OC	CEx
DC	CCr
	CF
	EC

Fixed assets (F)

OF	EF
CF	

Trading (T), profit and loss (Pl)

CsT	TS
ExPl	
CpPl	

Capital (Cp)

ECp	OCp
	CpPl

These relationships can now be expressed in algebraic form:

(i) $ESt = OSt + CrSt - StCs$
(ii) $ED = OD + SD - DC$
(iii) $ECr = OCr + CrSt - CCr$
(iv) $EC = OC + DC - CEx - CF - CCr$
(v) $CpPl = TS - CsT - ExPl$
(vi) $ECp = OCp + CpPl$
(vii) $EF = OF + CF$

The equations in themselves are not sufficient to produce a budgetary model; they are merely a reflection of a system of bookkeeping. The key to the transition is provided by examining the accounts (past experience) to ascertain what behavioural relationships obtain. For example, if we examine the debtors account it is apparent that, assuming sales levels are constant at £100 per month, debtors are allowed one month's credit, since the closing balance is exactly 1/12 of the annual sales. We can therefore calculate the amount of cash to be received from debtors as

(viii) $DC = OD + aSD$

where a is the proportion of current debtors (11/12) who will settle their accounts during the accounting period. Such assumptions about behaviour are called budgeting hypotheses. In our example we can observe more such hypotheses, one relating to creditors and the other to sales values. The creditors are similar to the debtors, so that we can write

(ix) $CCr = OCr + bCrSt$

where b is the proportion of creditors who have provided stock in the current period and who have been paid.

We will offer a simple hypothesis about the sales values, namely that all sales are made on the basis of cost plus a fixed percentage. (In the accounts, if we assume that 1,000 units of a homogeneous product were sold at £1.2 each, then the total cost of £1,000 is 100/120(%) of total revenue). Thus we write

(x) $StCs = \Sigma q_1 p_1$

where q_1 is the number of units sold, and p_1 is the cost price, and

(xi) $SD = \Sigma q_1 f p_1$

where f is the percentage mark up, e.g. 120/100.

Obviously more relationships exist. For example, the increasing of credit facilities to debtors from one to two months could result in a 10 per cent increase in sales. The consequence of this action can be worked through the model, given certain assumptions about minimum stock levels. We may write

(xii) $ESt \geqslant a\Sigma q_1$

where a is the percentage of total annual unit sales.

This book can provide no more than an introduction to budgetary models. The problems of model construction have been grossly simplified, but they nevertheless provide an indication of the sort of analytical tools which are now readily available to any business with reasonable computer facilities.

References and further reading

ANTON and FIRMIN (1972), *Contemporary Issues in Cost Accounting*. Houghton Mifflin.

ARGYRIS (1953), 'Human Problems with Budgets', *Harvard Business Review*, January 1953.

FREMGEN (1980), *Managerial Cost Analysis*. Irwin.

HAGUE (1971), *Managerial Economics*. Longmans.

HOPWOOD (1974), *Accounting and Human Behaviour*. Accountancy Age Books.

HORNGREN (1982), *Cost Accounting: A Managerial Emphasis*. Prentice-Hall.

HOTSTEDE (1968), *The Game of Budget Control*. Tavistock.

JOHNSTON (1967), *Statistical Cost Analysis*. McGraw-Hill.

SAVAGE and SMALL (1972), *Introduction to Managerial Economics.*
   Hutchinson.
WELSCH (1971), *Budgeting: Profit Planning and Control.* Prentice-Hall.

Questions for discussion

1   What benefits should accrue to a business from the installation of a budgetary control system?

2   The term 'budgetary control' may conjure up images of a dictatorial management which may either frighten or incense employees. How might management set about the task of reassuring employees that such control is a process of self-realization?

3   For the LM Co. Ltd, who produce a standard type of product, you are required to prepare at 1 January 1985 for each of the three months January, February and March 1985:

   (a) a budget of sales;
   (b) a budget of production, bought-out products, and stock of finished goods;
   (c) a budget of purchases of raw materials;
   (d) a statement showing the expected manufacturing contribution from sales if the above budgets are achieved and if costs are at standard.

The following data about the company are available:

(1) Sales

(i)   On 1 December each year the total sales for the ensuing year are estimated. Monthly sales are then budgeted by use of the pattern given in (iii) below.

(ii) During the 11 months to 30 November 1984 sales were 21,800 units. Sales in December 1984 were expected to be 2,200 units. For 1985 as a whole a 20 per cent increase over 1984 is expected.

(iii) The pattern of the company's sales is that 5 per cent of the annual total are made in each month except in:

   February, when 8% of annual sales are made
   March, when 22% of annual sales are made
   July, when 20% of annual sales are made
   September, when 10% of annual sales are made

(2) Production

(i)   The output capacity of the plant is 2,000 units per month.
(ii) Work put in hand one month is delivered to finished goods stores in the following month.
(iii) Raw material purchases are scheduled so that the material required for each month is on hand at the beginning of that month.

(3) Stocks and bought-out units

(i)   The minimum stock level is 5 per cent of the total sales for the previous year. This is also the desired level, but for seasonal requirements it may be built up by production to a maximum of 15 per cent of the previous year's sales.

(ii) If requirements for sales are above what production and stocks permit, it is possible to buy-out extra requirements for delivery in the month in which the goods are to be sold. The standard cost of such bought-out goods is £55 per unit.

(iii) Finished stock on 1 January 1985 is expected to be 2,500 units, all of which have been produced in the plant. The company operates a first in, first-out system for its finished stock, but regards finished goods of its own production in any month as having been received before units bought-out during that month.

(4) Selling price and marginal cost

The product sells at £80 each; its standard marginal cost, when produced in the factory, is as follows:

	£
Direct materials: 100 lb at £0.40 per lb	40.00
Direct labour: 6 hours at £1.00 per hour	6.00
Standard marginal cost, each	**£46.00**

There is no variable overhead.

4   Sizer Ltd has a budget target of 9,000 hours per period. However, as actual hours worked will tend to fluctuate a flexible budget is also to be produced for monitoring efficiency. The following information is available for dept. A which carries out 'widgeting', a process of finishing:

	£
	(per hour)
Direct labour	0.6
Indirect labour	0.25
Power	0.18
Miscellaneous	0.05
	(per period)
Supervision	2,200
Rent and rates	2,000
Depreciation	1,500
Administration	2,800

At above 9,000 hours per period, supervision and depreciation would each increase by 10 per cent.

Required:
Prepare a flexible budget for Sizer Ltd's dept. A at 80, 90, 100, and 110 per cent budgeted hours.

5   Next year's preliminary budget workings for Scrunchie, a breakfast cereal, the only product manufactured by H.F. Ltd, are shown below:

H.F. Ltd
Budgeted Revenue Account
for the year ending 30 September 1984

	£	£
Sales (20,000 boxes, containing standard packets)		600,000
Direct materials	240,000	
Direct labour	102,000	
Variable overhead	70,000	
Fixed overhead	122,200	
		534,200
Profit		**£65,800**

H.F. Ltd
Budgeted Net Assets
as at 30 September 1984

	£	£
Fixed assets (net of depreciation)		310,000
Working capital:		
Debtors	50,000	
Stocks	65,000	
Creditors	(25,000)	
		90,000
Net assets employed		**£400,000**

The existing plant and equipment is considerably under-utilized and a proposal being considered is to extend sales to supermarkets, where the product would be sold under a different brand name. Estimated effects of this proposal are

(i)   Additional annual sales, to supermarkets 8,000 boxes @ £25 per box.
(ii)   Cost of direct materials will be reduced as a result of a 5 per cent quantity discount on all purchases.
(iii) Extra supervisory and clerical staff will be required at a cost of £16,000 p.a.

(iv) Market research has indicated that sales to existing outlets will fall by approximately 10 per cent and there will be no change in selling price to these customers.

(v) Stocks and creditors will increase by £25,000 and £15,000, respectively, and the credit period extended to supermarkets will be double that given to existing customers.

Required:

Present data to assist in the evaluation of the proposal. Specifically you should

(a) Prepare a revised budgeted revenue account and statement of net assets employed incorporating the results of the proposal.

(b) Calculate the effect on profit of each of the changes resulting from the proposal and reconcile the total of these with the difference in budgeted profits.

(c) Advise management on the suitability of the proposal making any further calculations you consider necessary and adding any other comments or reservations you think relevant.

6   Shown below are graphs reflecting factory cost of expense data over varying production levels. The vertical axis of each graph represents total pounds (£) of expenses and the horizontal axis represents production levels.

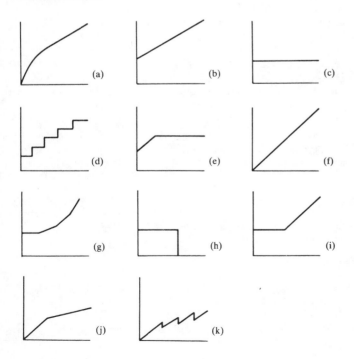

(a) You are required to indicate by letter which of the graphs represents each of the situations or items described below (the graphs may be used more than once or not at all):

(i) a royalty charge of £1 per unit produced up to 1,000 units, after which the charge is 60p per unit;
(ii) annual rent of the factory;
(iii) rates for a factory where a public authority waives the rates if 500 or more local men are employed;
(iv) material costs for production at £1.50 per unit of material;
(v) material costs for production based on the following scale of charges:

£8.00 for 1st unit produced
£7.50 for 2nd unit produced
£7.00 for 3rd unit produced, etc., reducing to a minimum cost per units produced of £4

(vi) electricity charge based on fixed charge plus £4 per unit of electricity used;
(vii) a water charge made up as follows:

1st 100 gal £1.00
next 100 gal 15p per gal
next 100 gal 20p per gal
all other gallonage 25p per gal

(b) For each of the graphs not associated with one of the given situations give a brief explanation of the cost behaviour and suggest what the cost might be.
(c) In what way does a knowledge of cost behaviour influence the usefulness of budgetary control?

7   Ideal Manufacturing Co. has prepared the following forecasts. From this information prepare a cash budget for three months ended 31 December.

Purchases

Month	Sales	Raw materials	Fuel and power	Other	Wages	Salaries	Direct expenses	Sundry expenses
July	29,800	14,400	1,305	2,050	3,124	2,010	426	1,876
Aug.	24,600	13,800	1,050	1,860	2,800	1,830	414	1,828
Sept.	27,000	14,400	780	2,020	3,128	1,950	432	1,952
Oct.	32,400	13,500	840	2,250	2,860	1,805	405	1,810
Nov.	36,000	12,600	1,020	2,400	3,550	2,280	378	1,822
Dec.	40,500	15,900	1,035	2,700	3,520	2,430	480	1,960

Notes

(i)   The anticipated cash balance at 1 October will be £5,000 overdrawn.

(ii) 80 per cent of debtors pay at the end of the month following sales; 10 per cent pay at the end of two months and the remainder after three months.

(iii) 50 per cent of raw materials are purchased from one supplier who allows 2 per cent cash discount for payment in same month. The remainder are paid in the month following.

(iv) Fuel and power costs are accumulated and paid at the end of every quarter beginning 1 April.

(v)   All other suppliers of goods and services allow one month's credit.

(vi) Included in sundry expenses is a standing charge for depreciation of £1,000 per month.

(vii) Wages are paid one week in arrears. August and November are five-week months, the remainder are four weeks. Salaries are paid monthly at the end of the period to which they refer.

(viii) New plant costing £50,000 will be paid for in December.

8   **Baker Ltd**
Balance Sheet
as at 30 June 1984

	£		
Issued share capital	60,000		
Profit and loss A/c	30,000		
	90,000		
8% debentures	10,000		
	100,000		

	Cost	Depreciation	Net
Fixed assets:	£	£	£
Plant and machinery	90,000	25,000	65,000
Motors	8,000	4,000	4,000
	98,000	29,000	69,000

Investments at cost (market value £11,000)		10,000
Current assets:		
Stock of raw material	10,000	
Stock of finished goods	20,000	
Debtors—May	13,000	
—June	15,000	
Bank	8,000	
	66,000	(*continued*)

Baker Ltd Balance Sheet
as at 30 June 1984 (*continued*)

Less:
Current liabilities:

Trade—creditors for materials—April	10,000	
—May	15,000	
—June	15,000	
Creditors for fixed expenses —June	5,000	
		45,000

Net current assets	21,000
	100,000

Required:
From this balance sheet, together with the following information which you have obtained, prepare

(a) a cash budget for the six months ending 31 December 1984 showing the cash balance at the end of each month;
(b) the forecast trading and profit and loss account for the six months ended 31 December 1984 and a balance sheet as at that date.

As the management accountant of Baker Ltd you have obtained the following information in respect of budgets and forecasts:

	July	Aug.	Sept.	Oct.	Nov.	Dec.
Sales (units)	4,500	4,500	6,000	4,500	3,000	3,000
Production (units)	4,000	4,500	4,500	4,000	4,000	4,000

The forecast selling price is £6 per unit—one-third of all sales will be paid by cash, debtors will pay two months after delivery. Trade creditors for materials are paid in the third month after the receipt of the goods. Materials are received in the month of production.
Production costs are expected to be

Direct materials	£1 per unit
Direct labour	£2 per unit
Indirect variable expenses	£1 per unit

Stock is valued at marginal cost.

Direct labour and indirect variable expenses are paid in the month of production.
Factory fixed expenses of £1,500 per month and administration fixed expenses of £3,500 are paid one month in arrears.
Depreciation on the plant and machinery is to be provided at the

rate of 10 per cent p.a. on the original cost and on the motors at the rate of 25 per cent p.a. using the reducing balance method.

The debenture interest is payable half-yearly on 30 June and 31 December.

The bank has set a limit on the overdraft of £5,000. If the cash budget is forecast to exceed that limit in any month, the investments would have to be sold in order to keep the overdraft below the limit. Assume that the profit on any investments sold is 10 per cent.

15 Standard costs and variance analysis

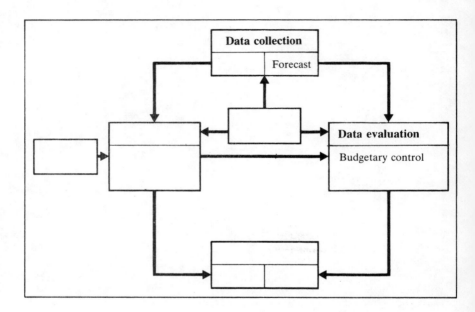

Data collection

Forecast

Data evaluation

Budgetary control

Nature and purpose of standard costs

In Chapter 13 we examined the elements of manufacturing costs and the methods by which such costs were accumulated. We observed that direct material and labour costs were collected on an actual basis, but that overhead costs were usually charged to production by means of a budgeted or normal overhead rate. Under this system the resulting budget costs are a combination of actual and predetermined costs. Many cost accounting systems, however, are based wholly on predetermined costs—costs that *should have been incurred* rather than the costs that *actually were incurred*. Such a system is called a standard cost system.

Each unit of production has a standard material cost, a standard labour cost and a standard overhead cost, determined for each production cost centre. Since standard costs are usually different from the actual costs incurred, the difference or variance is debited (if adverse) or credited (if favourable) to the profit and loss section of the income statement. A

338

standard cost system has several advantages:

(1) It is simpler to use once standards have been established, because there is no need to recalculate cost for each separate unit of production.
(2) Unit costs will be the same for each physically identical product, whereas under an actual cost system this may not be so. Under an actual job cost system, for example, two equally efficient men may be responsible for a particular operation. If one, because of seniority or some other reason, is paid a higher wage than the other, the cost of the product will vary—yet realistically there is no difference at all in the finished product.
(3) A standard cost system provides the basic control mechanism, in that any changes in efficiency will normally be automatically highlighted in the variance accounts.

The setting of standards

We have defined standard costs as costs which 'should be' incurred; what 'should be' incurred is determined by management who are subject to the same degree of fallibility which prescribes all human activity. Any analysis of variance must begin in practice with an examination of the accuracy of the standard. Standards may be inadequate because they were not set properly, or because conditions have changed so much that they have become obsolete.

Two types of standards are possible; standards of perfection and standards of attainability. Ideal standards are those which only allow those quantities of material or time which are absolutely essential to the task in hand; attainable or expected standards are based upon what can be achieved by efficient performance. For example, an ideal standard may suggest that it is possible for a worker to stamp out 50 parts from 50 metal sheets at the rate of 1 per 10 seconds. The expected standard will recognize that some material will be damaged, and some time will be lost, and so set the standard slightly lower. Motivation is critical, and, as we noted in Chapter 16, to set standards too high will discourage rather than encourage, frighten rather than motivate.

Standards for material and labour are concerned with prices and quantities. Material price standards are those prices which should be paid under the most favourable conditions possible. The standard price will include adjustments for any carriage charges and any quantity discounts. Standard wage rates (prices) are normally established as a result of negotiations between management and unions. Materials usage standards are established on the basis of theoretical input–output relationships, and also upon observations of experience which suggest certain allowances from the theoretical optimum relationship—notably adjustments for scrap.

Labour efficiency standards are the amount of time which particular productive operations should take, and are normally established on the basis of actual operation and a critical appraisal of whether or not those operations are being performed as efficiently as is feasible.

Standard costs for overhead are based on budgeted overhead and budgeted volume. Standard variable overhead costs are developed from past experience with adjustments for expected changes in conditions. Standard fixed overhead costs are only employed under absorption costing and are a function of budgeted fixed costs and budgeted volume.

Variance computation and analysis

The difference between actual and standard cost is called a variance. A variance is favourable when the actual cost is less than the standard. It is important to appreciate that, in this context, favourable and unfavourable are merely technical terms and do not denote good and bad. A qualitative statement can only be made after the underlying cause of the variance has been identified.

Variance computation is the mathematical technique for determining the amount of variance; given the standard and actual price and quantity, this is a logical but mechanical process. Variance analysis is the process of investigation which aims to determine the particular causes of variances the computations have identified. We will examine the cost elements—material, labour and overhead—in terms of standard and actual costs, assuming that the standard has been properly set, and also consider the computation and analysis of sales variances.

Material variances

(1) Computation

Material costs arise from the combination of price and quantity, so that any difference between standard and actual costs can arise because of price variances, usage variance or both. We may illustrate this as follows:

Material Y

Standard price per yard	£0.4
Standard usage per unit	3 yd
Actual price per yard	£0.5
Actual usage per unit	2 yd

The net variance may be computed as follows:

Actual cost per unit	$2 \times 0.5 = £1$
Standard cost per unit	$3 \times 0.4 = £1.2$
Variance (favourable)	**£0.2**

This net variance, however, is a combination of an adverse price and a favourable usage, as the diagram below may help to illustrate:

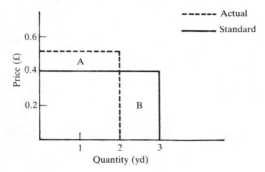

The material price variance is given by the quadrilateral A; the effect of the higher—and therefore unfavourable—price, is measured by multiplying the values of the two sides of the quadrilateral. In this case the value is

$$2 \times 0.1 = £0.2 \quad \text{(adverse)}$$

We may express this more formally and say that the material price variance is given by

Material price variance = (Actual price − Standard price) × Actual quantity used

The price variance may in fact be calculated at the time of purchase of the material, rather than at the time of issue to production. This situation arises if the material stocks are valued at a standard price rather than actual.

The material usage variance is given by quadrilateral B, the value being

$$1 \times 0.4 = 0.4 \quad \text{(favourable)}$$

or more formally

Material usage variance = (Quantity used − Standard quantity) × Standard price

The net result of the two calculations is

	£
Material price variance	(0.2)
Material usage variance	0.4
Net variance (favourable)	**£0.2**

When both price and usage variances are favourable or unfavourable, the rules above do not give such a clear-cut result. Consider the following:

Material X

Standard price per yard	£0.4
Standard usage per unit	3 yd
Actual price per yard	£0.5
Actual usage per unit	4 yd

Diagrammatically the result is

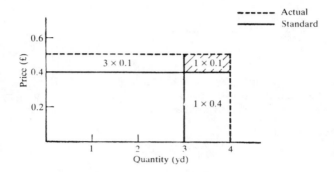

The net variance is $(4 \times 0.5) - (3 \times 0.4) = £0.8$ (unfavourable); of this $(3 \times 0.1) = £0.3$ is clearly a price variance, $(1 \times 0.4) = £0.4$ is clearly a usage variance, but the remaining area $(1 \times 0.1) = £0.1$ is an inextricable combination of the influence of higher prices and higher usage. The rules employed designate this entirely as a price variance.

(2) Analysis

Since the material price variance is simply the difference between the actual and standard price paid for materials purchased, it is tempting to assign all responsibility for the variance to the efficiency or otherwise of the purchasing department. Such a conclusion, however, might be completely erroneous. For example, a general price rise in an essential material is completely beyond the control and responsibility of the purchasing department. A favourable price variance may be achieved by purchasing cheaply from an unreliable supplier, and the poor quality of the goods result in a lot of waste which produces an adverse usage variance. An unfavourable variance may arise because material has been bought from a dearer source— but if this has been necessitated because of an emergency shortage on the production line which had not been notified in time to the purchasing department, then the responsibility must clearly fall on some other department.

Material usage variances can arise from a variety of causes. They may arise from a poor quality of production labour, from substandard machinery, through theft, through a poor quality of material, or an almost endless variety of circumstances. It is essential to trace responsibility, for until responsibility is determined, control is impossible.

Labour variances

(1)   Computation

The computation of labour variances is analogous to that of materials. The standard labour cost of a unit of production is constructed by multiplying the standard wage (price) per hour by the standard hours required to produce the unit. The variances can be attributed to difference in wages, and/or differences in time:

Product X

	Actual	Standard
Hours to produce	9	10
Rate per hour	£0.7	£0.5

The net labour variance becomes

Actual	9 × 0.7 = £6.3
Standard	10 × 0.5 = £5.0
Labour variance (adverse)	**£1.3**

The component variances are the wage rate variance and the labour efficiency variance:

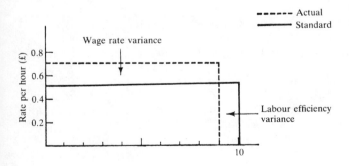

The wage rate variance is given by (9 × 0.2) = £1.8 (adverse), and the efficiency variance by (1 × 0.5) = £0.5 (favourable). More formally

Wage rate variance = (Actual rate per hour − Standard rate per hour) × Actual hours worked and

$$\text{Labour efficiency variance} = (\text{Actual hours worked} - \text{Standard hours allowed}) \times \text{Standard rate per hour}$$

As with material variances, the problem of entirely favourable or unfavourable variances is overcome by assuming that the portion of the variance which is an inextricable combination of higher/lower wages and higher/lower hours is attributable to the wage rate variance.

(2)   Analysis

The wage rate variance is probably the least susceptible to management control, since most wages are fixed by a process of negotiation. Changes in wage rates subsequent to the setting of standards are obviously uncontrollable at production level, and the standard should be adjusted. On the other hand, high actual wages in a department may arise because higher paid workers are engaged on a job normally done by lower paid employees. Such a practice may reflect necessity—to obviate a temporary bottleneck in production, for example—or they may be the result of poor labour recruitment policies.

Labour efficiency variances can arise for a multitude of reasons. Changes in a worker's operating effectiveness may be caused by his health, by family worries, by the nearness of holidays, by a football match, and a limitless number of other factors. The variance may be caused by the introduction of a new machine or tools into the production process, or by substandard materials, or by inadequate processing at an earlier stage. Finally it is worth noting that the standard hours were set having regard to the 'average' man in the 'average' conditions—and neither average really exists.

Overhead variances

The total overhead variances is the difference between the actual overhead costs incurred and the amount of overhead absorbed to production through use of the predetermined overhead rate (or rates if fixed and variable overhead are separated). The concept of volume is critical to all measurement of overhead; volume may be described in terms of output, i.e. number of units of product produced, or in terms of input, i.e. the productive efforts of the firm in labour hours or machine hours. Each unit of output demands a given input, and the *standard input volume* is the total quantity of labour hours (or some other input quantity) needed to produce the actual output of a period.

(1)   Computation

The calculation of overhead variances is not difficult provided the meaning of the variances is clearly understood. Unlike material and labour variance, where the significance is intuitively obvious, overhead variances are often more difficult to grasp conceptually. We will consider a numerical example in order to examine the procedure and its significance at every stage.

The Astra Manufacturing Co. Ltd prepares the following overhead budget:

(1) Total budgeted volume: 50,000 direct labour hours or 100,000 units of output
(2) Total budgeted variable overhead: £100,000
(3) Total budgeted fixed overhead: £250,000
(4) Standard variable overhead: 100,000/50,000 = £2 per direct labour hour
(5) Standard fixed overhead: 250,000/50,000 = £5 per direct labour hour

During the year the actual results are as follows:

(6) Actual volume = 30,000 direct labour hours, which produced 80,000 units of output
(7) Actual variable overhead: £120,000
(8) Actual fixed overhead: £180,000

It follows from (1) and (6) that the standard hours of the work actually done are

(9) $(50,000/100,000) \times 80,000 = 40,000$ standard hours

We can now compute the variances which have arisen, first in terms of the variable and then the fixed overhead. Since 30,000 hours were actually worked, the firm could have expected to spend $30,000 \times £2 = £60,000$ on variable overhead. But £120,000 was actually spent, and so there is a spending variance of £60,000. Thus

Spending (or budget) variance (variable)
 = Actual variable overhead − (Actual hours × Variable overhead rate)
 = 120,000 − (30,000 × 2)
 = **£60,000**

This variance is unfavourable in so far as actual costs exceed budgeted costs.

The firm spent 30,000 hours to produce 80,000 units of output; if it had worked at standard efficiency, it could only have produced $30,000 \times (100,000/50,000) = 60,000$ units. Since our measurement of input is labour hours, this overhead efficiency is caused directly by labour efficiency (assuming the standard input volume relationship was correctly established). Overhead is absorbed on the basis of standard hours, so Astra

Ltd will have absorbed 40,000 × 2 = £80,000, as opposed to 30,000 × 2 = £60,000—an efficiency variance of £20,000:

Efficiency variance = Variable overhead rate × (Actual hours
                          worked − Standard hours of work
                          completed)
                    = 2 × (30,000 − 40,000) = £20,000
                          (favourable)

A check on the individual computation can be provided by ascertaining the total variable overhead variance. As the variable rate was £2 per direct labour hour, and the standard hours of work done 40,000, the overhead absorbed (i.e. charged to work in progress) will be 40,000 × 2 = £80,000. The actual variable overhead was £120,000, giving a total adverse variance of £40,000, which consists of a £20,000 favourable efficiency variance and a £60,000 adverse budget variance.

The variance may be ascertained graphically, as shown, a device which may help the student to visualize the relationships that have been discussed:

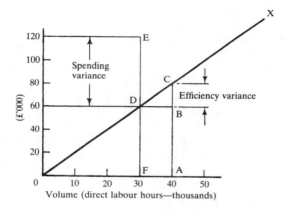

The line 0X is the variable overhead budget for different levels of activity and represents the amount that will be applied to production at those varying levels. The line FE indicates the actual variable overhead (£120,000) incurred in relation to the actual hours worked; its intersection with 0X at D provides the variable overhead which should have been incurred at that volume (30,000 × 2 = £60,000). The spending variance (ED) is thus the difference between what should have been incurred at that volume and what was actually incurred. AC shows the amount of overhead that will have been absorbed in relation to the standard hours of work done. As only 30,000 hours were actually worked, a saving of 10,000 hours or £20,000 was effected (CB).

Fixed overheads are fixed irrespective of volume, thus any difference between the budgeted fixed overhead and the actual fixed overhead will arise because of over- or under-spending. The spending variance is given by

Actual fixed overhead − Budgeted fixed overhead
$$= 180,000 - 250,000$$
$$= £70,000 \text{ (favourable)}$$

There is no measure of efficiency connected with fixed overhead; efficiency is connected with the concept of volume—the material usage variance reflects efficient or inefficient use of material for given volumes of production, the labour efficiency variance reflects the performance of the work base in relation to the standard time allowed, and the variable overhead efficiency variance indicates the efficient or inefficient use of labour (or other input) which makes possible savings or excess incurrence of overhead. Fixed costs are time costs, and as such are unconnected with volume of activity.

Since the absorption of fixed overhead is based on the relationship between budgeted costs and budgeted volume, any deviation from budgeted volume will result in more or less overhead being absorbed to production. The volume variance is given by

(Standard input volume of work done − Budgeted input volume) × Standard fixed overhead absorption rate
$$= (40,000 - 50,000) \times 5$$
$$= £50,000 \text{ (unfavourable)}$$

A check can be provided by computing the total fixed variance, which is similar to the variable overhead variance. The fixed overhead absorbed will be $40,000 \times 5 = 200,000$; since the actual overhead is £180,000, there is a total favourable variance of £20,000. This consists of a favourable spending variance (£70,000) and an adverse volume variance of £50,000.

The results can be determined graphically, as shown:

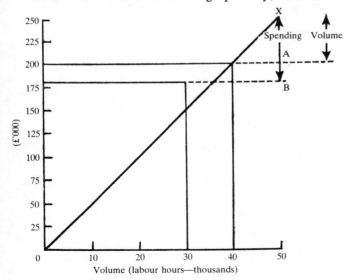

The line 0X represents the absorption rate of £5 per direct labour hour. XB is the spending variance, and XA the volume variance.

(2)   Analysis

(a) *Spending variances.* Whenever the actual cost differs from the budgeted cost, a spending variance will appear. To ascertain the nature of this item it will be necessary to examine the component parts of the overhead budgets to see which items of overhead have varied from expectations. Since overhead includes depreciation it is essential for management to know which variances are attributable to current spending on such things as indirect material and labour, and which to shifts in depreciation rates; the former may be controllable, the latter is a matter of accounting procedure.

(b) *Efficiency variance.* The causes of an efficiency variance are not changes in overhead costs but changes in the volume of activity. If activity is measured in labour hours, then the reason must be sought in terms of labour efficiency. It applies only to variable costs.

(c) *Volume variance.* The volume variance is caused uniquely by the mechanics of absorption costing, and is attributable solely to the fact that the volume of activity is greater or less than planned. The actual numerical result is virtually meaningless, but it does serve to draw attention to the vital question as to why planned and actual levels of production are different.

Sales variances

In general, the type of methodology used to compute and analyse cost variances is equally applicable to the computation and analysis of revenue (sales) variances. There are usually three main variances applied to the sales data, and these are: (i) sales price variance, (ii) sales volume variance, and (iii) sales mix variance.

(1)   Computation

The price and volume variances are analogous to the material cost price and usage variances, but the sales mix variance arises because a firm sells its products in different proportions than envisaged in the budget. We may illustrate the computation and analysis of these variances with the aid of the following data:

Product	Budget			Actual		
	unit price £	unit sales	total value £	unit price £	unit sales	total value £
A	8	10,000	80,000	9	11,000	99,000
B	4	10,000	49,000	3	10,500	31,500
		20,000	129,000		21,500	130,500

It will be seen that the business has a favourable total sales value variance of £130,500 − 120,000 = **£10,500**.

We may analyse this into its component parts, commencing with the sales price variance. If a unit is sold at a higher unit price than the original budget allowed, then there is a *favourable* price variance. Conversely, if a unit is sold at a lower price than originally intended, there is an *adverse* price variance. Thus, the sales price variances in this case are

Product A = 11,000 (9 − 8) =   £11,000 (Favourable)
Product B = 10,500 (3 − 4) =   £10,500 (Adverse)

+   £500 (Favourable)

More generally, we may write the sales price variance as

Sales price variance = Actual units sold × (Actual unit price − Standard unit price)

If the total volume of actual sales is greater than the budgeted volume of sales, there is a *favourable* volume variance, and, conversely, if the total volume of actual sales is less than the budgeted volume there is an *adverse* variance. However, in establishing this variance, we must be careful to isolate the effect of changes in volume from changes in the product mix. In the example, we expected to sell a total of 20,000 units but in fact sold 21,500 units. If this increase in volume of 1,500 units had been sold at the standard product mix, we would have sold 750 units more of A, and 750 units more of B. Hence, the volume variance is

Product A = 8 (750) = £6,000 (Favourable)
Product B = 4 (750) = £3,000 (Favourable)

£9,000 (Favourable)

More formally, we may write

Sales volume variance = Standard unit price × (Actual quantity in standard proportions − Budgeted unit quantity)

i.e.

A = 8 (10,750 − 10,000) = £6,000 (Favourable)
B = 4 (10,750 − 10,000) = £3,000 (Favourable)

If the product mix changes, we may isolate the effect of this by comparing the actual sales volume of each product with the actual total sales in the budgeted mix proportions. Thus

Product A = (8 × 11,000) − (8 × 10,750)
         = 8 (11,000 − 10,750) = £2,000 (Favourable)

$$\begin{aligned}
\text{Product B} &= (4 \times 10,500) - (4 \times 10,750) \\
&= 4\,(10,500 - 10,750) = \text{£1,000 (Adverse)}
\end{aligned}$$

$$+ \text{£1,000 (Favourable)}$$

More generally, we may write

Sales mix variance = Standard unit price × (Actual quantity −
Budget mix of the actual sales)

If we add together these three sales variances, we can return to our original total sales value variance, viz.:

Sales price variance	£500	(Favourable)
Sales volume variance	£9,000	(Favourable)
Sales mix variance	£1,000	(Favourable)
	£10,500	(Favourable)

(2)   Analysis

As with cost variances, there is little if any point in calculating the sales variances unless the causes are investigated and, if necessary and possible, corrected. Changes in sales prices from those established in the budget must be properly authorized. If the business is such that it gives its salesmen some discretion in price fixing, then the consequence of their decisions should be clearly established by considering the effect the changed price of a product has on volume and mix. Decreases in sales volume may not be attributable to the sales force, for it may be that the production is insufficient to meet demand. Changes in sales mix may occur because some products are substitutable and customers are shifting to the cheaper products.

Summary of variance formulae

For the sake of convenience the various formulae referred to in this chapter are summarized below. In each case, the formula is stated so that a positive answer is a favourable variance, and a negative answer, unfavourable.

___

Material

Price   = (Standard price − Actual price) × Actual quantity used

Usage = (Standard quantity − Actual quantity) × Standard price

Labour

Wage rate = (Standard wage rate − Actual wage rate) × Actual hours
worked

Efficiency = (Standard hours allowed − Actual hours
worked) × Standard wage rate

Variable overhead

Spending (budget) = (Actual input volume of work done × Standard variable overhead rate) − Actual variable overhead

Efficiency = (Standard input volume of work done[1] − Actual input volume) × Standard variable overhead rate

Fixed overhead

Spending (budget) = Budgeted costs − Actual costs

Volume = (Standard input volume of work done[1] − Budgeted input volume) × Standard fixed overhead rate

Sales

Price = (Actual unit price − Standard unit price) × Actual units sold

Volume = (Actual quantity in standard proportions − Budgeted unit quantity) × Standard unit price

Mix = (Actual quantity − Budget mix of actual sales) × Standard unit price

---

1   By labour hours or some other input method.

Recording standard costs

There is no universally agreed system by which standard costs are incorporated in the recording process. However, the differences between them are differences of practice and not of principle. We will use a system similar in cost flow to that illustrated in Chapter 13, the only difference being that material, labour and overhead are charged to production at standard cost, any variance being debited or credited to variance accounts.

Example

The Astra Manufacturing Co. Ltd produces a single product whose standard cost under the absorption costing method is as follows:

	£
Materials 4 lb at £0.5	2.0
Labour 10 hours at £0.4	4.0
Variable overhead 10 hours at 0.2	2.0
Fixed overhead 10 hours at 0.3	3.0
Standard Cost	**£11.0**

(1) Astra Ltd purchases 200,000 lb of material at £0.4935 per lb:

Material stock	Dr. 100,000	
Creditors		98,700
Price variance		1,300

The material is taken into stock at standard cost, and the resulting difference between purchase price and standard cost credited to the price variance account.

(2) During the year 47,000 units of the product are made; materials used for production amount to 199,000 lb:

Work in progress	Dr. 94,000	
Material usage variance	Dr. 5,500	
Material stock		99,500

The standard quantity of material for 47,000 units is $47,000 \times 4 = 188,000$ lb which, at standard cost, is £94,000. The difference between actual and standard quantities used provides the material usage variance.

(3) 460,000 labour hours are worked at a wage rate of £0.41 per labour hour:

Work in progress	Dr. 188,000	
Wage rate variance	Dr. 4,600	
Labour efficiency variance		4,000
Manufacturing wages		188,600

The work in progress is debited with the standard cost of the work done ($47,000 \times 10 \times 0.4$); the manufacturing wages (payroll) with the amount actually earned. The difference is analysed into the component variances.

(4) The actual overhead incurred was as follows:

Variable overhead	Dr. 99,000	
Fixed overhead	Dr. 170,000	
Sundry accounts		269,000

The sundry accounts will be cash, depreciation, etc.

(5) Since 47,000 units were produced, utilizing 470,000 standard hours, work in progress will be debited at the standard overhead rates:

Work in progress	Dr. 235,000	
Variable overhead		94,000
Fixed overhead		141,000

(6) Astra Ltd had expected to produce 50,000 units at a variable cost of £100,000 (£0.2 per direct labour hour), and at a fixed cost of £150,000

(£0.3 per direct labour hour). The overhead variances can therefore be identified:

Overhead spending variance (variable)	Dr. 7,000	
Variable overhead		5,000
Overhead efficiency variance (variable)		2,000
Overhead spending variance (fixed)	Dr. 20,000	
Overhead volume variance (fixed)	Dr. 9,000	
Fixed overhead		29,000

(7) Since 47,000 units were completed, the standard cost of those goods (47,000 × £11) can be transferred to finished goods:

Finished goods	Dr. 517,000	
Work in progress		517,000

The work in progress account (given there is no opening or closing work in progress) will now be cleared. The £517,000 consists of

Materials	94,000
Labour	188,000
Variable overhead	94,000
Fixed overhead	141,000
	£517,000

The question now arises as to how the balances on the variance accounts should be eliminated. In practice, in most cases they are debited or credited to either the trading account or to the profit and loss account in aggregate. If stock is disclosed in the balance sheet at standard cost it would seem logical to dispose of the variances through the profit and loss account in order to display the cost of goods sold at standard cost—a consistent treatment. This presupposes that the standards set are current and attainable; if they are not, they are not a satisfactory measure of current production costs, and the variances are not valid indicators of departure from costs of manufacture. In such circumstances it would seem reasonable to adjust the stock on the balance sheet and the manufacturing cost of the period by disposing of the variances through the manufacturing and trading accounts.

We may reflect the above transactions through the relevant ledger accounts as follows:

Material stock A/c

Creditors	98,700	WIP		94,000
Price		Usage		
variance	1,300	variance		5,500
	———	Balance		
	100,000	c/d		500
				———
				100,000

Work in progress A/c

Material	94,000	Finished	
Labour	188,000	goods	517,000
Variable			
overhead	94,000		
Fixed			
overhead	141,000		
	———		———
	517,000		**517,000**

Wages A/c

Bank	188,600	WIP	188,000
Efficiency		Rate	
variance	4,000	variance	4,600
	———		———
	192,600		192,600

Finished goods A/c

WIP	517,000

Variable overhead A/c

Bank/		WIP	94,000
creditors	99,000		
Efficiency		Spending	
variance	2,000	variance	7,000
	———		———
	101,000		101,000

Variance A/c

Material		Material	
usage	5,500	price	1,300
Labour		Labour	
rate	4,600	ef-	
Variable		ficiency	4,000
o/head		Variable	
spend-		o/head	
ing	7,000	ef-	
Fixed		ficiency	2,000
o/head		Trading	
—spend-		A/c	38,800
ing	20,000		
—volume	9,000		
	———		———
	46,100		46,100

Fixed overhead A/c

Bank/		WIP	141,000
creditors	170,000	Spending	
		variance	20,000
		Volume	
		variance	9,000
	———		———
	170,000		170,000

Standards and probability

In our discussion we have stressed the assumption that the standard set is correct; to measure the variance of an actual cost from an inaccurate standard cost produces a near meaningless result. But an error in the projected standard is almost certain to occur and, as Churchman observed, 'One does not measure unless one can also measure the error of the measurement'. One method of approaching the problem of errors in standards (or, for that matter, budgets) is to draw on probability statistics.

Any standard set can be presumed to represent that value most likely to occur; therefore any deviation from the standard is as likely to fall below as to fall above. Examination of past experience of variations from standard, and in particular of those variances which are controllable (i.e. not due to external factors), will indicate the expected percentage of deviation from standard. With knowledge of the value most likely to occur, and also of the percentage range of deviation, it is possible to calculate the probability of any given deviation being due to non-controllable factors.

For example, assume that the administration budget is £10,000 p.a. and that experience shows that controllable variation can be expected to fall within ± 10 per cent. If we further assume that the distribution around the mean value of £10,000 is normal, or nearly so (this assumption is not essential but in many cases it approximates close enough to reality to be acceptable), we can calculate the standard deviation by means of the formula

$$\frac{\frac{1}{2}\,(\text{range})}{3.09}$$

since the approximate limits of the distribution are 3.09 standard deviations above or below the mean. In our example

$$\begin{aligned}
\text{Standard deviation} &= \frac{\frac{1}{2}\,(11{,}000 - 9{,}000)}{3.09} \\
&= \frac{1{,}000}{3.09} \\
&= \pm\,\pounds324
\end{aligned}$$

By then expressing any variance in terms of the number of standard deviations from the mean standard, the probability of the variance being due to random non-controllable factors can be calculated. For example, if the actual administrative costs are £10,500, the number of standard deviations is

$$\frac{10{,}500 - 10{,}000}{324}$$
$$= 1.545$$

From statistical tables, the probability of the variance being due to non-controllable factors is only 0.11 (or 11 chances in 100).

Investigation will proceed whenever the probability reaches a level determined by management. In addition, management will also take account of the size of the variance if this has an important consequence relative to the overall financial position. The control system can be represented graphically, as shown:

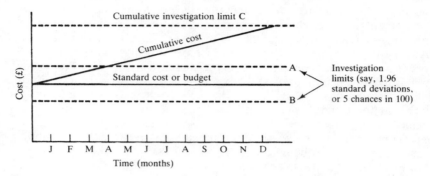

If the monthly variance falls above A or below B, investigation will take place. Furthermore, if the cumulative total of monthly variances exceeds the limit C, investigation will also take place.

This approach is, in effect, setting standards for variances', which are no longer favourable or unfavourable but simply greater or less than expected. Attention is focused not merely on some absolute level but also on the likely extent of deviations.

References and further reading

CHURCHMAN (1967), *Prediction and Optimal Decisions*. Prentice-Hall.
DYCKMAN (1969), 'The Investigation of Cost Variance', *Journal of Accounting Research*.
FREMGEN (1981), *Managerial Cost Analysis*. Irwin.
HORNGREN (1982), *Cost Accounting: A Managerial Emphasis*. Prentice-Hall.

Questions for discussion

1   Draw up a report for your managing director explaining the nature and purpose of a standard costing system, and the benefits which derive from its use.
2   Explain the term 'standard' as applied to standard costing. Is a standard cost what a product did, should, will, or might, cost?
3   What do you understand by the terms 'material price variance' and 'material usage variance', and give examples of their calculation? What action might be taken if there was an adverse material usage variance?

4 A product incorporates two materials, A and B. The standards are

A: Price £0.50 per kilo
Usage 4 kilos per unit
B: Price £1.80 per kilo
Usage 1.5 kilos per unit

During the month of December, 5,000 units are manufactured, the actual costs and quantities being

A: Cost £10,296
Quantity 19,800 kilos
B: Cost £13,416
Quantity 7,800 kilos

Required:
Calculate the material price and usage variances.

5 Salmon Electronics Ltd set the following standard costs per unit for 1984:

Direct materials:	Standard price per kilo	£1.20
	Standard usage per unit	5 kilos
Direct labour:	Standard wage rate per hour	£3.50
	Standard time per unit	1.5 hours

Factory overheads for 1984 were expected to be £27,000. Machine capacity was 18,000 machine hours p.a. and the standard machine time was also 1.5 hours per unit.
The actual results for 1984 were

Direct materials used 62,500 kilos costing £73,000
Direct labour cost £65,872 for 17,900 hours worked
Factory overheads amounted to £27,000

Maximum capacity was obtained from the machines. Actual output was 12,000 units.

Required:

(a) Calculate the standard cost of one unit and of 12,000 units.
(b) Calculate the actual cost of 12,000 units.
(c) Calculate the material and labour variances.

6 The Numas Co. Ltd prepared the following overhead budget for 1984:

1984 Budget

(1)	Output: 40,000 units	(160,000 labour hours)
(2)	Variable overhead	£400,000
(3)	Fixed overhead	£480,000

The actual output for the period was 39,000 units which took 162,000 labour hours, and actual variable and fixed overhead amounted to £380,000 and £490,000, respectively.

Required:
(a) Prepare a budget showing overhead costs per unit.
(b) Calculate the variable and fixed overhead absorption rates.
(c) Calculate and explain the significance of as many overhead variances as possible.

7 The Nomis Co. Ltd sells four standard products. At the end of March 1984 the following data was available for that month:

Product	Budget		Actual	
	unit price £	quantity (units)	total value £	quantity (units)
A	20	2,000	45,980	2,200
B	6	1,400	7,440	1,200
C	8	1,600	13,680	1,800
D	2	1,000	1,000	500

Required:
Calculate and explain the significance of the sales price, volume and mix variances for March 1984.

8 (i) 'Standards are neither good or bad *per se*, but are what people affected by them believe them to be.' Discuss the nature and purpose of standard costing in the light of this statement.
(ii) The Zee Co. Ltd operated a flexible budgetary system and planned to produce 10,000 units during the year 1984, and prepared the following standard cost statement:

	Unit cost £
Materials 3 lb @ £0.20 per lb	0.60
Labour 6 hrs @ £0.50 per hour	3.00
Fixed overhead	2.00
	£5.60

The actual results were:

Units produced	11,000
Material 44,000 @ £0.25	11,000
Labour 55,000 @ £0.70	38,500
Fixed overhead	21,000
	£70,500

Required:

(a) Calculate the variances, and prepare a statement reconciling budgeted costs with actual costs.
(b) Comment on the significance of the overhead variances.

9 On the basis of a production/sales level of 10,000 units a month, the standard unit cost of a carton of Gimmet which sells for £12 is

	£
Material: 12 kg at 50p	6.00
Labour: 1½ hours at £1.60	2.40
Fixed overhead	0.60

The operating statement for November 1984 was as follows:

	£	£	£
Budgeted profit			30,000
Add: Favourable variances			
Sales volume margin	1,500		
Materials price	1,268		
Wages efficiency	240		
Fixed overhead volume	300	3,308	
Less: Adverse variances			
Sales price	1,000		
Material usage	400		
Wages rates	780		
Fixed overhead expenditure	200	2,380	
Net favourable variance			928
Actual profit			**£30,928**

Required:

(a) Produce an operating statement in conventional accounting form, i.e. showing a trading, profit and loss account.
(b) Explain what is meant by 'interdependence' of variances, illustrating your answer by references to the above statement.

16 Accounting for business decisions—the capital investment decision

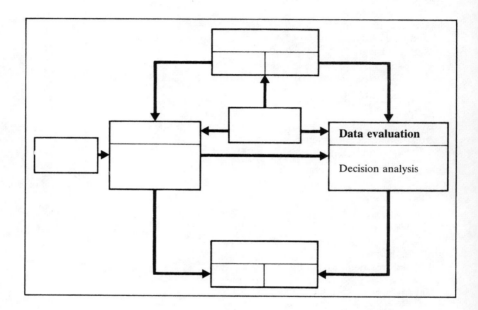

Business objectives

Economics is a social science concerned with the efficient allocation of scarce resources. Because resources such as men, materials or money are limited, the firm has to allocate them among alternative uses. If resources were unlimited, there would be no need for decisions, because all possible activities could be achieved. Scarce resources necessitate a choice, and the selection of one alternative implies the exclusion of others. In considering business decision-making, we must begin with the assumption that the firm behaves rationally, and that when faced at different times with identical problems, the decisions reached will be consistent.

Decisions must be made, therefore, on the basis of observable criteria, or, to put it in another way, the firm must have certain objectives in mind to enable it to make rational decisions. The vital question which is the logical precursor of any discussion of decision-making is whether or not it is possible to identify universal goals of economic activity. If every firm is striving to achieve different objectives, then any general analysis is impossible.

Economists have developed a theory of the firm which is based on the objective of profit maximization. The theory assumes that the firm must move towards its objectives in a rational manner, taking no action which will deprive it of its goal, and selecting from the range of alternative courses of action that alternative which will bring it nearer to profit maximization. Such a theory is heavily criticized on its motivational and cognitive assumptions. Motivational criticism argues that profit is only one of the objectives of the firm; the firm is also concerned with survival, with liquidity, with the welfare of employees, with maximizing revenue and with growth. It is important to recognize that these other motivational possibilities do not exclude profit as an objective, but rather they make it one of many objectives. Cognitive criticism points out that to maximize profits requires perfect knowledge—the firm must know exactly what expenses and revenues will stem from a particular action. As the future is uncertain it would seem impossible for the firm to plan to maximize its profits.

From this we may conclude that there is no simple or obvious business objective. Nevertheless, while profit is not the only goal of business activity, it is an extremely important one, and where a decision has to be made between profit and some alternative objective, profit is normally dominant. In our discussions of decision-making, therefore, we will assume that the firm is striving to earn as much profit as possible (i.e. to optimize profit), while ensuring that the solvency of the firm is maintained (since profit is not necessarily synonymous with cash). If faced with a decision which involves investment, the firm will choose that alternative which offers the higher profit relative to the investment; if the decision involves no investment, the firm will follow that course of action which leads to the highest profit.

The decision-making process

Whatever the nature of a decision, certain important generalizations can be made about the process by which the decision is reached. These are outlined in the following paragraphs.

(1) Define the problem

Unless the problem is clearly and precisely defined, an enormous amount of time can be wasted.

(2) Identify the alternatives

Once the problem is defined, the possible alternative solutions should be identified. Very often, in practice, the possible alternatives are not self-evident; it is all too easy to expend much effort in reaching a decision, only to find that another and better alternative invalidates the decision.

(3)   Measure the alternatives

Whenever possible, the various alternatives should be quantified, normally in monetary terms. It is important, however, not to become bemused by the apparent precision of a numerical solution. In the first place since all decisions are concerned with the future, the figures are estimates—and estimates can be wrong. Secondly we observed in Chapter 2 that the environmental postulate of money measurement, while convenient, results in the omission of all factors which cannot be described in money terms. Most decisions involve factors which can be measured, and those which cannot. Thus, the non-quantitative factors should be identified and presented to management along with the numerical assessment; management must then exercise their judgement.

(4)   Reach a decision

Having measured the alternatives, decide which is the best, and act on it. If the problem was of substance in the first instance, then delay in implementing a solution will be expensive.

In this and the following chapter, we will focus attention on specific business decision-making situations, seeking to identify the factors relevant in the particular situations. The treatment afforded is intended to provide an introduction to this important field. Specifically, we will consider in this chapter the capital investment decision and, in the following chapter, short-term decisions, pricing policies, break-even analysis and operational research.

Capital investment decisions

Any investment necessitates the commitment of funds now with the expectation of earning an acceptable stream of income over a period of time in the future. Capital investment is concerned with the allocation of resources to long-term assets in such a way as to optimize the return on the capital. The capital investment decision is important not only because it often involves very large sums of money, but also because the decision can influence the fortunes of the business for years to come.

Once made, capital investment decisions can seldom be reversed, so that the business is continually reminded of wrong or inadequate decisions made in the past. Sometimes, the scale of the investment is so large that its failure would mean the failure of the business. Moreover, capital investment is not only of significance to business itself, but also to the economy as a whole, for any investment has, through the 'multiplier' effect of economic analysis, a consequential generation of spending power well beyond the boundaries of the business.

Capital investment may involve such things as the acquisition or replacement of long-lived resources such as buildings, plant or machinery, the investment in another business which will earn revenue by way of dividends, the acquisition of another business, or the major extension of current activities through a new product. Investment will normally generate future cash flows into the business, but it is important to remember that some investment is designed to effect cash savings by reducing the scale of costs associated with a particular activity. For example, the modernization of manufacturing equipment may not result in any additional cash flow sales, but it may well increase the profitability by reducing the costs of manufacture.

Certain factors are common in differing degrees to all projects; in practice, it is the quantification of these factors which provides more difficulty than their evaluation. In this chapter, we will assume that data is readily available, focusing our attention on the methods of evaluation which can be employed.

(1) Payback

The payback method is probably the most popular method of investment appraisal. It is defined as the time period it takes for an investment to generate sufficient net cash income to recover its initial capital outlay in full. We may illustrate the method by comparing two projects:

Project	Initial cost	Net cash income (before depreciation) (£'000) Year							
		1	2	3	4	5	6	7	8
	£	£	£	£	£	£	£	£	£
A	10,000	2	2	2	4	1	–	–	–
B	10,000	4	3	1	1	1	1	1	1

Project A recovers its initial cost after four years, but project B requires five years; therefore project A would be selected. The method, however, has a number of important shortcomings:

(1) The timing of the cash flow is ignored. While project A may have the shorter payback period, inspection reveals that A has recovered 60 per cent of the initial cost after three years, but project B has recovered 80 per cent. If the projects become more risky with the passage of time, project B may have considerable attractions.
(2) By concentrating on a project's net cash flow only up to the point where it equals the initial cost, payback ignores overall profitability. After payback, project A is estimated to be capable of earning another £1,000, project B £3,000.
(3) Where the projects under comparison have widely differing lives, payback does not permit an intelligent choice. If, for example, the investment problem concerns the decision to ferry goods across a wide river by means of either (a) a bridge with a life of 100 years, or (b)

a ship with a life of 25 years, or (c) a hovercraft with a life of 15 years, knowledge of the respective paybacks will not greatly assist.

In spite of these weaknesses, payback has some useful limited applications, particularly where the projects under consideration have similar short lives (1–3 years), or similar lives greater than 10 years. The short life project is of particular importance in industries subject to rapid technological changes where high profits in the early years are essential.

(2) Rate of return

The rate of return on capital is defined as the ratio of profit to capital. Profit, which can either be gross or net of depreciation, is normally expressed as an average over the life of the project, and capital is usually taken to be the initial outlay.

We may illustrate this concept by reference to two projects, C and D, the data for which are given below:

Project	Initial cost	Net profit (£'000) Year						
		1	2	3	4	5	6	7
	£	£	£	£	£	£	£	£
C	25,000	4	6	7	8	6	5	2
D	35,000	5	9	10	11	8	9	1

Average profits:

$$C = £\frac{4 + 6 + 7 + 8 + 6 + 5 + 2}{7}$$

$$= £\frac{38}{7}$$

$$= £5,420$$

$$D = £\frac{5 + 9 + 10 + 11 + 8 + 9 + 1}{7}$$

$$= £\frac{53}{7}$$

$$= £7,570$$

Rate of return:

$$C = \frac{5,420}{25,000} \times 100\%$$

$$= 21.7\%$$

$$D = \frac{7,570}{35,000} \times 100\%$$
$$= 21.6\%$$

Project C would be chosen in preference to D.

The rate of return method overcomes one of the weaknesses of payback by taking into account all earnings, but nevertheless still ignores the incidence of the flow of profits and so fails to reflect the advantages of near, as opposed to distant, profit flows. As with payback, however, the method will produce acceptable results if similar short-term projects are under consideration.

(3)   Net present value

In the two methods outlined above, we have indicated that the major weakness is the failure to recognize that money available immediately is worth more than the equivalent amount received at some future date (*see* Chapter 12). The missing factor is the rate of compound interest which the money might be expected to earn between the present time and the date of receipt. If, for example, we invest £100 now at 7 per cent compound, then in one year's time the investment will be worth

$$100 + (100 \times 7\%)$$
$$= £107$$

In two years' time the investment will be worth

$$107 + (107 \times 7\%)$$
$$= £114.49$$

Conversely, we may observe that the present value of £114.49 received in two years' time (the interest rate being 7 per cent) is £100. More generally we write the end value of an investment made for n years at a given rate of interest as

$$S = C(1 + i)^n$$

where S is the value of investment of £C for n years at rate i; C the initial investment; i the rate of interest; and n the number of years.

The present value (PV) is given by

$$PV = \frac{C}{(1 + i)^n}$$

Tables are available to provide the value of both $(1 + i)^n$ and $1/(1 + i)^n$.

Provided the present value of the stream of net cash income exceeds the capital outlay, the firm can be assured of a surplus. When alternative projects are being considered, that project with the highest net present value will be selected. For example, using the data on page 363 we have

Interest rate = 7%

Year		A				B	
	Net cash income	Discount factor	PV	Net cash income	Discount factor	PV
	£		£	£		£
1	2,000	0.935	1,870	4,000	0.935	3,740
2	2,000	0.873	1,746	3,000	0.873	2,619
3	2,000	0.816	1,632	1,000	0.816	816
4	4,000	0.762	3,048	1,000	0.762	762
5	1,000	0.712	712	1,000	0.712	712
6	—	—	—	1,000	0.666	666
7	—	—	—	1,000	0.623	623
8	—	—	—	1,000	0.582	582
Total present value			9,008			10,520
Initial cost			10,000			10,000
Net present value			£(992)			£ 520

In these circumstances, and on financial grounds alone, the firm would undertake project B which has the highest net present value.

(4)   Yield

The yield on a project is defined as the rate of interest which discounts the future net cash flows of a project into equality with its capital cost, i.e. the rate of interest which results in a zero NPV. In an alternative choice situation, the firm will select that project which shows the highest yield or is equal to, or in excess of, the rate of return on the total capital. This method avoids the difficulty of selecting a rate of interest; rather it solves for the rate of interest.

To clarify this, we may return to our original statement that £100 invested at 7 per cent will produce £107 in a year's time, and that the present value of £107 in a year's time at 7 per cent is £100. We may rephrase this and ask 'What is the rate of interest (yield) which makes £107 in a year's time the equivalent of £100 now?' In practice, this will mean a process of trial and error using different interest rates. Using the data of project A as an example, we have

Year	Net cash income £	Discount factor ($i = 7\%$)	PV £
1	2,000	0.935	1,870
2	2,000	0.873	1,746

(continued)

(continued)

Year	Net cash income £	Discount factor (i = 7%)	PV £
3	2,000	0.816	1,632
4	4,000	0.762	3,048
5	1,000	0.712	712
			£9,008

Since £9,008 is less than £10,000, the yield must be less than 7 per cent. Using 2 per cent:

Year	Net cash income £	Discount factor (i = 2%)	PV £
1	2,000	0.980	1,960
2	2,000	0.961	1,922
3	2,000	0.942	1,884
4	4,000	0.924	3,696
5	1,000	0.906	906
			£10,368

By interpolation the required yield is

$$7 - \left[\frac{10,000 - 9,008}{10,368 - 9,008} \times (7 - 2) \right]$$
$$= 3.35\%$$

This particular project would not be undertaken on financial grounds since the firm could earn a greater yield by investing the funds externally.

The yield method encounters some difficulty in the presence of negative cash flows in the later life of the project, and also when the projects under consideration have very different lives. However, such situations form the minority of cases in practice; the interested student might well refer to more advanced texts.

Net present value and yield methods compared

In using the NPV method, the rate of interest applied is quite critical as can be seen from the following illustration:

Interest rate = 5%

| Year | Project | | | | | |
| | A | | | B | | |
	Net cash flow	V^n	PV	Net cash flow	V^n	PV
	£		£	£		£
1	200	0.95	190	800	0.95	760
2	300	0.91	273	100	0.91	91
3	400	0.86	344	100	0.86	86
4	200	0.82	164	100	0.82	82
5	200	0.78	156	100	0.78	78
Present value			1,127			1,097
Initial cost			1,000			1,000
Net present value			**127**			**97**

With $i = 5$ per cent, A would be selected having the highest NPV. But if we discount the two projects at 10 per cent we have

Interest rate = 10%

| Year | Project | | | | | |
| | A | | | B | | |
	Net cash flow	V^n	PV	Net cash flow	V^n	PV
	£		£	£		£
1	200	0.91	182	800	0.91	728
2	300	0.83	249	100	0.83	83
3	400	0.75	300	100	0.75	75
4	200	0.68	136	100	0.68	68
5	200	0.62	124	100	0.62	62
Present value			991			1,016
Initial cost			1,000			1,000
Net present value			**(9)**			**16**

Thus, discounting at 10 per cent suggests that project B would be preferred.

We may graph the results obtained, as illustrated on page 369, to show both the relationship between the two projects as different rates of interest and also the yield obtained by both projects.

On the vertical axis we measure the net present value of the project, plotting this against the discount rate of interest. The two points for each project are linked in a straight line. We can observe that any rate of interest less than about 9.0 per cent will lead to the selection of project A; any rate greater than 9.0 per cent will result in project B being selected.

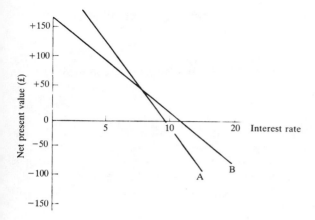

The point of intersection with the interest axis identifies the yield on the project—that rate of interest which provides a zero NPV. Quite clearly, project B has the highest yield.

The use of discounting methods leaves us, therefore, with two problems which must be resolved:

(1) Is the yield or the NPV the better method for project selection?
(2) In using the NPV method what is the 'correct' rate of interest?

Our decision rule for the yield method suggested that when comparing projects, the project with the highest yield should be undertaken. But this rule may lead to inconsistent investment decisions as between different accounting periods. For example, if in period 1 we evaluate two proposals A and B, A yielding 20 per cent and B 15 per cent, we would select A; if in a subsequent period two projects C and D yielded 6 per cent and 4 per cent, respectively, we would select C. But C yields far less than B, and also may be less than we could obtain from investing outside the company. In other words, there is need of a consistent yardstick, which is better provided by the use of a selected rate of interest in the NPV method. Moreover, the yield method presumes that the cash flow released each year by a project will be reinvested at the yield rate, and if a project is selected because of its high yield—say 30 per cent—there is a presumption that new projects will be found which will continue that yield.

What then is the relevant rate of interest to be employed in the NPV method? The choice lies basically between an external or internal rate of interest. The external rate of interest is the best rate the company could obtain by investing its funds in another organization. Quite clearly, if this external rate was greater and would remain greater than the rate which could be obtained by investing the funds within the company, then the company should go into liquidation and allow its shareholders to invest their funds more wisely.

Normally, therefore, the internal rate must be in excess of the external rate, the external rate providing a minimum cut off point. If projects are evaluated at the external rate of interest, then any project producing a negative NPV should not be undertaken.

This leaves us with the problem of defining and measuring the internal rate of interest, or 'cost of capital' as it is usually termed, and we now turn our attention to this problem.

The cost of capital

A company's funds come from a number of different sources—ordinary and preference shares, reserves, debentures, bank loans; each source has a cost, and the cost of the sources jointly is referred to as the company's 'cost of capital'. Since the company has to meet this cost, it will only undertake investment where the rate of return promised by the investment is in excess of or equal to the cost of capital.

The cost of capital is possibly the most controversial topic in financial theory. We will largely sidestep the theoretical problems in this book, and focus attention upon the practical problems of measuring the cost, both for specific sources and for the company as a whole.

(1)   The cost of debentures

The cost of debentures is the rate of interest to be paid, either gross or net of tax; 5 per cent debentures cost the company 5 per cent per annum of the nominal capital borrowed. We can write

$$K_d = \frac{I_d}{C_d}$$

where K_d is the cost of debt (gross of tax), I_d the interest payable, and C_d the net proceeds of the debenture issue. For example, if a company issues 100 £100 6 per cent debentures at 95 (i.e. at a discount of 5 per cent) then

$$K_d = \frac{I_d}{C_d}$$

$$= \frac{600}{9,500}$$

$$= 6.31\%$$

This calculation does assume, however, that the debentures will not be redeemed or at any rate if redeemed will merely be replaced by new debt. Where redemption is to take place at some stated future date, the cost of capital must be equated with the yield to redemption.

(2)   The cost of preference share capital

The cost of preference shares is a function of the rate of dividend which is, of course, fixed. We can write

$$K_p = \frac{D_p}{C_p}$$

where K_p is the cost of preference capital, D_p the dividend, and C_p the net proceeds of the preference issue. For example, the issue of 100,000 8 per cent £1 preference shares at a premium of 10 per cent:

$$K_p = \frac{D_p}{C_p}$$

$$= \frac{8,000}{110,000}$$

$$= 7.27\%$$

Preference dividends do not attract any tax relief and hence the cost is always 'gross'. Where preference shares are redeemable, then the cost of the shares should, like debentures, be obtained by calculating the yield to redemption.

(3) The cost of ordinary share capital

The cost of equity is the most difficult cost to measure. It may be defined in theory as that rate of return on equity which the company must earn in order to just satisfy the ordinary shareholder and so leave the market price of the shares unaltered. Since ordinary shares carry no fixed rate of dividend, the cost of the equity capital must be a function of expected dividends and the market price. The simplest equity model expresses the cost of equities as

$$K_e = \frac{D_0}{P_0} + g$$

where K_e is the cost of equity, D_0 the current dividend, P_0 the current market price, and g the expected annual rate of growth of dividends. For example, if a company's current dividend is 10p per share, the market price of the share £1.80 and the dividends are expected to increase by 3 per cent p.a., then

$$K_e = \frac{D_0}{P_0} + g$$

$$= \frac{10}{180} + 3$$

$$= 5.5\% + 3\%$$

$$= 8.5\%$$

Unless the company substantially alters its asset or financial structure, the cost of equity capital is likely to be relatively stable over time.

Digressing for a moment, it is interesting to note that since companies' dividend policies remain relatively stable over time, and it is observable that market prices do indeed fluctuate substantially, it follows that investors are constantly revising their growth expectations. It is in companies where growth expectations are highest that the greatest fluctuations in price occur. Consider two companies A and B, where A is the high growth company:

Company	D_0	P_0	g	$K_e = \dfrac{D_0}{P_0} + g$
A	15p	150p	10	20%
B	20p	160p	4	16.5%

Given that for company A, $K_e = 20$ per cent, and for B, $K_e = 16.5$ per cent and that in both cases K_e is stable, if investors revise their growth expectations downwards by 10 per cent, we have

A:
$$K_e = \frac{D_0}{P_0} + g$$

$$20 = \frac{15}{P_0} + \left[10 - \left(\frac{10}{100} \right) \right]$$

$$\therefore \quad P_0 = \frac{15}{20 - 9}$$

$$\therefore \quad P_0 = £1.36$$

B:
$$K_e = \frac{D_0}{P_0} + g$$

$$16.5 = 20 + \left[4 - \left(\frac{10}{100} \right) \right]$$

$$\therefore \quad P_0 = \frac{20}{16.5 - 3.6}$$

$$= £1.55$$

Thus, when growth expectations are revised downwards the price of growth stock A falls from £1.50 to £1.36—a fall of 9.3 per cent compared with the fall in B from £1.60 to £1.55, some 3.1 per cent.

(4)   The cost of retained earnings

It was observed in Chapter 10 that an important reason for retaining funds was to finance expansion. Since reserves are legally the property of the ordinary shareholder, it is normally assumed that their minimum cost is the cost of equity capital.

(5) The cost of capital

Once the cost of specific sources of finance have been ascertained the overall cost of capital, K_c, is calculated by means of a weighted average:

Issued capital	Book value £'000	Weight	Specific cost (%)	Weighted cost (%)
Ordinary shares	1,000	0.4	10	4.0
Preference shares	500	0.2	7.5	1.5
Reserves	750	0.3	10	3.0
Debentures	250	0.1	5	0.5
	2,500	1.0	$K_c =$	9.0

The weights are determined by relating the book value of the source to the total of capital employed. Each weight is then multiplied by the specific source cost, and the summation of these weighted costs provides the overall cost of capital. If the company undertakes an investment project which yields greater than 9 per cent (i.e. shows a positive net present value when discounted at 9 per cent), the ordinary shareholders will receive a return greater than is necessary to satisfy them since the return to preference and debenture holders is fixed and any surplus will accrue to the equity.

This method assumes that the capital structure (the gearing of the company) remains stable, and that investment projects will be financed in the same proportions as the capital structure.

Taxation and the investment proposal

Taxation affects the investment decision by reducing the cash flow left in the company's hands, and although this basic text cannot possibly encompass the many details and nuances of business taxation, it is nevertheless important that we recognize the substantial impact which taxation has on the viability of an investment proposal.

In principle, taxation affects the investment decision in two ways: first, it provides a system of 'capital allowances'—the equivalent of depreciation—which can be deducted from the net cash flow from the investment to arrive at the taxable profit. Secondly, this 'net cash flow after capital allowances' is subject, in the case of a limited company, to corporation tax, which reduces the amount of money left in the hands of the company.

The particular system of capital allowances varies in detail from Finance Act to Finance Act, but the basic framework has not changed much for many years. Most capital investments attract a substantial 'first year allowance' to encourage companies to invest by reducing their initial tax bill, which is then deducted from the initial investment in order to allow a diminishing balance system of annual 'writing down allowances' to take effect. If the asset is sold for an amount greater or less than its writing down value, the over or under allowance is adjusted as a 'balancing allowance or charge'.

Corporation tax is levied on the taxable profits, but most companies pay this tax one year in arrears, i.e. the tax payment on the taxable profits of 1984 is paid in 1985. As a simple illustration of this, assume the following investment profile:

Year 0 capital outlay	£1,000
Net cash flow: Year 1	800
Year 2	600
Year 3	600
Asset sold in Year 3	200
Capital allowance: 1st year	60%
Writing down allowance	25%
Corporation tax	50%

	(a)	(b)	(c)	(d)	(e)
	Net cash flow	Capital allowances	Taxable profit	Corporation tax	Cash flow after tax
Year 1	800	480	320	—	800
Year 2	600	80	520	160	440
Year 3	600	60	540	260	640
	300	−120	420		
Year 4				480	−480
	2,300	500			1,400

The capital allowances are computed thus:

Year 1	800 × 60%	= £480	WDV	320
Year 2	320 × 25%	= £ 80	,,	240
Year 3	240 × 25%	= £ 60	,,	180
Total allowances		£620		

Cost of asset 800 − 300	= £500	
Allowances	= £620	
So balancing charge	£120	

The taxable profit is arrived at by deducting column (b) from column (a) (note carefully the effect of the balancing charge), and the corporation tax at 50% is paid one year in arrears. The net cash flow after tax (column (e)) is reached by deducting (d) from (a).

The impact of the tax system is shown clearly by this illustration. The net cash flow from the investment of £2,300 is reduced, after taxation, to £1,400. However, the company enjoys the benefit of the entire net cash flow (£800) in year 1—an incentive to invest, but has to pay tax of £480 in year 4 when it receives no income from the investment.

We can now incorporate these ideas into our NPV analysis, by assuming the following data:

Initial investment	£1,000	
Expected net profits		
year 1	£100	
2	£300	
3	£400	
4	£400	
5	£300	
Depreciation	Straight line over 5 years	
Scrap value at end	Nil	
First-year allowance	60%	
Writing down allowance	25%	

Corporation tax at 52% is payable one year in arrears,
  and the company is earning taxable profits

The table which follows is calculated thus:

(1) Column c (cash flow) = a + b.
(2) Column d (written down value) = previous balance in column d −
     (e + f).
(3) Column g (taxable profits) = c − (e + f).
(4) Column h (corporation tax) = 52% × prior year's taxable profits (g).
(5) Column i (net cash flow after tax) = c − h.

	a	b	c	d	e	f	g	h	i
Year	Net profit	Depre- ciation	Profit before depre- ciation (cash flow)	Written down value at start	First- year all'nce 60%	Written down all'nce 25%	Taxable profits (loss)	Corpor- ation tax 52%	Net cash flow
	£	£	£	£	£	£	£	£	£
1	100	200	300	1,000	600	—	−300	—	300
2	300	200	500	400	—	100	400	−156	656
3	400	200	600	300	—	75	525	208	392
4	400	200	600	225	—	56	546	273	327
5	300	200	500	169	—	{ 42	331	284	216
6						{ 127		172	−172

Note that corporation tax (column h) is payable one year in arrears, and that
in the final year of the project there is a 'balancing allowance' such that the
total of all allowances—the first year allowance plus writing down allowances—equals the initial outlay on the asset. If the asset had in fact been sold
in year 5 for an amount exceeding £127, the business would suffer a 'balancing
charge' to keep the total allowances equal to the net outlay on the asset.

   If we compare the net present value of the project before and after tax
(with i = 10 per cent) we observe that the NPV after tax is £371 compared
with a before tax surplus of £856:

Year	Net cash flow before tax (column c) £	V^n	PV £	Net cash flow after tax (column i) £	V^n	PV £
1	300	0.91	273	300	0.91	273
2	500	0.83	415	656	0.83	544
3	600	0.75	450	392	0.75	294
4	600	0.68	408	327	0.68	222
5	500	0.62	310	216	0.62	134
6		0.56	—	−172	0.56	−96
			1,856			1,371
Initial cost			1,000			1,000
Net present value			**£856**			**£371**

Capital investment and risk

So far in this chapter, we have assumed that our knowledge about future cash flows generated by an investment project is perfect. Clearly this is not so in the real world, and in the remainder of this chapter we will consider, at an introductory level, methods of incorporating risk analysis into our investment decision.

Theoretically, there is a distinction between risk and uncertainty, for risk involves situations where the probability of alternative outcomes are known, and uncertainty is where it is impossible to place some measure of probability on the outcomes. For example, if we assume that a particular investment will generate a net cash flow of £1,000 in the first year, we cannot know for certain that that will be the outcome; what we are saying is that it is the most *probable* outcome. We may consider that, at the worst, the project will yield £900 and, at the best, £1,200. We can assign probabilities to these outcomes, viz.:

Net cash flow £	Probability of occurrence	Expected value (£)
900	0.1	90
1,000	0.8	800
1,200	0.1	120
	1.0	1,010

Thus, we profess ourselves 80 per cent confident, i.e. there are 8 chances in 10, that the outcome will be a net cash flow of £1,000, but there is a 1 in 10 chance that it could be £900 or £1,200. Since these values exhaust all possibilities, the total probability sums to one, i.e. 0.1 + 0.8 + 0.1 = 1, and the expected outcome is £1,010.

In this example, we have put a probability value on the outcome, and thus are dealing with a situation of risk. If the situation were uncertain, then we would find it impossible to establish or agree any such values. However, it must be said that the distinction is more theoretical than real, for it is nearly always possible to put some probability value on expected outcomes even if the quality of that judgement is open to question.

It is sometimes argued that assigning probabilities to outcomes may lead to a rather spurious precision, and that there are less complex and less misleading ways of allowing for risk. One possible method is to adjust the discount rate used to establish the net present value of a project. For example, if under conditions of certainty, the appropriate discount rate was 10 per cent, then, to allow for the degree of risk, the rate should be lifted to, say, 15 per cent which would set a more exacting requirement if the project were to show a positive net present value. The problem with this approach, however, is that it requires the establishment of different interest rates to compare a 'high risk' project with a 'low risk' project, and a judgement as to what is the difference between a 'high' and a 'low' risk. Moreover, since investment decisions are often made at different times by different people whose perception of what is 'high' and 'low' risk may vary, it is necessary to find some means of quantifying 'risk' in order to reduce the consequences of highly subjective and divergent judgements.

A slightly more sophisticated method of investment appraisal which does not make use of probability is that of 'sensitivity analysis', which is a critical analysis of all of the factors associated with a particular project in order to establish how 'sensitive' the net present value is to changes in any one of the variables. We may tabulate the results of such an inquiry in the following manner:

Maximum expected change in factor	Net present value		
	Original £	Adjusted £	Change %
10% decrease in sales value	10,000	9,500	5
2-year reduction in project life	10,000	7,000	30
15% increase in material costs	10,000	9,400	6
10% increase in capital costs	10,000	8,000	20

The table shows that the project is particularly sensitive to change in project life and capital costs, so that management would be well advised to investigate further the accuracy and reliability of the original estimates for these two factors before making any final decision.

This mode of analysis, however, is useful but limited because to make any judgement on the significance of the changes requires some estimate, however subjective, of their probability of occurrence. Secondly, this analysis considers the effect of changes in each factor in isolation, whereas, in practice, there may be simultaneous shifts in two or more of the variables.

A more fundamental approach to risk analysis is to incorporate our estimates of probable outcomes into the analysis and we will illustrate this with reference to two mutually exclusive projects, X and Y, for a company whose cost of capital is 10 per cent:

Period	X Net cash flow	V^n	PV	Y Net cash flow	V^n	PV
	£		£	£		£
1	4,000	0.95	3,800	3,000	0.95	2,850
2	3,000	0.91	2,730	2,000	0.91	1,820
3	2,000	0.86	1,720	3,000	0.86	2,580
			8,250			7,250
Capital outlay			7,000			6,000
Net present value			**1,250**			**1,250**

As the table shows the projects both result in a NPV of £1,250; if management is to choose between them it is necessary to evaluate the risk attached to each. The net cash flow data and hence the computed NPV represent management's belief about the *most likely* or *most probable* outcome of the projects. Management will have considered other possible cash flows but rejected them. Thus around each annual cash flow and the NPV there is a probability distribution.

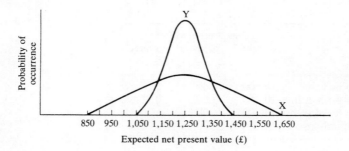

In the diagram, project Y is shown to have a greater dispersion around the mean value of £1,250 than project X. There is some probability that X will earn less than £1,050, while with Y the probability of earning less than £1,050 is zero. If we assume that management is risk averse when evaluating investment projects, it will select project Y as opposed to project X.

The conventional measure of dispersion of a probability distribution is the standard deviation, and to illustrate the use of this concept, we assume the following discrete probability distributions for the two projects:

| Project | | Period 1 | | | Period 2 | | | Period 3 | |
	D	NCF	EV	P	NCF	EV	P	NCF	EV
	0.3	3,000	900	0.3	2,000	600	0.3	1,000	300
X	0.4	4,000	1,600	0.4	3,000	1,200	0.4	2,000	800
	0.3	5,000	1,500	0.3	4,000	1,200	0.3	3,000	900
	1.0	—	4,000	1.0	—	3,000	1.0	—	2,000
	0.25	2,000	500	0.25	1,000	250	0.25	2,000	500
Y	0.50	3,000	1,500	0.50	2,000	1,000	0.50	3,000	1,500
	0.25	4,000	1,000	0.25	3,000	750	0.25	4,000	1,000
	1.00	—	3,000	1.00	—	2,000	1.00	—	3,000

Thus for project X in period 1 the probability that the net cash flow will be £3,000 is 0.3, and the expected value of £4,000 is obtained by summing the products.

If the cash flows of the different periods are independent of one another (i.e. the outcome of period n does not depend upon what happens in period $n - 1$), the expected net present value is given by

$$\text{ENPV} = \sum_{n=0}^{n=\infty} \frac{\bar{A}_n}{(1 + i)^n} = \sum_{n=0}^{n=\infty} \frac{C_n}{(1 + i)^n}$$

where $\bar{A}_n$ is the expected value in period n, i the discount rate, and C_n the capital outlay in period n.

For project X and with $i = 5$ per cent

$$\text{ENPV}_x = \frac{4,000}{1.05} + \frac{3,000}{1.05^2} + \frac{2,000}{1.05^3} - 7,000$$

$$= 3,800 + 2,730 + 1,720 - 7,000$$

$$= £1,250$$

and for project Y

$$\text{ENPV}_y = \frac{3,000}{1.05} + \frac{2,000}{1.05^2} + \frac{3,000}{1.05^3} - 6,000$$

$$= 2,850 + 1,820 + 2,580 - 6,000$$

$$= £1,250$$

The standard deviation has to be computed in two stages. First, we compute the standard deviation for each time period. We write

$$\sigma_n = \sqrt{\left(\sum_{x=1}^{x=\infty} (A_{xn} - \bar{A}_n)^2 P_{xn} \right)}$$

where

$$\sigma_n = \text{standard deviation for possible cash flows in period } n$$

$$A_{xn} = x\text{th net cash flow in period } n$$

$$A_n = \text{expected value of net cash for period } n$$

$$P_{xn} = \text{the probability of occurrence for } A_{xn}$$

Applying this to project X:

$$\text{Period 1} \quad \sigma_{1x} = \sqrt{\begin{array}{l}[0.3(3,000 - 4,000)^2 + 0.4(4,000 - 4,000)^2 \\ + 0.3(5,000 - 4,000)^2]\end{array}}$$

$$= \sqrt{(300,000 + 0 + 300,000)}$$

$$= £774.6$$

$$\text{Period 2} \quad \sigma_{2x} = \sqrt{\begin{array}{l}[0.3(2,000 - 3,000)^2 + 0.4(3,000 - 3,000)^2 \\ + 0.3(3,000 - 2,000)^2]\end{array}}$$

$$= £774.6$$

$$\text{Period 3} \quad \sigma_{3x} = \sqrt{\begin{array}{l}[0.3(1,000 - 2,000)^2 + 0.4(2,000 - 2,000)^2 \\ + 0.3(3,000 - 2,000)^2]\end{array}}$$

$$= £774.6$$

For project Y:

$$\sigma_{1x} = \sqrt{\begin{array}{l}[0.25(2,000 - 3,000)^2 + 0.50(3,000 - 3,000)^2 \\ + 0.25(4,000 - 3,000)^2]\end{array}}$$

$$= \sqrt{(250,000 + 0 + 250,000)}$$

$$= £707.1$$

and for

$$\sigma_{2x} = £707.1$$
$$\sigma_{3x} = £707.1$$

The final computation stage is the calculation of the standard deviation for the series as a whole. This is given by

$$\sigma = \sqrt{\left(\sum_{n=0}^{\infty} \frac{\sigma_n^2}{(1 + i)^{2n}}\right)}$$

where σ_n is the standard deviation for the probability distribution of possible net cash flows in period n.

For project X:

$$\sigma_x = \sqrt{\left(\frac{774.6^2}{1.05^2} + \frac{774.6^2}{1.05^4} + \frac{774.6^2}{1.05^6}\right)}$$

$$= \sqrt{\left(\frac{600,000}{1.10} + \frac{600,000}{1.22} + \frac{600,000}{1.40}\right)}$$

$$= \pm£1,211$$

For project Y:

$$\sigma_y = \sqrt{\left(\frac{707.1^2}{1.05^2} + \frac{707.1^2}{1.05^4} + \frac{707.1^2}{1.05^6}\right)}$$

$$= \sqrt{\left(\frac{500,000}{1.10} + \frac{500,000}{1.22} + \frac{500,000}{1.40}\right)}$$

$$= \pm£1,105$$

Note: The standard deviation for each period is the same in this example because the probability distributions for each period have been kept the same to simplify the illustration.

If the probability distribution is normal or approximately so, we are able to calculate the probability of a project earning more or less than a specific amount. One critical value is obviously a net present value of zero or less, for if management is risk averse, they will select that project which has the smallest probability of obtaining a negative result. To calculate the probability of project X earning zero or less, we calculate the number of standard deviations which separates the expected net present value from the value zero. This is

$$\frac{0 - 1250}{1211} = 1.0322 \text{ standard deviations}$$

Statistical tables inform us that the area under the normal curve contained by ±1.0322 standard deviations is 70 per cent. Thus, 30 per cent of the distribution lies outside of this range, and since we are concerned only with that half of the distribution which is less than the expected net present value it follows that 15 per cent of the distribution will have a value of £0 or less. Thus there is a 0.15 chance that project X will obtain a NPV of zero or less.

A similar calculation for project Y ($0 - 1250/1105 = 1.1312$ standard deviations) reveals a 0.13 chance of obtaining a NPV of zero or less, and hence we would expect management which is risk averse to select project Y.

References and further reading

BIERMAN and SMIDT (1966), *The Capital Budgeting Decision*. Macmillan.
FOGLER (1972), 'Ranking Techniques and Capital Budgeting',
   Accounting Review, January 1972.
ROBICHECK and MYERS (1975), *Optimal Financing Decisions*. Prentice-
   Hall.
VAN HORNE (1982), *Financial Management and Policy*. Prentice-Hall.

Questions for discussion

1   Three possible projects would each require an initial investment of
    £12,000. The expected net cash flows from each one are

	Years				
	1	2	3	4	5
	£	£	£	£	£
X	2,400	6,000	6,000	4,000	—
Y	6,000	6,000	3,600	1,200	—
Z	3,600	4,800	4,800	4,800	3,600

(a) Compare the three projects by means of

   (i)   payback;
   (ii) rate of return based on initial capital;
   (iii) net present value based on a cost of capital of 10 per cent;
   (iv) yield.

(b) Give reasoned advice to management on which project they should
     undertake.

2   A company which can borrow and lend money freely at 10 per cent
    p.a. is considering undertaking one of two investments. Information
    relating to these investments is given below:

Project	A	B
Capital outlay	£3,000	£2,000
Net cash flow		
year 1	500	200
2	700	300
3	1,000	500
4	1,100	800
5	900	900
6	100	900

Required:

(a) Calculate the payback period for each project.
(b) Calculate the net present value for each project.
(c) Advise the company which project it should undertake, stating your reasons and entering any caveats you consider necessary.

Do you consider the external rate of interest relevant to the company's decision-making process? If not, what alternative(s) would you suggest and why?

Present value table:

Year	6	7	8	9	10
1	0.94	0.94	0.93	0.92	0.91
2	0.89	0.87	0.86	0.84	0.83
3	0.84	0.82	0.79	0.77	0.75
4	0.79	0.76	0.74	0.71	0.68
5	0.75	0.71	0.68	0.65	0.62
6	0.70	0.67	0.63	0.60	0.57
7	0.67	0.62	0.58	0.55	0.51
8	0.63	0.58	0.54	0.50	0.47
9	0.59	0.54	0.50	0.46	0.42
10	0.56	0.51	0.46	0.42	0.39

3   A company has the following capital structure:

	£
£1 ordinary shares	100,000
6% £1 preference shares	20,000
Revenue reserves	50,000
10% debentures	50,000
	£220,000

The debentures were originally issued at 97; the ordinary dividend is currently 12p per share and the market price of the ordinary share is £2.20. The market expects that, given the recent relaxation of dividend constraint, dividends will grow at 1p per share per year.

Required:

Calculate the company's cost of capital, stating clearly any assumptions and limitations of your analysis.

4   A company is considering two alternative investment proposals, A and B, which are tabulated over the page:

	A £	B £
Initial investment	15,000	28,000
Net profit		
year 1	5,000	4,000
2	7,000	5,000
3	4,000	10,000
4	3,000	12,000
5	2,000	8,000
6	2,000	4,000
Depreciation	10% of original cost	25% diminishing balance
Scrap value in year 6	£3,000	£6,000
First-year allowance	60%	60%
WDA	25%	25%
Corporation tax	50%	50%
The company's cost of capital is 10%		

Required:
Advise management which project they should select.

5 Explain the different methods by which risk may be incorporated into the evaluation of investment proposals, and indicate the relative strengths and weaknesses of each method.

6 Far East Ltd is a manufacturing company which uses a variety of machines for its production programme. One of the machines has now to be replaced and the management of the company are considering which of two alternative machines should be acquired.

Details of the two machines (each of which has an estimated life of five years), and of the expected net return directly referable to them, are as follows:

	Machine X	Machine Y
Cost	£25,000	£30,000
Expected net returns:	£	£
End of year 1	4,000	6,000
2	8,000	12,000
3	10,000	10,000
4	5,000	6,000
5	4,000	4,000
Estimated trade-in value at end of year 5	3,000	5,000

Required:

(a) Calculate which of the two machines is likely to yield the better returns (based on discounted present value), using (i) 10 per cent and (ii) 15 per cent as the required rate.
(b) By interpolation, ascertain the true rate of interest for each machine.
(c) Comment briefly, in light of your answers to (a), on the problems arising from the use of discounted present value as a criterion for investment decisions.

Notes:

(i) Ignore taxation.
(ii) Except where otherwise indicated, assume that all inflows and outflows of cash take place at the end of the appropriate years.
(iii) The following table shows the present value of £1, using the rates of interest and the relevant years required by the question:

	10%	15%
End of 1 year	0.9091	0.8696
End of 2 years	0.8264	0.7561
End of 3 years	0.7513	0.6575
End of 4 years	0.6830	0.5718
End of 5 years	0.6209	0.4972

7   'In discounted cash flow appraisal of investment projects, future cash flows are discounted at the *relevant cost of capital*.'

What is meant by the term 'relevant cost of capital'? How is it computed?

17 Accounting for business decisions—short-term decisions

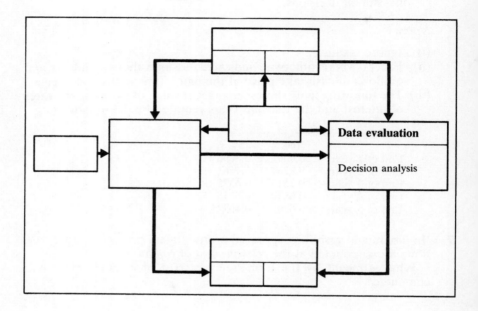

Costs and decision-making

Short-term decisions do not involve any long-term capital commitments, and are concerned either with choosing that alternative which is most profitable or that alternative which effects the greater savings. In our discussion of the nature of costs, in Chapter 13, we stressed the importance of the distinction between fixed and variable costs. For the purposes of decision-making this distinction is purely incidental; what matters is whether costs are relevant or irrelevant to the decision.

We can identify two types of cost: differential (or opportunity) costs, and sunk (or common) costs. Differential costs are those costs that will be different in one alternative as opposed to another. In general, variable costs will be differential in any decision which affects the volume of activity. Fixed costs will only be differential if they will be incurred as a consequence of the decision. In considering costs that are different, any costs allocated or apportioned should be viewed with considerable scepticism. For example, if the firm were considering whether to buy or make a particular item, the cost of making could include an allocation of overhead for such items as rent and factory services. All or part of these costs would still continue to be incurred irrespective of whether the item was bought out or made in the factory.

Sunk or common costs are those costs which will be the same regardless of the decision made; these costs are irrelevant to the decision. Depreciation of existing assets is a sunk cost, and is generally irrelevant to the short-term decision. Consider, for example, a decision to buy a new machine in place of an old one which has a current book value of £2,000. If the new machine is acquired the £2,000 will be treated as a loss; if the old machine continues in use then the £2,000 will be depreciated. The costs are the same (common) regardless of the decision and therefore can be ignored.

In general, differential costs are relevant, and sunk costs are not relevant to the short-term decision. What costs are, in fact, differential and which are sunk will depend on the nature of the problem. For example, consider some basic data about the running of a car:

Variable costs	*Pence per mile*
Petrol and oil	6.0
Maintenance	0.3
	6.3 pence

Fixed costs (annual)	£
Insurance	90.0
Licence	50.0
Depreciation	500.0
	£640.0

Decision A. The car is already insured and licensed. A journey of 50 miles by public transport would cost 200 pence; should the car be used (purely on the basis of cost)? The relevant costs are the variable cost of 6.3 pence per mile; the fixed costs have been incurred already. The cost by car is, therefore, 50 × 6.3 = 315 pence.

Decision B. The car is not yet insured and licensed. The relevant costs are therefore £140 + 6.3 pence per mile.

Decision C. The decision is whether to buy a car or to use public transport; the relevant costs are £640 + 6.3 pence per mile.

In all cases the relevant costs for the given decision are the costs affected by the decision; other costs may be ignored.

'Make or buy' decisions

A very common short-term problem facing a business is whether to sub-contract the making of components to specialist firms. We may illustrate the problem by means of the following data.

The Astral Co. produces part XK200 at the rate of 10,000 per month with the following unit cost:

XK200 unit cost	£
Material	3.50
Labour	2.10
Variable overhead	1.60
Fixed overhead	1.40
	8.60

A component manufacturer offers to supply the part at £7.80 per unit, and Astral estimates that, if accepted, the additional clerical costs (ordering, processing invoices, etc) would be £500, and that the handling and receiving bay costs would be £0.10 per unit.

At first sight the offer is attractive, for the apparent monthly costs would be

	Make £	Buy £
Additional handling costs	—	0.10
Buying in price	—	7.80
	8.60	**7.90**
Cost for 10,000 units	86,000	79,000
Additional clerical cost	—	500
Total cost	86,000	79,500

The saving would be £6,500 per month. However, the fixed overhead in the unit cost is an allocated cost, and will be incurred whether Astral manufactures the component or not; other products will have to absorb the fixed overhead currently absorbed by XK200. The only savings to Astral will be in the variable (and avoidable) costs of manufacture, £7.20 per unit. The decision will be analysed as follows:

	£	£
Monthly purchase cost		78,000
Additional costs		
Clerical	500	
Handling	1,000	1,500
		79,500
Less:		
Cost savings—variable costs (£7.20 × 10,000)		72,000
Net additional cost		**£7,500**

Hence, Astral would be £7,500 per month worse off if it bought in the component.

'Continue or abandon' decisions

A further but more complicated example of the need to indentify the costs relevant to decision-making may often be found in situations where a particular venture is partially complete and the business is trying to decide whether or not to continue or abandon the project. Such a decision requires the clear identification of the alternatives available (*see* Chapter 16), and then the recognition of the relevant costs. For example, the Summonal Co. has to date spent £75,000 on a research project, and it expects that when completed in a further year the results of that research can be sold for £100,000. In trying to decide whether to proceed, the business identifies the additional expenses necessary to complete the research:

Materials, £30,000. This material (already in store and paid for) is very toxic and will have to be disposed of in sealed containers at a cost of £2,500.

Labour, £20,000. The research project uses highly skilled labour taken from the production department of the company. If they were working on normal production, the company could earn £25,000 additional contribution to profit in the next year after paying the skilled labour.

Research staff, £30,000. The research unit will close down after the project has been completed, and redundancy pay has already been agreed at £12,500.

General overheads, £20,000. The research unit is apportioned a share of the total fixed costs of the business.

One again, at first sight, it might appear foolish to continue with the research. The tabulation could be

	Abandon now £	Complete £	£
Sales			100,000
Costs to date	75,000	75,000	
Additional costs:			
Materials		30,000	
Labour		20,000	
Research staff		30,000	
Overheads		20,000	
Redundancy		25,000	200,000
Net loss	75,000		100,000

This shows that the company would lose £25,000 more by continuing the project than by abandoning it now. However, the conclusion is incorrect as can be shown if we focus our attention on the costs that will be *different* as a consequence of a decision to abandon or complete.

We may note:

(1) The costs incurred to date, i.e. £75,000, are sunk costs and can have no bearing on any future decision.
(2) The additional materials (£30,000) have already been bought and paid for, so that the only cost which will change is the payment of £2,500 disposal cost if the project does not continue.
(3) The skilled labour will be paid £20,000 irrespective of whether the project continues or not—either as part of the research work or as normal production. As this cost is the same whatever the decision, it is not relevant. However, the 'opportunity' cost is £45,000 if the project continues, for that is the loss to the company of the production fore-gone—i.e. £25,000 + £20,000—for if the labour is transferred the con-tribution is greater by the amount of the labour cost. Another way of viewing this is to say that the cost of continuing the project is £20,000 labour plus the opportunity cost of £25,000, i.e. £45,000 in all.
(4) If the project continues, the research staff will be paid £30,000; if it ceases that money will be saved. Hence, as the cost will depend on the decision, it is a relevant cost. However, the decision on redundancy pay (£12,500) has already been taken, and, being the same whether the project continues or not, can be ignored.
(5) Apportioned overheads (£20,000) are irrelevant, for these costs will continue to be incurred by the rest of the business whether the research project continues or not.

We may retabulate these findings as follows:

	Abandon now	Complete	
	£	£	£
Sales	—		100,000
Material	(2,500)	—	
Labour	—	45,000	
Research		30,000	75,000
(Loss) Profit	(2,500)		25,000

The company should therefore continue with the project, for it will make a 'profit' of £25,000 compared with a 'loss' of £2,500 if it abandons the project now.

'Pricing' decisions

Price is of vital importance to the firm; if total revenues are not in excess of total expenses the firm must eventually go into liquidation. We could expect, therefore, that there are clearly defined rules of pricing; this is not so, since every firm and its product have some features which are unique. There are two broad avenues of approach, however, which encompass most varieties of pricing policy:

(1) Begin with the cost of the product, and add some margin of profit to the cost, thus determining price.
(2) Begin with the price (usually that set by similar products) and endeavour to keep costs below that level.

Whichever approach is adopted, the cost of the product is clearly quite critical. But which cost should be used? Should it be the 'full cost', that is all the variable costs plus some share of fixed costs, as provided by absorption costing, or should it be the variable costs alone, as provided by marginal costing?

Full-cost pricing is in widespread use by business, and is probably adopted because it is simple to apply. An example of a full-cost formula may be

  Direct materials and labour
   + Variable manufacturing overhead
   + Share of fixed manufacturing overhead
   + Percentage addition for selling and administration expenses
   + Percentage 'mark up' for profit

The approach is at first sight most appealing; provided the sales volume is adequate, profit is assured. Under this system, however, price becomes a function of the method of allocating fixed costs, which, as we observed in Chapter 13, is always arbitrary. Consider the situation of two firms, A and B, who both produce two identical products, with the unit costs given below:

	Firm A		Firm B	
	X	Y	X	Y
	£	£	£	£
Direct material	4.00	2.00	4.00	2.00
Direct labour	2.00	4.00	2.00	4.00
Variable overhead	1.00	2.00	1.00	2.00
	7.00	8.00	7.00	8.00
Fixed overhead	4.00	2.00	2.00	4.00
Full cost	11.00	10.00	9.00	12.00
Profit % (10)	1.10	1.00	0.90	1.20
Selling price	12.10	11.00	9.90	13.20

The variable costs for both firms are identical for each product, but the fixed costs, although similar in total, have been allocated on a different (yet still rational) basis. The consequence is different selling prices for identical products.

In practice, of course, this selling price is a first approximation; actual prices will take account of the strength of competition, and other marketing considerations. If the market is competitive the prices will adjust to some new intermediary levels, say £10 for X and £12 for Y. What will be the reaction of firms A and B in the face of these new prices? If they make use of the 'full cost' data, they will observe

	Firm A		Firm B	
	X	Y	X	Y
	£	£	£	£
Full cost	11.00	10.00	9.00	12.00
Selling price	10.00	12.00	10.00	12.00
Profit	—	2.00	1.00	—
Loss	1.00	—	—	—

As a consequence, A may be tempted to abandon product X, and B, product Y. To do so could be disastrous. Fixed costs will have to be incurred come what may. If A abandons product X, then Y will have to absorb all the fixed overhead costs, resulting in a loss of £2 per unit. The relevant figure for A to observe is the variable or marginal cost of £7 per unit for X. Any selling price in excess of this will contribute towards the fixed overhead, thus reducing the burden on product Y. The schedule may be rewritten as follows:

	X	Y
	£	£
Selling price	10	12
Marginal cost	7	8
Contribution to fixed overhead and profit	£3	£4

In considering pricing policy, it is important to consider the possible levels of activity when employing contribution pricing techniques. For example:

	X	Y	X	Y	X	Y	X	Y
Units sold	500	500	1,000	1,000	2,000	2,000	3,000	3,000
	£	£	£	£	£	£	£	£
Contribution	1,500	2,000	3,000	4,000	6,000	8,000	9,000	12,000
Total	3,500		7,000		14,000		21,000	
Fixed overhead	6,000		6,000		6,000		6,000	
Profit/loss	(2,500)		1,000		8,000		15,000	

Inspection will reveal that the firm must normally price the products in excess of their marginal costs, and that the total of the respective contributions at any given volume must exceed total fixed costs if the firm is to make a profit and survive in the long run.

Limiting factors

A further dimension to the 'contribution' problem occurs when a firm manufacturing a range of products is limited as to the quantity it can manufacture because of some restriction of the inputs available, perhaps a shortage of materials, or a lack of skilled labour. For example, consider the following data:

Product	A	B
	£	£
Selling price per unit	12	15
Marginal costs per unit		
Material (£0.3 per kilo)	5.4	1.2
Labour (£1.8 per hour)	3.6	10.8
Variable overhead	1.2	2.4
	10.2	14.4
Contribution	1.8	0.6

If A and B were substitutes for each other, and the firm could sell either A or B without restriction, their financial logic would dictate that it manufactures and sells only product A because it yields the highest contribution per unit. Or again, if the firm has the physical capacity to make up to 7,500 units in any combination of A or B, and the total market is 1,500 units for A and 8,000 for B, then the firm should produce:

$$A: \ 1,500 \ @ \ 1.8 = 2,700$$
$$B: \ 6,000 \ @ \ 0.6 = 3,600$$

Total contribution: £6,300

because that contribution will yield the greatest total contribution.

However, if only 20,000 kilos of the material needed for the product were available, then the firm has a choice which lies between producing:

$$A: \ \frac{20,000}{18} = 1,111 \text{ units}$$

$$\text{and} \ \ B: \ \frac{20,000}{4} = 5,000 \text{ units}$$

If we use all our limited supplies of material to produce A, the contribution will be:

$$1,111 \times 1.8 = £2,000$$

but if we were to produce only B with the limited material, the contribution would be:

$$5,000 \times 0.6 = £3,000$$

Clearly, our initial decision rule, that we make and sell the product with the highest contribution *per unit* would lead to an incorrect decision, and needs amendment. Where there is a limiting factor, then we should select that product which offers the highest contribution *per unit of the limiting factor*.

The contribution per unit of the limiting factor is:

For A: $\dfrac{£1.8}{18 \text{ kilos}} = £0.1$ per kilo

For B: $\dfrac{£0.6}{4 \text{ kilos}} = £0.15$ per kilo

This would correctly lead us to produce B, because the total contribution is

$$20,000 \text{ kilos} \times 0.15 = \underline{\underline{£3,000}}$$

compared with

$$20,000 \times 0.1 = \underline{\underline{£2,000}}$$

While there is more than one limiting factor e.g. material and labour, then our approach is still valid, but the solution can only be found by the use of equations and techniques of operational research, and this is dealt with briefly in the last section of this chapter.

Break-even analysis

In the preceding section we demonstrated the importance of marginal costing to pricing policy, and ended this discussion by pointing out the importance of levels of activity to the profitability of the firm. The analysis of revenues and costs in relation to volume is usually referred to a break-even analysis; specifically, the break-even point may be defined as that level of activity at which total revenue is equal to total expense, and hence net income is equal to zero.

For the single product firm, the break-even point may be computed in terms of product units. Assume that a firm sells a product at £3 per unit and that the variable costs are £1.20 per unit; the annual fixed costs are £36,000. In order to break even the firm must produce

$$\frac{36,000}{3-1.20} = 20,000 \text{ units}$$

More generally, the break-even point is given by

$$\frac{\text{Fixed costs}}{\substack{\text{Selling price} - \text{Variable costs} \\ \text{per unit} \qquad \text{per unit}}}$$

The analysis is often presented in graphical form, as illustrated. Units of production are measured on the horizontal axis, and costs and revenues on the vertical axis. Fixed costs are shown as a constant in a line parallel to the horizontal axis; the variable costs per unit are added to the fixed cost to provide the total cost line. The total revenue at any point is the selling price per unit multiplied by the number of units sold. The intersection of the total revenue and total cost line provides the break-even point.

The upper limits of the graph are determined by the productive capacity of the firm. Any point to the right of the break-even volume provides a

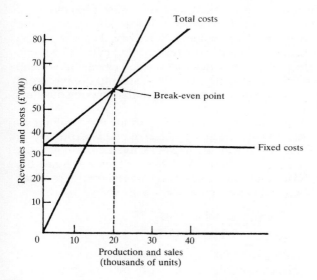

margin of safety; for example, if budgeted volume was 35,000 units the margin of safety would be 35,000 − 20,000 = 15,000 units. Profit (or loss) is measured by the vertical distance between the revenue and total cost lines.

This graph, which depicts the relationships between cost, revenues, volume and profit, is sometimes converted into a profit/volume chart. As with the break-even chart, the horizontal axis is still employed to measure volume of activity, but the vertical axis is now used to measure profit or loss. Using the information above, we can establish that at zero output the loss will be £36,000, i.e. the fixed costs, at 20,000 units of output the business will just break even, and at 35,000 units the profit will be

$$£35,000 \ (3 - 1.20) - 36,000 = £27,000$$

Once we have established these (or any other) three points, we may plot them on a profit value graph as follows:

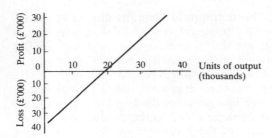

While this chart is obviously less detailed than the break-even chart—it compresses revenue and costs—it does serve to focus attention on the critical relationship between profit and volume of activity. The steeper the slope of the profit line, the more critical is the relationship between volume and profit, for while a steep slope indicates that a small change in volume can turn a loss into a profit, it is equally true that a steeply sloping profit line implies that small falls in volume will turn a profitable-making business into a loss-maker.

In a multi-product firm it is normally impossible to measure volume in terms of any common unit. In such circumstances volume is expressed in terms of sales values. Break-even will occur where fixed costs equal the revenues less the variable costs associated with those revenues. Since the variable profit is a known ratio, the sales ratio necessary to produce sufficient variable profit to cover fixed costs will be given by:

$$\text{Total fixed costs} \div \frac{\text{Sales} - \text{Variable costs}}{\text{Sales}}$$

If total sales are expected to be £105,000, total variable costs £42,000, and fixed costs £36,000, the break-even sales volume will be

$$36,000 \div \frac{105,000 - 42,000}{105,000}$$
$$= 36,000 \times \frac{105,000}{63,000}$$
$$= £60,000$$

Break-even analysis provides a useful way of studying the profit factors of the business. There are four ways in which profit can be increased (or loss decreased):

(1) Increase selling price per unit.
(2) Decrease variable costs per unit.
(3) Decrease fixed costs.
(4) Increase volume.

The effect of the change in any of the four variables can be depicted on the break-even graphs opposite, where (a) shows the increase in selling price,

(b) the decrease in variable costs, (c) the decrease in fixed costs and (d) the increase in volume.

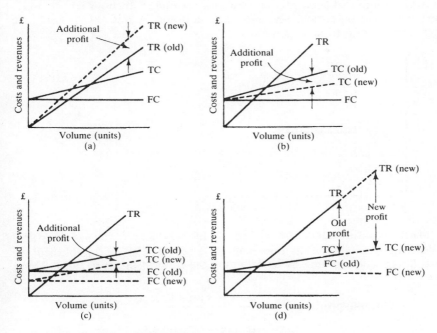

(a) (b) (c) (d)

Assumptions and limitations of break-even analysis

Break-even analysis is a useful tool of decision-making but not a sharp one. The analysis outlined above is conducted under a number of implicit assumptions.

(1) Conventional break-even analysis presumes that costs are either perfectly variable or absolutely fixed over all ranges of volume. In addition, variable cost is assumed to be a linear function of volume. As we observed in Chapter 14, the assumption of linear cost behaviour appears to be a fair approximation of the situation. Provided the relationship holds true over the critical volume—the minimum and maximum ranges of activity—what happens to cost outside of this range is not of any consequence in practical terms.

(2) A second assumption is that revenue is perfectly variable with volume, and is in a linear relationship. For many firms this will not be valid; for example, the same product may be sold at different prices to different customers, or lower prices may be necessary to achieve higher sales volumes. Once again, however, over the critical volume, the assumption may not be so unrealistic as to impair the analysis completely.

(3) The consequence of non-linear cost/revenue behaviour is that the revenue and cost lines will not be straight, and may produce multiple break-even points. We may illustrate this by means of a step function in fixed costs, a variable cost per unit which is not perfectly linear with respect

to volume, and a sales price that decreases above a certain volume. There are two break-even points displayed by the graph, and although in practice it may be impossible to predict cost and revenue behaviour so precisely, an awareness of critical volumes (i.e. between A and BE₂) would be extremely useful to management.

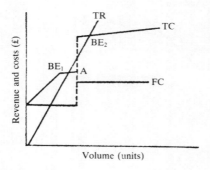

(4) In a multi-product firm, changes in the product mix can have a critical effect on profitability. In our example on page 396 we established the breakeven sales volume by ascertaining the ratio of profit to sales. Thus

$$\text{Variable profit ratio} = \frac{\text{Sales} - \text{Variable costs}}{\text{Sales}}$$
$$= \frac{105{,}000 - 42{,}000}{105{,}000}$$
$$= 60\%$$

We may assume that in the first instance this variable profit ratio was derived from the sales of four products:

Product	Budgeted sales	Variable cost	Variable profit	Variable profit/sales
	£	£	£	%
A	20,000	8,000	12,000	60
B	35,000	15,000	20,000	57
C	30,000	12,000	18,000	60
D	20,000	7,000	13,000	65
Total	105,000	42,000	63,000	

If the budgeted totals are achieved but a change in product mix takes place, it is possible to shift the break-even point without any change at all in sales volume:

Product	Actual sales	Variable cost	Variable profit	Variable profit/sales
	£	£	£	%
A	20,000	8,000	12,000	60
B	63,000	27,000	36,000	57
C	20,000	8,000	12,000	60
D	2,000	700	1,300	65
Total	105,000	43,700	61,300	

The average variable ratio is now

$$\frac{61,300}{105,000} = 58.4\%$$

and the break-even sales volume becomes

$$\frac{36,000}{58.4\%} = £61,700$$

(5) Break-even analysis assumes that everything produced is sold, and that there is no significant change in inventories. This assumption is necessary because costs and revenues are related to the same measure of volume. If inventories do change, then the sales volume of production will have to be substituted for current revenue to ascertain the break-even point. However, this in itself makes another assumption, namely that goods produced for inventory will eventually be sold at the current selling price.

(6) Finally, break-even analysis assures—as does most conventional accounting—that monetary values are stable. To establish a break-even point in real terms, it is necessary to adjust costs and revenues to uniform purchasing powers. In particular, the fixed costs which often include depreciation in terms of historic costs should be adjusted.

Operational research

Operational research (OR) is usually defined as the application of mathematical techniques to business problems. We have already met one application in the field of budgetary models, and in this chapter we will briefly consider three more. The use of a mathematical technique has three distinct stages: the collection of data, the construction of a model (hypothesis), and the testing of the model. In the context of business decision-making, all three stages present considerable difficulties.

(1)   Stock control

The field of stock control provides an interesting and important example of the use of OR techniques. As we will discuss in the next chapter, there are a number of important variables which will influence the level of investment in stock. There are a number of costs of holding stock—insurance, storage, obsolescence, and interest foregone, and there are a number of costs of being out of stock—ordering, interruption of production, loss of sales. These costs tend to move in opposite directions, because if the stock is large, holding costs will be high, and 'out-of-stock' costs low. We can express this relationship graphically:

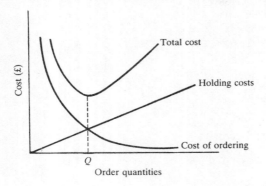

The minimum total cost will be at order quantity Q; if certain assumptions are made about stock usage and stock receipts[1] then an elementary mathematical model can be used to express the relationships and, by means of calculus, to determine the point of minimum total cost:

Let O be the cost of ordering, Q the order quantity, U the usage during period t, and H the holding cost per unit period t; then:

$$\text{Number of orders during period } t = \frac{U}{Q}$$

$$\text{Cost of ordering during period } t = \frac{(U)O}{(Q)}$$

$$\text{Average stock during period } t = \frac{Q}{2}$$

$$\text{Total holding costs} = \frac{(Q)}{(2)}H$$

$$\text{Total costs} = \frac{(U)}{(Q)}O + \frac{(Q)}{(2)}H$$

By differentiating this equation in respect of Q, we obtain the minimum total cost when

$$Q = \sqrt{\frac{2UO}{H}}$$

This particular model, because of the assumptions made, can be assailed as being unreal. Nevertheless, it is apparent that it is the square root of

1 Stock usage is even over time, and the time lag between ordering is insignificant.

the usage (or sales rate) which should determine the order qualities; this can provide a starting point for investigations by giving a figure which can be compared with current practice.

(2) Debtor and stock models

Stock models, almost without exception, focus attention upon the stock alone, ignoring the fact that most sales are for credit, and hence that a firm has to finance stock in the hands of debtors. The variables affecting the investment in debtors will be discussed in Chapter 18; at this point we will consider a model which links debtor *and* stock policy.

A simple form of the model assumes that a firm produces all stock on the first day of the month and delivers to customers on the last day; any stock unsold at month end is presumed valueless. The cash cost production function is given by

$$\text{Total cost} = £(10 + 3X)$$

i.e. a fixed cost of £10 and a variable cost of £3 per unit.

Each unit sells at £8 (all sales are on credit) and the firm faces a demand which is sensitive to changes in price through the manipulation of discount policy. There are two discount policies under review which have the following effect on demand:

(1) Discount 3 per cent for payment within 10 days

Rate of demand (units)	300	400
Probability of occurrence	0.5	0.5

(2) Discount 10 per cent for payment within 10 days

Rate of demand (units)	300	400
Probability of occurrence	0.3	0.4

If the first policy is adopted, 60 per cent in value of the debtors pay on the tenth day and the remainder at month end; if the second, the corresponding figures are 90 per cent and 10 per cent.

As with the stock control model, there is a cost of being unable to meet demand—referred to as the 'short cost'—which we will assume is £0.50 per unit per month. For example, if the firm produces 300 units and the demand is 400 units the short cost is £0.50 (400 − 300) = £50.

The stock is also subject to another cost; because the firm has tied up funds in stock it is forgoing returns which could have been earned by investing the money elsewhere; this 'opportunity' cost we will take as £0.05 per pound per month. For example, if there is £200 of stock for one month, the firm forgoes £200 (0.05) = £10. In addition, since stock is in the hands of debtors for 10 days of a month, there is an opportunity cost involved here as well.

There are four policies which the firm can adopt, and each of these has two possible outcomes:

Policy	Discount rate (D)	Stock (I)	Demand (d)
1	3%	300	300
			400
2	3%	400	300
			400
3	10%	300	300
			400
4	10%	400	300
			400

Each policy must be evaluated, the firm selecting that which will maximize the expected profits. The computation for each policy follows the pattern given below:

Policy I: D = 3%; I = 300; d = 300

		£	£
(a)	The gross revenue is	(300)(8)	2,400
(b)	The cost of production is (the fixed cost can be ignored since it is common to all policies)	(300) (3)	900
(c)	Since stock = demand, short cost is zero	(300 − 300) (0.50)	0
(d)	The stock is held for one month, hence the opportunity cost is	(300)(3)(0.05)	45
(e)	The gross revenue will be reduced by the discount taken. Since 60% of the debtors take discount, the cost is	(300)(8)(0.6)(0.03)	43.20
(f)	Stock is in the hands of *all* debtors for 10 days; this is financed *at cost* and the opportunity cost is	$(300)(3)\left(\dfrac{10}{30}\right)(0.05)$	15
(g)	Stock is in the hands of 40% of the debtors for an additional 20 days, and the opportunity cost is	$(300)(3)(0.4)\left(\dfrac{20}{30}\right)0.05$	12

The Gross Cost is   **£1,015.20**

Thus the outcome is   £2,400 − £1,015.20   **£1,384.80**

Policy I(a): D = 3%; I = 300; d = 400

The cost will be the same as above, except for a short cost of (400 − 300)(0.05) = £50, and hence the outcome will be £1,334.80. Since the probability of d = 300 when D = 3% is 0.5 and of d = 400 when D =

3% is also 0.5 the expected profit from producing and stocking 300 units and offering a discount of 3% is

$$1,384.80 \ (0.5) + 1,334.80 \ (0.5) = £1,359.80$$

Similar calculations for the other policies enable us to tabulate the expected values:

D(%)	I(units)	Expected value (£)
3	300	1,359.80
3	400	1,458.10
10	300	1,186.00
10	400	1,411.40

Hence the optimal policy is to produce and stock 400 units and offer a discount of 3 per cent.

The model can be generalized to incorporate other debtor variables and also the problem of uncertain cash flows from debtors.

(3) Linear programming and limiting factors

In Chapter 14, when discussing budgeting, we indicated that the firm should seek to identify the limiting factor—the factor which effectively restricts the total magnitude of operations in any given period. Restrictions will almost inevitably arise because resources are scarce, and earlier in this chapter (page 393) we discussed the need to calculate contribution per unit of the limiting factor in order to identify and select the highest. Where several limiting factors impinge on production, then we have recourse to linear programming, a name given to the mathematical technique which identifies the optimum contribution (in profit terms) of limited resources.

Consider, for example, a firm which produces two commodities, X and Y. Both products pass through two departments, A and B. Product X requires two hours in department A, and four hours in B; product Y requires six hours in A and four in B. Because of labour limitations department A has only 36 hours per week available, and B 40 hours per week. If product X makes a contribution to profit of £10 per unit, and Y of £7 per unit, how much of each should be produced?

We can specify the problem mathematically and write

Dept. A $2X + 6Y \leqslant 36$
Dept. B $4X + 4Y \leqslant 40$

The firm is seeking to maximize

£10X + 7Y

subject to

$X \geqslant 0$ and $Y \geqslant 0$

as it is impossible to produce a negative quantity.

We can obtain the answer to the above graphically, as illustrated. In dept. A, the production of X and Y can be between 18 units of X (when Y = 0) and six units of Y (when X is 0), in dept. B, 10 units of X can be produced (when Y = 0), and 10 units of Y (when X = 0).

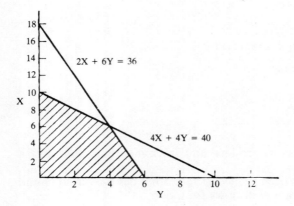

The feasibility area is shaded; outside of this area the constants are not satisfied. For example, although 18 units of X could be produced by dept. A, this would require 4 × 18 = 72 hours in dept. B—well above the constraint of 40 hours. To find the optimum profit position, it is necessary to calculate the profit at each corner of the feasibility area:

| Output | | Contribution | | Total |
X	Y	X	Y	
		£	£	£
0	0	0	0	0
10	0	100	0	100
6	4	60	28	88
0	6	0	42	42

Therefore, the firm should focus its resources on product X, producing ten units of X and none of Y. Notice that if the contribution of each product changes, the optimal solution may change with it. For example, if the contributions of X and Y were £6 and £8, respectively, the optimal solution would be to produce six units of X and four of Y.

In practice there are normally more than two variables, and techniques such as the 'simplex method' have been developed for solving such problems without recourse to graphical illustration.

References and further reading

DOPUCH, BIRNBERG and DEMSKI (1980), *Cost Accounting Data for Management's Decisions.* Harcourt Brace.

HILLIARD and LEITCH (1975), 'C.V.P. Analysis under Uncertainty', *Accounting Review*, January 1975.

HORNGREN (1982), *Cost Accounting: A Managerial Emphasis.* Prentice-Hall.

JAEDICKE and ROBICHEK (1964), 'Cost–Volume–Profit Analysis under Conditions of Uncertainty', *Accounting Review*, October 1964.

MARSLAND (1975), *Quantitative Techniques for Business.* Polytech Publishers.

Questions for discussion

1   Mrs Bland owns a small boarding house at a seaside resort. She takes up to 20 guests during the 'season' which lasts 14 weeks, and averages 15 guests per week who each pay £25 per week. The house, bought with her late husband's insurance monies, cost £14,000 in 1972. She occupies two rooms in the house herself, and during the season eats with the guests.

	Average total costs for 1 week in season	Annual costs
	£	£
Food	80	
Waitresses/cleaners	22	
Laundry	10	
Heating and lighting	8	
Depreciation of furniture, etc.		250
Rates		350
Telephone, advertising, postage, etc.		150
	120	750

Required:

(a) Estimate the annual profit, making any assumptions you think appropriate.
(b) What is the minimum average number of guests per week to just break even, and what is the average total cost per week per person?
(c) Some pensioners want to come for a week out of season. What is the minimum price Mrs Bland could charge?

2   A small company manufactures two products, selling 10,000 units of A and 30,000 units of B. The results in 1984 were

	A		B	
	£	£	£	£
Sales		25,000		40,000
Materials	8,000		18,000	
Labour	7,000		16,000	
Variable overhead	2,000		3,000	
Fixed overhead	4,000	21,000	5,000	42,000
Net Profit (Loss)		**4,000**		**(2,000)**

(i) The directors propose to abandon product B in order to increase the overall profit from £2,000 to £4,000. Advise them.

(ii) The company is approached by a new customer who offers to take 4,000 units of product A at £2.00 per unit. Should the company undertake the order, assuming it has spare capacity?

(iii) The company has already manufactured and has in store 2,000 units of product C—a line which it abandoned two years ago because there was no longer a market. The product costs had been:

	Cost per unit
	£
Material	0.75
Labour	1.20
Variable overhead	0.35
Fixed overhead	1.40
	£3.70

An offer is made to buy all 2,000 units for £4,400. Should the company accept?

3   A business makes one standard product with the following revenue and expense profile:

Selling price	£20 per unit
Direct labour	£5 per unit
Direct material	£4 per unit
Variable overhead	£3 per unit
Fixed overhead:	
0–4,999 units	£32,000
5,000–9,999 units	£44,000
Over 10,000 units	£60,000

Required:

(a) Prepare a break-even graph and read off the break-even point(s) in terms of volume and sales value.

(b) Convert the break-even chart into a profit volume chart.
(c) What is the margin of safety at 8,500 units?
(d) Calculate the profit which will be made if 14,000 units are sold.
(e) Explain the assumptions inherent in this type of analysis.

4   A business makes three products, X, Y and Z, and the revenues and expenses per unit are

	X	Y	Z
	£	£	£
Sales	8	4	7
Material	1.5	0.3	1.8
Labour	2.5	1.5	0.8
Variable overhead	2.0	1.0	1.4
Fixed overhead	1.0	0.5	0.5

The normal sales mix is in the ratio $X:Y:Z$ as $4:2:2$, and the fixed overheads have been absorbed on a budgeted combined sales volume of 24,000 units.

Required:

(a) Prepare a break-even chart to reflect the above information for the business as a whole (not by separate product line).
(b) What would be the effect on the break-even point if the sales mix became $X:Y:Z$ as $3:4:1$?

5   The Regent Co. Ltd is developing a new product called Scram, and has, to date, spent £50,000 on this project. Part of this development work has had a spin-off in material handling techniques which could be sold to a firm using similar materials for £20,000. The company is now considering whether to abandon the project, and submits the following information:

Material. The project needs two materials, X and Y. 2,000 kilos of X are already paid for and in store at a cost of £4.50 per kilo and this material is used in currently produced products. Recent sharp rises in material prices mean that the replacement cost would be £5.50 per kilo. Y is a highly specialist material already in store at a cost of £2,000. If it is not used for the project, it will be sold for at least £3,500.

Labour. Skilled and unskilled labour is used on the project. The skilled labour was specially hired at a cost of £10,000 p.a., and once the project (which will take a year to complete) is completed they will cease employment with the company, but receive redundancy pay of £5,000. The unskilled labour, which costs £5,000 p.a., will be reabsorbed within the general labour force.

Equipment. Equipment costing £20,000 was bought three years ago for the project, and is being depreciated at £5,000 p.a. over four years. If sold now the equipment would fetch £2,000, but in a year's time will not be worth anything.

Overhead. The company allocates £2,000 p.a. of general overhead to the project.

Sales. If completed, the company will sell the product patent for £30,000, but not manufacture it for itself.

Required:

Prepare a report showing whether the company should abandon or complete the project.

6   You are the independent auditor for the Scoopa Co. When you had completed your audit for the preceding year, management asked your assistance in arriving at a decision whether to continue manufacturing a part or to buy it from an outside supplier. The part, which is named Faktron, is a component used in some of the finished products of the company.

From your audit working papers and from further investigations you develop the following data relative to the company's operations:

(i) The annual requirement of Faktrons is 5,000 units. The lowest price quotation from a supplier was £8 per unit.

(ii) Faktrons have been manufactured in the Precision Machinery Department. Following are the total costs of this department during the preceding year when 5,000 Faktrons were produced:

	£
Materials	67,500
Direct labour	50,000
Indirect labour	20,000
Light and heat	5,500
Power	3.000
Depreciation	10,000
Property taxes and insurance	8,000
Payroll taxes and other fringe benefits	9,800
Miscellaneous	5,000

Discontinuing production of Faktrons would reduce the operation volume of the Precision Machinery Department but would not permit the disposal of any of the department's assets.

(iii) The following proportions of the variable costs in the Precision Machinery Department are directly traceable to Faktrons:

Materials	30%
Direct labour	40%
Indirect labour	30%
Power	10%

(iv) If Faktrons are purchased from an outside supplier, shipping charges would average £0.5 per unit and indirect labour in the Precision Machinery Department would be increased by £5,000 for receiving, inspecting, and handling.

Required:

(a) Prepare a schedule showing the relative costs of making and buying Faktrons to assist management in reaching a decision.
(b) Discuss the consideration in addition to costs that you would bring to the attention of management in helping them make a decision in this situation.

7   The Senslit Co. Ltd manufactures a range of light-sensitive papers used in photographic processes. The paper, once manufactured, is stored in specially constructed crates lined with 'photon'. These crates are manufactured and maintained by a special department within the company. During 1984 the department's operations cost £38,170 made up as follows:

	£	£
Direct materials (including 'photon')		14,000
Direct labour		10,000
		24,000
Overhead		
Departmental manager	1,600	
Depreciation of machinery	3,000	
Maintenance of machinery	720	
Rent (portion of warehouse)	900	
Other miscellaneous costs	3,150	9,370
		33,370
Administrative overhead		
(20% of direct costs)		4,800
		38,170

The Packaging Co. Ltd has approached the Senslit Co. offering to make all the crates required on a four-year contract for £25,000 p.a. and/or to maintain them for a further £5,000 p.a. Further investigation reveals that:

(a) The machinery used in the department cost £24,000 four years ago and will last for four more years. It could currently be sold for £5,000. It is needed in the manufacture of the crates but not for maintenance purposes.
(b) A stock of 'photon' was acquired last year for £20,000. One-fifth has been used this year (£4,000 has been included in the material cost). It originally cost £100 per ton but the replacement cost is £120 per ton, and it could currently be sold for £80 per ton.

(c) The Crate Department necessitates the renting of warehouse space for £1,800 p.a. The department only uses one-half of the space, the rest lies idle.

(d) If the department were closed all the labour force will be made redundant, but three of the men (current salary each £1,000 p.a.) will each receive a pension of £500 p.a.

(e) In the event of closure the manager will be transferred to another department.

(f) If Senslit continued to maintain the crates (while the Packaging Co. manufactured):

   (i) the machinery will not be required,
   (ii) the manager will remain in the department,
   (iii) the warehouse space requirements will not be reduced,
   (iv) only 10 per cent of *all* materials will be used,
   (v) only one employee earning £1,000 p.a. will be pensioned off at £500,
   (vi) the miscellaneous costs will be reduced by 80 per cent.

(g) If Senslit continued to manufacture (while the Packaging Co. maintained):

   (i) the machinery will be required,
   (ii) the manager will remain in the department,
   (iii) the warehouse space will be required,
   (iv) 90 per cent of all the materials will be required,
   (v) miscellaneous costs will be reduced by 20 per cent.

Required:
Evaluate the four possible courses of action by identifying the relevant cash flows over the four-year period, and advise management accordingly, indicating what other information may be relevant.

8 Wildcat Ltd had a bad strike in one of its many departments. By comparing budget and actual quantities for the strike period the firm's accountant prepared the following estimate of the cost of the strike:

	£	£
Sales: Number of units below budget		35,000
Budget unit selling price		£1.25
Total revenue lost because of strike		43,750
Less: Cost savings:		
Materials not used	8,750	
(35,000 units × budget unit material cost)		
Wages saved	17,500	
(35,000 units × budget unit labour cost)		
		26,250
		17,500

	£	£
Add: Wages paid during strike:		
Supervisory staff	500	
Workers in trade unions unaffected		
by strike	1,000	1,500
Fixed overhead not recovered		8,750
(35,000 units × budget overhead		
recovery rate)		
		£27,750

The department produces only one product, and keeps no stocks. At the time of the strike there was a temporary decline in demand for the product, and it is estimated that actual sales would in any case have been 10,000 units below budget. The sales manager has said that even to reach this volume of sales he would have to reduce the price of the last 25,000 units sold to £1.

The workers who came in during the strikes were used in maintenance work usually undertaken by an outside contractor. Materials costing £1,000 had to be specially bought for the maintenance work. The normal charge by the contractor is £3,000.

The budgeted fixed overhead rate is based solely on fixed costs that are unaffected by the activity of any one department.

It was agreed as part of the strike settlement to make up 10,000 of the units lost because of the strike by working exceptional overtime. For this work, there will be a special wage rate that will add 25 per cent to budgeted unit labour costs.

Required:

A report to Wildcat's board of directors showing the opportunity cost of the strike. Add a brief note explaining your treatment of fixed overheads. Explain any assumptions that you make.

9   S.S. Ltd manufacture perfumes. Their two products in the Brumiere range are made by the same process. Cost and price information is as follows:

	Normale		Super
	£		£
Selling price per unit	16.00		20.00
Labour: ¼ hour at £3 per hour	0.75		0.75
Materials: 3 litres at £2 per litre	6.00	4 litres at £2 per litre	8.00
Essence: 0.4 litres at £5 per litre	2.00	0.5 litres at £5 per litre	2.50
Packing	0.75		1.25

	Normale	*Super*
Share of research and development	4.00	2.00
Profit margin	2.50	5.50

£12,000 has been spent on research and development to perfect the common process.

| Current sales are: | Normale | 4,000 units |
| | Super | 2,000 units |

Super has the higher profit margin and £4,000 has just been spent on an advertising campaign which is expected to increase sales by 1,000 units. This would utilize all available capacity.

The current and projected demand curves for Super are as follows (D_1—D_1, without advertising, D_2—D_2, with advertising):

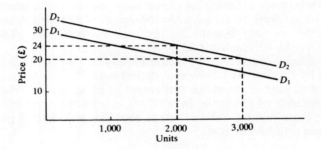

Unfortunately there is a drought in Borneo which is causing a shortage of essence, limiting supplies to 1,500 litres. Alternative supplies of Welsh essence could be obtained at £12 per litre. Advise management.

10 A firm manufactures three products, alpha, beta and gamma, with budgeted costs as follows:

Costs per unit	A	B	G
	£	£	£
Labour I £4/hr	5	8	10
Labour II £5/hr	6	4	6
Material X £4/kg	4	—	—
Material Y £6/kg	—	5	9
Power	1	2	3
Factory administration	2	4	8
	18	23	36

Factory administration has been apportioned to products on the basis of budgeted output based on last year's sales which is

A	B	G
80,000	120,000	150,000

Any change in budgeted output would require a reapportionment of these costs, but it is not anticipated that these sales volumes will be exceeded in the current year. Anticipated selling prices are

	A	B	G
	£	£	£
Sales 0–100,000	20	30	40
100,000–180,000	18	25	36

This year the firm expects output to be constrained by shortages of grade I labour and material Y:

Supply of grade I labour	720,000 h
Supply of material Y	200,000 kg

As the management accountant, advise the firm on production mix, providing supporting figures. Can you, as the management accountant, provide any information in consideration of the problem of overcoming the constraints?

18 The management of working capital

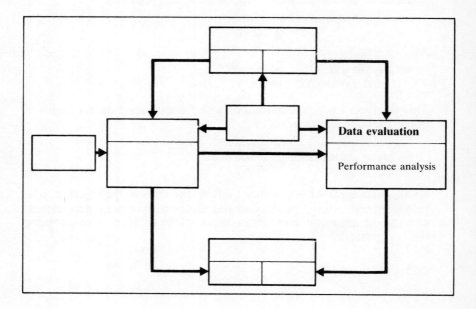

The need for funds in a business is affected by every activity of the business and by virtually everything that happens to the business. The old business adage 'You've got to have money to make money' is a simple recognition that most enterprises need funds in order to operate profitably. While the amounts needed in the individual firm are influenced by many factors, and fluctuate over a period of time, the typical business must maintain a substantial investment in the current assets of stock, customers (debtors), and cash, and also in fixed assets such as buildings, plant and equipment. For most, if not all, businesses, resources are scarce, and thus at any given point in time the assets disclosed on the balance sheet are a reflection of the cumulative investment decisions of management.

414

The working capital cycle

In Chapter 9 we drew a distinction between long- and short-term sources and uses of funds by means of the following table:

Time period	Source	Normal use
Long	Capital	Buildings
	Long-term loans	Plant, equipment
Short	Creditors	Stock, debtors
	Bank	Cash

The working capital of a business reflects the short-term uses of funds. It is said to 'work' because within the time span of one year there is a continuing cycle, or turnover, of these assets. The cash is used to acquire stock, which when sold will result in an inflow of cash either immediately or after a time lag if the sales were on credit.

The rate of turnover of current assets in relation to the total sales of a given time period is of critical importance to the total funds employed in those assets. Consider a firm which plans to make sales (at cost) of £1,000 during a given year. We will begin with the simplest case when all stock acquisitions and sales are for cash. Thus

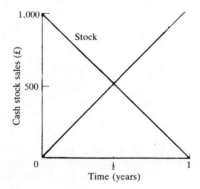

The firm could elect to buy the full £1,000 stock at the beginning of the year and gradually run down this stock as the sales are made. This would obviously require a maximum working capital of £1,000. The firm, however, could decide to buy stock twice a year; the funds then needed would be reduced to £500. In diagrammatic terms

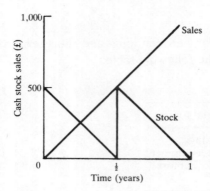

Obviously the more frequent the acquisition of stock, and the more rapidly the sales are made, the smaller the amount of working capital required. In practice there is a limit to the rapidity of turnover for a number of reasons, e.g. the time lag between the ordering and delivery of the stock, and between making the sale and receiving the cash.

The introduction of credit facilities both to and by the firm will have a considerable effect on the rate of turnover or rotation of the cycle. From the simple pattern of

we have moved to

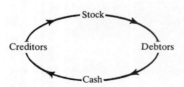

For any given annual sales volume the working capital required will depend on the time lags inherent in any stage of the cycle. The circulation of the working capital is not an automatic affair, but calls for close financial control and planning.

The rate of turnover of the current assets in relation to total sales can be calculated quite simply by dividing the annual sales by the average current assets for that year. For example, if sales were £200,000 and the current assets £30,000 the rate of turnover is

$$\frac{200,000}{30,000} = 6.66 \text{ times}$$

This may also be expressed in terms of sales days:

$$\frac{365}{6.66} = 54.8 \text{ days}$$

The resulting flow rate is, of course, an average of all current assets, and like any average may hide extremes.

Consider two companies, A and B:

| | Company A | | | Company B | | |
	£	Turnover times	days	£	Turnover times	days
Sales	200,000	—	—	400,000	—	—
Stock	35,000	5.7	64.0	38,000	10.5	34.8
Debtors	1,000	200.0	1.8	36,000	11.1	32.8
Cash	4,000	50.0	7.2	6,000	66.6	5.4
	40,000	5.0	73.0	80,000	5.0	73.0

Both companies have the same turnover rate for total current assets, but are considerably different in the manner in which they achieve this turnover. Company A with only 1.8 days' credit extended to debtors must make most of its sales for cash. Company B has lower stock levels—only 34.8 days' supply on hand as opposed to 64—and grants longer credit facilities to its customers.

With this general background in mind, we can now explore in some detail the factors affecting the investment in the various types of current assets. In this chapter we will seek to explore more fully some of the factors which, in the previous chapter, we built into mathematical models, enabling management to identify the optimal levels of investment in working capital.

The investment in stock

The book value of stocks held in the UK at the end of 1982 was £72,282 million; the very magnitude may give us some appreciation of the importance of investment in this asset. The statistics of National Income and Expenditure[1] indicate the distribution of this investment by industrial sector, as shown below.

1   National Income and Expenditure, 1982, Table 12.1.

Value of stocks held in UK at end of 1982

	£ million (book values)
Agriculture	3,032
Forestry	1,496
Mining and quarrying	1,178
Manufacturing	38,266
Gas, electricity and water	2,202
Retail distribution	7,611
Wholesale distribution	10,541
Other	7,118
Central Government	122
Adjustments	716
	£72,282

Within manufacturing industry stocks of material were valued at £12,755 million, work in progress at £13,806 million, and finished goods at £11,705 million.

Each of the categories differs significantly from the other, so that analysis of the stock investment and control is most meaningful if each category is treated separately. In general, work in progress is particularly important for the producers of durable goods, but for the non-durable producers (e.g. textiles, food, etc.) it is of much less consequence than raw materials or finished goods.

(1) Investment in raw materials

Virtually all manufacturing concerns must carry some stock of raw materials—those goods not yet put into the productive process—but what is judged sufficient—1 day's or 100 days' supply—is a matter for judgement in the light of a variety of considerations:

(a) *Safety or buffer stocks*. The basic justification for safety stocks is that they avoid the costly interruption of production which will result from being out of stock. How large this safety stock will be is a function of the usage rate and the conditions of supply—the speed and reliability with which suppliers can meet orders.

(b) *Purchase economy*. Buying in bulk can frequently result in more favourable prices. Management has to weigh the costs of holding stock (*see* (c) below) against the cost of savings inherent in the reduced prices.

(c) *Stock-holding costs*. Stock-holding costs are of major significance in determining the optimum inventory level. These costs include storage, insurance and losses through theft, obsolescence and physical deterioration.

(d) *Rate of production*. Since raw materials are incorporated in the productive process, the size of the stock will fluctuate with changes in the rate of production. Planned changes in production can be met with planned changes in stock-holding, but sudden unexpected declines or increases in sales volume with corresponding changes in the production rate will result in stocks significantly above or below the planned levels.

(e) *Efficient reporting*. To serve the purposes of financial accounting, the stock on hand need only be physically counted and valued once a year. In the intervening interval, unless there is a comprehensive stock record system, knowledge of stock levels is limited to 'informed' guesses. More rationally, the regulation of stock levels required a perpetual inventory system—the continuous record of stock levels and movements. Unless this information is reported to management it is difficult—if not impossible in large businesses—to maintain target stock levels.

(f) *Cost and availability of funds*. Resources of any firm are limited and the use of funds on stock will mean that other investment opportunities must be forgone. In economic terms, there is an opportunity cost involved. Such a cost is difficult to measure, for a firm can never know all the other alternatives open to them in order to identify the next best. In practice, when firms incorporate such a factor in their calculations of optimum stock levels, they normally use the prevailing external rate of interest as a measure of the opportunity cost.

(2)   The investment in work in progress

This category of stock comprises all goods in the process of production. The value of these goods from an accounting standpoint is the summation of the raw material costs transferred to work in progress (direct material) plus wages of those engaged in the production process (direct wages), together with an allocation of overhead costs such as heat, power, lighting and supervision. The accounting aspects of manufacturing concerns, together with the valuation of stocks, will be dealt with in subsequent chapters. Here we are primarily concerned with the main determinants of the amount of funds tied up in work in progress.

The volume of production is obviously a major determinant. Other things being equal, as production increases, the amount invested in work in progress increases. There is an evident connection with planned or anticipated sales in this respect, the volume of work in progress moving in sympathy with sales expectations.

The nature of the production process itself will also be a determinant of the work in progress investment; the larger the production process the greater the funds required. Two illustrations may clarify this point; contrast the instance of the daily newspaper where the length of the production process will not exceed 24 hours, and the example of shipbuilding where the time period from start to finish may be two or more years. While technological considerations will prescribe the length of the production process, management can also significantly influence the production time by altering the length of the production runs, or by instituting extra production shifts or authorizing overtime working, or by changes in production scheduling and control.

(3)   The investment in finished goods

The stock of finished goods is increased by additions from the completed work in progress or from purchases of finished goods, and diminished by sales. Fairly evidently, if sales and purchasing/production are fully coincident the investment in finished stock can be minimized. In practice, this can seldom if ever be achieved, and optimum finished stock levels are usually set in terms of so many days of anticipated sales. Over long periods these stocks tend to vary directly with the changes in sales volume.

The number of days' supply on hand will be determined by a combination of production and sales factors. On the production side, when sales demand is uneven (perhaps due to seasonal factors), an even production over the year will meet total annual demand at the price of higher stocks in the off-peak seasons. This is acceptable provided the savings in manufacturing costs are greater than the increased costs of holding stock.

Sales considerations may dictate an ability to meet demand quickly or lose the sales opportunity. In such circumstances a buffer stock of finished goods may be considered essential, and firms may be willing to acquire warehousing facilities for stock at strategic geographical locations.

Summary

All investment in stock carries risk. Prices can rise or fall—particularly in the commodity markets such as metals or foodstuffs—tastes can change, and new production techniques and product improvement can reduce the value of old stocks. In deciding the level of stock of all categories appropriate to the business, management has to evaluate the variables enumerated above. The task grows more complex with the size of the firm and many larger organizations are making use of mathematical models and computers to work out distribution patterns, production costs and stock levels that optimize the investment of funds in this area of the firm.

The investment in debtors

We observed earlier in this chapter that, for any given annual sales volume, the working capital required will be a function of the time lags inherent in any stage of the cycle. Most business sales are made on credit terms, and the investment in debtors represents an important and continuing commitment for most enterprises. The standard measure of control of the investment in debtors is that of turnover, i.e. debtors related to sales. Our earlier example of companies A and B yielded the following:

	A	B
Sales	£200,000	£400,000
Debtors	£1,000	£36,000
Turnover	200.0	11.1
Credit period	1.8 days	32.8 days

Policies which stress short credit terms, rigorous credit control and collection will clearly reduce the investment in debtors and losses through bad debts. But the corollary of this is normally restricted sales and profit margins, so that despite minimal debtor investment, the firm's rate of return on total investment is lower than if its credit facilities had been more lenient. Conversely, lenient or uncontrolled credit facilities will inflate debtors and increase bad debts without compensating increases in sales and in profit margins. The objective of the firm in relation to debtors is, therefore, to achieve a balance between the two extremes so that the investment in debtors contributes towards an optimum return on total investment.

Types of debtors

We have so far treated debtors as though they were a homogeneous entity, and our calculation of credit period (turnover) has ignored the existence of different debtor groups. It is customary to identify three main groups of debtors: (1) government (national and local), (2) trade, and (3) sundry.

(1)   Government (national and local)

Government debtors are normally isolated from the other groups because they are usually subject to terms which are not necessarily in accord with normal commercial practice. Credit terms are often extended and settlement may be delayed because of controls deemed necessary in the bureaucratic machine. Because government debtors may regularly take longer credit than other debtors it is useful for control purposes to clearly segregate them.

(2)   Trade

Trade debtors represent the indebtedness to the firm arising from the sale of its products to normal commercial customers. They are subject to the credit terms normally operative in that particular sector of industrial activity. Careful analysis will be required to ensure that credit terms are not violated. If, for example, a firm normally allows two months' credit it may be satisfied if the ratio of sales to debtors revealed

$$\frac{\text{Sales}}{\text{Debtors}} = £\frac{12,000}{2,000} = \frac{6}{1} = 2 \text{ months}$$

Further analysis on a time basis could indicate, however, that the average collection period is concealing vitally important facts:

Age (months)	Account No. of customers	Value £	% Value
Under 1	40	500	25
1 and under 2	80	800	40
2 and under 3	36	400	20
3 and over	10	300	15
	166	2,000	

The table shows that 15 per cent of customers by value have been owing money to the company for three months or more. Clearly the company should follow up these outstanding amounts without delay.

(3)   Sundry

Many firms engage in activities peripheral to their major purpose. For example, a car manufacturer at one time sold wine glasses to its dealers for advertising purposes. Such miscellaneous items will not normally be subject to the same credit conditions imposed on the trade debtors. Often the amounts involved on each individual account are insignificant, although considerable in total. The cost of collecting outstanding sundry debts is often in excess of their value; hence a separate policy needs to be laid down in respect of these items.

The determinants of investment in debtors

Whatever the type of debtor, the features influencing the size of the firm's investment will be similar. We will briefly identify the most important of these.

(1)   Volume of credit sales

Other factors being equal, the greater the volume of credit sales, the larger the investment in debtors.

(2)   Terms of credit

In theory, each firm is free to specify the terms of sale best suited to its circumstances. In practice, competitive pressures tend to push the individual firm to offer credit terms at least as generous as its competitors. In most long-established industries, credit terms have become a matter of tradition; customary terms may carry the notation EOM (end of month following delivery) or 5/10 net 30 (i.e. 5 per cent cash discount allowed for payment within 10 days, and payment within 30 days is required in any case).

Credit terms can be applied selectively even though custom dictates the general policy. Good (or large) customers can often expect and obtain more favourable credit facilities; new customers or customers with a poor payment record can expect minimal facilities.

(3)   Credit control

Credit control covers three policy aspects: (a) the decision to grant credit, (b) the monthly examination of debtors accounts, and (c) the collection of overdue accounts. The power to grant or refuse credit may be vested in either the marketing or financial function or, in larger firms, in a combination of the two. The marketing function is normally more willing to grant credit than the traditionally conservative financial function. In determining the credit worthiness of customers, attention will be paid to the financial resources of the firm, its capacity to operate efficiently, the reputation, and the particular economic circumstances affecting the trade or industry. The extent of the credit investigation will largely depend on the size of the credit facilities sought.

Once credit facilities have been extended, the accounts must be scrutinized to ensure that the credit terms are being followed. The analysis will Follow a pattern similar to that on page 421, but may well go further by breaking down sales by geographic area and product. Slow-paying customers can be promptly reminded (in a most polite manner) of their shortcomings.

The collection policy for long overdue accounts involves difficult problems. Sometimes threat of publicity will effect payment. Legal action will normally only be contemplated if the amount involved is in excess of the cost of the action, and also justifies the managerial effort involved.

The need for cash

If the daily cash receipts exactly matched the daily outflow, the need for cash investment in working capital would be restricted to reserves against unexpected contingencies. Such flows can seldom, if ever, be expected. Cash is of importance, because liabilities can only be paid in cash; the longer the time lags involved in the conversion of stock to debtors and debtors to cash, the greater the cash resources required to meet liabilities.

The management of cash is as critical to the firm as the management of stock and debtors. Too little cash, placing the firm in an illiquid position, could result in creditors forcing the firm to cease operations; too much cash will result in funds lying idle, and the overall return on capital employed falling below an acceptable level. The firm must plan its cash requirements on a day-to-day basis; it will do this by means of a cash budget or forecast, which was discussed in more detail in Chapter 14. To produce such a budget the firm must identify the sources and timing of all receipts, and the uses and timing of all payments. The budget will permit the business to estimate any cash surplus or deficit and to determine how best to eliminate these.

References and further reading

ARCHER and D'AMBROSIO (1980), *Business Finance*, Macmillan.
BERENEK (1968), *Working Capital Management*. Prentice-Hall.
GLAUTIER (1971), 'Towards a Reformulation of the Theory of Working Capital', *Journal of Business Finance*, Spring 1971.
HUNT, WILLIAMS and DONALDSON (1973), *Basic Business Finance*. Irwin.
KIRKMAN (1974), 'The Management of Trade Debtors', *Accountancy*, April 1974.

Questions for discussion

1   Define the term 'working capital'. Why does a business need working capital and what may be the consequences of having too much or too little?

2   What are the likely needs for working capital of the following:

(i)   A secondhand car dealer who buys for cash, and sells for cash or on hire purchase through a finance company. He employs two staff on premises which he rents, where he usually has 10–15 cars on display.

(ii)   A small builder who employs two permanent bricklayers, and hires other specialist labour as required. He normally completes two or three houses a year, each of which take 15 months to build.

(iii)   A coach operator who owns three coaches. He employs three drivers, and garages the coaches in a building he owns. He is in the tour and charter business; all tours are paid for in advance, and chartering is done on a monthly contract basis, the accounting being paid a month in arrears.

3   (a)   For each of the following *retail* businesses, make an estimate of what a reasonable rate of stock turnover would be (using sales divided by year end stocks):

(i)   department stores,
(ii)   electrical goods shops,
(iii)   butchers,
(iv)   greengrocers,
(v)   bakeries,
(vi)   tailors.

(b)   What would be the effect, if any, on these ratios of sales on hire purchase and seasonal fluctuations.

(c)   Obtain a copy of the most recent Census of Distribution, and contrast and compare your estimates of turnover with actual results.

4   Two similar retail businesses both had a sales turnover of £300,000 in 1984. An extract from the 1984 balance sheet reveals:

	A	B
	£	£
Stock	20,000	50,000
Debtors	12,000	3,000
Cash	3,000	4,000
	35,000	57,000
Creditors	10,000	17,000
	25,000	**40,000**

What conclusions can you draw from this data?

5   What factors influence the total investment a business must make in stock? How should the business seek to optimize the level of that investment?

6   'The level of investment in stock should not be determined without concurrently considering the level of investment in debtors.' Discuss.

7   Obtain the published accounts for three or four companies in different industries. Ascertain for each:

(a) The total investment in working capital, and its components.
(b) The ratio of current assets to current liabilities.
(c) The rate of stock and debtor turnover.

Comment on your findings.

8   At the beginning of January 1984, Solvency Ltd had a bank balance of £6,000. The budgeted operating statements for the next half-year show the following details:

	January	February	March	April	May	June
	£	£	£	£	£	£
Sales	84,000	96,000	100,000	108,000	108,000	120,000
Manufacturing expenses:						
Materials	34,000	38,000	40,000	42,000	42,000	46,000
Labour	18,000	21,000	21,000	22,000	22,000	23,000
Overhead	12,000	15,000	15,000	16,000	16,000	17,000
	64,000	74,000	76,000	80,000	80,000	86,000
Increase (−) or decrease (+) in stock of finished goods	(−) 2,000	(−) 2,000	(−) 2,000	—	—	(+) 4,000
	62,000	72,000	74,000	80,000	80,000	90,000
Expenditure on:						
Administration	8,000	8,000	8,000	9,000	9,000	9,000
Selling and distribution	6,000	6,000	6,000	7,000	7,000	7,000
Total expenses	76,000	86,000	88,000	96,000	96,000	106,000
Profit	8,000	10,000	12,000	12,000	12,000	14,000

The expense for materials is made up of:

	January	February	March	April	May	June
	£	£	£	£	£	£
Opening stock	4,000	6,000	8,000	8,000	10,000	8,000
Purchases	36,000	40,000	40,000	44,000	40,000	46,000
	40,000	46,000	48,000	52,000	50,000	54,000
Closing stock	6,000	8,000	8,000	10,000	8,000	8,000
	34,000	**38,000**	**40,000**	**42,000**	**42,000**	**46,000**

Materials bought are paid for in the month after delivery. The purchases made in December 1983 amounted to £32,000.

50 per cent of the debtors normally pay their accounts the month after being invoiced, the remainder pay the month after that; e.g. of invoices sent out in December 1983, category I pays in January 1984, category II pays in February 1984. Sales for November 1983 were £88,000 and those for December 1983 were £80,000.

The manufacturing overheads include depreciation at £2,000 per month.

Some of the overheads are paid other than monthly but have been averaged on a monthly basis for the budgeted operating statements. Details are:

	Averaged monthly amount £	Actually payable in (1984)
Manufacturing	600	Jan. £1,800, Apr. £1,800, July £1,800, Oct. £1,800
Administration	400	Apr. £2,400, Oct. £2,400

Apart from these (and depreciation) assume all expenses are paid in the month shown in the budgeted operating statements.

Payment of corporation tax is due in January 1984 in the sum of £30,000, but this will be partly paid by a cheque drawn on the company's building society account for £20,000.

The capital budget provides for payment of £8,000 in March and £16,000 in June, in respect of the purchase of new machinery.

Required:
Prepare a cash budget for the six months ended June 1984.

19 Performance analysis

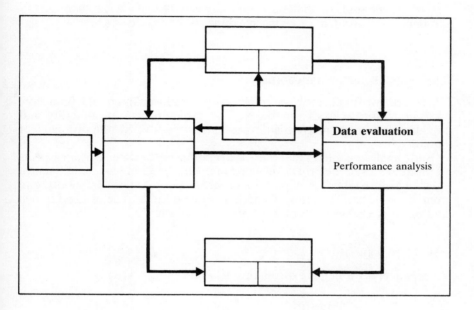

Business objectives

Most human activity is directed towards a particular objective or objectives, and the activity of business is no exception. To achieve a given objective requires two facets: first, the objective must be defined, and, secondly, measurements must be taken *en route* to the objective in order to ensure that it will eventually be attained. Thus for a business to evaluate its performance it must be aware of certain objectives, and have evolved analytical tools by which it can measure the extent to which the objectives have been achieved.

In an earlier chapter we observed that while profit was not the only objective of business activity it was, and is, an extremely important one which will normally be dominant in most situations. Since profit is not synonymous with cash, the firm must also ensure that it has sufficient liquid funds to meet its obligations when they fall due. As a generalization, therefore, the overall objectives of a business are to optimize profits and,

427

at the same time, maintain a satisfactory financial position. With the objectives stated we must now introduce analytical tools which will enable us to interpret profitability and liquidity. The problem encountered in Chapter 15 is in evidence again, namely, that there is no point in measuring anything unless we can ascribe meaning to the resulting measurement. For example, we may measure a firm's profit, but unless we have some basis of comparison we have no means of knowing whether the profit is good, bad or indifferent.

In the first part of this chapter we will concentrate our attention on describing the tools of analysis; with these established we can then turn to the important problem of giving meaning to the results.

The tools of performance analysis

There are two main tools in common use: ratio analysis and fund flow analysis. Ratio analysis can be used to evaluate both profitability and liquidity; fund flow analysis is directed primarily towards the problems of liquidity.

Ratio analysis assumes that there is a relationship between certain aspects of the activities of the firm as revealed in the income statement and balance sheet which establishes a pattern of behaviour. A ratio is simply one number expressed in terms of another. For example, if sales are £10,000 and profit is £1,000, then ratio of profit to sales is

$$\frac{1,000}{10,000} \text{ or } \frac{1}{10}$$

Alternatively, we might express this as a percentage, viz.:

$$\frac{1,000}{10,000} \times 100 = 10\%$$

Ratio analysis involves the careful selection of those ratios which will provide an insight into the performance of business. It is no substitute for management, but it can be a very considerable aid to management.

Tests of profitability

The broadest measure of overall performance is the ratio of net profit to net capital employed, the so-called 'return on investment'. For this purpose, net profit will be before any interest on loan capital or bank loan and either before or after tax, and net capital will include all borrowed money:

$$\text{Return on capital employed} = \frac{\text{Profit (before interest)}}{\text{Net capital employed}} \%$$

The reason for this is that both numerator and denominator must be composed of the same elements. For example, consider a company which has the following capital structure:

	£
Ordinary shares and reserves	20,000
10% Debentures	50,000
Net Capital Employed	70,000

If the company earns a net profit of £10,000, this is *after* the deduction of debenture interest, so that the total capital of 70,000 has earned

$$10,000 + (10\% \times 50,000) = 15,000$$

and the return on capital is

$$\frac{15,000}{70,000} = \textbf{21.4\%}$$

Further complications can arise; should bank overdrafts be included as part of the long-term capital, or a proportion of the creditors (since any business will always have a minimum base of creditors), or corporation tax owing (since some tax will always be owed)? These complications often lead some analysts to eschew the use of the 'ambiguous' net capital, and to use the return on tangible net assets as an overall measure of performance, i.e.

$$\frac{\text{Net profit (before or after tax)}}{\text{Tangible assets}}$$

Whatever the method, the percentage return can vary from year to year because of a change in either profit, or capital employed, or both. Critical to any firm's performance, is its sales; sales generate profit, and capital is employed in the various assets to generate sales. Sales, therefore, provide an analytical link between profit and capital employed.

For example, assume a firm makes a profit of £10,000 on a capital employed of £100,000 with sales of £80,000. The return on capital is

$$\frac{10,000}{100,000} \times 100 = 10\%$$

The ratio of net profit to sales is

$$\frac{10,000}{80,000} \times 100 = 12\tfrac{1}{2}\%$$

Net capital is merely another way of expressing the sum of assets less current liabilities. The net assets have generated £80,000 of sales, or have 'turned over' 80,000/100,000 = 0.8 times in the year. Linking the last two ratios we get

$$12\tfrac{1}{2}\% \times 0.8 = 10\%$$

or

$$\frac{\text{Net profit}}{\text{Sales}} \times \frac{\text{Sales}}{\text{Net capital (assets)}} = \text{Return on capital employed}$$

At first sight it may appear that this relationship is tautologous, for if we cancel out the sales value (which must be the same for the same business), the primary ratio must emerge. Thus

$$\frac{\text{Net profit}}{\text{Sales}} \times \frac{\text{Sales}}{\text{Net capital (assets)}} = \frac{\text{Net profit}}{\text{Net capital (assets)}}$$

However, the arithmetic hides a very important policy decision. We may compare, for example, a supermarket (A) with a small local retailer (B). At first, their performance may look similar, viz.:

$$\text{A: } \frac{\text{Net profit}}{\text{Net capital}} = \frac{£100}{1,000} = 10\%$$

$$\text{B: } \frac{\text{Net profit}}{\text{Net capital}} = \frac{£100}{1,000} = 10\%$$

The two businesses may have reached this position by totally different means. The supermarket achieves its overall return by keeping its prices low, thus achieving a very small margin of profit on each £1 of sales, and obtaining a large volume of business. The local retailer may seek a higher return per £1 of sales, but, because of the higher prices, will achieve a lower volume of business. Thus

$$\frac{\text{Net profit}}{\text{Sales}} \times \frac{\text{Sales}}{\text{Net capital}} = \frac{\text{Net profit}}{\text{Net capital}}$$

$$\text{A: } \frac{100}{4,000} \times \frac{4,000}{1,000}$$

or

$$2.5\% \quad \times \quad 4 \quad = \quad 10\%$$

$$\text{B: } \frac{100}{2,000} \times \frac{2,000}{1,000}$$

or

$$5\% \quad \times \quad 2 \quad = \quad 10\%$$

Businesses, therefore, have a most important policy decision to make, namely, to decide whether to seek lower sales margins in the hope that this will attract more customers and so, in the end, boost the return on capital.

This relationship opens the door to further analysis. We can explore the various expenses which were deducted from sales to establish the net profit. Usually, these expenses are expressed as a percentage of sales; thus working from the income statement, we recast it in terms of percentages.

Income Statement for the period ended 31 December 1984

	£	£	%	%
Sales		400,000		100
Less: Cost of sales		250,000		62.5
Gross Profit		150,000		37.5
Administration	32,000		8	
Selling	28,000		7	
		60,000	—	15
Net Profit		90,000		22.5
Tax		34,000		8.5
Net Profit after tax		**56,000**		**14.0**

The gross percentage indicates the average mark up on the products sold; the net profit percentage is a measure of overall profitability of sales. The net profit percentage is often regarded as the most important single measure of a firm's performance, but this is not so, for as we have seen it does not reflect the amount of investment utilized in earning the profit. For example, a high net profit percentage of, say, 50 per cent may appear extremely satisfactory, but if the turnover rate of net assets to sales is very low, say, 0.1, the return on capital employed would be only $50 \times 0.1 = 5\%$.

Because the sales/net assets relationship is so important, we can further explore the component parts of this ratio. Particularly critical is the way in which the firm employs its assets; each asset may be described in terms of turnover (i.e. sales/asset ratio) or in terms of sales days—the number of days it takes to generate sufficient sales to equal the value of the asset. This ratio is calculated by inverting the sales/asset ratio and multiplying by 365. We can analyse the use of assets as in the example below:

Astral Manufacturing Co. Ltd
Sales = £200,000

	£	£	Sales/asset ratio (rate of turnover)		Sales days	
Fixed assets	£	£				
Land and buildings	20,000		10.0		36.5	
Plant	40,000		5.0	3.33	73.0	
		60,000				109.5
Current assets						
Stock	50,000		4.0		91.3	
Debtors	25,000		8.0		45.6	
Cash	15,000		13.33	2.2	27.6	
		90,000				164.5
		£150,000		1.33		274

The sales/asset ratio or sales days ratio are only different ways of saying the same thing, and the only reason for using one of them in preference to another is that it conveys the significance of the ratio more easily. For example, it is probably more easily understood to say that debtors are being given an average of 45.6 days credit, rather than to say that the sales/debtors ratio is 8/1.

In the calculation of balance sheet ratios, certain limitations have to be borne in mind:

(1) The balance sheet represents the position of the firm at one moment in time; it may not be representative of the average position. For example, if the firm has strong seasonal sales patterns, the stock, the debtors and the cash may tend to fluctuate (with a time lag) in sympathy. If the balance sheet is prepared before the strong seasonal upsurge in sales, stocks will be high, and debtors and cash low; any ratios calculated at this point in time do not really represent the business. What is required is a set of *average* stock, debtors and cash balances. If the analysis is being conducted from outside of the firm, such detailed data is not normally available, however, and the analyst has to make do with second best. Nevertheless, if the ratios change substantially from year to year, there is a useful indication of a change in the firm's progress.

(2) The ratio of stock to sales, which is often used to provide an indication of average stock levels, is not strictly correct, since it is comparing sales at output prices with stock at input prices. If the information is available then it is more logical to relate stock to cost of sales. Provided profit margins remain constant, however, sale/stock ratios can be usefully compared over several years.

In the example above, if we assume that the cost of sales was £150,000 the rate of stock turnover is given by

$$\frac{\text{Cost of sales}}{\text{Stock}}$$

$$= \frac{150,000}{50,000}$$

$$= 3 \text{ times}$$

or 4 months stock-holding

(3) The sales/debtor ratio, which provides a measure of the average credit period, may be distorted by cash sales; credit sales will provide a better measurement if available.

It is sometimes useful to remember these ratios as a type of decision tree, all emanating from the overall measure of performance—the return on capital employed:

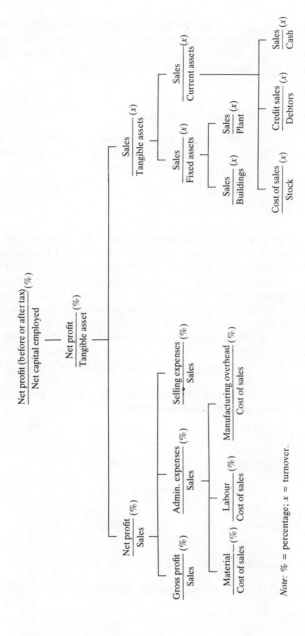

Relationship between financial ratios

The chart on page 433 can be further extended to provide more and more detailed analysis—for example, material can be sub-analysed into its different types—but analysis should only proceed so far as it will or is likely to produce information useful to management.

Profitability and capital structure

The overall measurement of performance was stated to be the ratio of profit to capital employed. In our exploration of this fundamental ratio we have progressed by expanding the formula to

$$\frac{\text{Net profit}}{\text{Sales}} \times \frac{\text{Sales}}{\text{Net assets}}$$

This enabled us to investigate the profitability of sales, and the profitable employment of the different types of assets. Any firm, however, not only has to decide how to allocate its resources among the different assets, but also has to decide how best to finance its operations. In the instance of the limited company, long-term finance can be provided by any combination of ordinary and preference shares and debentures (*see* Chapter 10). From the point of view of the equity (ordinary) shareholder, there is little point in the company borrowing money at fixed rates of interest and dividend unless profits earned are in excess of those fixed rates. Ratio analysis of the capital structure can indicate whether there is a gain or loss from such borrowing.

Consider, for example, the following data which reveals the profit and capital structure of a limited company:

AB Ltd
Income and Appropriation for the year ended 31 December 1984

	£
Net profit before tax	500,000
Taxation provision	200,000
Net profit after tax	300,000
Undistributed profit 1.1.83	350,000
Profit available for distribution	**£650,000**
Proposed dividends	£
10% final ordinary	100,000
5% preference	10,000
Undistributed profit 31.12.84	540,000
	£650,000

Balance Sheet as at 31 December 1984

	£	£
Authorized and issued share capital		
1,000,000 £1 ordinary	1,000,000	
200,000 5% preference	200,000	
		1,200,000
Capital reserve		
Share premium		50,000
Revenue reserves		
General reserve	110,000	
Undistributed profit	540,000	
		650,000
Loan capital		
600,000 4% debentures		600,000
Net Capital Employed		**2,500,000**

Ratio analysis yields the following results:

		£	%
(1)	Return on capital employed $\dfrac{\text{Profit before interest and tax}}{\text{Net capital employed}}$	$\dfrac{524,000^1}{2,500,000}$	20.96
(2)	Gain from using fixed interest loan capital $(3 - 1)$		+ 5.34
(3)	$\dfrac{\text{Profit after interest and before tax}}{\text{Shareholder's funds}}$	$\dfrac{500,000}{1,900,000}$	26.30
(4)	$\dfrac{\text{Tax}}{\text{Shareholders' funds}}$	$\dfrac{200,000}{1,900,000}$	− 10.50
(5)	$\dfrac{\text{Profit after interest and tax}}{\text{Shareholders' funds}}$	$\dfrac{300,000}{1,900,000}$	15.80
(6)	Gain from using fixed dividends preference shares $(7 - 5)$		+ 1.30
(7)	Return on equity funds $\dfrac{\text{Profit after interest and tax less preference dividend}}{\text{Equity funds}}$	$\dfrac{290,000}{1,700,000}$	
			17.10

The analysis reveals that the effect of the fixed interest/dividend funds is beneficial to the ordinary shareholder, as he gains both from the employment of loan capital and from preference shares.

Tests of liquidity

Liquidity refers to the ability of the firm to meet its current obligations when they become due. Current obligations are recorded as current lia-

1   Since debenture interest is $4\% \times 600,000 = £24,000$.

bilities, which must presumably be met from current assets, unless the productive capacity of the business in the form of fixed assets is to be eroded.

The current ratio is the most commonly used of all balance sheet ratios. It is computed as

$$\frac{\text{Current assets}}{\text{Current liabilities}}$$

Unless there are exceptional circumstances, that ratio must be greater than $1:1$ in the long run. If this were not so, and creditors pressed for payment, some fixed assets would have to be sold, eroding productive capacity (unless, of course, some loan could be negotiated).

Consideration of the proportion of various types of current assets is also necessary. A ratio such as

$$\frac{\text{Current assets}}{\text{Current liabilities}} = \frac{£30,000}{£15,000} = 2 \text{ to } 1$$

may appear satisfactory, but if the structure of the current assets was

Stock	22,000
Debtors	7,500
Cash	500
	£30,000

the situation would be difficult, for it takes time to turn stock into cash. As a consequence, the so-called acid-test is often used:

$$\frac{\text{Quick assets}}{\text{Current liabilities}}$$

where quick assets are those which are immediately available (or very nearly so) to meet current obligations. In practice, this normally requires the exclusion of stock, so in our example the acid-test ratio is

$$\frac{8,000}{15,000} = 0.54 \text{ to } 1$$

Investment ratios

Quite apart from the important measurements of profitability and liquidity outlined above, certain other ratios are of use to the investor.

(1)   Dividend yield

$$\frac{\text{Par value} \times \text{Dividend \%}}{\text{Market value}}$$

The dividend yield is an important measure (*see* Chapter 10) because it indicates to a potential investor what rate of return he can expect on his investment.

(2) Ordinary dividend cover

$$\frac{\text{Profit after tax } - \text{ Preference dividend (gross)}}{\text{Amount of gross dividend on ordinary shares}}$$

The dividend cover provides a measure of the security of the dividend; the higher the cover, the more likely the company is to able to maintain its dividends, and, at the same time, internally reinvest funds for the benefit of the ordinary shareholder.

(3) Earnings per share

$$\frac{\text{Profit after tax } - \text{ Preference dividend (gross)}}{\text{Number of ordinary shares issued}}$$

The market value of an ordinary share is closely related to earnings per share, and this ratio is often used as a predictor of the future value of the ordinary shares. There are, in practice, considerable difficulties in using this ratio for any purposes of inter-company comparison, in part because of the difficulties of establishing comparable treatment of taxation in the accounts.

(4) Price–earnings ratio

There is clearly a connection between the dividends paid and the market price of the share; this as we have seen is expressed by the yield. Most, if not all, companies, however, do not distribute all profits by way of dividend. Earnings, after tax and preference dividends, benefit the ordinary shareholder partly through providing their dividend, and partly through retention to promote future growth. The price–earnings ratio (P/E ratio) is a measure of the relationship between earnings and market price. It is given by

$$P/E = \frac{\text{Market price per share}}{\text{Earnings per share}}$$

The inversion of this ratio provides the capitalization rate, the rate at which the market is capitalizing the value of current earnings:

$$\text{Capitalization rate} = \frac{\text{Earnings per share}}{\text{Market price per share}} \times 100$$

Cash flow analysis

Cash flow analysis has found increasing popularity in America, and has gained much ground in this country. A measure of its increased popularity is the fact that an Accounting Standard—*Statements of Source and Application of Funds*—took effect on 1 January 1976. The analysis can be used in two ways: first, it is employed as a historical tool, when it seeks to answer such questions as, 'from where did the funds (cash) come, and to where did the funds (cash) go?'; secondly, it may be used as a forecasting tool when it closely resembles the cash budget described in Chapter 16. Our discussion here will be confined to the historical sphere.

We have constantly reiterated that profit is not necessarily synonymous with cash, but it is often confusing for the layman to find that a firm which makes a substantial profit can also be short of cash and may even be running an overdraft. The reason for this is that accounting measures income according to the accrual concept—matching revenues and expenses, and not receipts and expenditures. Fund flow analysis seeks to recast the income statement and balance sheet as prepared in accordance with accounting postulates, and describe the events of an accounting period in terms of sources of additional funds, and the uses to which these were put. The Accounting Standard expresses it thus: 'A funds statement should show the sources from which funds have flowed into the company and the way in which they have been used. It should show clearly the funds generated or absorbed by the operations of the business and the manner in which any resulting surplus of liquid assets has been applied or any deficiency of such assets has been financed, distinguishing the long term from the short term. The statement should distinguish the use of funds for the purchase of new fixed assets from funds used in increasing the working capital of the company.'

To reconstruct the flow of funds, three basic sets of information must be available: balance sheets at the beginning and end of the period under review, and an income statement linking the two balances sheets. In Chapter 2 we introduced the basic balance sheet relationship of Assets = Liabilities, indicating that the assets represented use of funds, and liabilities sources of funds. It follows, therefore, that as between two balance sheet dates, the change in assets must equal the change in liabilities:

$$\Delta A = \Delta L \text{ (between time } T_0 \text{ and } T_1)$$

The change can be either an increase in both, or a decrease in both. If an increase in assets is a use of funds, then a decrease in assets must provide a source; conversely, an increase in liabilities is a source of fund, and a decrease, a use. For example, the sale of equipment will reduce the asset of plant thus providing a source of cash, and a reduction in creditors means that cash has been used to pay them. Summarizing this then, we have

$$\text{Change in sources} = \text{Change in uses}$$

or

$$\frac{\text{Increase in liabilities}}{+ \text{ Decrease in assets}} = \frac{\text{Increase in assets}}{+ \text{ Decrease in liabilities}}$$

Since increases in liabilities and decreases in assets are both credits, and increases in assets and decreases in liabilities are both debits, the above equation merely reflects the duality postulate that debits must equal credits.

With this in mind, we can now turn to a series of examples which demonstrate, step by step, the fund flow analysis procedure.

Example 1
X Co. Ltd

	Balance sheets		Analysis of change	
	1983	1984	Source	Use
Ordinary shares	30,000	35,000	5,000	—
Retained profit	12,500	14,200	1,700	—
Creditors	9,500	6,300	—	3,200
	£52,000	**55,500**		
Land and buildings	11,400	11,400	—	—
Equipment	19,300	20,300	—	1,000
Stock	12,100	11,500	600	—
Debtors	4,200	11,300	—	7,100
Cash	5,000	1,000	4,000	—
	£52,000	**55,500**	**11,300**	**11,300**

Income Statement (1983) Profit **£1,700**

The analysis reveals clearly why, although a profit of £1,700 was made, cash has fallen by £4,000—the prime cause is the startling increase in debtors. We can formally prepare the cash flow statement:

X Co. Ltd
Cash Flow Statement

Sources:	£	£
During the year the company		
(1) Issued additional shares		5,000
(2) Reduced stock by		600
(3) Earned an operating revenue		1,700
Thus providing funds of		7,300
Uses:		
These were applied in		
(4) Acquiring additional equipment	1,000	
(5) Providing additional credit to debtors	7,100	
(6) Reducing creditors by	3,200	
		11,300
Leaving a deficit of		**£4,000**
to be provided by reducing cash.		

Our first example assumes that the profit of £1,700 was all equated by cash. Obviously the assumption is unreal; in particular, certain non-cash expenses such as depreciation will have been deducted in arriving at the profit. If we wish to establish the net cash flow (rather than the income flow) arising from operations, we must add back such expenses to the accounting profit.

Example 2

X Co. Ltd

	Balance sheets		Analysis of Change		Adjustments
	1983	1984	Source	Use	
Ordinary shares	30,000	35,000	5,000	—	
Retained profit	12,500	14,200	1,700	—	+900
Creditors	9,500	6,300	—	3,200	
	£52,000	55,500			
Land and buildings (cost)	11,400	11,400	—	—	
Equipment (cost)	27,800	29,700	—	1,900	
Less: Depreciation	(8,500)	(9,400)	900	—	−900
Stock	12,100	11,500	600	—	
Debtors	4,200	11,300	—	7,100	
Cash	5,000	1,000	4,000	—	
	£52,000	55,500	12,200	12,200	—

Income Statement (1984)

	£	£
Sales		85,000
Less: Cost of sales		65,000
Gross Profit		20,000
Administration	6,300	
Depreciation	900	
Selling	11,100	
		18,300
Net Profit		**£1,700**

In the first analysis of change, the profit is treated as cash flow, and the depreciation as an additional source. Since depreciation is not a cash source, and operation profit understates cash inflow by the amount of depreciation, an adjustment is made in the final column. Notice that adjustments must *always* sum to zero. Recasting our source and application statement we have the following result:

X Co. Ltd

Cash Flow Statement

	£	£
Sources:		
During the year the company		
(1) Issued additional shares		5,000
(2) Reduced stock by		600
(3) Received a net cash inflow from operations		2,600
Thus providing funds of		8,200
These were applied in		
(4) Acquiring additional equipment	1,900	
(5) Increasing debtors by	7,100	
(6) Reducing creditors by	3,200	
		12,200
Leaving a deficit of		**£4,000**
to be financed by a reduction in cash		

This example illustrates the basic procedure which can be followed even in the most complex situations. Stage one is the arithmetic operation of identifying balance sheet changes without recourse to any additional information which may be available; the totals of changes of uses and sources must *always* agree. Stage two is incorporating any additional information which necessitates adjustment to the apparent cash flow as revealed by the balance sheet analysis. The third example (below) introduces different types of adjustment.

Example 3

Bloomer Co. Ltd

	Balance sheets		Analysis of change	
	1983	1984	Source	Use
Ordinary shares	107,000	127,000	20,000	—
Share premium	—	5,000	5,000	—
Revenue reserves	93,500	109,600	16,100	—
Loan capital	20,000	4,000	—	16,000
Taxation	7,000	6,000	—	1,000
Creditors	24,000	16,000	—	8,000
Dividend proposed	10,700	12,700	2,000	—
	£262,200	**280,300**		

(*continued*)

Bloomer Co. Ltd *(continued)*

	Balance sheets		*Analysis of Change*	
	1983	1984	Source	Use
Buildings (cost)	55,700	82,700	—	27,000
Plant (cost)	87,000	92,000	—	5,000
Depreciation	(21,000)	(25,000)	4,000	—
Vans (cost)	5,000	6,000	—	1,000
Depreciation	(1,600)	(2,400)	800	—
Investments (cost)	25,800	30,200	—	4,400
Stock	41,300	59,800	—	18,500
Debtors	20,000	27,000	—	7,000
Cash	50,000	10,000	40,000	—
	£262,200	280,300	87,900	87,900

Income Statement (1983)

	£	£
Sales		280,000
Less: Cost of sales		210,000
Gross Profit		70,000
Profit on debenture redemption		500
		70,500
Depreciation: Plant	4,000	
Vans	800	
Loss on sale of plant	2,000	
Administration	14,600	
Selling	12,100	
Finance	2,200	
		35,700
Net Profit		34,800
Tax provision		6,000
Net Profit after Tax		28,800
Unappropriated profit (1.1.84)		93,500
Profit available for distribution		£122,300
Dividend proposed:		
10% final ordinary		12,700
Unappropriated profit		109,600
		£122,300

Note: The loss on sale of plant arose because plant costing £9,000 (depreciation accumulated £6,000) was sold for £1,000.

The following adjustments are necessary:

		£	£
(1)	Balance of plant 1.1.84		87,000
	Less: Sales at cost		9,000
			78,000
	Balance of plant 31.12.84		92,000
	Purchase during year		**£14,000**
(2)	Balance of plant depreciation 1.1.84		21,000
	Less: Depreciation of plant sold		6,000
			15,000
	Balance of plant depreciation 31.12.84		25,000
	Depreciation provided during year		**£10,000**
(3)	Non-cash expense, revenue and appropriation is added back to the accounting unappropriated profit:		
	Balance per balance sheet 31.12.84		109,600
	Add: Dividend proposed	12,700	
	Tax provision	6,000	
	Loss on plant	2,000	
	Depreciation—plant (see above)	10,000	
	—vans	800	
			31,500
			141,100
	Less: Profit on debentures		500
			140,600
	Less: Balance at 1.1.84		93,500
	Net operating receipts		**£47,100**

The cash flow statement will now appear as follows:

Bloomer Co. Ltd
Cash Flow Statement

Sources:	£	£
During the year Bloomer Co.		
(1) Issued new shares		25,000
(2) Sold plant		1,000
(3) Earned net operating receipts		47,100
Providing funds of		73,100

Cash Flow Statement (*continued*)

	£	£
Uses:		
These funds were applied in		
(1) Buying additional plant	14,000	
(2) Redeeming debentures	15,500	
(3) Buildings	27,000	
(4) Vans	1,000	
(5) Paying tax	7,000	
(6) Reducing creditors	8,000	
(7) Paying dividends	10,700	
(8) Acquiring new investments	4,400	
(9) Increasing investment		
—in stock	18,500	
—and debtors	7,000	
		113,100
Requiring a reduction in cash of		**£40,000**

The Appendix to the Accounting Standard uses a slightly different format which highlights the effect on working capital, and is called a fund flow statement, viz.:

Source of funds	£	£
Net operating receipts		47,100
Funds from other sources:		
Sale of plant	1,000	
Issue of shares for cash	25,000	26,000
		73,100
Application of funds		
Purchase of fixed assets	42,000	
Redemption of debentures	15,500	
Tax paid	7,000	
Dividends paid	10,700	75,200
		(2,100)
Increase/decrease in working capital		
Increase in stock	18,500	
Increase in debtors	7,000	
Decrease in creditors	8,000	
Movement in net liquid funds:		
Decrease in cash (40,000)		
Short-term investments 4,400	(35,600)	**(2,100)**

The foregoing description of fund flow analysis has assumed that the analyst has access to detailed records, but detailed information about such events as sale of plant is not normally available to the outsider. A good analyst, however, can often do a fairly accurate job of deducing what probably took place. Fund flow analysis, therefore, is a useful managerial tool in so far as it can help to highlight reasons for changes in the liquidity of the firm.

Bases for comparison

To become meaningful, all data requires comparison. To state that profit is £100,000, or that return on capital is 9 per cent, is not of itself meaningful. We must have a yardstick by which we can judge whether the ratios calculated are good, bad or indifferent. There are three types of yardstick or standards against which actual performance may be evaluated: a budget, a past performance, other firms. We have considered the question of budgets in Chapter 16, so here we will consider past performance and other firms as possible bases for comparison.

(1) Past performance

The accounts for Bartor Ltd for 1983 and 1984 are as follows:

	1983 £'000	1983 £'000	1984 £'000	1984 £'000
Credit sales		50		80
Cost of sales		40		66
Gross profit		10		14
Administration	5		6	
Selling	2	7	2	8
Net profit		3		6
Dividends proposed		2		5
Unappropriated profit for year		£1		£1

Balance Sheets

	1983 £'000	1983 £'000	1984 £'000	1984 £'000
Ordinary shares		20		50
Reserves		13		14
Net capital employed		£33		£64

Balance Sheets (*continued*)

	1983		1984	
	£'000	£'000	£'000	£'000
Buildings	5		15	
Plant	10		23	
		15		38
Stock	8		14	
Debtors	5		12	
Cash	12		9	
		25		35
		40		73
Less:				
Creditors	(5)		(4)	
Dividends	(2)		(5)	
		(7)		(9)
		£33		**£64**

From the accounts, we may derive the important ratios:

	Ratio		1983	1984
(1)	$\dfrac{\text{Net profit}}{\text{Net capital employed}}$	%	9.1	9.4
(1a)	$\dfrac{\text{Net profit}}{\text{Tangible assets}}$	%	7.5	8.3
(2)	$\dfrac{\text{Net profit}}{\text{Sales}}$	%	6.0	7.5
(3)	$\dfrac{\text{Cost of sales}}{\text{Sales}}$	%	80.0	82.5
(3a)	$\dfrac{\text{Gross profit}}{\text{Sales}}$	%	20.0	17.5
(4)	$\dfrac{\text{Administration}}{\text{Sales}}$	%	10.0	7.5
(5)	$\dfrac{\text{Selling expenses}}{\text{Sales}}$	%	4.0	2.5
(6)	$\dfrac{\text{Credit sales}}{\text{Tangible assets}}$	Turnover	1.25	1.10
(7)	$\dfrac{\text{Sales}}{\text{Fixed assets}}$	Turnover	3.33	2.10
(8)	$\dfrac{\text{Cost of sales}}{\text{Stock}}$	Days	73	77
(9)	$\dfrac{\text{Credit sales}}{\text{Debtors}}$	Days	36	55
(10)	$\dfrac{\text{Sales}}{\text{Cash}}$	Days	88	41

	Ratio		1983	1984
(11)	$\dfrac{\text{Current assets}}{\text{Current liabilities}}$		3.6 : 1	3.9 : 1
(12)	$\dfrac{\text{Quick assets}}{\text{Current liabilities}}$		2.4 : 1	2.3 : 1
(13)	Dividend rate		10%	10%
(14)	Dividend cover	Times	1.5	1.2

On the basis of these ratios, we may offer the following observations:

(1) Although profits have doubled (from £3,000 to £6,000), the rate of return on capital has only risen marginally from 9.1 per cent to 9.4 per cent.

(2) The company has improved its profitability on each £1 of sales from 6p to 7½p. This, however, has been achieved by more efficient general and sales administration—the cost of those functions has fallen by 4 per cent relative to total sales in the period, but these savings were partially offset by a reduction in the gross profit margin from 20 per cent to 17.5 per cent.

(3) The company's policy regarding profitability of sales and use of assets seems to have changed, viz.:

$$\frac{\text{NP}}{\text{S}} \times \frac{\text{S}}{\text{TA}} = \frac{\text{NP}}{\text{TA}}$$

1978   6% × 1.25   = 7.5%

1979 7.5% × 1.1   = 8.3%

The company is making less efficient use of its assets, but this may be because the substantial additional investment in fixed assets (see (4) below) of £23,000 net is not yet fully operational.

(4) The company is using its fixed resources much less efficiently—the turnover ratio is down from 3.3 to 2.1 times per year, although it may be that the new assets were acquired too late in the year to have become fully utilized.

(5) Stock control has marginally worsened; there are now 77 days of stock on hand, as opposed to 73 in 1983. The absolute level of stockholding, viz. 11 weeks, may be rather too high for the type of business.

(6) Debtors are now being allowed 8 weeks to pay compared with 5 weeks in 1983. This increase means that the company has tied up an additional £4,000 of funds in debtors during the year compared with what it would have been if the same control had been exercised.

(7) The current ratio is falling within an acceptable band (between 2 : 1 and 5 : 1 is normally regarded as reasonable), although the acid-test ratio would suggest that the company is rather too liquid (the 'normal' range is between 1 : 1 and 2 : 1), but this seems to be primarily caused by the extension of credit to debtors. If the debtors were restored *pro*

rata to their 1983 level, viz. £8,000, this would provide a cash balance of £13,000—which at 18 per cent of the tangible assets seems a rather high proportion of 'idle' funds to leave in the company, unless the management have further investment plans.

(8) Dividends have remained constant during the year, in spite of a £30,000 increase in issued capital. Whilst this is laudable, the dividend cover has fallen from 1.5 to 1.2 which must give rise to some concern for the future security of dividends.

(9) The company, therefore, needs to tighten its debtor and stock control, restore the effective use of its fixed resources, obtain a better gross (and, therefore, net) margin on sales, and give careful consideration as to the best means of employing its liquid resources.

Comparison with past performance can clearly indicate whether the firm is doing 'better' or 'worse' than in the past, but it still cannot demonstrate whether the performance is acceptable. If a firm increases its return on investment from 2 per cent to 3 per cent, it is still not doing very well.

(2)   Inter-firm comparison

An external yardstick is provided by comparing the performance of firms similar in size in the same sector of industry. There are often serious problems of compatibility which arise because of differing accounting practices and environmental circumstances. Nevertheless a good analyst can make some allowance for these differences and obtain a reasonable external check on performance.

In this country, the Centre for Inter Firm Comparisons provides a valuable service for many sectors of industry in collecting and relating comparative information for subscribing firms.

Problems of analysis and comparisons

The mechanics of analysis are relatively straightforward; the difficulties arise in the interpretation of the results. A number of factors create difficulties in any performance analysis situation, and these must be borne in mind when attempting to interpret the findings.

(1)   The meaning of ratio changes

In analysing a situation, an attempt is being made to establish whether performance has improved, but in many business situations it is difficult to tell whether a higher ratio represents a better performance than a lower ratio. For example, a higher net profit percentage is normally better than a low one, but a too high ratio may indicate that the firm has a considerable demand for its products even at a high price, and that if the price were lowered and sales increased, the total return on investment would improve even if the net profit ratio dropped.

Or again, a high current ratio is not necessarily better than a low one.

Consider the following statement of current assets and current liabilities:

	£	£
Current assets		
Stock	9,000	
Debtors	7,000	
Cash	4,000	
		20,000
Less: Current liabilities—creditors		5,000
Net Working Capital		**£15,000**

The current ratio is £20,000 to £5,000 or 4:1. The firm could now pay off it creditors by utilizing its cash and taking a bank overdraft of £1,000. Thus

	£	£
Current assets		
Stock	9,000	
Debtors	7,000	
		16,000
Less: Current liabilities—overdraft		1,000
Net Working Capital		**£15,000**

The current ratio has increased to 16:1; yet one could hardly say that a firm without any cash was in a 'better' position.

Many ratios can usefully be considered as a quality range, within which performance is satisfactory. If the ratios move outside of this range—whether below or above—there is an indication of an unsatisfactory situation which needs careful consideration.

(2)   Money measurement

As we have observed, accounting assumes that money values are stable. This assumption can cause particular difficulties in ratios which include assets at historical cost less depreciation. A firm which has acquired its assets some years ago when prices were lower, or had almost completely depreciated them, would have much smaller net money capital than a similar firm which had acquired its assets more recently. To achieve meaningful ratios and comparisons it is essential, wherever possible, to make adjustments to the changing price levels (see Chapter 12).

(3)   Consistency

Changes in accounting practice within a company can lead to changes in ratios which are the function of the practice rather than performance. The problem of consistency is even more acute when making inter-firm comparisons, for accounting terms are by no means precisely defined, and there is considerable diversity as to how income and value should be measured. For a comparison to be valid, like must be compared with like.

(4)   Short run changes

Earlier on in this chapter, we indicated that the balance sheet, representing one moment in time, may not reflect the average or typical situation. Many retail stores, for example, prepare their accounts to 31 January; Christmas stocks have been sold out, debtors have settled their accounts, and the spring stocks have not started to arrive. Current assets and current liabilities therefore are likely to be considerably lower than at any other time in the year.

Summary

Performance analysis is no substitute for management, but it can be a very considerable aid to management. Ratios, properly selected, can reveal much about the financial behaviour of the firm. Ratio or fund flow analyses cannot in themselves provide answers, but they highlight the areas in which further investigation is necessary as a prelude to management action.

References and further reading

ACCOUNTING STANDARDS COMMITTEE (1975), *Statements of Source and Application of Funds.*
BEAVER (1966), 'Financial Ratios as Predictors of Failure', *Journal of Finance.*
BEVAN (1969), *The Use of Ratios in the Study of Business Fluctuations and Trends.* Institute of Chartered Accountants.
BUCKLEY (1975), 'Company Liquidity', *Accountancy,* February 1975.
ELAM (1975), 'Predictive Ability of Financial Ratios', *Accounting Review,* January 1975.
FITZGERALD (1972), *Analyses and Interpretation of Financial Ratios.* Butterworths.
HOFSTEDT (1972), 'Some Behavioural Parameters of Financial Analysis', *Accounting Review,* October 1972.
HOPWOOD (1972), 'An Empirical Study of the Role of Accounting Data in Performance Evaluation', *Empirical Research in Accounting.*
KIRKMAN (1973), 'Function and Future of Liquidity Ratios', *Accountancy,* May 1973.

Questions for discussion

1   'Ratio analysis is an aid but not a substitute for management.' Discuss.

2   Squeezie owns a retail shop and has recently asked you to prepare his accounts. From his records you are able to prepare the following trading account for the year ended 31 December 1984 and to compare it with the account for the previous year, prepared by Squeezie himself:

	1984		1983	
	£	£	£	£
Sales		176,000		150,000
Cost of goods sold				
Opening stock	30,000		10,000	
Purchases	142,000		120,000	
	172,000		130,000	
Less: Closing stock	40,000	132,000	30,000	100,000
Gross Profit		**44,000**		**50,000**

In explaining the reason for the fall in gross profit, Squeezie informs you that on 1 January 1984 the cost of goods from his suppliers was increased by 20 per cent, but because of competition he could increase his selling prices by only 10 per cent from that date.

Required:

(a) Outline the significance of the 'gross profit percentage' in examining a trading account.
(b) Work out whether the explanation given by Squeezie would fully account for the decrease in the gross profit.
(c) Give four other possible reasons for the decrease in the gross profit.

3   A, B and C are three companies in the same industrial sector:

Capital employed:	A (£)		B (£)		C (£)	
Issued £1 ordinary shares	70,000		40,000		100,000	
Retained profits	60,000		40,000		20,000	
	130,000		80,000		120,000	
10% debentures	10,000		60,000		—	
	140,000		**140,000**		**120,000**	
Represented by:						
Fixed assets						
(at cost less depn.)		52,000		111,000		69,000
Current assets						
Stock	48,000		66,000		64,000	
Debtors	30,000		30,000		80,000	
Cash	42,000	120,000	—	96,000	1,000	145,000
		172,000		207,000		214,000

		A (£)		B (£)		C (£)
Less: Current liabilities:						
Overdraft	—		16,000		—	
Creditors	25,000		45,000		64,000	
Proposed dividends	7,000	(32,000)	6,000	(67,000)	30,000	(94,000)
		140,000		**140,000**		**120,000**
Average stock		50,000		72,000		60,000
Sales (credit)		250,000		240,000		800,000
Gross profit		50,000		60,000		80,000
Net profit (after interest)		30,000		30,000		30,000
Overdraft interest		—		1,000		—

Required:

Write a report comparing the financial performance of the three companies.

4   X Ltd was incorporated at the beginning of 1975 and has produced gradually improving results since then. On examining the accounts for 1984, the managing director is puzzled by the fact that the bank balance has fallen by £1,500, even though undistributed profits have increased.

Prepare:

(a) A cash flow statement, explaining the reason for the fall in the bank balance.
(b) A brief memorandum to the managing director, commenting on the information revealed by this statement.
(c) What further information would you like?

The following information was extracted from the accounts for 1984:

Balance Sheets
as at 31 December

	1983 £	1984 £		1983 £	1984 £
Ordinary share			Land and buildings	20,000	32,000
capital	85,000	110,000			
Undistributed			Plant and machinery		
profits	11,000	22,000	cost	35,000	65,500
Creditors	13,500	16,500			
Current taxation	8,500	13,500			
Proposed dividend	7,000	10,000	*Less:* Depreciation	(15,000)	(22,500)
Fixed asset					
replacement			Stock	50,000	61,000
reserve	10,000	12,000	Debtors	31,500	46,000
			Cash at bank	13,500	2,000
	£135,000	**£184,000**		**£135,000**	**£184,000**

Profit Statement Extract
for year ended 31 December 1984

		£
Net profit before taxation after charging depreciation of £7,500		36,500
Less: Corporation tax		13,500
Net profit after taxation		23,000
Less: Proposed dividend	10,000	
Transfer to reserve—fixed asset replacement	2,000	12,000
Retained Profit		**11,000**

5   As accountant for Capone Enterprises Ltd, a firm of soft drink distributors, you have received the following information about the performance of competitors in the trade:

Return on ownership capital employed	60%
Return on capital employed, including loans	20%
Sales to capital employed, including loans	4 times
Returns on sales	5%
Current ratio	3 : 4 : 1
Cash and debtors: creditors	0 : 6 : 1
Stock turnover ratio	2.6 times
Debtors turnover ratio	15 times
Creditor payment ratio	3 times

Before the directors make policy decisions regarding their competitive position they would like you to explain what the above information means. (Note that they want to understand how meaningful the information is, rather than be given a detailed description of each ratio.)

They are particularly aware of the fact that, through a series of unfortunate accidents, their competitors have recently had to replace their fixed assets at the high prices now ruling, whereas Capone Enterprises is still utilizing fixed assets acquired cheaply some time ago, and they would like you to include in your explanations the effect of this on comparisons.

Historic cost is the basis of accounting throughout the trade, including Capone Enterprises Ltd.

6   The following are the summarized trading and profit and loss accounts for the year 1984, and the balance sheets as at 31 December 1984, of A Ltd and B Ltd:

Trading and Profit and Loss A/cs

	A Ltd £'000	B Ltd £'000		A Ltd £'000	B Ltd £'000
Stock at 1.1.84	96	16	Sales	720	720
Purchases	638	648	Stock at 31.12.84	104	24
Gross profit	90	80			
	824	**744**		**824**	**744**
General expenses	32	35	Gross profit	90	80
Net profit	58	45			
	90	**80**		**90**	**80**
Issued share capital	200	200	Fixed assets	256	215
Reserves	160	32	Stock	104	24
Profit and loss A/c	120	48	Debtors	80	48
Creditors	128	81	Bank	168	74
	608	**361**		**608**	**361**

Required:

(a) Set out and complete the following table:

		A Ltd	B Ltd
(i)	Rate of stock turnover		
(ii)	Average credit period allowed to debtors (in months)		
(iii)	Average credit period allowed by creditors (in months)		
(iv)	Current ratio		
(v)	Return on tangible assets		
(vi)	Acid test ratio		
(vii)	Gross profit as a percentage of sales		
(viii)	Net profit to sales percentage		
(ix)	Return on net capital employed		

You may assume that the stock of each company has been built up from the amount at 1 January to the amount at 31 December at an even rate during the year. As regards the calculation of the liquid ratio, debtors are to be treated as liquid assets.

(b) State concisely the conclusions which may be drawn from the comparison of the above data relating to A Ltd with that concerning B Ltd. Assume that both companies sell the same kind of products to the same type of customers.

7   From the following information you are required to prepare a statement of sources and application of funds (working capital):

Constructors Ltd
Comparative Balance Sheets at

	£'000	31 March 1983 £'000	£'000	31 March 1984 £'000
Share capital—ordinary shares		7,854		8,220
Revenue reserves				
General reserve		1,242		1,278
Profit and loss A/c		24,372		26,664
6% Debentures		3,174		3,318
Current liabilities		6,834		7,548
		43,476		**47,028**
Plant and machinery	37,116		40,002	
Less: Accumulated depreciation	20,088		21,936	
		17,028		18,066
Other fixed assets		726		768
Investments (long-term)		3,018		3,312
Current assets				
Cash	2,406		2,520	
Other current assets	20,298	22,704	22,362	24,882
		43,476		**47,028**

Trading and Profit and Loss A/c
for the year ended 31 March 1984

	£'000	£'000
Sales		76,788
Dividends from investments		336
Profit on sale of plant		60
Profit on sale of investment		36
		77,220
Less: Expenses	68,939	
Depreciation	2,328	
Debenture interest	199	
		71,466
Net Profit		5,754
Add: Brought forward from last year		24,372
		30,126
Less: Dividends paid		3,426
		26,700
Transfer to general reserve		36
		26,664

Plant and machinery costing £600,000 with a written down value of £120,000 was sold for £180,000.

An investment in a subsidiary company was sold for £54,000. It had cost £18,000.

8 Two retail firms, A and B, are of similar size and were capitalized for similar amounts. Firm A paid £100,000 for a freehold property; firm B rented its property and invested £100,000 in a government security yielding 10 per cent. The following are the abridged trading results for 1984:

		A		B
	£	£	£	£
Gross profit		100,000		100,000
Expenses (other than rent)	60,000		60,000	
Rent	—		10,000	
Trading profit		40,000		30,000
Investment income				10,000
Net Profit		**40,000**		**40,000**

(a) Do you envisage any problems in comparison of the trading results of the two companies?
(b) How might such problems be overcome?
(c) What reservations might you thus have when making inter-firm comparisons?

Part IV

Accounting and society

The final chapter of the book explores the relationship between accounting and the growing concern for the broad social responsibilities of business activity, a relationship which challenges the basis of conventional accounting concepts and procedures and which points to some possible exciting developments in accounting.

20 Accounting and society

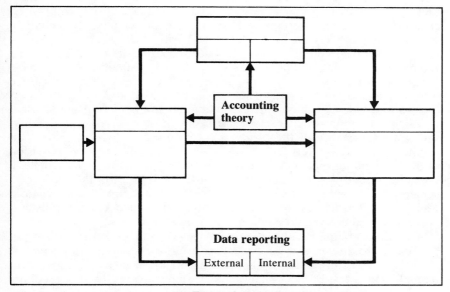

External environment

The accounting environment

Accounting does not exist in a vacuum; it reflects the activities of the business which reacts and interacts with an external environment shaped by economic, political, social, legal, environmental and technological forces. Traditionally, accounting has particularly related to the economic implications of business activity but now, with a growing awareness of a business's social responsibilities—for the environment, for the use of scarce resource, for employment opportunity, for product safety—accounting too is beginning to reflect a new social awareness. This is a dimension of accounting which may hold many exciting developments in the future.

As yet, the term 'social responsibility' has no precise or agreed meaning, but tends to convey the philosophy that no person or business should undertake activities without consideration for the impact which those activities might have on others. This philosophy of the business represents a considerable conceptual shift from the traditional economic view of the

459

firm which saw profit maximization as the only goal of consequence. In our earlier deliberations (*see* Chapter 16), we modified this traditional view to suggest a business strives to earn as much profit as possible (i.e. profit optimizing rather than profit maximizing), whilst ensuring that it remains solvent. This modification, however, still perceives the business as an economic rather than a social unit, and stresses the business's relationship to the economic environment to the virtual exclusion of the other forces which shape and are shaped by the business's activities.

A further modification this economic view is that economic goals can only be pursued in a manner constrained by consideration of the different sectors of society with which the business deals—shareholders, employees, customers, etc. There are some sectors of society which have an immediate and personal concern in the business's activities: the shareholders of a company are vitally interested in management's decisions, but so too are the employees without whom the business could not survive. A ruthless pursuit of profit maximization might put such stresses on the work-force that they would either strike or leave—and that would deny the business the profits which it was pursuing. Customers are another important segment of society, and unless they remain satisfied with such things as the quality, safety and durability of the product, the business will be no more. But product quality and safety has a cost, and it could well be that the provision of these attributes means the sacrifice of some profitability. Nevertheless, it can be argued that this pursuit of 'constrained' profit in the short term is merely a device for ensuring long-term survival and profit maximization. The economic goals still remain the focus, and the other social considerations are merely being pressed into serving their needs.

A fundamental departure from these views is that which regards profit as a means to an end and not an end in itself. Profit is only important to the extent that, in earning it and in using it, the business has striven to treat all of the contributors—shareholders, employees, customers, creditors and the general public who are affected by the business's activities—as co-equal partners, demonstrating an equal responsibility to all. Management is held responsible for retaining the level of profit which is compatible with the pursuit and attainment of socially acceptable goals.

It is this latter ethos which has given birth to 'social responsibility accounting', and in the remainder of this chapter we will explore some of the byways—which may yet turn out to be highways—along which accounting is travelling. This area of accounting is in its infancy, and is fraught with difficulties. There is, as yet, no agreement as to what social goals and responsibilities should be undertaken by the business, or what order of priorities should be given to them. Moreover, since many of these goals are about 'satisfying' needs, there are considerable conceptual problems in devising adequate devices for measuring 'satisfaction'.

The 'quality of life'

A major preoccupation of western civilization for over 100 years has been the pursuit of economic growth, partly in the belief that its attainment would automatically solve or provide the wealth to solve the urgent social problems and needs of the time—unemployment, poverty, hunger, disease, housing, education and so on. In more recent years, however, the apparently axiomatic relationship between economic growth and social progress has come under close scrutiny. In the first place, the rate of economic growth has slowed appreciably—some economists believe that we are in a permanent 'no growth' situation—and, therefore, the pressing social problems cannot be solved by creating new wealth, but by reallocating existing wealth. Secondly, different pressure groups have argued that economic growth may not be synonymous with improvements in the quality of life, for some economic growth may destroy those very resources and facilities which are required to enhance life. For example, the quarrying of minerals in a national park may enhance a company's income, but may well destroy the very environment which the recipients of the income—employees, suppliers and shareholders—would wish to and could visit as a consequence of their additional income.

There are many different pressure groups seeking to maintain and improve the 'quality of life' as they see it. Some notable groups are concerned with the environmental aspects of business activity. Consider, for example, the lengthy, protracted and often heated debates which surround the potential building of new motorways, the disposal of nuclear waste, the building of nuclear power stations, or more recently the slaughter of whales. Another pressure group, given legal recognition through the establishment of the Equal Opportunities Commission, has been concerned to ensure that women have equal employment opportunities with men, which, because of the need to equalize salaries, has had important implications for the cost structures in certain industries. Discrimination on the grounds of race or religion is now illegal, and this has had an impact upon the costs of recruitment, training and the maintenance of good labour relations.

Consumer protection movements have had a major impact upon product design and safety, and the quality of after-sales service—an outstanding example would be the consequences, in America, of Ralph Nader on car safety design. Many of the nationalized industries now have consumer councils with powers, *inter alia,* to take up with the industry complaints from dissatisfied customers. A particular target for these movements has been the control of advertising standards, and, partly as a result of their pressure, there are now strict codes of conduct to be observed. Regard for the health and safety of employees and consumers has also been an important concern; the linking of smoking and cancer and the severe restrictions on cigarette advertising has had a major effect upon tobacco revenues, and legislation relating to 'Health and Safety at Work' has, and is, resulting in substantial safety expenditure by many employers.

One general consequence of all these various pressure groups is to focus attention upon 'externalities'—the external effects of a business's activities which occur whenever there is an effect, negative or positive, on society. These social costs or benefits accrue directly to society, so that conventional accounting does not even recognize their existence. For example, the discharge of toxic wastes or effluent into a river by a chemical manufacturing company may result in additional water purification costs for the water boards who draw water from that river. These costs fall on society at large through the water rate, and are not taken into account in establishing the cost of the original chemical product. On the other hand, substantial social benefits may accrue if a new factory offers employment in an area of high unemployment. Many of the burdens which have fallen upon both ratepayer and taxpayer are removed, but these benefits are not added to the revenue of the business.

Much of the debate about externalities has been concentrated on the 'bad' things—the social costs rather than the social benefits—and considerable effort has gone into either removing the source of the social cost or measuring its value and charging it to the business which gave rise to it. Removing the source can be very expensive for the business; indeed, at an extreme, the business will cease to exist. The banning of many asbestos products on health grounds forced some businesses into liquidation, and costs of rendering some toxic wastes harmless before discharging them into rivers and sewers can be almost prohibitive. To re-charge the business for the social cost of its actions is a more difficult proposition. In the first place, there is no direct suppression of the cause of the social cost—many pressure groups would argue that social costs should not be institutionalized but eradicated—and, secondly, there are considerable difficulties in measuring the cost. For example, lead additives in petrol have been shown to be a dangerous health hazard to people living near a heavily used road system, but how is such an externality to be costed?

The extent of social responsibility in business

Almost any action by business can be deemed to have an effect on the 'quality of life', and the potential range of social responsibilities which may accrue to a business or be forced upon it by pressure groups or government legislation is virtually limitless. Clearly, however, a business cannot solve all social problems, and there is a need to find some framework which will define and limit the potential responsibilities. Social responsibility in business may be said to extend to four main areas: (1) employment, (2) environment, (3) community, and (4) product.

(1)   Employment

The responsibilities of the business towards its employees embrace welfare, training and economic dimensions. The welfare dimension includes such matters as health and safety, medical care, recreational facilities and a concern not only for the well-being of the employee but also for his family. In this country, companies such as Cadbury's and Bata have a long-established tradition of care for the general welfare of their employees, and in the USA companies like Quaker Oats exhibit similar concern. Training, education and promotion prospects are equally important, as are wage and salary levels and fringe benefits. Job security, the stability of employment levels and lay-off practices are important to the employee, and the employment of minority groups such as the physically handicapped, or racial minorities, forms part of the business's wider social responsibilities.

(2)   Environment

Environmental responsibilities are of growing importance to industrial activity. Much effort and investment is now directed towards abating the polluting effects of production, and products themselves are being improved in order to reduce their pollutive effects, e.g. the development of bio-degradable plastics. Particular attention is focused on the extractive industries, and considerable monies are spent to minimize the ugliness of waste deposits from mining activity and to restore the landscape when natural deposits are exhausted. With an increasing recognition that natural resources are finite, more effort is redirected to recycling of waste materials.

(3)   Community

Community responsibilities are those which the business has towards individuals or groups who are, in fact, outside of the immediate sphere of the business's activities. The acceptance of this type of responsibility represents an important shift in attitudes, for funds spent in this way might narrowly be conceived as *ultra vires* the objectives of a company as laid down in the Memorandum of Association. Community care can embrace a general philanthropy—donations to cultural, educational or other organizations in the area; financial or manpower support to assist in the public services; housing, transport and, perhaps, the payment of local and national taxes.

(4)   Product

This area embraces the qualitative aspects of the business's products or services—safety, durability, after-sales service and utility. It includes also the manner in which the product is marketed—the truthfulness of advertising, the accuracy and completeness of the product labelling. Much legislation is already directed at food and drink products, where standards of advertising and labelling demanded by law go far beyond what could be regarded as necessary for mere marketing purposes.

Accounting and social responsibility

If business is to embrace these various social responsibilities, then it must be held accountable for its actions and, as part of its reporting process, inform those to whom it is accountable of the success or otherwise it has had in meeting those responsibilities. At present, company reporting is virtually synonymous with financial reporting, and financial reporting rests heavily upon the postulates and conventions outlined in the early parts of this book. As we have stressed, however, accounting is a normative discipline, and the various principles it has adopted are a reflection of the needs of society as perceived at the time of their inception and modified in the light of experience and changing needs. Accounting principles were designed to meet economic needs and goals; to what extent have they to be modified to meet the reporting requirements of both economic and social goals?

Underpinning much of accounting is the concept of the business entity—an institution which may own and owe economic resources (*see* Chapter 2). Such a concept, however, cannot fully incorporate externalities—social costs and benefits. Social costs could be incorporated in so far as they are measurable and charged (invoiced) to the company, but the social benefits are for the most part immeasurable, and, even if measured, are unlikely to be paid to the business. Social costs and benefits cannot therefore be 'matched' as is required by the accrual postulate (*see* Chapter 3), and so the accounting concepts of income would not be satisfactorily applied.

A rather more subtle point is that social benefit is derived from activity designed to improve the quality of life, not merely to maintain it. Once such activity is institutionalized (i.e. measured and formally incorporated into the financial accounts) it reflects the steady state—maintaining but not improving—so is no longer a social benefit. If this view is correct—and it is much in dispute—then it is not the inability to apply the matching concept which is of consequence, it is that the matching concept itself is not relevant for the reporting of social responsibilities.

The accounting recognition of costs and revenues leans heavily upon the criteria of objectivity; historic cost is the preferred method of valuation because it is independently verifiable, and revenue is recognized as soon as it is capable of objective measurement. The whole concept of social costs and benefits denies this objectivity; in the first place, it is often difficult to agree what social costs and benefits have accrued to a particular activity, and, even if agreed, they are most difficult to measure. Many such costs and benefits cannot really be translated into monetary terms—can a monetary value be put on the quality of life?—so that the money measurement convention is an inadequate vehicle for conveying both economic and social messages.

If accounting principles as currently conceived cannot adequately reflect the dimensions of social responsibility as outlined in this text, should accounting principles be changed? One view is that the information necessary to judge and evaluate social performance should not be integrated with reports designed and needed for economic decisions; economic and social responsibility reporting should be maintained in parallel and derived from the principles applicable to each system. Is this separation ultimately desirable? Social and economic goals are becoming increasingly intertwined—economic goals constrain the realization of social goals, and social goals constrain the economic goals—so that the maintenance and development of two independent reporting systems would deny the essential interdependence of the various organizational goals.

Social responsibility accounting is, as yet, in its infancy, and many of the profound conceptual and methodological problems are barely identified let alone explored. This is one of the frontiers of accounting theory and practice which is likely to attract much attention in the next decade. Since no formal theory has yet evolved, we will turn our attention finally to outline some practices which begin, in part, to take accounting beyond the economic frontiers and into the realms of social responsibility.

Developments in accounting practice

As we have seen, social and economic objectives are interdependent, so that the growing emphasis upon reporting social goals in no way diminishes the importance of the economic objectives. A business cannot survive in the long run without profitability and liquidity. However, the conventional means of reporting profit through the profit and loss account does emphasize the recipients of the profit—the shareholders—as being the primary focus of concern. A representation of this statement which treats all of the beneficiaries—employees, shareholders, creditors and government—of business activity as co-equal partners is an important shift of emphasis.

The Corporate Report recommended the publication of a 'Statement of Added Value', that is the value added to materials and services acquired by the business's activities, this being 'the simplest way of putting profit into proper perspective *vis-à-vis* the whole enterprise'. Such a statement could appear in the following form:

Statement of added value

	£'000
Sales	800
Less: Materials and services acquired	500
Value Added	300
Which was applied to:	
Employees	170
Shareholders' dividends	40
Loan interest	10
Taxation	60
Asset maintenance and expansion	20
Value Added	300

Some companies have already adopted this value added statement as part of their annual report, which is itself undergoing a remarkable transformation. In particular, employees, the most important asset of any business, are being brought more and more into the picture, through the use of 'employee profiles'. These profiles, which include such things as statistics, turnover, net capital employed and wages expressed per employee, are a growing feature of many company accounts, and are a reflection of a growing awareness of the importance of the human asset.

This leads us finally to the development of human resource accounting, which involves 'measuring the costs incurred by businesses to recruit, select, hire, train and develop assets, and an evaluation of their economic value'. This development did not particularly evolve out of concern for people *per se,* but for what those people could do for the business. The most well-known attempt to incorporate human asset values into conventional accounts is found in the American R. G. Barry Corporation. This company capitalized the costs of recruiting, training and development of management personnel, expensing it over the expected useful life of the investment. Several methods have been suggested for valuing the human asset—replacement cost, present value of future earnings, and subjective or behavioural valuation based upon the employee's contribution to profitability, man management, solvency, physical resource management, and consumer satisfaction—but none of them can be regarded as completely or even partially satisfactory. Nevertheless, the willingness of both practitioners and theorists to explore this area is yet another indication of the widening frontiers of accounting.

References and further reading

ACCOUNTING STANDARDS STEERING COMMITTEE (1975), *The Corporate Report.*

BRUMMET (1973), 'Total Performance Measurement', *Management Accounting N.A.A.,* November 1973.

CAPLAN and LANDEKICH (1974), *Human Resource Accounting: Past, Present and Future.* National Association of Accountants.

COMMITTEE FOR ECONOMIC DEVELOPMENT (1971), *Social Responsibilities of Business Corporations.*

ESTES (1973), *Accounting and Society.* Melville Publishing Co.

HOPWOOD (1974), *Accounting and Human Behaviour.* Accountancy Age Books.

LICKERT (1967), *The Human Organisation: Its Management and Value.* McGraw-Hill.

LIVINGSTONE and GUNN (1974), *Accounting for Social Goals.* Harper and Row.

STEINER (1971), *Business and Society.* Random House.

WOLFE (1973), *Cost Benefit and Cost Effectiveness.* Allen and Unwin.

Questions for discussion

1   'The limited company has only one duty—to look after its shareholders.' Discuss.

2   'The corporate goal should be to obtain that level of profit which is compatible with its meeting its social responsibilities.' Discuss.

3   List as many major 'pressure groups' as you can, and consider to what extent their actions have caused modifications—through legislation or otherwise—in business behaviour.

4   'The failure of business to identify the costs and benefits of externalities is directly traceable to the accountant's search for objectivity.' Discuss.

5   Select any 5–10 company reports and analyse the extent to which there is awareness of 'social responsibilities'.

6   To what extent are accounting principles and conventions inconsistent or inadequate with a need for a company to report upon its success (or otherwise) in meeting its social responsibilities?

7   Using the data provided in question 10 of Chapter 10, prepare a statement of added value. To what extent do you consider that this statement assists in 'putting profit in perspective'?

8   How would you set about placing a monetary value on your worth? Does human asset accounting, in attempting to measure the worth of an employee to the business, reflect too narrow a view of worth?

Suggested solutions to numerical questions

Chapter 2   The Balance Sheet

Q 6

	(i)	(ii)	(iii)	(iv)	(v)	(vi)	(vii)
	£	£	£	£	£	£	£
Ownership Interest	12,000	12,000	12,000	12,200	12,100	12,100	11,900
Current Liabilities							
Creditors			1,500	1,500	1,500	1,100	1,100
	12,000	12,000	13,500	13,700	13,600	13,200	13,000
Fixed Assets							
Premises		6,000	6,000	6,000	6,000	6,000	6,000
Car	2,000	2,000	2,000	2,000	2,000	2,000	2,000
Current Assets							
Stock			1,500	800	800	800	800
Debtors				900	900	900	900
Cash	10,000	4,000	4,000	4,000	3,900	3,500	3,300
	£12,000	£12,000	£13,500	£13,700	£13,600	£13,200	£13,000

Q 12(a)

	1983		1984	
	£	£	£	£
Ownership Interest		21,350		22,320
Current Liabilities				
Wages owed	175		180	
Creditors	1,600	1,775	1,800	1,980
		£23,125		£24,300
Fixed Assets				
Freehold shop	13,500		13,500	
Delivery van	2,000	15,500	2,000	15,500
Current Assets				
Stock	2,900		3,200	
Debtors	2,125		2,650	
Cash at bank	2,500		2,900	
Cash in till	100	7,625	50	8,800
		£23,125		£24,300

Q 14

	1	2	2a	7	7a	7b	14	14a	14b	20	21	21a	26	28	28a	28b
	£	£	£	£	£	£	£	£	£	£	£	£	£	£	£	£
Ownership Interest	7,500	7,500	7,500	7,610	7,610	7,550	7,690	7,740	7,680	7,640	7,640	7,570	7,570	7,830	7,830	7,770
Current Liabilities																
Creditors			1,250	1,250	1,570	1,570	1,570	1,570	1,570	1,570	570	570	570	570	1,070	1,070
	7,500	7,500	8,750	8,860	9,180	9,120	9,260	9,310	9,250	9,210	8,210	8,140	8,140	8,400	8,900	8,840
Fixed Assets																
Shop	5,000	5,000	5,000	5,000	5,000	5,000	5,000	5,000	5,000	5,000	5,000	5,000	5,000	5,000	5,000	5,000
Office fixtures															500	500
Current Assets																
Stock		300	1,550	1,300	1,620	1,620	1,460	1,360	1,360	1,390	1,390	1,390	1,390	1,090	1,090	1,090
Debtors							300	300	300	230	230	230				
Cash	2,500	2,200	2,200	2,560	2,560	2,500	2,500	2,650	2,590	2,590	1,590	1,520	1,750	2,310	2,310	2,250
	7,500	7,500	8,550	8,860	9,180	9,120	9,260	9,310	9,250	9,210	8,210	8,140	8,140	8,400	8,900	8,840

Chapter 3   Income Measurement—Expenses

Q 8

Item	Payment during 1983/84	Expenses 1983/84	Unexpired expenses 31.3.84	Expenses 1984/85	Unexpired expenses 31.3.85
	£	£	£	£	£
(a)	500	500			
(b)	220		220	220	
(c)	180	36	144	36	112
(d)	96	24	72	72	
(e)	8,200		8,200		8,200
(f)	2,400	600	1,800	1,200	600

Q 9

		£				£	
Van	(5)	500		Ownership interest	(11)		660
					(15)	15	
Debtors	(3)	143			(30)	20	
	(9)	115					
	(23)		180	Creditors	(2)		500
	(27)	400			(11)		366
					(18)	300	
Bank	(1)	600					
	(5)		500				
	(7)		18				
	(13)	200					
	(18)		300				
	(23)	180					
	(28)		90				
Cash	(1)	60					
	(4)		23				
	(13)	200	200				
	(14)		15				
	(15)		15				
	(24)	60					
	(30)		20				
Purchases	(2)	500					
	(4)	23		Sales	(3)		143
					(9)		115
Rent	(28)	90			(13)		200
					(24)		60
Petrol	(7)	18			(27)		400
Sundry	(14)	15					

(summary overleaf)

Summarizing the above we have:

	£			£
	+	−		−	+
Van	500		Ownership interest	625
Debtors	478		Creditors	566
Bank	72			
Cash	47			
	£1,097			**£1,191**
Purchases	889		Sales	918
Rent	90			
Petrol	18			
Sundry	15			
	£1,012			**£ 918**

	A	+	E		L	+	R
	1,097	+	1,012	≠	1,191	+	918
		£2,109		≠		**£2,109**	

H. Smith
Income Statement for the period ended 30 June 1984

	£	£	£
Revenues			
Sales			918
Expenses			
Purchases	889		
Less: Closing stock	329	560	
Rent		90	
Petrol		18	
Sundry		15	683
Net Profit			**£235**

H. Smith
Balance Sheet as at 30 June 1984

	£	£		£	£
Fixed Assets			**Ownership Interest**		
Van		500	Balance at 1 June		660
			Net profit	235	
			Less: Drawings	35	200
					860
Current Assets			**Current Liabilities**		
Stock	329		Creditors		566
Debtors	478				
Bank	72				
Cash	47	926			
		£1,426			**£1,426**

Q 10

Clifton
Income Statement for the period ended 31 December 1984

	£	£	£
Revenues			
Sales			69,300
Discounts received			925
Rent received			415
			70,640
Expenses			
Stock at 1.1.84	6,100		
Purchases	58,700		
	64,800		
Less: Stock at 31.12.84	8,500	56,300	
Discounts allowed		1,320	
Bad debts		325	
Wages and salaries	7,045		
Add: Owing	415	7,460	
General expenses		865	
Rates and insurances	300		
Less: Prepaid	50	250	
Depreciation (10%)		140	66,660
Net Profit			**£ 3,980**

Clifton
Balance Sheet as at 31 December 1984

	£	£		£	£
Fixed Assets			**Ownership Interest**		
Land and buildings		7,000	Balance at 1 January 84		15,000
Furniture and			Profit	3,980	
fittings	1,400		*Less:* Drawings	1,600	2,380
Less: Depreciation	140	1,260			17,380
		8,260			
Current Assets			**Current Liabilities**		
Stock	8,500		Creditors and accruals		5,960
Debtors and					
prepayments	5,900				
Bank	680	15,080			
		£23,340			**£23,340**

Chapter 4   Income Measurement Revenue

Q 3

(a) (i) Point of Sale

	(i)	(ii)	(iii)	(iv)	(v)	(vi)
Capital	1,000	1,000	1,000	1,000	1,000	1,000
Profit			(40)	60	60	260
	£1,000	1,000	960	1,060	1,060	1,260
Stock		500	500	400	400	200
Debtors				200	150	550
Cash	1,000	500	460	460	510	510
	£1,000	1,000	960	1,060	1,060	1,260

(a) (ii) Completion of Production

	(i)	(ii)	(iii)	(iv)	(v)	(vi)
Capital	1,000	1,000	1,000	1,000	1,000	1,000
Profit		500	460	460	460	460
	£1,000	1,500	1,460	1,460	1,460	1,460
Stock		1,000	1,000	800	800	400
Debtors				200	150	550
Cash	1,000	500	460	460	510	510
	£1,000	1,500	1,460	1,460	1,460	1,460

(a) (iii) Receipt of Cash

	(i)	(ii)	(iii)	(iv)	(v)	(vi)
Capital	1,000	1,000	1,000	1,000	1,000	1,000
Profit			(40)	(40)	(15)	(15)
	£1,000	1,000	960	960	985	985
Stock		500	500	400	400	200
Debtors				100	75	275
Cash	1,000	500	460	460	510	510
	£1,000	1,000	960	960	985	985

Q 6
Yama Co.,
Trading, Profit and Loss Account
for the period ended 31 December 1984

	£	£
Sales		42,400
Stock at 1 January 1984	4,400	
Purchases	21,600	
	26,000	
Less: Stock at 31 December 1984	6,000	20,000
Less: **Gross Profit**		22,400
Provision for doubtful debts	220	
Depreciation on fixtures	200	
Administrative expenses	5,600	
Selling expenses	5,600	
Distribution expenses	3,000	
Financial expenses	900	15,520
Net Profit		**£ 6,880**

Yama Co.
Balance Sheet as at 31 December 1984

	£	£	£
Ownership Equity			
Balance at 1 January 1984			7,000
Profit		6,880	
Less: Drawings		3,000	3,880
Net Capital Employed			**£10,880**
Represented by:			
Fixed Assets			
Buildings (cost)			6,000
Fixtures (cost)		2,000	
Less: Depreciation		800	1,200
			7,200
Current Assets			
Stock		6,000	
Debtors and prepayments	11,200		
Less: Provision	220	10,980	
Bank		4,100	
		21,080	
Less: **Current Liabilities**			
Creditors and accruals		17,400	3,680
			£10,880

Q 7
Fletcher
Trading, Profit and Loss Account
for the period ended 31 December 1984

	£	£	£	£
Sales				70,900
Stock at 1 January 1984		6,300		
Purchases	56,500			
Less: Drawings	200	56,300	62,600	
Less: Stock at 31 December 1984			8,000	54,600
Gross Profit				16,300
Discounts Received			814	
Provision no longer required			40	854
Less:				17,154
Repairs			198	
Car expenses (less private use)			212	
Wages and salaries			8,924	
Discounts allowed			1,061	
Rates and insurance			203	
Bad debts			359	
General expenses			1,586	
Depreciation of furniture			200	12,743
Net Profit				**£ 4,411**

Fletcher
Balance Sheet as at 31 December 1984

	£	£	£
Ownership Equity			
Balance at 1 January 1984			30,500
Profit for the year		4,411	
Less: Drawings		2,706	1,705
			£32,205
Represented by:			
Fixed Assets			
Freehold land and buildings			20,650
Furniture and fittings		2,000	
Less: Depreciation		740	1,260
Car			950
			22,860
Current Assets			
Stock		8,000	
Debtors and prepayments	5,258		
Less: Provision	100	5,158	
Bank		540	
		13,698	
Less: **Current Liabilities**			
Creditors and accruals		4,353	9,345
			£32,205

Chapter 5   Accounting Records—An Introduction to Bookkeeping

Q 4

(a)   Journal

		Dr. £	Cr. £
(i)	A. Jones A/c J. Jones A/c Goods sold to A. Jones incorrectly debited to J. Jones	35	35
(ii)	Bad debts A/c J. Jones A/c J. Jones declared bankrupt	27	27
(iii)	Office expenses A/c Office equipment A/c Purchase of stationery incorrectly debited to Office Equipment A/c	12	12
(iv)	Drawings A/c Wages A/c Drawings made by Mr. Goodhope incorrectly debited to the Wages A/c	40	40

(b)

J. Jones

Balance	27	A. Jones	35
Sales	35	Bad debts	27

A. Jones

Balance	92	
Sales	28	
J. Jones	35	

Office Equipment

Balance	212	Office expenses	12
Cash	97		
Cash	12		

Office Expenses

Balance	128	
Cash	8	
Office equipment	12	

Wages

Balance	100	Drawings	40
Cash	40		

Bad Debts

J. Jones	27	

Drawings

Wages	40	

Q 5

Corrections to Trial Balance

	£ Dr.	£ Cr.
(i)		+20
(ii)	+180	−180
(iii)	+80	+80
(iv)		+75
(v)	—	—
(vi)	—	—
	+260	−5

In the original trial balance the credits exceeded the debits by £255.

Note: Item (v) will involve only a switch between debtors—it will not affect the trial balance, and item (vi) will involve only a switch between two debit balances.

Q 6

Rent A/c

10.7.84 Bank	125	31.12.84 P. & L.	375
10.10.84 Bank	125		
31.12.84			
Balance c/d	125		
	375		375
7.1.85 Bank	125		
7.4.85 Bank	125	1.1.85	
8.7.85 Bank	150	Balance b/d	125
4.10.85 Bank	150	31.12.85	
31.12.85		P. & L.	575
Balance c/d	150		
	£700		£700
		1.1.86	
		Balance b/d	150

Rates A/c

30.4.84 Bank	300	31.12.84 P. & L.	450
30.10.84 Bank	300	31.12.84	
		Balance c/d	150
	600		600
1.1.85		31.12.85 P. & L.	675
Balance b/d	150	31.12.85	
30.4.85 Bank	350	Balance c/d	175
31.10.85 Bank	350		
	£850		£850
1.1.86			
Balance b/d	175		

Q 7

Motor Expense A/c

Bank (Petrol)	400	P. & L.	547
Bank (License)	40	Balance c/d	
Bank (Tyres)	90	(36 + 25 + 22)	83
Bank (Insurance)	100		
	£630		£630
Balance c/d	83		

Q 8

Commission A/c

Balance	2,600	P. & L.	3,100
Balance c/d (accrual)	500		
	3,100		3,100
		Balance b/d	500

Insurances A/c

Balance	230	P. & L.	170
		Balance c/d (prepaid)	60
	230		230
Balance b/d	60		

Provision for Doubtful Debts A/c

P. & L. (provision no longer required)	44	Balance	210
Balance c/d	166		
	210		210
		Balance b/d	166

Bad Debts A/c

Debtors	200	P. & L.	200

Provision for Depreciation A/c

		Balance	9,000
Balance c/d	13,100	P. & L.	4,100
	13,100		13,100
		Balance b/d	13,100

Debtors A/c

Balance c/d	8,500	Bad debts	200
		Balance c/d	8,300
	8,500		8,500
Balance b/d	8,300		

Stock A/c

Balance	3,650	Trading A/c	3,650
Trading A/c	4,310	Balance c/d	4,310
Balance b/d	4,310		

Rent A/c

Balance	390	P. & L.	486
Balance c/d (accrual)	96		
	486		486
		Balance b/d	96

Extract

Trading, Profit and Loss Account

Opening stock	3,650	Closing stock	4,310
Commission	3,100	Provision for	
Insurance	170	doubtful debts	
Bad debts	200	not required	44
Depreciation	4,100		
Rent	486		

Q 9

Capital A/c

		1 Jan. Cash	500
		1 Jan. Bank	2,500
		1 Jan. Van	1,200
			4,200

Bank A/c

1 Jan. Capital	2,500	2 Jan. Furniture	250
22 Jan. Brown	100	16 Jan. Squires	384
		31 Jan. Balance c/d	1,966
	2,600		2,600
1 Feb. Balance b/d	1,966		

Drawings A/c

12 Jan. Cash	60		

Van A/c

1 Jan. Capital	1,200		

Rent A/c

1 Jan. Cash	180		

Cash A/c

1 Jan. Capital	500	1 Jan. Rent	180
5 Jan. Sales	100	4 Jan. Wages	40
10 Jan. Sales	130	11 Jan. Wages	40
		12 Jan. Drawings	60
		14 Jan. Sundry	35
		19 Jan. Wages	40
		26 Jan. Wages	40
		31 Jan. Balance c/d	295
	730		730
1 Feb. Balance b/d	295		

Furniture A/c

2. Jan. Bank	250		

Purchases A/c

2 Jan. Squires	400		
9 Jan. Guy	280		
	680		

Sales A/c

		3 Jan. Brown	350
		5 Jan. Cash	100
		10 Jan. Cash	130
		24 Jan. Jones	110
			690

Squires A/c

18 Jan. Bank	384	2 Jan. Purchases	400
18 Jan. Discount received	16		
	400		400

Wages A/c

4 Jan. Cash	40		
11 Jan. Cash	40		
19 Jan. Cash	40		
26 Jan. Cash	40		
	160		

Guy A/c

		8 Jan. Purchases	280

Sundry A/c

14 Jan. Cash	35		

Brown A/c

3 Jan. Sales	350	22 Jan. Bank	100
		31 Jan. Balance c/d	250
	350		350
1 Feb. Balance b/d	250		

Discounts Received A/c

		18 Jan. Squires	16

Jones A/c

24 Jan. Sales	110		

Mr. Smith
Trial Balance as at 31 January

	Dr. £	Cr. £
Capital		4,200
Bank	1,966	
Drawings	60	
Van	1,200	
Rent	180	

(cont'd right)

(*Trial Balance cont'd*)

Cash	295	
Creditors—Guy		280
Furniture	250	
Purchases	680	
Sales		690
Debtors—Brown	250	
—Jones	110	
Wages	160	
Sundry	35	
Discounts Received		16
	£5,186	**£5,186**

Q 10

Capital A/c

30 June Drawings	34		1 June Bank	600	
30 June Balance c/d			1 June Cash	50	
			30 June Net profit	182	
	832			832	
			1 July Balance b/d	798	

Drawings A/c

20 June Cash	10	30 June Capital	34	
27 June Cash	24			
	34		34	

Motor Insurance A/c

15 June Bank	84	30 June P. & L.	7
		30 June Balance c/d	77
	84		84
1 July Balance b/d	77		

Van A/c

5 June Bank	256	30 June Balance c/d	256
1 July Balance b/d	256		

Purchases A/c

2 June Jones	130		
4 June Cash	23		
11 June Jones	240	30 June Trading A/c	501
Moss	62		
Huggins	46		
	501		501

Purchases Returns A/c

30 June Trading A/c	67	13 June Jones	25
		28 June Jones	42
	67		67

Rent A/c

30 June Balance c/d	50	30 June P. & L.	50
		1 July Balance b/d	50

Provision for Depreciation A/c

30 June Balance c/d	30	30 June P. & L.	30
		1 July Balance b/d	30

Bank A/c

1 June Capital	600	5 June Van	256
25 June Potter	43	7 June Motor exp.	12
		15 June Insurance	84
		21 June Moss	62
		21 June Huggins	46
		30 June Balance c/d	183
	643		643
1 July Balance b/d	183		

Cash A/c

1 June Capital	50	4 June Purchases	23
23 June Heaton	66	15 June Motor exp.	5
26 June Sales	34	20 June Drawings	10
		27 June Drawings	24
		29 June Office exp.	4
		30 June Balance c/d	84
	150		150
1 July Balance b/d	84		

Jones A/c

13 June Purchases ret.	25	2 June Purchases	130
28 June Purchases ret.	42	11 June Purchases	240
30 June Balance c/d	303		
	370		370
		1 July Balance b/d	303

Moss A/c

21 June Bank	62	11 June Purchases	62

Huggins A/c

21 June Bank	46	11 June Purchases	46

Motor Expenses A/c

7 June Bank	12	30 June P. & L.	17
15 June Cash	5		
	17		17

Office Expenses A/c

29 June Cash	4	30 June P. & L.	4

Sales A/c

		3 June Heaton	66
		Norris	25
		Potter	43
		9 June Barnes	24
		Listen	26
30 June Trading A/c	435	Moores	65
		26 June Cash	34
		30 June Norris	40
		Edgar	67
		Listen	45
	435		435

Sales Returns A/c

19 June Norris	11	30 June Trading A/c	11

Moores A/c

9 June Sales	65	30 June Balance c/d	65
1 July Balance b/d	65		

Edgar A/c

30 June Sales	67	30 June Balance c/d	67
1 July Balance b/d	67		

Heaton A/c

3 June Sales	66	23 June Cash	66

Norris A/c

3 June Sales	25	19 June Sales	
30 June Sales	40	returned	11
		30 June Balance c/d	54
	65		65
1 July Balance b/d	54		

Potter A/c

3 June Sales	43	25 June Bank	43

Barnes A/c

9 June Sales	24	30 June Balance c/d	24
1 July Balance b/d	24		

Listen A/c

9 June Sales	26	30 June Balance c/d	71
30 June Sales	45		
	71		71
1 July Balance b/d	71		

Trial Balance as at 30 June

	Dr. £	Cr. £
Capital		650
Bank	183	
Van	256	
Drawings	34	
Cash	84	
Purchases	501	
Purchases returns		67
Debtors: Norris	54	
Barnes	24	
Listen	71	
Edgar	67	
Moores	65	
Sales		435
Creditors: Jones		303
Sales returns	11	
Motor expenses	17	
Motor insurance	84	
Office expenses	4	
	£1,455	£1,455

Trading, Profit and Loss Account for the period ended 30 June

	£	£		£	£
Purchases	501		Sales	435	
Less: Returns	67		*Less:* Returns	11	424
	434				
Less: Closing stock	300	134			
Gross Profit c/d		290			
		£424			**£424**
			Gross Profit b/d		290
Provision for depreciation		30			
Rent		50			
Motor expenses		17			
Motor insurance		7			
Office expenses		4			
Net Profit		182			
		£290			**£290**

Balance Sheet as at 30 June

	£	£		£	£
Capital			**Fixed Assets**		
Balance at 1 June		650	Van	256	
Profit for period	182		*Less:* Depreciation	30	226
Less: Drawings	34	148			
		798			
			Current Assets		
			Stock	300	
			Debtors	281	
Current Liabilities			Prepayments	77	
Creditors	303		Bank	183	
Accruals	50	353	Cash	84	925
		£1,151			**£1,151**

Chapter 6   The Valuation and Depreciation of Fixed Assets

Q 5

(a) (i) Straight Line

	Year 1	Year 2	Year 3	Year 4	Year 5
	£	£	£	£	£
Depreciation	900	900	900	900	900
Net Book Value	4,100	3,200	2,300	1,400	500

$$\textbf{Annual depreciation} = \frac{£5,000 - 500}{5} = \textbf{£900}$$

(a) (ii) Reducing Balance

	Year 1	Year 2	Year 3	Year 4	Year 5
	£	£	£	£	£
Depreciation	1,845	1,164	735	463	294
Net Book Value	3,155	1,991	1,257	794	500

$$\text{Annual Depreciation} = \left(1 - \sqrt[5]{\frac{500}{5,000}}\right) 100\%$$
$$= (5,000 - 0.631)\,100$$
$$= \mathbf{36.9\%}$$

(a) (iii) Sum of the Digits

	Year 1	Year 2	Year 3	Year 4	Year 5
	£	£	£	£	£
Depreciation	1,500	1,200	900	600	300
Net Book Value	3,500	2,300	1,400	800	500

$$
\textbf{Annual Depreciation} \quad
\begin{array}{ll}
\text{Year} & 1 \\
& 2 \\
& 3 \\
& 4 \\
& 5 \\
\hline
& 15 \\
\end{array}
\quad
\left.
\begin{array}{l}
5/15 \\
4/15 \\
3/15 \\
2/15 \\
1/15 \\
\end{array}
\right\} \times (5,000 - 500)
$$

Q 7

(a) (i)

Year	Cost/WDV	Depreciation
	£	£
1978/79	3,000	300
1979/80	2,700	270
1980/81	2,430	243
1981/82	2,187	219
1982/83	1,968	197
1983/84	1,771	177
1984/85	1,594	—
		£1,406

Plant at cost	£3,000
Less: Depreciation	1,406
WDV	1,594
Sale price	600
Loss on plant sold	£ 994

(a) (ii)

	£	£
1982/83	3,000	300
1983/84	2,700	270
1984/85	2,430	—
		£570

WDV		£2,430
Sale price		1,500
Loss on plant sold		£ 930

	£	£
Plant at cost 1 July 1984	30,000	
Less: Sales at cost	6,000	24,000
Depreciation on plant at 1 July 1984	15,000	
Less: Depreciation on plant sold	1,976	13,024
WDV at 1 July 1984		10,976
(a) (iii) Additions during year		10,000
		20,976
Thus, depreciation for year @ 10%		£ 2,098

(a) (iv)

Year	Cost/WDV	Depreciation
	£	£
1978/79	3,000	750
1979/80	2,250	750
1980/81	1,500	750
1981/82	750	750
1982/83	—	—
		£3,000

WDV	nil
Trade in	500
Profit on sale	£500

	£	£
Vehicles at cost 1 July 1984	25,000	
Less: Sales at cost	3,000	22,000
Additions at cost		3,870
		£25,870
Thus, depreciation at 25%		£ 6,468
Depreciation of vehicles at 1 July 1984		15,000
Less: Depreciation at 1 July 1984 on vehicles sold		3,000
		£12,000

Balance Sheet Extract at 30 June 1985

	Cost	Valuation on 30 June 1985	Depreciation	Net
	£	£	£	£
Freehold property	10,000	150,000	—	150,000
Plant and machinery	34,000	—	15,122	18,878
Motor vehicles	25,870	—	18,468	7,402
			£23,590	**£176,280**

(b)

Depreciation for 1984/85: Plant	£ 2,098
Vehicles	£ 6,468
Loss on sale of plant	£ 1,924
Profit on sale of vehicle	£ 500
Gain on revaluation	£50,000

Q 8

(a) (1)   **Motor Vehicle Register as at 1 January 1985**

Register number	Cost	Date of purchase	Depreciation	Net book value at 1.1.85
	£		£	£
Car 3	2,000	1.7.82	1,500	500
Car 4	2,500	1984	625	1,875
Car 5	2,500	1984	625	1,875
Van 2: (cab)	2,000	1.7.83	1,000	1,000
(trailer)	1,500	30.6.84	375	1,125
Van 3	4,000	30.9.84	1,000	3,000
	£14,500		**£5,125**	**£9,375**

(a) (2)

		£	£
Profit on disposals: Car 1		100	
Car 2		200	
Van 1		200	500
Loss on disposals: Van 2 (trailer)			250
Net Profit			**£250**

(a) (3)

Depreciation for year: Car 3	500
Car 4/5	1,250
Van 2: (cab)	500
(trailer)	375
Van 3	1,000
	£3,625

Q 9

(a)   Workings

	Year	Cost/WDV	Depreciation
		£	£
Buildings	1982	100,000	2,000
	1983	98,000	2,000
	1984	96,000	2,000
	1985	94,000	
			£ 6,000
Plant	1982	75,000	11,250
	1983	63,750	9,563
	1984	54,187	8,128
	1985	46,059	
			£28,941
Motor cars	1982	15,000	3,750
	1983	11,250	2,813
	1984	8,437	2,109
	1985	6,328	
			£ 8,672
Office	1982	5,000	1,250
	1983	3,750	938
	1984	2,812	703
	1985	2,109	
			£ 2,891

Ledger Accounts for 1984

Freehold Land A/c

1.1.84 Balance b/d	20,000	31.12.84 Balance c/d	20,000
1.1.85 Balance b/d	20,000		

Freehold Buildings A/c

1.1.84 Balance b/d	100,000	31.12.84 Balance c/d	100,000
1.1.85 Balance b/d	100,000		

Plant & Machinery A/c

1.1.84 Balance b/d	75,000	31.12.84 Balance c/d	75,000
1.1.85 Balance b/d	75,000		

Provision for Depreciation on Buildings A/c

		1.1.84 Balance b/d	4,000
31.12.84 Balance c/d	6,000	31.12.84 P. & L. A/c	2,000
	6,000		6,000
		1.1.85 Balance b/d	6,000

Provision for Depreciation on Plant & Machinery A/c

		1.1.84 Balance b/d	20,813
31.12.84 Balance c/d	28,941	31.12.84 P. & L. A/c	8,128
	28,941		28,941
		1.1.85 Balance b/d	28,941

Motor Cars A/c

1.1.84 Balance b/d	15.000	31.12.84 Balance c/d	15,000
1.1.85 Balance b/d	15,000		

Provision for Depreciation on Motor Cars A/c

		1.1.84 Balance b/d	6,563
31.12.84 Balance c/d	8,672	31.12.84 P. & L. A/c	2,109
	8,672		8,672
		1.1.85 Balance b/d	8,672

Office Appliances A/c

1.1.84 Balance b/d	5,000	31.12.84 Balance c/d	5,000
1.1.85 Balance b/d	5,000		

Provision for Depreciation on Office Appliances A/c

		1.1.84 Balance b/d	2,188
31.12.84 Balance c/d	2,891	31.12.84 P. & L. A/c	703
	2,891		2,891
		1.1.85 Balance b/d	2,891

(b) (1)

	Year	Cost/WDV £	Depreciation £
Plant	1982	500	75
	1983	425	64
	1984	361	54
	1985	307	—
			£193

Plant & Machinery A/c

1.1.85 Balance b/d	75,000	1.1.85 Sale of plant	500

Provision for Depreciation A/c

1.1.85 Sale of plant	193	1.1.85 Balance b/d	28,941

Sale of Plant A/c

Plant A/c	500	Depreciation A/c	193
		Loss—P. & L. A/c	307
	£500		£500

(b) (2)

	Year	Cost/WDV £	Depreciation £
Motor Car	1982	800	200
	1983	600	150
	1984	450	113
	1985	337	—
			£463

Motor Cars A/c

| 1.1.85 Balance b/d | 15,000 | 1.1.85 Sale of car | 800 |

Provision for Depreciation A/c

| 1.1.85 Sale of car | 463 | 1.1.85 Balance b/d | 8,672 |

Sale of Car A/c

Car A/c	800	Depreciation A/c	463
Profit—P. & L. A/c	13	Bank	350
	£813		£813

Chapter 7   The Valuation of Current Assets

Q 1

(a) FIFO

	Purchases				Cost of Sales		
Date	Units	Unit price	Total	Date	Units	Unit price	Total
		£	£			£	£
6.1	30	10	300	15.1	50	$(30 \times 10) + (20 \times 12)$	540
13.1	40	12	480	22.1	50	$(20 \times 12) + (30 \times 15)$	690
18.1	50	15	750				
			£1,530				£1,230

		£	£
Sales (100×20)			2,000
Purchases		1,530	
Less: Closing stock		300*	1,230
Gross Profit			**£ 770**

*$20 \times 15 = £300$

(b) LIFO

	Cost of Sales		
Date	Units	Unit price	Total
		£	£
15.1	50	$(40 \times 12) + (10 \times 10)$	580
22.1	50	(50×15)	750
			£1,330

		£	£
Sales			2,000
Purchases		1,530	
Less: Closing stock		200*	1,330
Gross Profit			**£ 670**

*$20 \times 10 = £200$

(c) Weighted Average

		Cost of Sales		
Date	Units	Unit price		Total
		£		£
15.1	50	$\dfrac{(300+480)}{70} \times 50$		557
22.1	50	$\dfrac{((20 \times 11.14)+750)}{70} \times 50$		695
				£1,252

	£	£
Sales		2,000
Purchases	1,530	
Less: Closing stock	278*	1,252
Gross Profit		**£ 748**

*20 × 13.9 = £278

Q 5

(i)   FIFO

			£	£
Upright:	Sales			2,700
	Purchases		2,000	
	Less: Closing stock		250	1,750
	Gross Profit			**£ 950**
Grand:	Sales			3,200
	Purchases		3,600	
	Less: Closing stock		1,700	1,900
	Gross Profit			**£1,300**

(ii)   LIFO

			£	£
Upright:	Sales			2,700
	Purchases		2,000	
	Less: Closing stock		250	1,750
	Gross Profit			**£ 950**
Grand:	Sales			3,200
	Purchases		3,600	
	Less: Closing stock		1,500	2,100
	Gross Profit			**£1,100**

(iii)   Weighted Average
Upright: as for FIFO

		£	£
Grand:	Sales		3,200
	Purchases	3,600	
	Less: Closing stock	1,589	2,011
	Gross Profit		**£1,189**

Q 6

Rawhide & Co.
Trading, Profit and Loss Account for the period ended 31 March 1984

	£	£
Sales		1,200,000
Purchases	1,000,000	
Less: Closing stock	200,000	800,000
Gross Profit		**400,000**
Less:		
Salaries	7,500	
Depreciation on vehicles	1,200	
Loss on investments	5,000	
R. & D.	15,000	
Other expenses	162,300	191,000
Net Profit		**£ 209,000**

Balance Sheet as at 31 March 1984

	£	£
Capital	150,000	
Net Profit	209,000	
	£ 359,000	
Fixed Assets		
Motor vehicles (cost)	6,000	
Less: Depreciation	1,200	4,800
Current Assets		
Stock	200,000	
Investments (M.V. £10,000)	5,000	
Investments in subsidiary	20,000	
Debtors	143,200	
	368,200	
Less: **Current Liabilities**		
Bank overdraft	14,000	354,200
		£ 359,000

Q 9

Fletcher

Trading, Profit and Loss Account for the period ended 31 December 1984

	£	£	£
Sales			50,900
Opening stock		6,300	
Purchases	36,500		
Less: Goods for owner	200	36,300	
		42,600	
Less: Closing stock		8,800	33,800
Gross Profit			**17,100**
Discounts received		814	
Provision no longer required		40	854
			17,954
Less:			
Repairs to buildings		198	
Car expenses		212	
Depreciation on car		190	
Depreciation on fittings		200	
Wages and salaries		8,924	
Discounts allowed		1,061	
Rates and insurances		203	
Bad debts		359	
General expenses		1,586	12,933
Net Profit			**£ 5,021**

Balance Sheet as at 31 December 1984

	£	£	£
Capital			
Balance at 1 January 1984			30,500
Profit		5,021	
Less: Drawings		2,706	2,315
Net Capital Employed			**£32,815**
Represented by:			
Fixed Assets			
Land and buildings			20,650
Furniture and fittings (cost)		2,000	
Less: Depreciation		740	1,260
Car		950	
Less: Depreciation		190	760
			22,670
Current Assets			
Stock		8,800	
Debtors and prepayments	5,258		
Less: Provision	100	5,158	
Bank		540	
		14,498	
Less: **Current Liabilities**			
Creditors and accruals		4,353	10,145
			£32,815

Q 10(a)

Jim
Trial Balance as at 31 March 1984

	£	£
Capital		50,000
Property	50,000	
Plant and machinery	10,000	
Depreciation		6,000
Sales		200,000
Purchases	100,000	
Stock	30,000	
Debtors and creditors	40,000	15,000
Wages	15,000	
Heat, etc	2,000	
General expenses	17,000	
Discounts	900	
Carriage inwards	800	
Carriage outwards	700	
Returns	600	500
Provision for bad debts		400
Sale of plant		900
Cash and bank	2,800	
Drawings	4,000	
	£273,800	**£273,800**

Jim
Trading, Profit and Loss Account for the period ended 31 March 1984

	£	£	£
Sales		200,000	
Less: Returns		600	199,400
Opening stock		30,000	
Purchases	100,000		
Carriage inwards	800		
	100,800		
Less: Goods taken by owner	100		
	100,700		
Less: Returns	500	100,200	
		130,200	
Less: Closing stock		35,000	95,200
Gross Profit			**£104,200**
Discounts received		1,000	
Provision no longer required		10	
Profit on sale of plant		300	1,310
			105,510
Less:			
Bad debts		1,000	
Depreciation on plant		340	
Wages		15,000	
Heat, etc		2,000	
General expenses $(17,000-25-25+20-8)$		16,962	
Carriage outwards		700	
Discounts allowed		900	36,902
Net Profit			**£ 68,608**

Jim
Balance Sheet as at 31 March 1984

	£	£	£
Capital			
Balance at 1 April 1983			50,000
Profit		68,608	
Less: Drawings		4,125	64,483
Net Capital Employed			**£114,483**
Represented by:			
Fixed Assets			
Property			50,000
Plant and machinery (cost)		9,000	
Less: Depreciation		5,940	3,060
			53,060
Current Assets			
Stock		35,000	
Debtors and prepayments	39,033		
Less: Provision	390	38,643	
Cash and bank		2,800	
		76,443	
Less: **Current Liabilities**			
Creditors and accruals		15,020	61,423
			£114,483

Chapter 8   Further Aspects of Financial Records

Q 3

Bert Huggings
Trading, Profit and Loss Account for the period ended 31 December 1984

	£	£
Sales		7,800
Purchases	7,400	
Less: Closing stock	1,700	5,700
Gross Profit		**2,100**
Less:		
Petrol	400	
Interest	100	
Rent	350	
Provision for doubtful debts	50	
Expenses	250	
Depreciation of lorry	210	1,360
Net Profit		**£ 740**

Balance Sheet as at 31 December 1984

	£	£	£
Capital			
Balance at 1 January 1984			5,000
Profit		740	
Less: Drawings		1,640	(900)
			4,100
Loan			1,000
Net Capital Employed			**£5,100**
Represented by:			
Fixed Assets			
Lorry			840
Less: Depreciation			210
			630
Current Assets			
Stock		1,700	
Debtors and prepayments	550		
Less: Provision	50	500	
Bank		4,900	
Cash		310	
		7,410	
Less: **Current Liabilities**			
Creditors and accruals		2,940	4,470
			£5,100

(N.B. There are several possible 'solutions' to this question)

Q 4

Wilson
Trading, Profit and Loss Account for the period ended 30 June 1984

	£	£
Sales		22,000*
Opening stock	950	
Purchases	17,900	
	18,850	
Less: Closing stock	1,250	17,600
Gross Profit		**4,400**
Less:		
Accounting fees	125	
Rates	170	
Rent	800	
Electricity	132	
Sundry	100	
Wages	1,500	
Depreciation of fixtures	250	3,077
Net Profit		**£ 1,323**

* Ascertained by calculating cost of sales and applying mark up.

Balance Sheet as at 30 June 1984

	£	£	£
Capital			
Balance at 1 July 1983			4,095
Profit		1,323	
Less: Drawings (2894* + 830 + 490)		4,214	(2,891)
			£1,204
Fixed Assets			
Fixtures *less* depreciation			750
Current Assets			
Stock		1,250	
Debtors and prepayments		400	
Cash		190	
		1,840	
Less: **Current Liabilities**			
Creditors and accruals	1,301		
Bank overdraft	85	1,386	454
			£1,204

* Balancing figure on Cash A/c, after obtaining cash sales received from customers as a balancing figure on the Sales/Debtors A/c.

Q 5

(a) (i)

Debtors Control A/c

	£		£
Balance b/d	1,891	Bad debts	68
Unpaid cheque	110	Discounts allowed	43
A. Jones	97	Balance c/d	1,987
	£2,098		£2,098
Balance b/d	1,987		

(a) (ii)

Creditors Control A/c

	£		£
Error	9	Balance b/d	2,130
Balance c/d	2,121		
	£2,130		£2,130
		Balance b/d	2,121

		£	£
(b) (iii)	Office equipment A/c DR	240	
	Purchases A/c		240
	Acquisition of fixed assets incorrectly treated as purchases		
(iv)	Drawings A/c DR	320	
	Wages A/c		320
	Drawings incorrectly treated as wages		
(v)	Capital A/c DR	40	
	Provision for depreciation A/c		40
	Underprovision in 1983		
(vi)	Drawings A/c DR	45	
	Stationery A/c		45
	Purchase of private stationery		
(vii)	Returns inwards A/c DR	90	
	Returns outwards A/c		90
	Goods returned to supplier incorrectly credited to returns inwards A/c		

(c)   Trial Balance as at 31 December 1984

	£	£
Premises	7,000	
Capital		8,400
Drawings	2,300	
Provision for depreciation		520
Debtors and creditors	1,987	2,121
Stock	1,200	
Purchases	9,240	
Sales		14,003
Returns inwards and outwards	400	90
Office equipment	1,840	
Wages	1,220	
Commission	160	
Discounts	210	121
Bank		980
Cash	56	
Heating and lighting	375	
Postage and stationery	179	
Bad debts	68	
	£26,235	**£26,235**

(d)   **Perrod & Co.**
Baiance Sheet as at 31 December 1984

	£	£	£
Capital			8,400
Profit		2,332	
Less: Drawings		2,300	32
			£8,432

	£	£	£
Fixed Assets			
Premises			7,000
Equipment (cost)		1,840	
Less: Depreciation		750	1,090
			8,090
Current Assets			
Stock		1,400	
Debtors		1,987	
Cash		56	
		3,443	
Less: **Current Liabilities**			
Creditors	2,121		
Bank overdraft	980	3,101	342
			£8,432

Q 7

(a)
Sales Ledger Control A/c

Balance b/d	33,041	Cash	215,164
Sales	232,183	Bad debts	750
Bank	125	Discounts allowed	2,475
		Allowances	2,354
		Contra	565
		Balance c/d	44,041
	£265,349		**£265,349**
Balance b/d	44,041		

Differences: Sales Ledger Control A/c = £74

Purchases Ledger Control A/c

Bank	131,643	Balance b/d	23,214
Discounts received	1,742	Purchases	162,175
Allowances	2,858		
Contra	565		
Balance c/d	48,581		
	£185,389		£185,389
		Balance b/d	48,581

Q 8

	£	£
Balance per Bank A/c		1,310.40
Less: Charges		12.80
		1,297.60
Add: Incorrect amount on cheque No. 236130		9.90
Corrected Bank A/c		**£1,307.50**
Balance per Bank Statement		1,166.45
Add: Cheque charged*	19.47	
Standing Order*	32.52	51.99
		1,218.44
Less: Giro Credit*		21.47
		1,196.97
Less: Cheques drawn not presented	30.00	
	52.27	82.27
		1,114.70
Add: Lodgement not yet credited by bank		192.80
Balance per Bank A/c		**£1,307.50**

* Items requiring further investigation before amending Bank A/c

Q 11

Bank A/c

Casting error	100	Balance	1,210
Dividend	30	Bank charges	76
		Cheque dishonour	70
Balance c/d	1,244	Error	18
	£1,374		£1,374
		Balance b/d	1,244

	£
Balance per Bank Statement	(706)
Add: Cheques not yet presented	(420)
	(1,126)
Less: Lodgements not yet credited	360
	(766)
Add: Cheque not yet charged	
(incorrectly charged to No. 2)	(520)
	(1,286)
Less: Cheque charged in error	42
Balance per Bank Account	(£1,244)

Chapter 9   The Partnership

Q 4

Alexander and Arnold
Trading, Profit and Loss, and Appropriation Account
for the period ended 30 September 1984

	£	£
Sales		62,300
Purchases	55,800	
Less: Closing stock	6,000	49,800
Gross Profit		**13,500**
Sundry expenses	4,870	
Bad debts	200	
Depreciation provision	160	5,230
Net Profit		**£ 8,270**
Salary—Arnold		1,490
Interest on capital—Arnold	420	
—Alexander	350	770
Share of profits—Arnold (2/5)	2,404	
—Alexander (3/5)	3,606	6,010
		£ 8,270

Balance Sheet as at 30 September 1984

	£	£
Capital		
Alexander	8,400	
Arnold	7,200	15,600
Current Accounts		
Alexander	2,626	
Arnold	3,044	5,670
Current Liabilities		
Creditors and Accruals		3,150
		£24,420
Fixed Assets	£	£
Premises		11,000
Van at cost	1,600	
Less: Depreciation	160	1,440
		12,440
Current Assets		
Stock	6,000	
Debtors	5,400	
Bank	250	
Cash	330	11,980
		£24,420

Q 5

Smith and Jones
Trading, Profit and Loss, and Appropriation Account
for the period ended 31 March 1984

	£	£
Sales		27,590
Purchases	9,450	
Less: Closing stock	660	8,790
Gross Profit		**18,800**
Less:		
Discounts allowed	192	
Lease amortization	600	
Depreciation—machinery	1,000	
—van	160	
Gas and electricity	185	
Insurance	140	
Wages	2,100	
Packages	1,624	
Postage	2,582	
Advertising	620	
Telephone	760	
Petrol	248	
Motor repairs	170	10,381
Net Profit		**£ 8,419**
Salary—Jones		1,000
Interest on capital—Jones	300	
—Smith	480	780
Share of profits—Smith (2/3)	4,626	
—Jones (1/3)	2,213	6,639
		£ 8,419

Balance Sheet as at 31 March 1984

	£	£		£	£
Captial			**Fixed Assets**		
Smith	8,000		Leases (cost)	6,000	
Jones	5,000	13,000	*Less:* amortization	600	5,400
			Machinery (cost)	5,000	
			Less: Depreciation	1,000	4,000
Current Accounts			Van (cost)	800	
Smith	2,766		*Less:* Depreciation	160	640
Jones	1,993	4,759			10,040
Current Liabilities			**Current Assets**		
Creditors		3,250	Stock	660	
			Debtors and prepayments	170	
			Bank	10,091	
			Cash	48	10,969
		£21,009			**£21,009**

Q 6 (a)

	£
Net profit before appropriation	8,780
(i)	−35
(ii)	−350
(iv)	+100
(vi)	−33
(vii)	−82
Revised net profit	**£8,380**

Current Accounts

	£ Webb	£ Guy		£ Webb	£ Guy
Drawings	4,280	3,950	Balance at 1.1.83	900	100
Goods		65	Salary		2,350
Balance	1,055	30	Interest	400	250
			Profits	4,035	1,345
	5,335	4,045		5,335	4,045

Balance Sheet as at 31 December 1983

	£	£		£	£
Capital Accounts			Premises		10,400
Webb	8,000		Equipment	4,000	
Guy	5,000	13,000	*Less:* Depreciation	2,300	1,700
					12,100
Current Accounts					
Webb	1,055				
Guy	30	1,085	Stock	2,450	
			Debtors *less* provision	1,067	
Creditors and accruals		1,732	Cash	200	3,717
		£15,817			**£15,817**

Q 9

		£		£
(i)	Capital A	28,000	Goodwill	16,000
	B	28,000		
	C	10,000	Cash	13,000
	Current A/cs A	1,500	Other assets	41,500
	B	1,000		
	Creditors	2,000		
		£70,500		£70,500

		£		£
(ii)	Capital A	22,000	Cash	17,000
	B	22,000	Other assets	41,500
	C	10,000		
	Current A/cs A	1,500		
	B	1,000		
	Creditors	2,000		
		£58,500		£58,500

		£		£
(iii)	Capital A	20,000	Cash	13,000
	B	20,000	Other assets	41,500
	C	10,000		
	Current A/cs A	1,500		
	B	1,000		
	Creditors	2,000		
		£54,500		£54,500

Q 10

(a) Journal

	£	£
Goodwill Dr.	12,000	
Capital—Brown		9,000
—Allen		3,000
Share of goodwill credited to partners in *old* profit-sharing ratios		
Cash Dr.	4,000	
Capital—Campbell		4,000
Capital introduced by Campbell		

(b) Campbell, Brown & Allen
Trading, Profit and Loss and Appropriation Account
for the period ended 31 December 1983

	£	£
Sales		50,630
Opening stock	9,250	
Purchases	47,300	
	56,550	
Less; Closing stock	14,200	42,350
Gross Profit		£8,280
Discount received		950
		9,230
Less;		
Interest on loan	200	
Discounts allowed	650	
Wages	2,200	
Lighting and heating	860	
Rates	790	
Depreciation—buildings	460	
—vehicles	500	
Provision for doubtful debts	29	
Bad debts	150	
Vehicle running expenses	680	
Miscellaneous	471	6,990
Net Profit		£2,240
Net Profit Jan—June 1983		1,120
Interest on capital ($\frac{1}{2}$ year)—Brown	450	
—Allen	360	
Share on profits ($\frac{1}{2}$ year) —Brown ($\frac{3}{4}$)	$232\frac{1}{2}$	
—Allen ($\frac{1}{4}$)	$77\frac{1}{2}$	1,120
Net Profit July—Dec 1983		1,120
Interest on capital—Brown	720	
—Allen	450	
—Campbell	120	
Share of loss —Brown ($\frac{1}{2}$)	(85)	
Share of loss —Allen ($\frac{1}{3}$)	$(56\frac{2}{3})$	
Share of loss —Campbell (1/6)	$(28\frac{1}{3})$	1,120

Current Accounts

	£ B	£ A	£ C		£ B	£ A	£ C
Balance	–	259	–	Balance	1,600		
Loss	85	56.6	28.4	Interest	450	360	–
				Profit	232.5	77.5	–
Balance	2,917.5	571.9	91.6	Interest	720	450	120
	3,002.5	887.5	120.0		3,002.5	887.5	120

Balance Sheet as at 31 December 1983

	£	£		£	£
Capital			Goodwill		12,000
Brown	24,000		Buildings	23,000	
Allen	15,000		*Less:* Depreciation	3,560	19,440
Campbell	4,000	43,000	Vehicles	9,000	
			Less: Depreciation	4,500	4,500
					35,940
Current Accounts				£	
Brown	2,917.5				
Allen	571.9		Stock		14,200
Campbell	91.6	3,581	Debtors :5,300		
Loan		4,000	*Less:* 159	5,141	
Creditors		5,300	Prepayments	80	
Accruals		80	Bank	600	20,021
		£55,961			£55,961

Chapter 10   The Public Limited Company—Capital Structure and Financial Reporting

Q 10

(a)

Ordinary Share Capital A/c			**Cash A/c**		
	Cash	50,000	Ordinary shares	50,000	

Share Premium A/c

	Cash	10,000
	Cash	1,000

5% Preference Share A/c

| | Cash | 20,000 |

10% Debenture A/c

	Cash	28,000
	Discount	1,200

Cash A/c:
- Ordinary shares 50,000
- Share premium 10,000
- Preference shares 20,000
- Share premium 1,000
- Debenture 28,800

Discount on Debenture A/c

Debenture A/c   1,200

(b)   **Balance Sheet extract**

		£
Called-up share capital		
50,000 £1 Ordinary shares		50,000
20,000 5% £1 Preference shares		20,000
		70,000
Share Premium		11,000
		£81,000

Creditors: Amounts falling due after one year		
30,000 10% Debentures		30,000
and, under the assets:		
Fixed assets		
Intangible assets		
Discount on debentures		1,200

Note: this would normally be written off through the appropriation account

Q 11

Cash A/c

		Debenture interest	1,500
		Ordinary dividend	2,500
		Preference dividend	500

Ordinary Dividend A/c

Cash	2,500	Appropriation A/c	
Balance c/d	3,750	—Dividend paid	2,500
		—Dividend proposed	3,750
	£6,250		£6,250
		Balance b/d	3,750

Preference Dividend A/c

Cash	500	Appropriation A/c	
Balance c/d	500	—Dividends paid	500
		—Dividends proposed	500
	£1,000		£1,000
		Balance b/d	500

Debenture Interest A/c

Cash A/c	1,500	P. & L. A/c	3,000
Accrual c/d	1,500		
	£3,000		£3,000
		Balance b/d	1,500

Appropriation A/c

Dividends paid			
5% Ordinary	2,500		
2½% Preference	500		
Dividends proposed			
7½% Ordinary	3,750		
2½% Preference	500		

Q 12
(i) Newman PLC
Trading, profit and Loss, and Appropriation Account for the period ended 31 December 1984

	£'000	£'000	£'000
Sales			964
Less: Returns outwards			28
			936
Opening stock		66	
Purchases	501		
Less: Returns inwards	25		
	476		
Add: Carriage inwards	1	477	
		543	
Less: Closing stock		90	453
Gross Profit			**483**
Less:			
Carriage outwards	10		
Salesmen's salaries	64		
General distribution expenses	23		
Depreciation—vehicles	15	112	
Administrative wages and salaries	59		
Depreciation—plant	25		
General administrative expenses	22		
Directors' remuneration	30		
Auditors' fees	3	139	251
			232
Rent			8
			240
Debenture interest			2
Net profit before taxation			238
Provision for taxation			45
Net profit after taxation			**193**
Profit undistributed at 1 January 1984			58
			£251
Dividends proposed			
10% Ordinary		25	
8% Preference		4	29
Transfer to general reserve			40
Undistributed profit 31 December 1984			182
			£251

Newman PLC
Balance Sheet as at 31 December 1984

	£'000	£'000	£'000
Fixed Assets			
Intanglible Assets			
Goodwill			85
Tangible Assets			
Plant and machinery (cost)		125	
Less: Depreciation		84	41
Vehicles (cost)		90	
Less: Depreciation		45	45
			171
Current Assets			
Stock		90	
Debtors		310	
Prepayments		1	
Cash at bank and in hand		140	
		541	
Creditors (amount falling due within one year)			
Creditors	59		
Other creditors—dividends	29		
—taxation	45		
Accruals	5	138	403
	—		
		£403	**£574**
Net current assets			
Total Assets *less* **Current Liabilities**			
Creditors (Amounts falling due after one year)			
Debenture loans			
Capital and Reserves			
Called-up share capital			
250,000 £1 Ordinary		250	
50,000 8% £1 Preference		50	
		300	
Share premium		20	
Other reserves—general		52	
Profit and Loss account		182	554
			£574

(ii) Published Profit and Loss (abridged)

	£'000	£'000
Turnover		936
Cost of Sales		453
Cross Profit		483
Distribution costs	112	
Administrative costs	139	251
		232
Other operating income		8
		240
Interest payable		2
		238
Tax on profit on ordinary activities		45
Profit on Ordinary Activities		**£193**

(Appropriation Account and Balance Sheet as above)

Q 13

Undercliffe PLC
Trading, Profit and Loss and Appropriation Account for the period ended 31 December 1984

	£'000	£'000	£'000
Sales			900
Less: Returns			22
			878
Opening stock		220	
Purchases		513	
		733	
Less: Closing stock		288	455
Gross Profit			433
Selling wages and salaries	60		
Motor expenses	32		
General distribution expenses	16		
Depreciation—motor vehicles	14	122	
Administrative wages and salaries	69		
General administrative expenses	18		
Auditors' fees	4		
Directors' remuneration	38		
Bad debts	6		
Provision for doubtful debts	2		
Depreciation—plant and equipment	25		
Discounts allowed	10		
	172		
Less: Discounts received	9	163	285
			148
Royalties			10
			158
Debenture interest			20
Net profit before taxation			138
Provision for taxation			60
Net profit after taxation			78
Undistributed profit 1 January 1984			40
			£118
Dividends proposed			
6% Preference		6	
20% Ordinary		24	30
Transfer to general reserve			25
Undistributed profit at 31 December 1984			63
			£118

Balance Sheet as at 31 December 1984

	£'000	£'000	£'000
Fixed Assets			
Intangible Assets			
Goodwill		55	
Development costs		38	93
Tangible Assets			
Land and buildings (valuation)		200	
Plant and equipment (cost)	250		
Less: Depreciation	145	105	
Motor vehicles (cost)	70		
Less: Depreciation	42	28	333
			426
Current Assets			
Stock		288	
Debtors	50		
Less: Provision	2	48	
		336	
Creditors (amount falling due within one year)			
Trade creditors	65		
Other creditors—dividends	30		
—taxation	60		
Accruals	4		
Bank overdraft	20	179	
Net Current Assets		157	157
Total Assets less Current Liabilities			**£583**
Creditors (amount falling due after one year)			
Debenture loans			160
Capital and Reserves			
50p Ordinary shares		120	
6% £1 Preference shares		100	
		220	
Revaluation reserve		25	
Other reserves—general		115	
Profit and Loss Account		63	423
			£583

Chapter 11   The Public Limited Company—Changes in Capital Structure and Groups of Companies

Q 2   (f)

Ordinary Share Capital A/c

		Balance b/d	60,000
		Share premium	20,000
Balance c/d	100,000	General reserve	20,000
	£100,000		£100,000

Share Premium A/c

Ordinary share Capital A/c	£20,000	Balance b/d	£20,000

General Reserve A/c

		Balance b/d	40,000
Ordinary share Capital A/c	20,000		
Balance c/d	20,000		
	£40,000		£40,000

(g)
Balance Sheet

	£		£
Ordinary shares	100,000		
General reserve	20,000	Sundry assets	195,000
Profit & Loss	60,000		
Current liabilities	15,000		
	£195,000		£195,000

Q 5 (c)

Ordinary Share Capital A/c

		Balance b/d	20,000
Balance c/d	30,000	Bank	10,000
	£30,000		£30,000

Share Premium A/c

		Balance b/d	2,000
Balance c/d	5,000	Bank	3,000
	£5,000		£5,000

Bank A/c

Balance b/d	5,000		
Ordinary share A/c	10,000		
Share premium	3,000	Balance c/d	18,000
	£18,000		£18,000

(d)
Eaton PLC

30,000 £1 Ordinary	30,000	Sundry assets	35,000
Share premium	5,000	Bank	18,000
Undistributed profit	14,000		
Current liabilities	4,000		
	£53,000		£53,000

Q 8   (i) (a)

Preference Share A/c

Cash	£30,000	Balance b/d	£30,000

Share Premium A/c

Cash	3,000	Balance b/d	5,000
Balance c/d	2,000		
	£5,000		£5,000

Capital Redemption Reserve A/c

		Undistributed profit A/c	£30,000
Balance c/d	£30,000		

Undistributed Profit (P. & L.) A/c

Capital redemption Reserve A/c	30,000	Balance b/d	35,000
Balance c/d	5,000		
	£35,000		£35,000

Cash A/c

Balance b/d	35,000	Preference share A/c	30,000
		Share premium A/c	3,000
		Balance c/d	2,000
	£35,000		£35,000

(i) (b)
Tarns   PLC
Balance Sheet

	£		£
£1 Ordinary shares	50,000	Cash	2,000
Share premium	2,000	Other net	
Capital redemption reserve	30,000	assets	85,000
Undistributed profits	5,000		
	£87,000		£87,000

(ii) (a)

Preference Share A/c

Preference share redemption A/c	£30,000	Balance b/d	£30,000

Capital Redemption Reserve A/c

		Undistributed profit A/c	£30,000
Balance c/d	£30,000		

Undistributed Profits A/c

Capital redemption		Balance b/d	35,000
reserve A/c	30,000		
Preference share			
redemption A/c	3,000		
Balance c/d	2,000		
	£35,000		£35,000

Preference Share Redemption A/c

		Preference share	
		A/c	30,000
Cash	33,000	Undistributed	
		profit A/c	3,000
	£33,000		£33,000

(ii) (b)

Tarns PLC

	£		£
£1 Ordinary shares	50,000	Cash	2,000
Share premium	5,000	Other net assets	85,000
Capital redemption			
reserve	30,000		
Undistributed profit	2,000		
	£87,000		£87,000

Q 11

(a) Book value of B

Assets		60,000
Less: Creditors		5,000
		£55,000
A has acquired 9/10 × 55,000	=	49,500
but paid		75,000
Therefore, goodwill on acquisition		£25,000

(b) Value of minority interest:

Total equity value of B	55,000
Less: Value acquired by A	49,500
Therefore, minority interest	£5,500

(c) A
Consolidated Balance Sheet

£1 Ordinary shares	200,000	Assets	255,000
Reserves	50,000	Goodwill	25,500
Current liabilities	25,000		
Minority interest	5,500		
	£280,500		£280,500

Q 12

(a) Minority interest in current profits of B:

Ordinary dividend 12,000 × $\frac{1}{4}$	= 3,000	
Retained profits in 4,000 × $\frac{1}{4}$	= 1,000	4,000

Minority interest in current loss of C:

Retained loss 4,000 × 2/5	=	(1,600)

So, minority interest in current group profits   £2,400

(b) Cost of control/goodwill

Book value of B at 1.1.84 = 80,000 + 12,000	=	£92,000
So, value of equity acquired by A = $\frac{3}{4}$ × 92,000	=	69,000
Price paid	=	74,000
So goodwill	=	£ 5,000
Book value of C at 1.1.84 = 50,000 + 2,800	=	£52,800
So, value of equity acquired by A = 3/5 × 52,800	=	31,680
Price paid	=	40,000
So, goodwill	=	£ 8,320
So, total goodwill = 5,000 + 8,320	=	£13,320

(c) Minority interest at date of acquisition

In B 92,000 − 69,000	=	23,000
In C 52,800 − 31,680	=	21,120
		£44,120

(d) Total minority interest:

44,120 + 2,400	=	£46,520

(e) Consolidated Profit and Loss Account

Group profit (58,500 + 16,000 − 4,000)	**£70,500**
Dividends proposed	36,000
Retained profits	
($\frac{3}{4}$ × 16,000 − 3/5 × 4,000 + 22,500)	32,100
Minority interest (see (a) above)	2,400
	£70,500

(f) A

Consolidated Balance Sheet as at 31 December 1984

Ordinary shares	156,000	Fixed assets	180,000
Retained profits		Goodwill	13,320
(29,000 + 32,100)	61,100	Stock	86,000
Creditors	54,700	Debtors	44,000
Dividends proposed	36,000	Cash	31,000
Minority interest	46,520		
	£354,320		**£354,320**

Chapter 12   Value and Income Measurement

Q 10

Trading , Profit and Loss Account
for the period ended 31 December 1984

	Unadjusted		Factor	Adjusted to 31.12.84	
	£'000	£'000		£'000	£'000
Sales		100	125/118		105.9
Opening stock	30		125/114	32.9	
Purchases	61		125/118	64.6	
	91			97.5	
Less: Closing stock	40	51	125/118	42.4	55.1
Gross Profit		**49**			**50.8**
Expenses	10		125/118	10.6	
Depreciation					
— Buildings	4		125/105	4.8	
— Equipment	10	24	125/80	15.6	31.0
Net Profit		**25**			**19.8**
Dividends proposed		15			15.0
Balance c/f		£10			£ 4.8

Balance Sheet as at 31 December 1984

	Unadjusted		Factor	Adjusted to 31.12.84	
	£'000	£'000		£'000	£'000
Ordinary shares		150	125/80		234.4
Reserves		70	Residual		38.7
Debentures		20	125/125		20.0
		£240			£293.1
Land (less depreciation)	148		125/105	176.2	
Equipment (less depreciation)	40	188	125/80	62.5	238.7
Stock	40		125/118	42.4	
Debtors	28		125/125	28.0	
Bank	14		124/125	14.0	
	82			84.4	
Less:					
Creditors	(15)		125/125	(15.0)	
Dividends Proposed	(15)	52	125/125	(15.0)	54.4
		£240			£293.1

Note: Gain from holding money

Net monetary assets at 31.12.83 stated in 31.12.84 pounds	£'000
$(13-(10+10+15))=-22 \times 125/116$	(23.7)
Net monetary assets at 31.12.84	
$(28+14)-(20+15+15)=-8$	
Hence, increase in net monetary assets	
$-8-(-22)=14 \times 125/118$	14.8
	(8.9)
Net monetary assets at 31.12.84	(8.0)
So, gain from owing money	0.9

This can be formally reconciled by re-working the 1983 balance sheet in terms of 1984 pounds. This gives a 'residual' reserve of £33.8.

Hence: Reserves 31.12.84	£38.7
Reserves 31.12.83	34.8
Profit	3.9
Add: gain from owing money	0.9
Increase in reserves per adjusted P. & L. A/c	£ 4.8

Q 12

Trading, Profit and Loss Account
for the period ended 31 December 1984

	£'000
Profit on historical cost basis	25.0
Less: Current cost operating adjustment	9.9
Current cost profit	15.1
Add: Gearing adjustment	0.3
Current cost profit attributable to shareholders	15.4
Dividends proposed	15.0
Transfer to reserves	0.4

Balance Sheet as at 31 December 1984

	£'000	£'000
Ordinary shares		150.0
Current cost reserve		62.7
Profit and loss (60 + 0.4)		60.4
		£273.1
Land (less depreciation)		176.2
Equipment (less depreciation)		62.5
		238.7
Stock	42.4	
Debtors	28.0	
Bank	14.0	
	84.4	
Less: Creditors	(15.0)	
Dividends	(15.0)	54.4
		293.1
Less: Debentures		20.0
		£273.1

Notes:

1. *Cost of sales adjustment*

	£'000
Increase in stock holdings at historic cost (40 − 30)	10.0
Increase in stock holdings at average current cost	
$(40 \times 118/125 - 30 \times 118/116) = 37.8 - 30.5 =$	7.3
Holding gain from increase in stock prices: (i.e. the current cost of sales is £53.7)	£ 2.7
The current cost value of the closing stock is $40 \times 125/118 =$	£42.4

2	*Depreciation adjustment*	£'000

Depreciation charge for the year = (As for CPP, given the same index)	£20.4
Adjustment to historic depreciation is £20.4 − 14 =	£ 6.4

The fixed asset replacement reserve (i.e. the difference between the current and historic values of the fixed assets) will stand at
£238.7 − 188 = £50.7
as part of the current cost reserve (see Note 5).

3	*Monetary working capital adjustment*	£'000

Increase in monetary working capital at historic cost $(28 − 15) − (13 − 10) =$	10
Increase in MWC at average current cost $13 \times 118/125 − 3 \times 118/116$ $12.3 − 3.1 =$	9.2
Loss from increase in MWC	£ 0.8

(For the sake of simplicity, no part of the cash balances has been included in MWC).

4	*Gearing adjustment*	£'000

Cost of sales adjustment	2.7
Depreciation adjustment	6.4
MWC adjustment	0.8
Total current cost adjustment	£ 9.9

Net operating assets	£'000
Fixed assets	188
Stock	40
Net MWC	13
	£241

Net borrowing	£'000
Debentures	20
Less: Bank	14
	£ 6

Gearing adjustment $= 9.9 \times 6/241 = £0.3$

5	*Current cost reserve*	£'000

This is composed of:	
Current cost of adjustment less gearing adjustment	9.6
Fixed asset replacement reserve	50.7
Stock replacement reserve $(42.4 − 40.0)$	2.4
	£62.7

Chapter 14   Elements of Cost Accounting

Q 3

Manufacturing, Trading, Profit and Loss Account
for the period ended 31 December 1984

	£	£	£
Opening stock of materials	1,400		
Purchases	7,800	9,200	
Less: Closing stock		1,000	8,200
Factory wages			4,980
Prime cost of manufacture			13,180
Factory overhead			
Expenses		4,040	
Depreciation—machinery		900	4,940
			18,120
Work in progress 1.1.84		2,250	
Less: W.I.P. 31.12.84		1,500	750
Factory cost of production			18,870
Stock of finished goods 1.1.84		9,760	
Purchases		1,400	
		11,160	
Less: Stock of finished goods 31.12.84		10,500	660
Warehouse wages		2,030	
Warehouse expenses		3,270	5,300
			£24,830

	£	£
Sales		37,330
Less: Returns		400
		36,930
Cost of Sales		24,830
Gross Profit		**12,100**
Distribution costs		
Selling expenses	3,900	
Depreciation—vans	600	
Administration expenses		
Depreciation—buildings	240	
—equipment	100	
General	1,550	6,390
		5,710
Other operating income		220
Net Profit		**£5,930**

Balance Sheet as at 31 December 1984

	£	£
Capital		23,400
Reserves		7,930
		£31,330
Fixed Assets		
Land and buildings (net)		7,760
Machinery (net)		4,660
Office equipment (net)		200
Vans (net)		1,200
		13,820

(cont'd)

				(*cont'd*)
Current Assets				
Stock—raw material		1,000		
—W.I.P		1,500		
—finished goods		10,500		
Debtors less provision		5,580		
Prepayments		100		
Cash		700		
		19,380		
Less: **Current liabilities**	£			
Creditors	1,000			
Accruals	870	1,870	17,510	
			£31,330	

Q 8(a)

				Absorption			Marginal	
	Units	£	£	£	£		£	£
1983								
Sales	5,000	20			100,000			100,000
Cost of Sales								
Variable costs	6,000	9		54,000			54,000	
Fixed costs	6,000	4		24,000			—	
				78,000			54,000	
Less: **Closing stock**								
Variable costs	1,000	9	9,000				9,000	
Fixed costs	1,000	4	4,000	13,000	65,000		—	45,000
					35,000			55,000
Fixed costs					—			24,000
Gross Profit					**£ 35,000**			**£ 31,000**
1984								
Sales	8,000	30			240,000			240,000
Cost of sales								
Opening stock	1,000			13,000			9,000	
Variable costs	10,000	15	150,000				150,000	
Fixed costs	10,000	8	80,000	230,000			—	
				243,000			159,000	
Less: **Closing stock**								
Variable costs	3,000	15	45,000				45,000	
Fixed costs	3,000	8	24,000	69,000	174,000			114,000
					66,000			126,000
Fixed costs					—			80,000
Gross Profit					**£ 66,000**			**£ 46,000**

Q 9

	Group 1	Group 2	Group 3	Total	Basis of apportionment
	£	£	£	£	
Consumables	200	400	500	1,100	
Maintenance	500	1,000	800	2,300	
Power	750	1,000	1,250	3,000	Effective H.P.
Rent & rates	200	150	250	600	Area
Heat & light	600	450	750	1,800	Area
Insurance of buildings	100	75	125	300	Area
Insurance of machinery	150	450	400	1,000	Book value
Depreciation of machinery	2,400	4,000	1,600	8,000	Machine hours
Supervision	540	900	360	1,800	Machine hours
	£5,440	£8,425	£6,035	£19,900	
Machine hours	**12,000**	**20,000**	**8,000**	**40,000**	
Machine hour rate	**£0.45**	**£0.42**	**£0.75**		

Q 10

Job Cost Sheet

	£	£
Materials		90.00
Direct labour		30.00
Overhead: Group 1 4 @ 0.45	1.80	
Group 2 7 @ 0.42	2.94	
Group 3 5 @ 0.75	3.75	8.49
Job Cost		£128.49

Q 11

	A	B	Assembly	Pack.
	£	£	£	£
Indirect wages	7,600	8,700	8,250	4,600
Maintenance wages	2,000	4,000	1,000	1,000
Indirect materials	5,400	7,200	3,600	5,400
Power	4,800	4,800	—	1,200
Rent & rates	3,200	2,400	4,800	2,400
Light & heat	800	600	1,200	600
Insurance	600	800	100	100
Depreciation	12,000	16,000	2,000	2,000
	36,400	44,500	20,950	17,300
Maintenance	4,000	8,000	2,000	2,000
Stores	1,800	2,400	1,200	1,800
General	3,360	2,520	1,680	840
	£45,560	£57,420	£25,830	£21,960
Overhead absorption rate:				
machine hours	£0.46	£0.48	—	—
labour hours	—	—	£0.17	£0.22

(cont'd next page)

(cont'd from previous page)

Maint.	Stores	General	Total	Basis of apportionment
£	£	£	£	
4,500	2,300	4,850	40,800	Actual
1,000	500	900	10,400	Actual
1,800	1,350	800	25,550	Actual
1,200	—	—	12,000	H.P.
960	1,640	640	16,000	Area
240	400	160	4,000	Area
300	50	50	2,000	Value
6,000	1,000	1,000	40,000	Value
16,000	7,200	8,400	150,750	
(16,000)				Maintenance wages
	(7,200)			Indirect materials issued to production
		(8,400)		Direct labour cost (£21,600)
—	—	—	£150,750	

Q 12

Process I A/c

	litres	£		litres	£
Materials	16,000	47,400	Normal loss	1,560	—
Labour		4,880	Abnormal loss	840	2,751
Expenses		4,270	Transfer to Proc. II	8,000	40,264
Overhead		12,200	Closing W.I.P.	5,600	25,735
	16,000	**£68,750**		**16,000**	**£68,750**

Note: Equivalent units:

	litres
Material: Begun and complete	8,000
In process	5,600
Abnormal loss	840
Equivalent units	14,440
Normal loss (16,000 × 0.85)	1,560
	£16,000

Therefore, material unit cost $= \dfrac{47,400}{14,440}$ =   £3.283

	litres
Labour, expense, O/H: Begun and complete	8,000
In process 5,600 × 75%	4,200
Equivalent units	12,200

Therefore, unit costs: Labour $\dfrac{4,880}{12,200}$ =   £0.4

Expenses $\dfrac{4,270}{12,200}$ =   £0.35

Overhead $\dfrac{12,200}{12,200}$ =   £1.0

Value of W.I.P. = Material: 5,600 × 3.283   =   £ 18,385

Labour/exp/O/H: 4,200 × 1.75   =   7,350

5.033   25,735

Value of completed units = 8,000 × 5.033   =   £40,264

Value of abnormal loss = 840 × 3.283   =   £2,751

Process II A/c

	litres	£		litres	£
Process I	8,000	40,264	Normal loss	800	—
Labour		6,000			
Overhead		6,000	Finished goods	7,500	54,442
Abnormal gain	300	2,178			
	8,300	£54,442		8,300	£54,442

		litres
Equivalent units: Begun and complete		7,500
Abnormal gain		(300)
Equivalent units		7,200
Normal loss (10%)		800
Input volume		8,000

	£
Unit cost: Process I	40,264
Labour	6,000
Overhead	6,000
	52,264 ÷ 7,200 = £7.258

Chapter 15   Budgets and Budgetary Control

Q 3 (a) Sales

Volume: 1984 Sales = 21,800 + 2,200 = 24,000 units
1985 Sales = 24,000 + 20% = 28,800 units

Sales 1985:	January	= 1,440 (5%)
	February	= 2,304 (8%)
	March	= 6,336 (22%)

(b) Production and stock, 1985

	January	February	March	April
Opening stock	2,500	1,200	1,200	1,200
Production to stock	—	2,000	2,000	2,000
Bought in:	140	304	4,336	—
	2,640	3,504	7,536	3,200
Sales	1,440	2,304	6,336	1,440
Closing stock	1,200	1,200	1,200	1,760

Minimum stock = 5% × 24,000 = 1,200 units
Maximum stock = 15% × 24,000 = 3,600 units

i.e. January production = 2,000 (given one month time lag)

(c) Raw material purchases:	January	2,000
	February	2,000
	March	2,000

		£
(d) Sales (10,080 × 80)		806,400
Less: Cost of sales (marginal)		
Jan.	1,440 × £46	
Feb.	140 × 55	
	2,164 × 46	
Mar.	304 × 55	
	2,896 × 46	
	3,136 × 55	495,900
(see Note 3(iii))		
Contribution		£310,500

Q 4
Sizer Ltd
Flexible Budget

Capacity %	80%	90%	100%	110%
Budgeted hours	7,200	8,100	9,000	9,900
	£	£	£	£
Direct labour	4,320	4,860	5,400	5,940
Indirect labour	1,800	2,025	2,250	2,475
Power	1,296	1,458	1,620	1,782
Miscellaneous	360	405	450	495
	7,776	8,748	9,720	10,692
Supervision	2,200	2,200	2,200	2,420
Rent and rates	2,000	2,000	2,000	2,000
Depreciation	1,500	1,500	1,500	1,650
Administration	2,800	2,800	2,800	2,800
	£16,276	£17,248	£18,220	£19,562

Q 5
(a)

H. F. Ltd
Revised Profit Budget for the year ending 30 September 1984

	£	£
Sales		740,000
Material	296,400	
Labour	132,600	
Variable overhead	91,000	520,000
Contribution		220,000
Fixed overhead		138,200
Net Profit		**£ 81,800**

Budgeted Net Assets as at 30 September 1984

	£	£
Fixed Assets		310,000
Stocks	90,000	
Debtors*	78,333	
Creditors	(40,000)	128,333
Net assets employed		**£438,333**

* $540,000/12 + 200,000/6 = £78,333$

(b)

	Revised	Original	Difference	
Sales	£740,000	£600,000	+£140,000	$=8,000 \times 25 - 2,000 \times 30$
Materials	296,400	240,000	+ 56,400	$=6,000 \times 11.4 - 20,000 \times 0.6$
Labour	132,600	102,000	+ 30,600	$=6,000 \times 5.1$
Variable	91,000	70,000	+ 21,000	$=6,000 \times 3.5$
	520,000	412,000	108,000	
Fixed	138,200	122,200	+ 16,000	
	£658,200	**£534,200**	**+£124,000**	
Profit	£ 81,800	£ 65,800	+£ 16,000	

Q 7

Cash Budget

	October	November	December
Receipts	£	£	£
Opening balance	(5,000)	258	9,129
Cash from sales	27,040	31,080	34,740
	£22,040	**£31,338**	**£43,869**
Payments			
Materials	13,815	12,924	14,091
Fuel	—	—	2,895
Other	2,020	2,250	2,400
Wages	2,927	3,555	3,350
Salaries	1,805	2,280	2,430
Direct expenses	405	378	480
Sundry	810	822	960
Plant	—	—	50,000
	£21,782	**£22,209**	**£ 76,606**
Closing Balance	£ 258	£ 9,129	£(32,737)

Q 8

Baker Ltd
Cash Budget for the six months ending 31 December 1984

	July	Aug.	Sept.	Oct.	Nov.	Dec.
Opening Balance	8,000	3,000	(5,000)	(5,000)	1,000	9,500
Sales	22,000	24,000	30,000	27,000	30,000	24,000
Investments	—	1,500	3,500	—	—	—
	30,000	28,500	28,500	22,000	31,000	33,500
Materials	10,000	15,000	15,000	4,000	4,500	4,500
Labour	8,000	9,000	9,000	8,000	8,000	8,000
Indirect expenses	4,000	4,500	4,500	4,000	4,000	4,000
Factory—fixed	5,000	5,000	5,000	5,000	5,000	5,000
Admin —fixed	—	—	—	—	—	—
Debenture interest	—	—	—	—	—	400
	£27,000	**£33,500**	**£33,500**	**£21,000**	**£21,500**	**£21,900**
Balance c/f	£ 3,000	£ (5,000)	£ (5,000)	£ 1,000	£ 9,500	£11,600

Budgeted, Trading, Profit and Loss Account
for the period ended 31 December 1984

	£	£	£
Sales			153,000
Opening stock materials	10,000		
Purchases	25,000		
	35,000		
Less: Closing stock	9,500		
		25,500	
Labour		50,000	
		75,500	
Indirect variable		25,000	
Marginal cost of production		100,500	
Opening stock of finished goods		20,000	
Cost of production		100,500	
		120,500	
Less: Closing stock		18,000	
		102,500	
Depreciation—plant		9,000	
Factory expenses		9,000	120,500
			32,500
Profit on investments			500
			33,000
Administration		21,000	
Depreciation—motors		1,000	
Debenture interest		400	22,400
Net profit			**£ 10,600**

Budgeted Balance Sheet as at 31 December 1984

	£	£		£	£
Share capital		60,000	Plant (W.D.V.)		56,000
Profit & Loss		40,600	Motors (W.D.V.)		3,000
		100,600			59,000
Debentures		10,000	Investment		5,500
Creditors: goods	12,000		Stock: materials	9,500	
other	5,000	17,000	finished goods	18,000	
			Debtors	24,000	
			Bank	11,600	63,100
		£127,600			**£127,600**

Chapter 16   Standard Costs and Variance Analysis

Q 4

			£	£
Material price variances:				
A: £(0.50—0.52) 19,800		=	(396)A	
B: £(1.80—1.72) 7,800		=	642F	228
Material usage variances:				
A: (20,000—19,800) 0.5		=	100F	
B: (7,500—7,800) 1.8		=	(540)A	(440)
Total adverse variance				**£212**

			£	£
Note: Standard cost: A: 20,000 × 0.5	=	10,000		
B: 7,500 × 1.8	=	13,500	23,500	
Actual cost: A:	=	10,296		
B:	=	13,416	23,712	
Adverse variance				**£ (212)**

Q 5

			1 unit	12,000 units
			£	£
(a)	Material	5 × 1.20	6.00	72,000
	Labour	1.5 × 3.5	5.25	63,000
	Overhead	1.5 × 1.5	2.25	27,000
			13.50	**£162,000**

				Variance
			£	£
(b)	**Actual Costs:**			
	Material	1.168 × 62,500	73,000	(1,000)
	Labour	3.68 × 17,900	65,872	(2,872)
	Overhead	1.5 × 18,000	27,000	—
			165,872	**£(3,872)**

		£	£
(c)	**Material variances:**		
	Price (1.20—1.168) 62,500	2,000	
	Usage (60,000—62,500) 1.20	(3,000)	(1,000)
	Labour variances:		
	Wages (3.5—3.68)17,900	(3,222)	
	Efficiency (18,000–17,900) 3.5	350	(2,872)
	Total adverse variance		**£(3,872)**

Q 6

			£		£
(a)	**Budgeted overhead cost per unit:**				
	Variable overhead	=	400,000	=	10.00
			40,000		
	Fixed overhead	=	480,000	=	12.00
			40,000		
					£22.00

(b) Variable overhead absorption rate $= \dfrac{400,000}{160,000}$ $= £2.5$ per direct labour hr.

Fixed overhead absorption rate $= \dfrac{480,000}{160,000}$ $= £3.0$,,

(c) Variable overhead variances:

	£	£
Budget (162,000 × 2.5) − 380,000	25,000F	
Efficiency (156,000 − 162,000) 2.5	15,000A	10,000

Fixed overhead variances:

Spending (480,000 − 490,000)	10,000A	
Volume (156,000 − 160,000)3	12,000A	(22,000)
Total adverse variance		**£(12,000)**

	£	£

Note: Overhead absorbed:

Variable: 156,000 × 2.5	390,000	
Fixed: 156,000 × 3.0	468,000	858,000

Actual overhead:

Variable	380,000	
Fixed	490,000	870,000
Total adverse variance		**£(12,000)**

Q 7

	Budget				Actual			
	Unit price	Quantity	%	Total	Unit price	Quantity	Total	Actual quantities in budget proportions
	£			£	£		£	
A	20	2,000	33⅓	40,000	20.9	2,200	45,980	1,900
B	6	1,400	23⅓	8,400	6.2	1,200	7,440	1,330
C	8	1,600	26⅔	12,800	7.6	1,800	13,680	1,520
D	2	1,000	16⅔	2,000	2.0	500	1,000	950
		6,000	100	£63,200		5,700	£68,100	5,700

Hence, total sales variance = £63,200 − 68,100 = **£4,900** favourable

					£	£
£						
Price variances:	A	(20.9 − 20.0)	× 2,200		1,980F	
	B	(6.2 − 6.0)	× 1,200		240F	
	C	(7.6 − 8.0)	× 1,800		(720)A	
	D	(2 − 2)	× 500		—	1,500F
Volume variances:	A	(1,900 − 2,000)	× 20		(2,000)A	
	B	(1,300 − 1,400)	× 6		(420)A	
	C	(1,520 − 1,600)	× 8		(640)A	
	D	(950 − 1,000)	× 2		(100)A	(3,160)A
Misc variances:	A	(2,200 − 1,900)	× 20		6,000F	
	B	(1,200 − 1,330)	× 6		(780)A	
	C	(1,800 − 1,520)	× 8		2,240F	
	D	(500 − 950)	× 2		(900)A	6,560F
						£4,900F

Q 8

	Flexible Budget	Actual	Variance
	£	£	£
Material	6,600	11,000	(4,400)A
Labour	33,000	38,500	(5,500)A
Fixed overhead	20,000	21,000	(1,000)A
	£59,600	**£70,500**	**£(10,900)A**

		£	£
Material variances:			
Price (0.2–0.25) 44,000		(2,200)A	
Usage (33,000–44,000) 0.2		(2,200)A	(4,400)A
Labour variances:			
Wage rate (0.5–0.7) 55,000		(11,000)A	
Efficiency (66,000–55,000) 0.5		5,500F	(5,500)A
Fixed overhead*:			
Spending 20,000–21,000		(1,000)A	
Volume (66,000–66,000) 0.30		—	(1,000)A
			£(10,900)A

* The fixed overhead absorption rate will be adjusted through the flexible budget from 20,000/60,000 to 20,000/66,000—hence there will be no volume variance

Q 9

(i)   **Fixed overhead volume variance:**
        $(X - 10,000) 0.6 = 300F$
        X (standard input volume of work done) = **10,500 units**

(ii)   **Fixed overhead spending variance:**
        $6,000 - X = (200)A$
        Actual fixed overhead = **£6,200**

(iii)   **Material variances:**
        Usage: $((10,500 \times 12) - X) 0.5 = £(400)A$
        Actual usage = 126,800 kg
        Price: $(0.5 - X) 126,800 = £1,268F$
        Actual price = **£0.49 per kilo**

(vi)   **Labour variances:**
        Efficiency: $((10,500 \times 1.5) - X) 1.6 = £240F$
        Actual hours worked = 15,600
        Wage rate: $(1.6 - X) 15,600 = £(780)A$
        Actual Wage Rate = **£1.65 per labour hour**

(v)   **Sales variance:**
        Price $= (Y - 12) 10,500 = (1,000)A$
        Actual sales price = **£11.90476 per unit**
        (Volume margin $= (10,500 - 10,000) \times (12.00 - 9.00) = 1,500F$)

(a)   **Operating statement**

	£	£
Sales (10,500 × 11.90476)		125,000
Materials (126,800 × 0.49)	62,132	
Labour (15,600 × 1.65)	25,740	
Overhead	6,200	94,072
Operating profit		**£30,928**

Chapter 17   Accounting for Business Decisions—The Capital Investment Decision

Q 1

(a) (i)   Payback

X: $2 + \dfrac{12,000 - 8,400}{6,000} = 2.6$ years ✓

Y: 2.0 years ✓

Z: $2 + \dfrac{12,000 - 8,400}{4,800} = 2.75$ years ✓

(a) (ii)   Rate of return (original investment)

X: $\dfrac{18,400}{4} = \dfrac{4,600}{12,000} = 38.33\%$ ✓

Y: $\dfrac{16,800}{4} = \dfrac{4,200}{12,000} = 35.0\%$ ✓

Z: $\dfrac{21,600}{5} = \dfrac{4,320}{12,000} = 36.0\%$ ✓

(a) (iii) Net present value (i = 10%)

	X		Y		Z	
	Actual	*NPV*	*Actual*	*NPV*	*Actual*	*NPV*
	£	£	£	£	£	£
1	2,400	2,184	6,000	5,460	3,600	3,276
2	6,000	4,980	6,000	4,980	4,800	3,984
3	,000	4,500	3,600	2,700	4,800	3,600
4	4,000	2,720	1,200	816	4,800	3,264
5	—	—	—	—	3,600	2,232
		14,384		13,956		16,356
Less:		12,000		12,000		12,000
NPV		£ 2,384		£ 1,956		£ 4,356

(a) (iv)   Yield (i = 15%)

	X		Y		Z	
	Actual	*NPV*	*Actual*	*NPV*	*Actual*	*NPV*
	£	£	£	£	£	£
1	2,400	2,088	6,000	5,220	3,600	3,132
2	6,000	4,560	6,000	4,560	4,800	3,648
3	6,000	3,960	3,600	2,376	4,800	3,168
4	4,000	2,280	1,200	111684	4,800	2,736
5	—	—	—	—	3,600	1,800
		12,888		12,840		14,484
Less:		12,000		12,000		12,000
		£ 888		£ 840		£ 2,484

By interpolation the yields are:

X: $15 + \left(\dfrac{888}{2,384 - 888} \right) 5 = 17.97\%$

Y: $15 + \left(\dfrac{840}{1,956 - 840} \right) 5 = 18.76\%$

Z: $15 + \left(\dfrac{2,484}{4,356 - 2,484} \right) 5 = 21.63\%$

Q 2

(a) Payback

$$A = 3 + \frac{800}{1,100} = 3.73 \text{ years}$$

$$B = 4 + \frac{200}{900} = 4.22 \text{ years}$$

(b) Net present value $(i = 10\%)$

	A		B		
	Actual	*NPV*	*Actual*	*NPV*	*NPV Factor*
	£	£	£	£	£
1	500	455	200	182	.91
2	700	581	300	249	.83
3	1,000	750	500	375	.75
4	1,100	748	800	544	.68
5	900	558	900	558	.62
6	100	57	900	513	.57
		3,149		2,421	
Less:		3,000		2,000	
NPV	£	149	£	421	

Q 3

Cost of debentures: $K_d = \dfrac{5,000}{48,500}$

$= 10.31\%$

Cost of preference share capital: $K_p = \dfrac{1,200}{20,000}$

$= 6\%$

Cost of ordinary share capital: $K_e = \dfrac{12}{220} + 8.33\%$

$= 5.45 + 8.33$

$= 13.78\%$

Cost of capital:

Source	Book value	Weight	Cost %	Weighted Cost %
	£'000			
Ordinary	100	0.45	13.78	6.20
Preference	20	0.09	6.00	0.54
Reserves	50	0.23	13.78	3.17
Debentures	50	0.23	10.31	2.37
	220	1.00		12.28

Therefore, $K_c = 12.28\%$

Q4

Project A

Year	Net profit	Depre'n	Net cash flow before tax	WDV at start	1st year allowance	Writing down allowance	Taxable profits	Corp'n tax	Net cash flow after tax
	£	£	£	£	£	£	£	£	£
1	5,000	1,500	6,500	15,000	9,000	—	-2,500	—	6,500
2	7,000	1,500	8,500	6,000	—	1,500	6,000	-1,250	9,750
3	4,000	1,500	6,500	4,500	—	1,125	5,375	3,000	3,500
4	3,000	1,500	4,500	3,375	—	844	3,656	2,688	1,812
5	2,000	1,500	3,500	2,531	—	633	2,867	1,828	1,672
6	2,000	1,500	{3,500 / 3,000	1,898	—	{475 / 1,423*	4,602	1,434	5,066
7	—							2,301	-2,301

* Balancing allowance or, alternatively, show a balancing charge of 3,000 − 1,423 = £1,577, and delete £3,000 from cash flow.

Project B

Year	Net profit	Depre'n	Net cash flow before tax	WDV at start	1st year allowance	Writing down allowance	Taxable profits	Corp'n tax	Net cash flow after tax
	£	£	£	£	£	£	£	£	£
1	4,000	7,000	11,000	28,000	16,800	—	-5,800	—	11,000
2	5,000	5,250	10,250	11,200	—	2,800	7,450	-2,900	7,350
3	10,000	3,938	13,938	8,400	—	2,100	11,838	3,725	10,213
4	12,000	2,953	14,953	6,300	—	1,575	13,378	5,919	9,034
5	8,000	2,215	10,215	4,725	—	1,181	9,034	6,689	3,526
6	4,000	1,661	{5,661 / 6,000	3,544	—	{886 / 1,017*	9,758	4,517	7,144
7	—							4,879	-4,879

* Balancing allowance.

		A		B	
		NCF	NPV	NCF	NPV
		£	£	£	£
1	.91	6,500	5,915	11,000	10,010
2	.83	9,750	8,093	7,350	6,101
3	.75	3,500	2,625	10,213	7,660
4	.68	1,812	1,232	9,034	6,143
5	.62	1,672	1,037	3,526	2,186
6	.57	5,066	2,888	7,144	4,072
7	.51	−2,301	−1,174	−4,879	−2,488
			20,616		33,684
Less:			15,000		28,000
NPV			£5,616		£5,684

Q 6

(a)

		X		Y		X	Y	
		i = 10%				i = 15%		
		NCF	NPV	NCF	NPV		NPV	NPV
		£	£	£	£	£	£	£
1	.91	4,000	3,640	6,000	5,460	.87	3,480	5,220
2	.83	8,000	6,640	12,000	9,960	.76	6,080	9,120
3	.75	10,000	7,500	10,000	7,500	.66	6,600	6,600
4	.68	5,000	3,400	6,000	4,080	.57	2,850	3,420
5	.62	4,000	2,480	4,000	2,480	.50	2,000	2,000
6	.62	3,000	1,860	5,000	3,100	.50	1,500	2,500
			25,520		32,580		22,510	28,860
Less:			25,000		30,000		25,000	30,000
NPV			520		2,580		(2,490)	(1,140)

	X	Y
NPV (10%)	520	2,580
(15%)	(2,490)	(1,140)

(b) Yield (internal rate of return)

X: $10 + \left(\dfrac{520}{3,010}\right) 5 = \underline{\underline{\mathbf{10.86\%}}}$

Y: $10 + \left(\dfrac{2,580}{3,720}\right) 5 = \underline{\underline{\mathbf{13.47\%}}}$

Chapter 18   Accounting for Business Decisions – Short-term Decisions

Q 1

		£	£
(a)	Revenue (15 × 25 × 14)		5,250
	Variable costs:*		
	Food (80 × 14)	1,120	
	Waitresses (22 × 14)	308	
	Laundry (10 × 14)	140	
	Heating & lighting (8 × 14)	112	1,680
			3,570
	Fixed costs:		
	Depreciation	250	
	Rates	350	
	Advertising etc.	150	750
	Net profit		**£2,800**

* Part of waitresses' cost is probably fixed

(b)   To just cover costs:

Average variable costs per person per week $\dfrac{1,680}{14 \times 15} = £8$

Revenue per person per week = £25

Hence, contribution per person per week = $25 - 8 = £17$

Fixed costs = £750

So, total number of guests in season to break even: $\dfrac{750}{17} = 44.1 = 45$ guests

Hence, minimum average guests per week to break even $\dfrac{45}{14} = 3.2 = $ **4 guests**

(c)   A price equal to marginal cost, i.e. £8 per week

Q 2

(i)

	A Unit price			B Unit price		
	£	£	£	£	£	£
Sales	2.5		25,000	1.33		40,000
Material	0.8	8,000		0.6	18,000	
Labour	0.7	7,000		0.53	16,000	
Variable O/H	0.2	2,000	17,000	0.1	3,000	37,000
	1.7			1.23		
Contribution	0.8		8,000	0.1		3,000

Total contribution	11,000	
Fixed costs	9,000	
Profit	**£2,000**	

To abandon B would result in a loss of £3,000 contribution, so the result would be:

Contribution (A)	8,000	
Fixed costs	9,000	
Loss	**£(1,000)**	

(ii) At £2 per unit the contribution is:
2 − 1.7 = £0.3, and 4,000 units will add:
0.3 × 4,000 = £1,200 to contribution and profit

(iii) The costs are 'sunk' – sell for £4,400

N.B.: From a 'financial accounting' standpoint the alternatives are:

(a) Do not sell – and eventually write the stock off as a loss
    £3.7 × 2,000 = £7,400 loss
OR
(b) sell – and lose £7,400 − 4,400 = £3,000 loss

Hence the 'gain' to the company is **£4,400**

Q 3 (a)

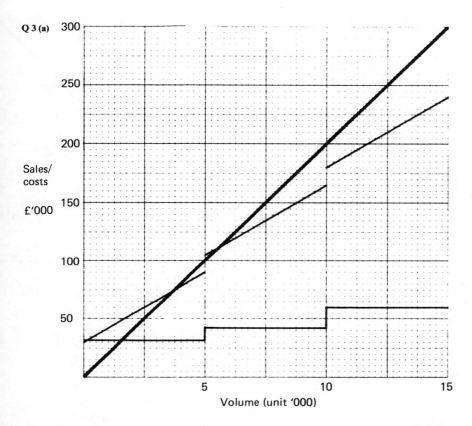

Volume (unit '000)

Q 3

(a) Break-even 4,000 units 5,500 units
(c) Margin of safety at 8,500 units = 3,000 units
(d) At 14,000 units profit = £14,000 (20 − 12) − 60,000 = **£52,000**

Q 3(b)

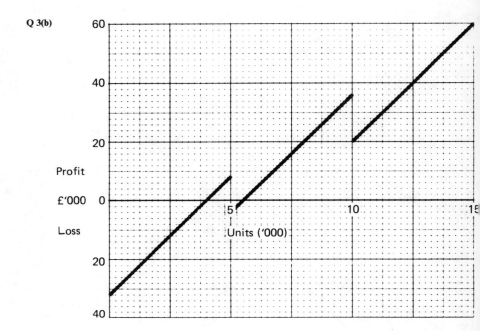

Q 4(a)

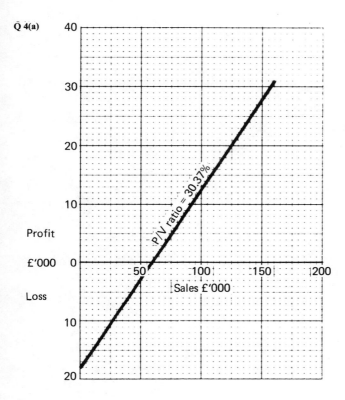

Note: Total contribution £24,000 + 7,200 + 18,000 = £49,200

Total sales £96,000 + 24,000 + 42,000 = £162,000

Therefore, P/V ratio = $\dfrac{49,200}{162,000}$ = 30.37%

Therefore, break-even = $\dfrac{18,000}{30.37\%}$ = **£59,347 sales**

(b)   If sales mix changes:

Total contribution £18,000 + 14,400 + 9,000 = £41,400

Total sales   £72,000 + 48,000 + 21,000 = £141,000

Therefore, P/V ratio = $\dfrac{41,400}{141,000}$ = 29.36%

Therefore, break-even = $\dfrac{18,000}{29.36\%}$ = **£61,308 sales**

Q 5

Differential costs/(benefits)

	Abandon £	Complete £
Material X	—	2,000
Y	(3,500)	—
Labour – skilled	—	10,000
Equipment	(2,000)	—
Overhead	—	—
	(5,500)	12,000
Sales	(20,000)	(30,000)
	(25,500)	(18,000)

So, abandon now.

Q 6

Variable costs of manufacturing faktrons:

$20,250 + 20,000 + 6,000 + 300 = £46,550$

Other costs born by department whether faktrons are made or not:

$5,500 + 10,000 + 8,000 + 9,800 + 5,000 = £39,300$

Savings if faktrons are not manufactured:

Variable costs	£46,500
Less: Shipping charges	(2,500)
Indirect labour	(5,000)
Net savings	£39,000

Cost of buying out:
5,000 × 8	£40,000

So, increase in costs   £1,000

Therefore, continue to manufacture.

Q 7

Four-Year Cash Flow

	S–make S–maintain £	S–make P–maintain £	S–maintain P–make £	P–make P–maintain £
Materials–Senslit	19,200	19,200	(12,800)	(12,800)
–Other	40,000	36,000	5,600	—
Labour	40,000	40,000	38,000	6,000
Manager (i.e. £1,600 p.a. whatever the choice)	—	—	—	—
Machinery	—	—	(5,000)	(5,000)
Rent	7,200	7,200	7,200	—
Other	12,600	10,080	2,520	—
Admin.	—	—	—	—
P.C. Ltd	—	20,000	100,000	120,000
Total costs	**£119,000**	**£132,480**	**£135,520**	**£108,200**

Therefore, P.C. Ltd to make and maintain.

Q 8

Opportunity Cost of Strike

	£	£
Loss in revenue 25,000 × £1		25,000
Less:		
Material (25,000 × 0.25)	6,250	
Wages (25,000 × 0.5)	12,500	
Savings on contractor	2,000	20,750
		4,250
Add:		
Maintenance materials	1,000	
Loss of contribution (10,000 × 0.125)	1,250	2,250
Opportunity cost of strike		**£6,500**

Q 9

Normale: Contribution per unit	£6.50
Super: ,, ,, ,,	£7.50

Normale: Contribution per unit of limiting factor £6.50/0.4 = £16.25
Super: ,,   ,,   ,, ,,   ,,   ,,   £7.50/0.5 = £15.00

Therefore, use scarce essence for Normale

Maximum production of Normale 1,500/0.4 = 37,500 units

All other production will involve an essence cost of £12 per litre. Since this still gives a positive contribution for Normale, i.e. £3.7 per unit, and there is no limit on purchase, then:

Contribution – Normale =	3,750	× 6.5 =	24,375
	250	× 3.7 =	925
	4,000		**£25,300**

There are two alternatives for Super—either sell

  (a) 2,000 units at £24 per unit, or
  (b) 3,000 units at £20 per unit.

(a)	Contribution 2,000 (24 − 16)	= £16,000
(b)	Contribution 3,000 (20 − 16)	= £12,000

Therefore, sell 2,000 units of Super

Hence, total contribution—Normale	25,300
—Super	16,000
	£41,300

Q 10

The two sales levels need to be investigated separately.

(i) Sales: 0–100,000 units

	A	B	G
	£	£	£
Sales	20	30	40
V.C.	16	19	28
Contribution per unit	4	11	12
Contribution per labour hour	£3.2	£5.5	£4.8
Contribution per kg of Y	—	£13.2	£8

Hence, produce B before G before A.

	A	B	G
Maximum sales	80,000	100,000	100,000
Labour hours	100,000	200,000	250,000 = 555,000 < 720,000
Material Y kg	—	83,333	116,667 = 200,000 = 200,000
			i.e. 77,777 units

Therefore, total contribution:

A	80,000 × 4 =	320,000
B	83,333 × 11 =	916,663
G	77,777 × 12 =	933,324
		£2,169,987

(ii) Sales: 100,000 – 180,000 units

	A	B	G	
	£	£	£	
Sales	20*	25	36	*max = 80,000 units
V.C.	16	19	28	
Contribution per unit	4	6	8	
Contribution per labour hour	£3.2	£3	£3.2	
Contribution per kg of Y	—	£5	£5.33	

Hence, produce G before A before B.

	A	B	G
Maximum sales	80,000	120,000	150,000
Labour hours	100,000	240,000	375,000 = 725,000 > 720,000
Material Y kg	—	—	200.000 = 200,000
			i.e. 133,333 units

Therefore, total contribution:

A	80,000 × 4 =	320,000
B	—	—
G	133,333 × 8 =	1,066,666
		£1,386,666

Therefore, best product mix is:

A	80,000 units
B	83,333 units
G	77,777 units

Chapter 19 The Management of Working Capital

Q 8

Cash Budget, January–June 1984

	J	F	M	A	M	J
	£	£	£	£	£	£
Opening balance	6,000	12,200	11,200	6,200	9,000	18,000
Sales receipts	44,000	40,000	42,000	48,000	50,000	54,000
	40,000	42,000	48,000	50,000	54,000	54,000
	90,000	94,200	101,200	104,200	113,000	126,000
Purchases	32,000	36,000	40,000	40,000	44,000	40,000
Labour	18,000	21,000	21,000	22,000	22,000	23,000
Overheads	9,400	12,400	12,400	13,400	13,400	14,400
	1,800	—	—	1,800	—	—
Admin.	7,600	7,600	7,600	8,600	8,600	8,600
				2,400		
Selling	6,000	6,000	6,000	7,000	7,000	7,000
Tax	10,000					
Machinery			8,000			16,000
	77,800	83,000	95,000	95,200	95,000	109,000
Balance c/f	£12,200	£11,200	£ 6,200	£ 9,000	£18,000	£ 17,000

Chapter 20　Performance Analysis

Q 3

	A		B		C	
Net profit before interest	31,000	22.1%	37,000	23.7%	30,000	25%
Net Capital Employed	140,000		156,000		120,000	
Net profit after interest	30,000	23.1%	30,000	37.5%	30,000	25%
Shareholders' Funds	130,000		80,000		120,000	
Net Profit	30,000	17.4%	30,000	14.5%	30,000	14%
Tangible Assets	172,000		207,000		214,000	
Net Profit	30,000	12%	30,000	12.5%	30,000	3.75%
Sales	250,000		240,000		800,000	
Gross Profit	50,000	20%	60,000	25%	80,000	10%
Sales	250,000		240,000		800,000	
Sales	250,000	4.8X	240,000	2.2X	800,000	11.6X
Fixed Assets	52,000		111,000		69,000	
Sales	250,000	2.1X	240,000	5.2X	800,000	5.5X
Current Assets	120,000		96,000		145,000	
Cost of Sales	200,000	3 mths	180,000	4.8 mths	720,000	1 mth
Average Stock	50,000		72,000		60,000	
Sales	250,000	1.4 mths	240,000	1.5 mths	800,000	1.2 mths
Debtors	30,000		30,000		80,000	
Current Assets	120,000	3.75/1	96,000	1.4/1	145,000	1.5/1
Current Liabilities	32,000		67,000		94,000	
Quick Assets	72,000	2.25/1	30,000	0.4/1	81,000	0.9/1
Current Liabilities	32,000		67,000		94,000	
Ordinary Dividend %	7,000	10%	6,000	15%	30,000	30%
	70,000		40,000		100,000	
Ordinary Dividend cover	30,000	4.3X	30,000	5X	30,000	1X
	7,000		6,000		30,000	

Q 4

Sources of Funds	£	£
Net cash flow from operations		
Increase in reserves: replacement	2,000	
P. & L.	11,000	
Taxation provision	13,500	
Dividends proposed	10,000	
Depreciation	7,500	44,000
Issue of ordinary shares		25,000
Increase in creditors		3,000
		72,000
Application of Funds		
Investment in: buildings	12,000	
plant	30,500	
Increase in current assets: stock	11,000	
debtors	14,500	
Payment of: taxation	8,500	
dividends	7,000	83,500
Reduction in cash		**£11,500**

Q 6(a)

	A		B	
(i)	$\dfrac{830}{100}$	8.3X	$\dfrac{840}{20}$	42X
(ii)	$\dfrac{720}{80}$	1.3 mths	$\dfrac{720}{48}$	0.8 mths
(iii)	$\dfrac{638}{128}$	2.4 mths	$\dfrac{648}{81}$	1.5 mths
(iv)	$\dfrac{352}{128}$	2.75/1	$\dfrac{146}{81}$	1.8/1
(v)	$\dfrac{58}{608}$	9.5%	$\dfrac{45}{361}$	12.5%
(vi)	$\dfrac{248}{128}$	1.9/1	$\dfrac{122}{81}$	1.5/1
(vii)	$\dfrac{90}{720}$	12.5%	$\dfrac{80}{720}$	11.1%
(viii)	$\dfrac{58}{720}$	8.1%	$\dfrac{45}{720}$	6.3%
(ix)	$\dfrac{58}{480}$	12.1%	$\dfrac{45}{280}$	16.1%

Q 8

Constructors Ltd
Sources and Applications of Funds
for the year ended 31 March 1984

	£'000	£'000
Sources of funds		
Net operating receipts		
(2,292 + 3,426 − 60 − 36 + 2,328 + 36)		7,986
Funds from other sources:		
Issue of ordinary shares	366	
Issue of debentures	144	
Sale of plant	180	
Sale of investment	54	744
		8,730
Application of funds		
Purchase of plant	3,486	
Purchase of other fixed assets	42	
Investments	312	
Dividends paid	3,426	7,226
		£1,464
Increase/decrease in working capital		
Increase in non-cash current assets	2,064	
Increase in creditors	(714)	
Movements in net liquid funds		
Increase in cash	114	**£1,464**

Index

Journal of International Money and Finance

Editor
Professor Michael R Darby
Department of Economics
University of California
Los Angeles CA 90024, USA

In recent years the field of international finance, and its study, have greatly expanded. There has been a marked increase in interest among all economists in international monetary arrangements, exchange rate determination, and macro-economic adjustments in open economies. The result has been a remarkable rise in the quality and quantity of research dealing with these issues.

The *Journal of International Money and Finance* brings together the work of many thinkers and academics who have made a study of the following branches of international economics.

Foreign exchange markets
Balance of payments
International monetary arrangements
International interactions of prices, incomes and money
Finance of multi-national corporations
Foreign aid
International economic institutions

The journal is committed to publication of the best available research in the field of international finance thus broadly defined. Each issue carries five or six major papers, as well as review articles, and notices of new books and literature in the field.

For further information and specimen copy, please contact

Sheila Smith
Butterworth Scientific Ltd – Journals Division,
P O Box 63, Westbury House, Bury Street, Guildford, Surrey, GU2 5BH, UK.
Telephone 0483 31261   Telex 859556 Scitec G